CAMBRIDGE LIBRARY COLLECTION

Books of enduring scholarly value

Religion

For centuries, scripture and theology were the focus of prodigious amounts
of scholarship and publishing, dominated in the English-speaking world
by the work of Protestant Christians. Enlightenment philosophy and
science, anthropology, ethnology and the colonial experience all brought
new perspectives, lively debates and heated controversies to the study of
religion and its role in the world, many of which continue to this day. This
series explores the editing and interpretation of religious texts, the history of
religious ideas and institutions, and not least the encounter between religion
and science.

The Acts of the Apostles

This annotated edition of The Acts of The Apostles was prepared for
classroom use by Thomas Ethelbert Page, a schoolmaster at Charterhouse,
and published in 1886. The text is taken directly from the critical edition
of the New Testament in Greek published by Fenton Hort and Brooke
Westcott in 1881, the most authoritative version then available. Page's
extensive annotations (over two hundred pages to accompany seventy pages
of text) aimed to provide an explanation of the Greek text free of doctrinal
discussions and moral reflections, unlike most existing commentaries which
Page found 'quite unadapted for practical work with boys'. Page endeavoured
to make the translation process as straightforward as possible and his
extensive commentary offers a clear and simple understanding of the text.
His book is still a useful guide for those approaching the Greek text for the
first time.

T0382236

Cambridge University Press has long been a pioneer in the reissuing of out-of-print titles from its own backlist, producing digital reprints of books that are still sought after by scholars and students but could not be reprinted economically using traditional technology. The Cambridge Library Collection extends this activity to a wider range of books which are still of importance to researchers and professionals, either for the source material they contain, or as landmarks in the history of their academic discipline.

Drawing from the world-renowned collections in the Cambridge University Library, and guided by the advice of experts in each subject area, Cambridge University Press is using state-of-the-art scanning machines in its own Printing House to capture the content of each book selected for inclusion. The files are processed to give a consistently clear, crisp image, and the books finished to the high quality standard for which the Press is recognised around the world. The latest print-on-demand technology ensures that the books will remain available indefinitely, and that orders for single or multiple copies can quickly be supplied.

The Cambridge Library Collection will bring back to life books of enduring scholarly value (including out-of-copyright works originally issued by other publishers) across a wide range of disciplines in the humanities and social sciences and in science and technology.

The Acts of the Apostles

Being the Greek Text as Revised by
Drs Westcott and Hort

EDITED BY FENTON JOHN ANTHONY HORT,
BROOKE FOSS WESTCOTT
AND THOMAS ETHELBERT PAGE

CAMBRIDGE UNIVERSITY PRESS

Cambridge, New York, Melbourne, Madrid, Cape Town, Singapore,
São Paolo, Delhi, Dubai, Tokyo

Published in the United States of America by Cambridge University Press, New York

www.cambridge.org
Information on this title: www.cambridge.org/9781108007504

© in this compilation Cambridge University Press 2009

This edition first published 1886
This digitally printed version 2009

ISBN 978-1-108-00750-4 Paperback

THE

ACTS OF THE APOSTLES.

PARENTIBUS OPTIMIS

QUIBUS

SI QUID HABEO

ACCEPTUM REFERO.

THE

ACTS OF THE APOSTLES,

BEING

THE GREEK TEXT

AS REVISED BY

DRS WESTCOTT AND HORT,

WITH EXPLANATORY NOTES

BY

THOMAS ETHELBERT PAGE, M.A.

ASSISTANT MASTER AT CHARTERHOUSE, AND FORMERLY
FELLOW OF ST JOHN'S COLLEGE, CAMBRIDGE.

’Ιᾶταί σε ’Ιησοῦς.

London:
MACMILLAN AND CO.
1886

Λουκᾶς ὁ ἰατρὸς ὁ ἀγαπητός.
Col. iv. 14.

Λουκᾶς ἐστὶν μόνος μετ᾽ ἐμοῦ.
2 Tim. iv. 11.

Μάρκος, Ἀρίσταρχος, Δημᾶς, Λουκᾶς, οἱ συνεργοί μου.
Phil. 24.

THE COLLECT FOR ST LUKE'S DAY.

Almighty God, who calledst Luke the Physician, whose praise is in the Gospel, to be an Evangelist, and Physician of the soul; May it please thee, that, by the wholesome medicines of the doctrine delivered by him, all the diseases of our souls may be healed; through the merits of thy Son Jesus Christ our Lord. *Amen.*

PREFACE.

THIS edition is intended chiefly for use in Schools, at the same time I am not without hope that in some points it may be of service to other students. Certainly, after a careful examination of the Revised Version, I am justified in saying that there are some passages in the Acts the meaning of which is not generally understood even by scholars. It may suffice to refer to the unintelligible renderings given of such important passages as i. 16—22 and x. 34—39, to the less obvious but clear errors pointed out in the note on μὲν οὖν ii. 41, and to the direct violation of the laws of language in the translation of xix. 2 and xxvii. 12.

That there is room for a useful School edition of the Acts, and indeed of any portion of the New Testament, few with any experience in teaching will deny. Schoolboys are for the most part grievously ignorant of the subject. For this two main reasons may be assigned.

(1) Being conversant with the English version they are able to translate the Greek with fatal facility, and fall into the common error of supposing that they understand the meaning of words, the sound of which has been familiar to them from infancy.

(2) Most commentaries are quite unadapted for practical work with boys. Their fault is this. The editors do not confine themselves chiefly to explanation of the text, which is the first and strictly the only duty of a commentator, but encumber their notes with doctrinal discussions and moral reflections. Such additions are at best out of place, even where the doctrinal arguments are not wholly one-sided and the moral disquisitions not trite and mediocre: in a scholar they usually create irritation; schoolboys soon cease to read the notes altogether.

In the present edition the notes with some few exceptions—which will I hope justify themselves— are confined to explanation and illustration of the text. By thus limiting myself I have been enabled to make the notes comparatively short and at the same time fairly thorough. I have moreover carefully studied brevity: it would have taken me half the time to write twice as much. In one point too much space has been saved. Passages of the Bible referred to are rarely quoted. This is done deliberately. I know that as a rule boys will not look up references. This is only natural where the references are to a variety of books, and in such cases passages referred to should usually be quoted; but to read the Greek Testament without a Bible at hand is useless, and it is most important that boys should become accustomed to working with it and examining passages referred to in it.

Allusion has been made not unfrequently to the views of other commentators. The limits however of my work preclude any but a brief examination of

conflicting opinions except in important cases. Perhaps
it is well that this is so. The number of commentators is immense, and there is no possible or impossible
view of even simple passages which has not found
advocates. To have overloaded the notes throughout with a discussion of the views, which seemed
to me plainly erroneous, would have made them
useless for their purpose. Indeed even now, after
cutting out all that seemed possible, I much doubt
whether they are as simple as they should be.
Certainly some of them can be of little use to any
but advanced boys, but I trust that this may be due
rather to the complexity of the subject than to a lack
of clearness or brevity on my part: at any rate I do
not hold that even in a school-book difficult passages
should be slurred over, exactly because they are
difficult.

I have not written an 'Introduction'. It would
be fairly easy to compile one similar to those which
are to be found in many English editions. The pro-
blems however presented by the Acts are so many
and so complex, that an Introduction worthy of the
name would require a separate volume and a capacity
immeasurably exceeding mine.

It is right however that I should refer to my
personal opinions on one or two points. One is that
I consider that on critical grounds the writer of the
Acts is to be identified with the writer of the third
Gospel, and that I see no reason whatever why he
should not be St Luke. Another point is that I
regard the writer as an *honest* writer, and my notes
are written on that supposition: they are an endeavour

ACTS OF THE APOSTLES.

to make clear the meaning of a writer, who is, I consider, endeavouring honestly to lay before his readers certain facts which he himself believes. This declaration is, I think, required from me in this preface, for it is clear that the whole character of my notes would be altered if I started from the supposition that the writer either wilfully misrepresented facts or was influenced by such a strong bias or tendency as to render his narrative continually open to suspicion. Beyond this, however, I do not think it necessary for a commentator to go in expressing his personal opinions: if he does, he passes from exegesis into criticism, and these two subjects should, where possible, be kept entirely apart. I will endeavour to illustrate my meaning by two instances.

(1) It does not seem to me that it lies within my province to discuss the exact details and evidence of the miracles related in the Acts. That miracles are impossible or, under certain circumstances, improbable, cannot logically be asserted except from the premises of pure materialism; *a priori* they are exactly as possible as any act of human volition. Moreover they form an integral part of Christianity; the claims of Christianity as a religion essentially rest on the miraculous. It is obvious however that the miracles related in the Acts stand on a different footing to those ascribed to Christ: it would be perfectly reasonable to fully accept the latter and at the same time hold that some of the former are related on insufficient evidence or are based on exaggerated reports. The examination, however, of such questions is entirely without the range of my duty as a commentator: my

duty is only clearly to point out that the writer is
describing a miracle, when I judge from his words
that he is doing so.

(2) In dealing with the argument of certain
speeches I have endeavoured to bring out the meaning
of the text. In doing so I have at times spoken of
the argument as 'clear' or 'telling', but this does not
imply or require that I should hold any special views
as to the method of Messianic interpretation of the
Old Testament which is employed, but only that, the
legitimacy of that method being presupposed, the
argument founded on it appears to me valid.

Moreover, all questions about the exact nature of
inspiration seem to lie outside my work. I have commented on the Acts as on a work written by a man
for men, that is to say, produced in accordance with
the laws of human thought and to be examined and
understood by human intelligence. Nor indeed is there
any clear ground of reason or authority for any other
supposition. That the preservation of an adequate
record of the life of Jesus and the foundation of the
Christian Church would be ensured by God, may be
safely maintained by any believer, and that record is
justly regarded with a reverence such as can attach to
no other human writings: on the other hand the
assertion of higher claims serves no necessary end and
involves many difficulties.

Lastly I may add that I have not attempted in
any way to use my notes to support any particular
form of dogmatic teaching. Legitimate exegesis has
no concern with the opinions which may be founded
on the results at which it arrives. It is the duty of a

commentator to examine the facts before him, and to decide upon them with judicial impartiality. To the easy triumphs which await the impassioned advocate of a popular cause he has no right: if he makes them his aim, he may indeed gain the cheap applause of partisans but he will forfeit the esteem of sober seekers after truth.

On these points I have endeavoured to express myself clearly. It is distinctly not my wish that any one should use my notes without knowing the principles on which I have proceeded. I have therefore thus far been personal and possibly controversial. From this point, however, I believe that the reader will find little to which those adjectives can justly be applied. My one object has been to elucidate the text: occasionally I have had to express a decided opinion that certain views were erroneous, but nowhere have I willingly written a word except in charity.

Of the text which I am enabled to employ it would be impertinent in me to speak critically. This much I may say, that, as is the case with everything of real excellence, its merits are clear even to one who is not an expert.

A list of the works principally used by me will be found facing the notes. References to such works will frequently be found in the margin as nearly as possible parallel to that part of the note which is borrowed from them or in agreement with them. It must not be assumed however that the commentators so referred to are (except when marks of quotation are given) in exact accord with my notes: it is rather my object to indicate to those, who wish to examine more fully the grounds on which a note is based, in what books they will find similar views maintained. As I am ignorant of Hebrew, explanations given of Hebrew words or phrases are in no case original.

I owe my best thanks to my friend the Rev. C. C. Tancock for looking over the proofs of the notes, but he is in no way responsible for any errors or opinions to be found in them.

T. E. PAGE.

CHARTERHOUSE, GODALMING.

The following explanation of the notation employed in the text is copied from the smaller edition of the Greek Testament by Drs Westcott and Hort, pp. 580—3.

"The primary place in the text itself is assigned to those readings which on the whole are the more probable, or in cases of equal probability the better attested. The other alternative readings occupy a secondary place, with a notation which varies according as they differ from primary readings by Omission, by Addition, or by Substitution.

A secondary reading consisting in the Omission of words retained in the primary reading is marked by simple brackets [ ] in the text.

A secondary reading consisting in the Addition of words omitted in the primary reading is printed at the foot of the page without any accompanying marks, the place of insertion being indicated by the mark ⊤ in the text.

A secondary reading consisting in the Substitution of other words for the words of the primary reading is printed at the foot of the page without any accompanying mark, the words of the primary reading being included within the marks ⌐ ¬ in the text.

Wherever it has appeared to the editors, or to either of them, that the text probably contains some primitive error, that is, has not been quite rightly preserved in any existing documents, or at least in any existing document of sufficient authority, the marks †† are placed at the foot of the page, the extreme limit of the words suspected to contain an error of transcription being indicated by the marks ⌐ ¬ in the text. Where either of two suspected extant readings might legitimately have been printed in the text, one of them is printed as an alternative reading between the ††: where there is no such second reading entitled to be associated with the text, the †† are divided only by dots. All places marked with †† are the subject of notes in the Appendix to the larger edition."

ERRATUM.

On p. 255, line 10,
    For, which you sail into from the W.
    read, which you sail into from the E.

ΠΡΑΞΕΙΣ ΑΠΟΣΤΟΛΩΝ

1 ΤΟΝ ΜΕΝ ΠΡΩΤΟΝ ΛΟΓΟΝ ἐποιησάμην περὶ
πάντων, ὦ Θεόφιλε, ὧν ἤρξατο Ἰησοῦς ποιεῖν τε καὶ
2 διδάσκειν ἄχρι ἧς ἡμέρας ἐντειλάμενος τοῖς ἀποστόλοις διὰ
3 πνεύματος ἁγίου οὓς ἐξελέξατο ἀνελήμφθη· οἷς καὶ παρέστησεν ἑαυτὸν ζῶντα μετὰ τὸ παθεῖν αὐτὸν ἐν πολλοῖς
τεκμηρίοις, δι᾽ ἡμερῶν τεσσεράκοντα ὀπτανόμενος αὐτοῖς
4 καὶ λέγων τὰ περὶ τῆς βασιλείας τοῦ θεοῦ. καὶ συναλιζόμενος παρήγγειλεν αὐτοῖς ἀπὸ Ἰεροσολύμων μὴ χωρίζεσθαι, ἀλλὰ περιμένειν τὴν ἐπαγγελίαν τοῦ πατρὸς ἣν
5 ἠκούσατέ μου· ὅτι Ἰωάνης μὲν ἐβάπτισεν ὕδατι, ὑμεῖς δὲ
ἐν πνεύματι βαπτισθήσεσθε ἁγίῳ οὐ μετὰ πολλὰς ταύτας
6 ἡμέρας. Οἱ μὲν οὖν συνελθόντες ἠρώτων αὐτὸν
λέγοντες Κύριε, εἰ ἐν τῷ χρόνῳ τούτῳ ἀποκαθιστάνεις τὴν
7 βασιλείαν τῷ Ἰσραήλ; εἶπεν πρὸς αὐτούς Οὐχ ὑμῶν
ἐστὶν γνῶναι χρόνους ἢ καιροὺς οὓς ὁ πατὴρ ἔθετο ἐν τῇ
8 ἰδίᾳ ἐξουσίᾳ, ἀλλὰ λήμψεσθε δύναμιν ἐπελθόντος τοῦ ἁγίου
πνεύματος ἐφ᾽ ὑμᾶς, καὶ ἔσεσθέ μου μάρτυρες ἔν τε Ἰερουσαλὴμ καὶ [ἐν] πάσῃ τῇ Ἰουδαίᾳ καὶ Σαμαρίᾳ καὶ ἕως
9 ἐσχάτου τῆς γῆς. καὶ ταῦτα εἰπὼν βλεπόντων αὐτῶν
ἐπήρθη, καὶ νεφέλη ὑπέλαβεν αὐτὸν ἀπὸ τῶν ὀφθαλμῶν
10 αὐτῶν. καὶ ὡς ἀτενίζοντες ἦσαν εἰς τὸν οὐρανὸν πορευο-
μένου αὐτοῦ, καὶ ἰδοὺ ἄνδρες δύο παριστήκεισαν αὐτοῖς ἐν

P.   I

ἐσθήσεσι λευκαῖς, οἳ καὶ εἶπαν "Ανδρες Γαλιλαῖοι, τί ἑστή- 11
κατε βλέποντες εἰς τὸν οὐρανόν; οὗτος ὁ Ἰησοῦς ὁ ἀναλημ-
φθεὶς ἀφ' ὑμῶν εἰς τὸν οὐρανὸν οὕτως ἐλεύσεται ὃν τρόπον ἐθεάσασθε αὐτὸν πορευόμενον εἰς τὸν οὐρανόν. Τότε 12
ὑπέστρεψαν εἰς Ἰερουσαλὴμ ἀπὸ ὄρους τοῦ καλουμένου
Ἐλαιῶνος, ὅ ἐστιν ἐγγὺς Ἰερουσαλὴμ σαββάτου ἔχον
ὁδόν.   Καὶ ὅτε εἰσῆλθον, εἰς τὸ ὑπερῷον ἀνέβη- 13
σαν οὗ ἦσαν καταμένοντες, ὅ τε Πέτρος καὶ Ἰωάνης καὶ Ἰάκωβος καὶ Ἀνδρέας, Φίλιππος καὶ Θωμᾶς, Βαρθολομαῖος
καὶ Μαθθαῖος, Ἰάκωβος Ἀλφαίου καὶ Σίμων ὁ ζηλωτὴς
καὶ Ἰούδας Ἰακώβου. οὗτοι πάντες ἦσαν προσκαρτεροῦντες 14
ὁμοθυμαδὸν τῇ προσευχῇ σὺν γυναιξὶν καὶ Μαριὰμ τῇ
μητρὶ [τοῦ] Ἰησοῦ καὶ σὺν τοῖς ἀδελφοῖς αὐτοῦ.

ΚΑΙ ΕΝ ΤΑΙΣ ΗΜΕΡΑΙΣ ταύταις ἀναστὰς Πέτρος 15
ἐν μέσῳ τῶν ἀδελφῶν εἶπεν (ἦν τε ὄχλος ὀνομάτων ἐπὶ τὸ
αὐτὸ ὡς ἑκατὸν εἴκοσι) "Ανδρες ἀδελφοί, ἔδει πληρωθῆναι 16
τὴν γραφὴν ἣν προεῖπε τὸ πνεῦμα τὸ ἅγιον διὰ στόματος
Δαυεὶδ περὶ Ἰούδα τοῦ γενομένου ὁδηγοῦ τοῖς συλλαβοῦσιν
Ἰησοῦν, ὅτι κατηριθμημένος ἦν ἐν ἡμῖν καὶ ἔλαχεν τὸν 17
κλῆρον τῆς διακονίας ταύτης. – Οὗτος μὲν οὖν ἐκτήσατο 18
χωρίον ἐκ μισθοῦ τῆς ἀδικίας, καὶ πρηνὴς γενόμενος
ἐλάκησεν μέσος, καὶ ἐξεχύθη πάντα τὰ σπλάγχνα αὐτοῦ.
καὶ γνωστὸν ἐγένετο πᾶσι τοῖς κατοικοῦσιν Ἰερουσαλήμ, 19
ὥστε κληθῆναι τὸ χωρίον ἐκεῖνο τῇ διαλέκτῳ αὐτῶν Ἀκελδαμάχ, τοῦτ' ἔστιν Χωρίον Αἵματος. – Γέγραπται γὰρ 20
ἐν Βίβλῳ Ψαλμῶν
    Γενηθήτω ἡ ἔπαυλις αὐτοῦ ἔρημος
    καὶ μὴ ἔστω ὁ κατοικῶν ἐν αὐτῇ,
καὶ
    Τὴν ἐπισκοπὴν αὐτοῦ λαβέτω ἕτερος.
                    5 εἰς

21 δεῖ οὖν τῶν συνελθόντων ἡμῖν ἀνδρῶν ἐν παντὶ χρόνῳ ᾧ
22 εἰσῆλθεν καὶ ἐξῆλθεν ἐφ' ἡμᾶς ὁ κύριος Ἰησοῦς, ἀρξάμενος
ἀπὸ τοῦ βαπτίσματος Ἰωάνου ἕως τῆς ἡμέρας ἧς ἀνελήμφθη ἀφ' ἡμῶν, μάρτυρα τῆς ἀναστάσεως αὐτοῦ σὺν ἡμῖν
23 γενέσθαι ἕνα τούτων. καὶ ἔστησαν δύο, Ἰωσὴφ τὸν καλούμενον Βαρσαββᾶν, ὃς ἐπεκλήθη Ἰοῦστος, καὶ Μαθθίαν.
24 καὶ προσευξάμενοι εἶπαν Σὺ κύριε καρδιογνῶστα πάντων,
25 ἀνάδειξον ὃν ἐξελέξω, ἐκ τούτων τῶν δύο ἕνα, λαβεῖν τὸν
τόπον τῆς διακονίας ταύτης καὶ ἀποστολῆς, ἀφ' ἧς παρέβη
26 Ἰούδας πορευθῆναι εἰς τὸν τόπον τὸν ἴδιον. καὶ ἔδωκαν
κλήρους αὐτοῖς, καὶ ἔπεσεν ὁ κλῆρος ἐπὶ Μαθθίαν, καὶ
συνκατεψηφίσθη μετὰ τῶν ἕνδεκα ἀποστόλων.

1 Καὶ ἐν τῷ συνπληροῦσθαι τὴν ἡμέραν τῆς πεντηκοστῆς
2 ἦσαν πάντες ὁμοῦ ἐπὶ τὸ αὐτό, καὶ ἐγένετο ἄφνω ἐκ τοῦ
οὐρανοῦ ἦχος ὥσπερ φερομένης πνοῆς βιαίας καὶ ἐπλήρω-
3 σεν ὅλον τὸν οἶκον οὗ ἦσαν καθήμενοι, καὶ ὤφθησαν αὐτοῖς διαμεριζόμεναι γλῶσσαι ὡσεὶ πυρός, καὶ ἐκάθισεν
4 ἐφ' ἕνα ἕκαστον αὐτῶν, καὶ ἐπλήσθησαν πάντες πνεύματος
ἁγίου, καὶ ἤρξαντο λαλεῖν ἑτέραις γλώσσαις καθὼς τὸ
5 πνεῦμα ἐδίδου ἀποφθέγγεσθαι αὐτοῖς. Ἦσαν
δὲ ⌜ἐν⌝ Ἰερουσαλὴμ κατοικοῦντες Ἰουδαῖοι, ἄνδρες εὐλαβεῖς
6 ἀπὸ παντὸς ἔθνους τῶν ὑπὸ τὸν οὐρανόν· γενομένης δὲ τῆς
φωνῆς ταύτης συνῆλθε τὸ πλῆθος καὶ συνεχύθη, ὅτι ἤκου-
7 σεν εἷς ἕκαστος τῇ ἰδίᾳ διαλέκτῳ λαλούντων αὐτῶν· ἐξίσταντο δὲ καὶ ἐθαύμαζον λέγοντες ⌜Οὐχὶ⌝ ἰδοὺ πάντες
8 οὗτοί εἰσιν οἱ λαλοῦντες Γαλιλαῖοι; καὶ πῶς ἡμεῖς ἀκούομεν ἕκαστος τῇ ἰδίᾳ διαλέκτῳ ἡμῶν ἐν ᾗ ἐγεννήθημεν;
9 Πάρθοι καὶ Μῆδοι καὶ Ἐλαμεῖται, καὶ οἱ κατοικοῦντες τὴν
Μεσοποταμίαν, Ἰουδαίαν τε καὶ Καππαδοκίαν, Πόντον καὶ
10 τὴν Ἀσίαν, Φρυγίαν τε καὶ Παμφυλίαν, Αἴγυπτον καὶ τὰ
μέρη τῆς Λιβύης τῆς κατὰ Κυρήνην, καὶ οἱ ἐπιδημοῦντες
11 Ῥωμαῖοι, Ἰουδαῖοί τε καὶ προσήλυτοι, Κρῆτες καὶ Ἄραβες,

7 Οὐχ

ἀκούομεν λαλούντων αὐτῶν ταῖς ἡμετέραις γλώσσαις τὰ
μεγαλεῖα τοῦ θεοῦ. ἐξίσταντο δὲ πάντες καὶ διηποροῦντο, 12
ἄλλος πρὸς ἄλλον λέγοντες Τί θέλει τοῦτο εἶναι; ἕτεροι 13
δὲ διαχλευάζοντες ἔλεγον ὅτι Γλεύκους μεμεστωμένοι
εἰσίν. Σταθεὶς δὲ ὁ Πέτρος σὺν τοῖς ἕνδεκα 14
ἐπῆρεν τὴν φωνὴν αὐτοῦ καὶ ἀπεφθέγξατο αὐτοῖς ῎Ανδρες
᾿Ιουδαῖοι καὶ οἱ κατοικοῦντες ᾿Ιερουσαλὴμ πάντες, τοῦτο
ὑμῖν γνωστὸν ἔστω καὶ ἐνωτίσασθε τὰ ῥήματά μου. οὐ 15
γὰρ ὡς ὑμεῖς ὑπολαμβάνετε οὗτοι μεθύουσιν, ἔστιν γὰρ
ὥρα τρίτη τῆς ἡμέρας, ἀλλὰ τοῦτό ἐστιν τὸ εἰρημένον διὰ 16
τοῦ προφήτου ᾿Ιωὴλ

Καὶ ἔϲται ἐν ταῖϲ ἐϲχάταιϲ ἡμέραιϲ, λέγει ὁ θεόϲ, 17
ἐκχεῶ ἀπὸ τοῦ πνεύματόϲ μου ἐπὶ πᾶϲαν ϲάρκα,
καὶ προφητεύϲουϲιν οἱ υἱοὶ ὑμῶν καὶ αἱ θυγατέρεϲ
ὑμῶν,
καὶ οἱ νεανίϲκοι ὑμῶν ὁράϲειϲ ὄψονται,
καὶ οἱ πρεϲβύτεροι ὑμῶν ἐνυπνίοιϲ ἐνυπνιαϲθή-
ϲονται·
καί γε ἐπὶ τοὺϲ δούλουϲ μου καὶ ἐπὶ τὰϲ δούλαϲ 18
μου
ἐν ταῖϲ ἡμέραιϲ ἐκείναιϲ ἐκχεῶ ἀπὸ τοῦ πνεύματόϲ μου,
καὶ προφητεύσουσιν.
Καὶ δώϲω τέρατα ἐν τῷ οὐρανῷ ἄνω 19
καὶ ϲημεῖα ἐπὶ τῆϲ γῆϲ κάτω,
αἷμα καὶ πῦρ καὶ ἀτμίδα καπνοῦ·
ὁ ἥλιοϲ μεταϲτραφήϲεται εἰϲ ϲκότοϲ 20
καὶ ἡ ϲελήνη εἰϲ αἷμα
πρὶν ᵀ ἐλθεῖν ἡμέραν Κυρίου τὴν μεγάλην
καὶ ἐπιφανῆ.
Καὶ ἔϲται πᾶϲ ὃϲ ἐὰν ἐπικαλέϲηται τὸ ὄνομα 21
Κυρίου ϲωθήϲεται.
῎Ανδρες ᾿Ισραηλεῖται, ἀκούσατε τοὺς λόγους τούτους. ᾿Ιη- 22

20 ἤ

σοῦν τὸν Ναζωραῖον, ἄνδρα ἀποδεδειγμένον ἀπὸ τοῦ θεοῦ
εἰς ὑμᾶς δυνάμεσι καὶ τέρασι καὶ σημείοις οἷς ἐποίησεν
23 δι᾽ αὐτοῦ ὁ θεὸς ἐν μέσῳ ὑμῶν, καθὼς αὐτοὶ οἴδατε, τοῦτον
τῇ ὡρισμένῃ βουλῇ καὶ προγνώσει τοῦ θεοῦ ἔκδοτον διὰ
24 χειρὸς ἀνόμων προσπήξαντες ἀνείλατε, ὃν ὁ θεὸς ἀνέστησεν
λύσας τὰς ὠδῖνας τοῦ θανάτου, καθότι οὐκ ἦν δυνατὸν
25 κρατεῖσθαι αὐτὸν ὑπ᾽ αὐτοῦ· Δαυεὶδ γὰρ λέγει εἰς αὐτόν
     Προορώμην τὸν κΫριον ἐνώπιόν μοΥ διὰ παντόσ,
     ὅτι ἐκ δεξιῶν μοΥ ἐστιν ἵνα μὴ σαλεΥθῶ.
26 διὰ τοῦτο ηὐφράνθη μοΥ ἡ καρδία καὶ ἠγαλλιάσατο
                             ἡ γλῶσσά μοΥ,
     ἔτι δὲ καὶ ἡ σάρξ μοΥ κατασκηνώσει ἐπ᾽ ἐλπίδι·
27 ὅτι οὐκ ἐνκαταλείψεις τὴν ψΥχήν μοΥ εἰς ᾅδην,
     οὐδὲ δώσεις τὸν ὅσιόν σοΥ ἰδεῖν διαφθοράν.
28 ἐγνώρισάς μοι ὁδοΥσ ζωῆσ,
     πληρώσεις με εὐφροσΥνησ μετὰ τοΥ προσώποΥ
                                  σοΥ.
29 Ἄνδρες ἀδελφοί, ἐξὸν εἰπεῖν μετὰ παρρησίας πρὸς ὑμᾶς
περὶ τοῦ πατριάρχου Δαυείδ, ὅτι καὶ ἐτελεύτησεν καὶ
ἐτάφη καὶ τὸ μνῆμα αὐτοῦ ἔστιν ἐν ἡμῖν ἄχρι τῆς ἡμέρας
30 ταύτης· προφήτης οὖν ὑπάρχων, καὶ εἰδὼς ὅτι ὅρκῳ ὤμοσεν αὐτῷ ὁ θεὸς ἐκ καρποΥ τῆσ ὀσφΥοσ αὐτοΥ καθίσαι
31 ἐπὶ τὸν θρόνον αὐτοΥ, προιδὼν ἐλάλησεν περὶ τῆς ἀναστάσεως τοῦ χριστοῦ ὅτι οὔτε ἐνκατελείφθη εἰσ ᾅδην
32 οὔτε ἡ σὰρξ αὐτοῦ εἶδεν διαφθοράν. τοῦτον τὸν Ἰησοῦν
33 ἀνέστησεν ὁ θεός, οὗ πάντες ἡμεῖς ἐσμὲν μάρτυρες. τῇ
δεξιᾷ οὖν τοῦ θεοῦ ὑψωθεὶς τήν τε ἐπαγγελίαν τοῦ πνεύματος τοῦ ἁγίου λαβὼν παρὰ τοῦ πατρὸς ἐξέχεεν τοῦτο ὃ
34 ὑμεῖς [καὶ] βλέπετε καὶ ἀκούετε. οὐ γὰρ Δαυεὶδ ἀνέβη εἰς
τοὺς οὐρανούς, λέγει δὲ αὐτός
     Εἶπεν κΥριοσ τῷ κΥρίῳ μοΥ   ΚάθοΥ ἐκ δεξιῶν
                                          μοΥ
35 ἕωσ ἂν θῶ τοΥσ ἐχθροΥσ σοΥ ὑποπόδιον τῶν
                                 ποδῶν σοΥ.

ἀσφαλῶς οὖν γινωσκέτω πᾶς οἶκος Ἰσραὴλ ὅτι καὶ κύριον 36
αὐτὸν καὶ χριστὸν ἐποίησεν ὁ θεός, τοῦτον τὸν Ἰησοῦν ὃν
ὑμεῖς ἐσταυρώσατε.   Ἀκούσαντες δὲ κατενύγησαν 37
τὴν καρδίαν, εἶπάν τε πρὸς τὸν Πέτρον καὶ τοὺς λοιποὺς
ἀποστόλους Τί ποιήσωμεν, ἄνδρες ἀδελφοί; Πέτρος δὲ 38
πρὸς αὐτοὺς Μετανοήσατε, καὶ βαπτισθήτω ἕκαστος ὑμῶν
ἐν τῷ ὀνόματι Ἰησοῦ Χριστοῦ εἰς ἄφεσιν τῶν ἁμαρτιῶν
ὑμῶν, καὶ λήμψεσθε τὴν δωρεὰν τοῦ ἁγίου πνεύματος·
ὑμῖν γάρ ἐστιν ἡ ἐπαγγελία καὶ τοῖς τέκνοις ὑμῶν καὶ πᾶσι 39
τοῖς εἰς μακρὰν ὅσους ἂν προσκαλέσηται Κύριος
ὁ θεὸς ἡμῶν.   ἑτέροις τε λόγοις πλείοσιν διεμαρτύρατο, καὶ 40
παρεκάλει αὐτοὺς λέγων Σώθητε ἀπὸ τῆς γενεᾶς τῆς σκολιᾶς ταύτης. Οἱ μὲν οὖν ἀποδεξάμενοι τὸν λόγον αὐτοῦ 41
ἐβαπτίσθησαν, καὶ προσετέθησαν ἐν τῇ ἡμέρᾳ ἐκείνῃ ψυχαὶ
ὡσεὶ τρισχίλιαι. ἦσαν δὲ προσκαρτεροῦντες τῇ διδαχῇ τῶν 42
ἀποστόλων καὶ τῇ κοινωνίᾳ, τῇ κλάσει τοῦ ⌈ἄρτου⌉ καὶ ταῖς
προσευχαῖς.   Ἐγίνετο δὲ πάσῃ ψυχῇ φόβος, 43
πολλὰ δὲ τέρατα καὶ σημεῖα διὰ τῶν ἀποστόλων ἐγίνετο.
πάντες δὲ οἱ πιστεύσαντες ⌈ἐπὶ τὸ αὐτὸ⌉ εἶχον ἅπαντα κοινά, 44
καὶ τὰ κτήματα καὶ τὰς ὑπάρξεις ἐπίπρασκον καὶ διεμέριζον 45
αὐτὰ πᾶσιν καθότι ἄν τις χρείαν εἶχεν· καθ᾽ ἡμέραν τε 46
προσκαρτεροῦντες ὁμοθυμαδὸν ἐν τῷ ἱερῷ, κλῶντές τε
κατ᾽ οἶκον ἄρτον, μετελάμβανον τροφῆς ἐν ἀγαλλιάσει καὶ
ἀφελότητι καρδίας, αἰνοῦντες τὸν θεὸν καὶ ἔχοντες χάριν 47
πρὸς ὅλον τὸν λαόν. ὁ δὲ κύριος προσετίθει τοὺς σωζομένους καθ᾽ ἡμέραν ἐπὶ τὸ αὐτό.   1

Πέτρος δὲ καὶ Ἰωάνης ἀνέβαινον εἰς τὸ ἱερὸν ἐπὶ τὴν
ὥραν τῆς προσευχῆς τὴν ἐνάτην, καί τις ἀνὴρ χωλὸς ἐκ 2
κοιλίας μητρὸς αὐτοῦ ὑπάρχων ἐβαστάζετο, ὃν ἐτίθουν
καθ᾽ ἡμέραν πρὸς τὴν θύραν τοῦ ἱεροῦ τὴν λεγομένην
Ὡραίαν τοῦ αἰτεῖν ἐλεημοσύνην παρὰ τῶν εἰσπορευομένων
εἰς τὸ ἱερόν, ὃς ἰδὼν Πέτρον καὶ Ἰωάνην μέλλοντας εἰσιέ- 3

42 ἄρτου,

4 ναι εἰς τὸ ἱερὸν ἠρώτα ἐλεημοσύνην λαβεῖν. ἀτενίσας δὲ
Πέτρος εἰς αὐτὸν σὺν τῷ Ἰωάνῃ εἶπεν Βλέψον εἰς ἡμᾶς.
5 ὁ δὲ ἐπεῖχεν αὐτοῖς προσδοκῶν τι παρ' αὐτῶν λαβεῖν.
6 εἶπεν δὲ Πέτρος Ἀργύριον καὶ χρυσίον οὐχ ὑπάρχει μοι,
ὃ δὲ ἔχω τοῦτό σοι δίδωμι· ἐν τῷ ὀνόματι Ἰησοῦ Χριστοῦ
7 τοῦ Ναζωραίου περιπάτει. καὶ πιάσας αὐτὸν τῆς δεξιᾶς
χειρὸς ἤγειρεν αὐτόν· παραχρῆμα δὲ ἐστερεώθησαν αἱ
8 βάσεις αὐτοῦ καὶ τὰ σφυδρά, καὶ ἐξαλλόμενος ἔστη καὶ
περιεπάτει, καὶ εἰσῆλθεν σὺν αὐτοῖς εἰς τὸ ἱερὸν περιπατῶν
9 καὶ ἀλλόμενος καὶ αἰνῶν τὸν θεόν. καὶ εἶδεν πᾶς ὁ λαὸς
10 αὐτὸν περιπατοῦντα καὶ αἰνοῦντα τὸν θεόν, ἐπεγίνωσκον δὲ
αὐτὸν ὅτι οὗτος ἦν ὁ πρὸς τὴν ἐλεημοσύνην καθήμενος ἐπὶ
τῇ Ὡραίᾳ Πύλῃ τοῦ ἱεροῦ, καὶ ἐπλήσθησαν θάμβους καὶ
11 ἐκστάσεως ἐπὶ τῷ συμβεβηκότι αὐτῷ.   Κρατοῦντος δὲ αὐτοῦ τὸν Πέτρον καὶ τὸν Ἰωάνην συνέδραμεν
πᾶς ὁ λαὸς πρὸς αὐτοὺς ἐπὶ τῇ στοᾷ τῇ καλουμένῃ Σολομῶν-
12 τος ἔκθαμβοι. ἰδὼν δὲ ὁ Πέτρος ἀπεκρίνατο πρὸς τὸν λαόν
Ἄνδρες Ἰσραηλεῖται, τί θαυμάζετε ἐπὶ τούτῳ, ἢ ἡμῖν τί
ἀτενίζετε ὡς ἰδίᾳ δυνάμει ἢ εὐσεβείᾳ πεποιηκόσιν τοῦ περι-
13 πατεῖν αὐτόν; ὁ θεὸς Ἀβραὰμ καὶ Ἰσαὰκ καὶ Ἰακώβ,
ὁ θεὸς τῶν πατέρων ἡμῶν, ἐδόξασεν τὸν παῖδα αὐτοῦ Ἰησοῦν, ὃν ὑμεῖς μὲν παρεδώκατε καὶ ἠρνήσασθε κατὰ
14 πρόσωπον Πειλάτου, κρίναντος ἐκείνου ἀπολύειν· ὑμεῖς δὲ
τὸν ἅγιον καὶ δίκαιον ἠρνήσασθε, καὶ ᾐτήσασθε ἄνδρα
15 φονέα χαρισθῆναι ὑμῖν, τὸν δὲ ἀρχηγὸν τῆς ζωῆς ἀπεκτείνατε, ὃν ὁ θεὸς ἤγειρεν ἐκ νεκρῶν, οὗ ἡμεῖς μάρτυρές ἐσμεν.
16 καὶ τῇ πίστει τοῦ ὀνόματος αὐτοῦ τοῦτον ὃν θεωρεῖτε καὶ
οἴδατε ἐστερέωσεν τὸ ὄνομα αὐτοῦ, καὶ ἡ πίστις ἡ δι' αὐτοῦ
ἔδωκεν αὐτῷ τὴν ὁλοκληρίαν ταύτην ἀπέναντι πάντων
17 ὑμῶν. καὶ νῦν, ἀδελφοί, οἶδα ὅτι κατὰ ἄγνοιαν ἐπράξατε,
18 ὥσπερ καὶ οἱ ἄρχοντες ὑμῶν· ὁ δὲ θεὸς ἃ προκατήγγειλεν
διὰ στόματος πάντων τῶν προφητῶν παθεῖν τὸν χριστὸν
19 αὐτοῦ ἐπλήρωσεν οὕτως. μετανοήσατε οὖν καὶ ἐπιστρέψατε

44 ἦσαν ἐπὶ τὸ αὐτὸ καὶ

πρὸς τὸ ἐξαλιφθῆναι ὑμῶν τὰς ἁμαρτίας, ὅπως ἂν ἔλθωσιν 20
καιροὶ ἀναψύξεως ἀπὸ προσώπου τοῦ κυρίου καὶ ἀποστείλῃ
τὸν προκεχειρισμένον ὑμῖν χριστὸν Ἰησοῦν, ὃν δεῖ οὐρανὸν 21
μὲν δέξασθαι ἄχρι χρόνων ἀποκαταστάσεως πάντων ὧν ἐλάλησεν ὁ θεὸς διὰ στόματος τῶν ἁγίων ἀπ᾽ αἰῶνος αὐτοῦ
προφητῶν. Μωυσῆς μὲν εἶπεν ὅτι Προφήτην ὑμῖν ἀνα- 22
cτήcει Κύριοc ὁ θεὸc ἐκ τῶν ἀδελφῶν ὑμῶν ὡς ἐμέ·
αὐτοῦ ἀκούcεcθε κατὰ πάντα ὅcα ἂν λαλήcῃ πρὸc
ὑμᾶc. ἔcται δὲ πᾶcα ψυχὴ ἥτιc ἂν μὴ ἀκούcῃ τοῦ 23
προφήτου ἐκείνου ἐξολεθρευθήcεται ἐκ τοῦ λαοῦ.
καὶ πάντες δὲ οἱ προφῆται ἀπὸ Σαμουὴλ καὶ τῶν καθεξῆς 24
ὅσοι ἐλάλησαν καὶ κατήγγειλαν τὰς ἡμέρας ταύτας. ὑμεῖς 25
ἐστὲ οἱ υἱοὶ τῶν προφητῶν καὶ τῆς διαθήκης ἧς ὁ θεὸς διέθετο πρὸς τοὺς πατέρας ⌜ὑμῶν⌝, λέγων πρὸς Ἀβραάμ Καὶ
ἐν τῷ cπέρματί cου εὐλογηθήcονται πᾶcαι αἱ πα-
τριαὶ τῆc γῆc. ὑμῖν πρῶτον ἀναστήσας ὁ θεὸς τὸν παῖδα 26
αὐτοῦ ἀπέστειλεν αὐτὸν εὐλογοῦντα ὑμᾶς ἐν τῷ ἀποστρέφειν
ἕκαστον ἀπὸ τῶν πονηριῶν [ὑμῶν]. Λαλούν- 1
των δὲ αὐτῶν πρὸς τὸν λαὸν ἐπέστησαν αὐτοῖς οἱ ⌜ἀρχιερεῖς⌝
καὶ ὁ στρατηγὸς τοῦ ἱεροῦ καὶ οἱ Σαδδουκαῖοι, διαπονού- 2
μενοι διὰ τὸ διδάσκειν αὐτοὺς τὸν λαὸν καὶ καταγγέλλειν
ἐν τῷ Ἰησοῦ τὴν ἀνάστασιν τὴν ἐκ νεκρῶν, καὶ ἐπέβαλον 3
αὐτοῖς τὰς χεῖρας καὶ ἔθεντο εἰς τήρησιν εἰς τὴν αὔριον, ἦν
γὰρ ἑσπέρα ἤδη. πολλοὶ δὲ τῶν ἀκουσάντων τὸν λόγον ἐπί- 4
στευσαν, καὶ ἐγενήθη ἀριθμὸς τῶν ἀνδρῶν ὡς χιλιάδες πέντε.
Ἐγένετο δὲ ἐπὶ τὴν αὔριον συναχθῆναι αὐτῶν τοὺς 5
ἄρχοντας καὶ τοὺς πρεσβυτέρους καὶ τοὺς γραμματεῖς ἐν
Ἰερουσαλήμ (καὶ Ἄννας ὁ ἀρχιερεὺς καὶ Καιάφας καὶ 6
Ἰωάννης καὶ Ἀλέξανδρος καὶ ὅσοι ἦσαν ἐκ γένους ἀρχιερα-
τικοῦ), καὶ στήσαντες αὐτοὺς ἐν τῷ μέσῳ ἐπυνθάνοντο Ἐν 7
ποίᾳ δυνάμει ἢ ἐν ποίῳ ὀνόματι ἐποιήσατε τοῦτο ὑμεῖς;
τότε Πέτρος πλησθεὶς πνεύματος ἁγίου εἶπεν πρὸς αὐτούς 8
Ἄρχοντες τοῦ λαοῦ καὶ πρεσβύτεροι, εἰ ἡμεῖς σήμερον 9

25 ἡμῶν

ἀνακρινόμεθα ἐπὶ εὐεργεσίᾳ ἀνθρώπου ἀσθενοῦς, ἐν τίνι
10 οὗτος σέσωσται, γνωστὸν ἔστω πᾶσιν ὑμῖν καὶ παντὶ τῷ
λαῷ Ἰσραὴλ ὅτι ἐν τῷ ὀνόματι Ἰησοῦ Χριστοῦ τοῦ Ναζωραίου, ὃν ὑμεῖς ἐσταυρώσατε, ὃν ὁ θεὸς ἤγειρεν ἐκ νεκρῶν,
11 ἐν τούτῳ οὗτος παρέστηκεν ἐνώπιον ὑμῶν ὑγιής. οὗτός
ἐστιν ὁ λίθος ὁ ἐξογθενηθεὶς ὑφ' ὑμῶν τῶν οἰκοδό-
12 μων, ὁ ɼενόμενος εἰς κεφαλὴν ɼωνίας. καὶ οὐκ ἔστιν
ἐν ἄλλῳ οὐδενὶ ἡ σωτηρία, οὐδὲ γὰρ ὄνομά ἐστιν ἕτερον
ὑπὸ τὸν οὐρανὸν τὸ δεδομένον ἐν ἀνθρώποις ἐν ᾧ δεῖ σωθῆ-
13 ναι ἡμᾶς. Θεωροῦντες δὲ τὴν τοῦ Πέτρου παρρησίαν
καὶ Ἰωάνου, καὶ καταλαβόμενοι ὅτι ἄνθρωποι ἀγράμματοί
εἰσιν καὶ ἰδιῶται, ἐθαύμαζον, ἐπεγίνωσκόν τε αὐτοὺς ὅτι σὺν
14 τῷ Ἰησοῦ ἦσαν, τόν τε ἄνθρωπον βλέποντες σὺν αὐτοῖς
15 ἑστῶτα τὸν τεθεραπευμένον οὐδὲν εἶχον ἀντειπεῖν. κελεύ-
σαντες δὲ αὐτοὺς ἔξω τοῦ συνεδρίου ἀπελθεῖν συνέβαλλον
16 πρὸς ἀλλήλους λέγοντες Τί ποιήσωμεν τοῖς ἀνθρώποις
τούτοις; ὅτι μὲν γὰρ γνωστὸν σημεῖον γέγονεν δι' αὐτῶν
πᾶσιν τοῖς κατοικοῦσιν Ἰερουσαλὴμ φανερόν, καὶ οὐ δυνά-
17 μεθα ἀρνεῖσθαι· ἀλλ' ἵνα μὴ ἐπὶ πλεῖον διανεμηθῇ εἰς τὸν
λαόν, ἀπειλησώμεθα αὐτοῖς μηκέτι λαλεῖν ἐπὶ τῷ ὀνόματι
18 τούτῳ μηδενὶ ἀνθρώπων. καὶ καλέσαντες αὐτοὺς παρήγγειλαν καθόλου· μὴ φθέγγεσθαι μηδὲ διδάσκειν ἐπὶ τῷ
19 ὀνόματι [τοῦ] Ἰησοῦ. ὁ δὲ Πέτρος καὶ Ἰωάνης ἀποκρι-
θέντες εἶπαν πρὸς αὐτούς Εἰ δίκαιόν ἐστιν ἐνώπιον τοῦ
20 θεοῦ ὑμῶν ἀκούειν μᾶλλον ἢ τοῦ θεοῦ κρίνατε, οὐ δυνάμεθα
21 γὰρ ἡμεῖς ἃ εἴδαμεν καὶ ἠκούσαμεν μὴ λαλεῖν. οἱ δὲ
προσαπειλησάμενοι ἀπέλυσαν αὐτούς, μηδὲν εὑρίσκοντες
τὸ πῶς κολάσωνται αὐτούς, διὰ τὸν λαόν, ὅτι πάντες
22 ἐδόξαζον τὸν θεὸν ἐπὶ τῷ γεγονότι· ἐτῶν γὰρ ἦν πλειόνων
τεσσεράκοντα ὁ ἄνθρωπος ἐφ' ὃν γεγόνει τὸ σημεῖον τοῦτο
23 τῆς ἰάσεως. Ἀπολυθέντες δὲ ἦλθον πρὸς τοὺς
ἰδίους καὶ ἀπήγγειλαν ὅσα πρὸς αὐτοὺς οἱ ἀρχιερεῖς καὶ οἱ
24 πρεσβύτεροι εἶπαν. οἱ δὲ ἀκούσαντες ὁμοθυμαδὸν ἦραν

1 ἱερεῖς

φωνὴν πρὸς τὸν θεὸν καὶ εἶπαν Δέσποτα, σὺ ὁ ΠΟΙΗϹΑϹ
ΤΟΝ ΟΥΡΑΝΟΝ ΚΑΙ ΤΗΝ ΓΗΝ ΚΑΙ ΤΗΝ ΘΑΛΑϹϹΑΝ ΚΑΙ
ΠΑΝΤΑ ΤΑ ΕΝ ΑΥΤΟΙϹ, ⌈ὁ τοῦ πατρὸς ἡμῶν διὰ πνεύματος 25
ἁγίου στόματος⌉ Δαυεὶδ παιδός σου εἰπών
    Ἵ ΝΑ ΤΙ ΕϹΦΡΥΑΞΑΝ ΕΘΝΗ
    ΚΑΙ ΛΑΟΙ ΕΜΕΛΕΤΗϹΑΝ ΚΕΝΑ ;
    ΠΑΡΕϹΤΗϹΑΝ ΟΙ ΒΑϹΙΛΕΙϹ ΤΗϹ ΓΗϹ   26
    ΚΑΙ ΟΙ ΑΡΧΟΝΤΕϹ ϹΥΝΗΧΘΗϹΑΝ ΕΠΙ ΤΟ ΑΥΤΟ
    ΚΑΤΑ ΤΟΥ ΚΥΡΙΟΥ ΚΑΙ ΚΑΤΑ ΤΟΥ ΧΡΙϹΤΟΥ ΑΥΤΟΥ.
ϹΥΝΗΧΘΗϹΑΝ γὰρ ἐπ᾽ ἀληθείας ἐν τῇ πόλει ταύτῃ ἐπὶ τὸν 27
ἅγιον παῖδά σου Ἰησοῦν, ὃν ἔχρισας, Ἡρῴδης τε καὶ
Πόντιος Πειλᾶτος σὺν ΕΘΝΕϹΙΝ καὶ λαοῖϲ Ἰσραήλ, ποιῆσαι 28
ὅσα ἡ χείρ σου καὶ ἡ βουλὴ προώρισεν γενέσθαι. καὶ τὰ 29
νῦν, κύριε, ἔπιδε ἐπὶ τὰς ἀπειλὰς αὐτῶν, καὶ δὸς τοῖς δούλοις
σου μετὰ παρρησίας πάσης λαλεῖν τὸν λόγον σου, ἐν τῷ 30
τὴν χεῖρα ἐκτείνειν σε εἰς ἴασιν καὶ σημεῖα καὶ τέρατα
γίνεσθαι διὰ τοῦ ὀνόματος τοῦ ἁγίου παιδός σου Ἰησοῦ.
καὶ δεηθέντων αὐτῶν ἐσαλεύθη ὁ τόπος ἐν ᾧ ἦσαν συνη- 31
γμένοι, καὶ ἐπλήσθησαν ἅπαντες τοῦ ἁγίου πνεύματος,
καὶ ἐλάλουν τὸν λόγον τοῦ θεοῦ μετὰ παρρησίας.

Τοῦ δὲ πλήθους τῶν πιστευσάντων ἦν καρδία καὶ ψυχὴ 32
μία, καὶ οὐδὲ εἷς τι τῶν ὑπαρχόντων αὐτῷ ἔλεγεν ἴδιον εἶναι,
ἀλλ᾽ ἦν αὐτοῖς πάντα κοινά. καὶ δυνάμει μεγάλῃ ἀπεδί- 33
δουν τὸ μαρτύριον οἱ ἀπόστολοι τοῦ κυρίου Ἰησοῦ τῆς
ἀναστάσεως, χάρις τε μεγάλη ἦν ἐπὶ πάντας αὐτούς. οὐδὲ 34
γὰρ ἐνδεής τις ἦν ἐν αὐτοῖς· ὅσοι γὰρ κτήτορες χωρίων ἢ
οἰκιῶν ὑπῆρχον, πωλοῦντες ἔφερον τὰς τιμὰς τῶν πιπρα-
σκομένων καὶ ἐτίθουν παρὰ τοὺς πόδας τῶν ἀποστόλων· 35
διεδίδετο δὲ ἑκάστῳ καθότι ἄν τις χρείαν εἶχεν. Ἰωσὴφ δὲ 36
ὁ ἐπικληθεὶς Βαρνάβας ἀπὸ τῶν ἀποστόλων, ὅ ἐστιν μεθερ-
μηνευόμενον Υἱὸς Παρακλήσεως, Λευείτης, Κύπριος τῷ
γένει, ὑπάρχοντος αὐτῷ ἀγροῦ πωλήσας ἤνεγκεν τὸ χρῆμα 37

                          25 †...†

καὶ ἔθηκεν παρὰ τοὺς πόδας τῶν ἀποστόλων.

1 Ἀνὴρ δέ τις Ἀνανίας ὀνόματι σὺν Σαπφείρῃ τῇ γυναικὶ
2 αὐτοῦ ἐπώλησεν κτῆμα καὶ ἐνοσφίσατο ἀπὸ τῆς τιμῆς,
συνειδυίης καὶ τῆς γυναικός, καὶ ἐνέγκας μέρος τι παρὰ
3 τοὺς πόδας τῶν ἀποστόλων ἔθηκεν. εἶπεν δὲ ὁ Πέτρος
Ἀνανία, διὰ τί ἐπλήρωσεν ὁ Σατανᾶς τὴν καρδίαν σου
ψεύσασθαί σε τὸ πνεῦμα τὸ ἅγιον καὶ νοσφίσασθαι ἀπὸ
4 τῆς τιμῆς τοῦ χωρίου; οὐχὶ μένον σοὶ ἔμενεν καὶ πραθὲν
ἐν τῇ σῇ ἐξουσίᾳ ὑπῆρχεν; τί ὅτι ἔθου ἐν τῇ καρδίᾳ σου
τὸ πρᾶγμα τοῦτο; οὐκ ἐψεύσω ἀνθρώποις ἀλλὰ τῷ θεῷ.
5 ἀκούων δὲ ὁ Ἀνανίας τοὺς λόγους τούτους πεσὼν ἐξέψυξεν·
6 καὶ ἐγένετο φόβος μέγας ἐπὶ πάντας τοὺς ἀκούοντας. ἀναστάντες δὲ οἱ νεώτεροι συνέστειλαν αὐτὸν καὶ ἐξενέγκαντες
7 ἔθαψαν. Ἐγένετο δὲ ὡς ὡρῶν τριῶν διάστημα
8 καὶ ἡ γυνὴ αὐτοῦ μὴ εἰδυῖα τὸ γεγονὸς εἰσῆλθεν. ἀπεκρίθη δὲ πρὸς αὐτὴν Πέτρος Εἰπέ μοι, εἰ τοσούτου τὸ
9 χωρίον ἀπέδοσθε; ἡ δὲ εἶπεν Ναί, τοσούτου. ὁ δὲ Πέτρος πρὸς αὐτὴν Τί ὅτι συνεφωνήθη ὑμῖν πειράσαι τὸ
πνεῦμα Κυρίου; ἰδοὺ οἱ πόδες τῶν θαψάντων τὸν ἄνδρα
10 σου ἐπὶ τῇ θύρᾳ καὶ ἐξοίσουσίν σε. ἔπεσεν δὲ παραχρῆμα
πρὸς τοὺς πόδας αὐτοῦ καὶ ἐξέψυξεν· εἰσελθόντες δὲ οἱ
νεανίσκοι εὗρον αὐτὴν νεκράν, καὶ ἐξενέγκαντες ἔθαψαν
11 πρὸς τὸν ἄνδρα αὐτῆς. Καὶ ἐγένετο φόβος μέγας ἐφ᾽ ὅλην
τὴν ἐκκλησίαν καὶ ἐπὶ πάντας τοὺς ἀκούοντας ταῦτα.

12 Διὰ δὲ τῶν χειρῶν τῶν ἀποστόλων ἐγίνετο σημεῖα καὶ
τέρατα πολλὰ ἐν τῷ λαῷ· καὶ ἦσαν ὁμοθυμαδὸν πάντες ἐν
13 τῇ Στοᾷ Σολομῶντος· τῶν δὲ λοιπῶν οὐδεὶς ἐτόλμα κολ-
14 λᾶσθαι αὐτοῖς· ἀλλ᾽ ἐμεγάλυνεν αὐτοὺς ὁ λαός, μᾶλλον δὲ
προσετίθεντο πιστεύοντες τῷ κυρίῳ πλήθη ἀνδρῶν τε καὶ
15 γυναικῶν· ὥστε καὶ εἰς τὰς πλατείας ἐκφέρειν τοὺς ἀσθενεῖς
καὶ τιθέναι ἐπὶ κλιναρίων καὶ κραβάττων, ἵνα ἐρχομένου
16 Πέτρου κἂν ἡ σκιὰ ἐπισκιάσει τινὶ αὐτῶν. συνήρχετο δὲ

καὶ τὸ πλῆθος τῶν πέριξ πόλεων Ἰερουσαλήμ, φέροντες ἀσθενεῖς καὶ ὀχλουμένους ὑπὸ πνευμάτων ἀκαθάρτων, οἵτινες ἐθεραπεύοντο ἅπαντες.

Ἀναστὰς δὲ ὁ ἀρχιερεὺς καὶ πάντες οἱ σὺν αὐτῷ, ἡ 17 οὖσα αἵρεσις τῶν Σαδδουκαίων, ἐπλήσθησαν ζήλου καὶ 18 ἐπέβαλον τὰς χεῖρας ἐπὶ τοὺς ἀποστόλους καὶ ἔθεντο αὐτοὺς ἐν τηρήσει δημοσίᾳ. Ἄγγελος δὲ Κυρίου διὰ νυκτὸς ἤνοιξε 19 τὰς θύρας τῆς φυλακῆς ἐξαγαγών τε αὐτοὺς εἶπεν Πο- 20 ρεύεσθε καὶ σταθέντες λαλεῖτε ἐν τῷ ἱερῷ τῷ λαῷ πάντα τὰ ῥήματα τῆς ζωῆς ταύτης. ἀκούσαντες δὲ εἰσῆλθον ὑπὸ 21 τὸν ὄρθρον εἰς τὸ ἱερὸν καὶ ἐδίδασκον. Παραγενόμενος δὲ ὁ ἀρχιερεὺς καὶ οἱ σὺν αὐτῷ συνεκάλεσαν τὸ συνέδριον καὶ πᾶσαν τὴν γερουσίαν τῶν υἱῶν Ἰσραήλ, καὶ ἀπέστειλαν εἰς τὸ δεσμωτήριον ἀχθῆναι αὐτούς. οἱ δὲ παραγενόμενοι 22 ὑπηρέται οὐχ εὗρον αὐτοὺς ἐν τῇ φυλακῇ, ἀναστρέψαντες δὲ ἀπήγγειλαν λέγοντες ὅτι Τὸ δεσμωτήριον εὕρομεν 23 κεκλεισμένον ἐν πάσῃ ἀσφαλείᾳ καὶ τοὺς φύλακας ἑστῶτας ἐπὶ τῶν θυρῶν, ἀνοίξαντες δὲ ἔσω οὐδένα εὕρομεν. ὡς δὲ 24 ἤκουσαν τοὺς λόγους τούτους ὅ τε στρατηγὸς τοῦ ἱεροῦ καὶ οἱ ἀρχιερεῖς, διηπόρουν περὶ αὐτῶν τί ἂν γένοιτο τοῦτο. Παραγενόμενος δέ τις ἀπήγγειλεν αὐτοῖς ὅτι Ἰδοὺ οἱ 25 ἄνδρες οὓς ἔθεσθε ἐν τῇ φυλακῇ εἰσὶν ἐν τῷ ἱερῷ ἑστῶτες καὶ διδάσκοντες τὸν λαόν. τότε ἀπελθὼν ὁ στρατηγὸς σὺν 26 τοῖς ὑπηρέταις ἦγεν αὐτούς, οὐ μετὰ βίας, ἐφοβοῦντο γὰρ τὸν λαόν, μὴ λιθασθῶσιν· ἀγαγόντες δὲ αὐτοὺς ἔστησαν 27 ἐν τῷ συνεδρίῳ. καὶ ἐπηρώτησεν αὐτοὺς ὁ ἀρχιερεὺς λέγων Παραγγελίᾳ παρηγγείλαμεν ὑμῖν μὴ διδάσκειν ἐπὶ 28 τῷ ὀνόματι τούτῳ, καὶ ἰδοὺ πεπληρώκατε τὴν Ἰερουσαλὴμ τῆς διδαχῆς ὑμῶν, καὶ βούλεσθε ἐπαγαγεῖν ἐφ᾽ ἡμᾶς τὸ αἷμα τοῦ ἀνθρώπου τούτου. ἀποκριθεὶς δὲ Πέτρος καὶ οἱ 29 ἀπόστολοι εἶπαν Πειθαρχεῖν δεῖ θεῷ μᾶλλον ἢ ἀνθρώποις. ὁ θεὸς τῶν πατέρων ἡμῶν ἤγειρεν Ἰησοῦν, ὃν ὑμεῖς διεχει- 30 ρίσασθε κρεμάσαντες ἐπὶ ξύλου· τοῦτον ὁ θεὸς ἀρχηγὸν 31

32 ἐν αὐτῷ v. ἐσμὲν αὐτῷ

καὶ σωτῆρα ὕψωσεν τῇ δεξιᾷ αὐτοῦ, [τοῦ] δοῦναι μετάνοιαν
32 τῷ Ἰσραὴλ καὶ ἄφεσιν ἁμαρτιῶν· καὶ ἡμεῖς ⌈ἐσμὲν⌉ μάρτυρες τῶν ῥημάτων ⌈τούτων, καὶ τὸ πνεῦμα τὸ ἅγιον ὃ⌉
33 ἔδωκεν ὁ θεὸς τοῖς πειθαρχοῦσιν αὐτῷ. οἱ δὲ ἀκούσαντες
34 διεπρίοντο καὶ ἐβούλοντο ἀνελεῖν αὐτούς. Ἀναστὰς δέ τις
ἐν τῷ συνεδρίῳ Φαρισαῖος ὀνόματι Γαμαλιήλ, νομοδιδάσκαλος τίμιος παντὶ τῷ λαῷ, ἐκέλευσεν ἔξω βραχὺ τοὺς
35 ἀνθρώπους ποιῆσαι, εἶπέν τε πρὸς αὐτούς Ἄνδρες Ἰσραηλεῖται, προσέχετε ἑαυτοῖς ἐπὶ τοῖς ἀνθρώποις τούτοις τί
36 μέλλετε πράσσειν. πρὸ γὰρ τούτων τῶν ἡμερῶν ἀνέστη
Θευδᾶς, λέγων εἶναί τινα ἑαυτόν, ᾧ προσεκλίθη ἀνδρῶν
ἀριθμὸς ὡς τετρακοσίων· ὃς ἀνῃρέθη, καὶ πάντες ὅσοι
37 ἐπείθοντο αὐτῷ διελύθησαν καὶ ἐγένοντο εἰς οὐδέν. μετὰ
τοῦτον ἀνέστη Ἰούδας ὁ Γαλιλαῖος ἐν ταῖς ἡμέραις τῆς
ἀπογραφῆς καὶ ἀπέστησε λαὸν ὀπίσω αὐτοῦ· κἀκεῖνος
ἀπώλετο, κ.ὶ πάντες ὅσοι ἐπείθοντο αὐτῷ διεσκορπίσθη-
38 σαν. καὶ [τὰ] νῦν λέγω ὑμῖν, ἀπόστητε ἀπὸ τῶν ἀνθρώπων τούτων καὶ ἄφετε αὐτούς· (ὅτι ἐὰν ᾖ ἐξ ἀνθρώπων
39 ἡ βουλὴ αὕτη ἢ τὸ ἔργον τοῦτο, καταλυθήσεται· εἰ δὲ ἐκ
θεοῦ ἐστίν, οὐ δυνήσεσθε καταλῦσαι αὐτούς·) μή ποτε καὶ
40 θεομάχοι εὑρεθῆτε. ἐπείσθησαν δὲ αὐτῷ, καὶ προσκαλεσάμενοι τοὺς ἀποστόλους δείραντες παρήγγειλαν μὴ λαλεῖν
41 ἐπὶ τῷ ὀνόματι τοῦ Ἰησοῦ καὶ ἀπέλυσαν. Οἱ μὲν οὖν
ἐπορεύοντο χαίροντες ἀπὸ προσώπου τοῦ συνεδρίου ὅτι
42 κατηξιώθησαν ὑπὲρ τοῦ ὀνόματος ἀτιμασθῆναι· πᾶσάν τε
ἡμέραν ἐν τῷ ἱερῷ καὶ κατ᾽ οἶκον οὐκ ἐπαύοντο διδάσκοντες καὶ εὐαγγελιζόμενοι τὸν χριστὸν Ἰησοῦν.

1   ΕΝ ΔΕ ΤΑΙΣ ΗΜΕΡΑΙΣ ταύταις πληθυνόντων τῶν
μαθητῶν ἐγένετο γογγυσμὸς τῶν Ἑλληνιστῶν πρὸς τοὺς
Ἑβραίους ὅτι παρεθεωροῦντο ἐν τῇ διακονίᾳ τῇ καθημερινῇ

32 τούτων· καὶ τὸ πνεῦμα τὸ ἅγιον

αἱ χῆραι αὐτῶν. προσκαλεσάμενοι δὲ οἱ δώδεκα τὸ πλῆ- 2
θος τῶν μαθητῶν εἶπαν Οὐκ ἀρεστόν ἐστιν ἡμᾶς καταλεί-
ψαντας τὸν λόγον τοῦ θεοῦ διακονεῖν τραπέζαις· ἐπισκέ- 3
ψασθε ⌈δέ⌉, ἀδελφοί, ἄνδρας ἐξ ὑμῶν μαρτυρουμένους ἑπτὰ
πλήρεις πνεύματος καὶ σοφίας, οὓς καταστήσομεν ἐπὶ τῆς
χρείας ταύτης· ἡμεῖς δὲ τῇ προσευχῇ καὶ τῇ διακονίᾳ τοῦ 4
λόγου προσκαρτερήσομεν. καὶ ἤρεσεν ὁ λόγος ἐνώπιον 5
παντὸς τοῦ πλήθους, καὶ ἐξελέξαντο Στέφανον, ἄνδρα
⌈πλήρη⌉ πίστεως καὶ πνεύματος ἁγίου, καὶ Φίλιππον καὶ
Πρόχορον καὶ Νικάνορα καὶ Τίμωνα καὶ Παρμενᾶν καὶ
Νικόλαον προσήλυτον Ἀντιοχέα, οὓς ἔστησαν ἐνώπιον τῶν 6
ἀποστόλων, καὶ προσευξάμενοι ἐπέθηκαν αὐτοῖς τὰς χεῖρας.
Καὶ ὁ λόγος τοῦ θεοῦ ηὔξανεν, καὶ ἐπληθύνετο ὁ ἀρι- 7
θμὸς τῶν μαθητῶν ἐν Ἰερουσαλὴμ σφόδρα, πολύς τε ὄχλος
τῶν ἱερέων ὑπήκουον τῇ πίστει.

Στέφανος δὲ πλήρης χάριτος καὶ δυνάμεως ἐποίει τέρατα 8
καὶ σημεῖα μεγάλα ἐν τῷ λαῷ. Ἀνέστησαν δέ τινες τῶν 9
ἐκ τῆς συναγωγῆς τῆς λεγομένης Λιβερτίνων καὶ Κυρη-
ναίων καὶ Ἀλεξανδρέων καὶ τῶν ἀπὸ Κιλικίας καὶ Ἀσίας
συνζητοῦντες τῷ Στεφάνῳ, καὶ οὐκ ἴσχυον ἀντιστῆναι τῇ 10
σοφίᾳ καὶ τῷ πνεύματι ᾧ ἐλάλει. τότε ὑπέβαλον ἄνδρας 11
λέγοντας ὅτι Ἀκηκόαμεν αὐτοῦ λαλοῦντος ῥήματα βλά-
σφημα εἰς Μωυσῆν καὶ τὸν θεόν· συνεκίνησάν τε τὸν λαὸν 12
καὶ τοὺς πρεσβυτέρους καὶ τοὺς γραμματεῖς, καὶ ἐπιστάντες
συνήρπασαν αὐτὸν καὶ ἤγαγον εἰς τὸ συνέδριον, ἔστησάν 13
τε μάρτυρας ψευδεῖς λέγοντας Ὁ ἄνθρωπος οὗτος οὐ παύε-
ται λαλῶν ῥήματα κατὰ τοῦ τόπου τοῦ ἁγίου [τούτου] καὶ
τοῦ νόμου, ἀκηκόαμεν γὰρ αὐτοῦ λέγοντος ὅτι Ἰησοῦς ὁ 14
Ναζωραῖος οὗτος καταλύσει τὸν τόπον τοῦτον καὶ ἀλλάξει
τὰ ἔθη ἃ παρέδωκεν ἡμῖν Μωυσῆς. καὶ ἀτενίσαντες εἰς 15
αὐτὸν πάντες οἱ καθεζόμενοι ἐν τῷ συνεδρίῳ εἶδαν τὸ πρόσωπον αὐτοῦ ὡσεὶ πρόσωπον ἀγγέλου. Εἶπεν 1

3 [δή]   5 πλήρης MSS

2 δὲ ὁ ἀρχιερεύς Εἰ ταῦτα οὕτως ἔχει; ὁ δὲ ἔφη Ἄνδρες
ἀδελφοὶ καὶ πατέρες, ἀκούσατε. Ὁ θεὸς τῆϲ Δόξηϲ
ὤφθη τῷ πατρὶ ἡμῶν Ἀβραὰμ ὄντι ἐν τῇ Μεσοποταμίᾳ
3 πρὶν ἢ κατοικῆσαι αὐτὸν ἐν Χαρράν, καὶ εἶπεν πρὸϲ
αὐτόν Ἔξελθε ἐκ τῆϲ γῆϲ ϲου καὶ ᵀ τῆϲ ϲυγγενείαϲ
4 ϲου, καὶ Δεῦρο εἰϲ τὴν γῆν ἣν ἄν ϲοι Δείξω· τότε ἐξελθὼν ἐκ γῆς Χαλδαίων κατῴκησεν ἐν Χαρράν. κἀκεῖθεν μετὰ
τὸ ἀποθανεῖν τὸν πατέρα αὐτοῦ μετῴκισεν αὐτὸν εἰς τὴν γῆν
5 ταύτην εἰς ἣν ὑμεῖς νῦν κατοικεῖτε, καὶ οὐκ ἔδωκεν αὐτῷ
κληρονομίαν ἐν αὐτῇ οὐδὲ βῆμα ποδόϲ, καὶ ἐπηγγείλατο
Δοῦναι αὐτῷ εἰϲ κατάϲχεϲιν αὐτὴν καὶ τῷ ϲπέρματι
6 αὐτοῦ μετ᾽ αὐτόν, οὐκ ὄντος αὐτῷ τέκνου. ἐλάλησεν δὲ
οὕτως ὁ θεὸς ὅτι ἔϲται τὸ ϲπέρμα αὐτοῦ πάροικον ἐν
γῇ ἀλλοτρίᾳ, καὶ Δουλώϲουϲιν αὐτὸ καὶ κακώϲουϲιν
7 ἔτη τετρακόϲια· καὶ τὸ ἔθνοϲ ᾧ ἂν Δουλεύϲουϲιν
κρινῶ ἐγώ, ὁ θεὸς εἶπεν, καὶ μετὰ ταῦτα ἐξελεύϲονται
8 καὶ λατρεύϲουϲίν μοι ἐν τῷ τόπῳ τούτῳ. καὶ ἔδωκεν
αὐτῷ Διαθήκην περιτομῆϲ· καὶ οὕτως ἐγέννησεν τὸν
Ἰσαὰκ καὶ περιέτεμεν αὐτὸν τῇ ἡμέρᾳ τῇ ὀγδόῃ,
καὶ Ἰσαὰκ τὸν Ἰακώβ, καὶ Ἰακὼβ τοὺς δώδεκα πατριάρ-
9 χας. Καὶ οἱ πατριάρχαι ζηλώϲαντες τὸν Ἰωϲὴφ ἀπέ-
10 Δοντο εἰϲ Αἴγυπτον· καὶ ἦν ὁ θεὸϲ μετ᾽ αὐτοῦ, καὶ
ἐξείλατο αὐτὸν ἐκ πασῶν τῶν θλίψεων αὐτοῦ, καὶ ἔδωκεν
αὐτῷ χάριν καὶ σοφίαν ἐναντίον Φαραὼ βαϲιλέωϲ
Αἰγύπτου, καὶ κατέϲτηϲεν αὐτὸν ἡγούμενον ἐπ᾽ Αἴ-
11 γυπτον καὶ ᵀ ὅλον τὸν οἶκον αὐτοῦ. ἦλθεν δὲ λιμὸϲ
ἐφ᾽ ὅλην τὴν Αἴγυπτον καὶ Χανάαν καὶ θλίψιϲ
μεγάλη, καὶ οὐχ ηὕρισκον χορτάσματα οἱ πατέρες ἡμῶν·
12 ἀκούϲαϲ δὲ Ἰακὼβ ὄντα ϲιτία εἰϲ Αἴγυπτον ἐξαπέ-
13 ϲτειλεν τοὺς πατέρας ἡμῶν πρῶτον· καὶ ἐν τῷ δευτέρῳ
ἐγνωρίϲθη Ἰωϲὴφ τοῖϲ ἀδελφοῖϲ αὐτοῦ, καὶ φα-
14 νερὸν ἐγένετο τῷ Φαραὼ τὸ γένος Ἰωϲήφ. ἀποστείλας δὲ
Ἰωϲὴφ μετεκαλέσατο Ἰακὼβ τὸν πατέρα αὐτοῦ καὶ πᾶσαν

3 ἐκ   10 ἐφ᾽   13 ἀνεγνωρίσθη

τὴν συγγένειαν ἐν ψυχαῖς ἑΒΔΟΜΗΚΟΝΤΑ ΠΕΝΤΕ, ⌐ΚΑΤΕΒΗ 15
δὲ⌐ ᾿Ιακὼβ [εἰϲ ΑΙΓΥΠΤΟΝ]. καὶ ἐΤΕΛΕΥΤΗϹΕΝ ΑΥΤΟϹ καὶ
οἱ πατέρες ἡμῶν, καὶ ΜΕΤΕΤΕΘΗϹΑΝ εἰϲ ϹΥΧΕΜ καὶ ἐτέθη- 16
σαν ἐν τῷ ΜΝΗΜΑΤΙ ᾧ ὠΝΗϹΑΤΟ᾿ΑΒΡΑᾺΜ τιμῆς ἀργυρίου
παρὰ ΤΩΝ ΥΙΩΝ ῾ΕΜΜῺΡ ἐΝ ϹΥΧΕΜ. Καθὼς δὲ ἤγγιζεν 17
ὁ χρόνος τῆς ἐπαγγελίας ἧς ὡμολόγησεν ὁ θεὸς τῷ ᾿Αβραάμ,
ΗΥΞΗϹΕΝ ὁ λαὸς καὶ ἐΠΛΗΘΥΝΘΗ ἐν Αἰγύπτῳ, ἄχρι οὗ 18
ἀΝΕϹΤΗ ΒΑϹΙΛΕΥϹ ἕτεροϲ ἐπ᾿ ΑΙΓΥΠΤΟΝ, ὃϲ ΟΥΚ ΗΔΕΙ
ΤΟΝ ᾿ΙΩϹΗΦ. οὗτος ΚΑΤΑϹΟΦΙϹΑΜΕΝΟϹ τὸ ΓΕΝΟϹ ἡμῶν 19
ἐΚΑΚΩϹΕΝ τοὺς πατέρας τοῦ ποιεῖν τὰ βρέφη ἔκθετα αὐτῶν
εἰς τὸ μὴ ΖΩΟΓΟΝΕΙϹΘΑΙ. ἐν ᾧ καιρῷ ἐγεννήθη Μωυσῆς, καὶ 20
ἦν ἀϹΤΕΙΟϹ τῷ θεῷ· ὃϲ ἀνετράφη ΜΗΝΑϹ ΤΡΕΙϹ ἐν τῷ οἴκῳ
τοῦ πατρός· ἐκτεθέντος δὲ αὐτοῦ ἀΝΕΙΛΑΤΟ αὐτὸν Η ΘΥΓΑ- 21
ΤΗΡ ΦΑΡΑῺ καὶ ἀνεθρέψατο αὐτὸν ἑαυτῇ εἰϲ ΥΙΟΝ. καὶ 22
ἐπαιδεύθη Μωυσῆς πάσῃ σοφίᾳ Αἰγυπτίων, ἦν δὲ δυνατὸς
ἐν λόγοις καὶ ἔργοις αὐτοῦ. ῾Ως δὲ ἐπληροῦτο αὐτῷ τεσσε- 23
ρακονταετὴς χρόνος, ἀνέβη ἐπὶ τὴν καρδίαν αὐτοῦ ἐπισκέψασθαι τοὺϲ ἀΔΕΛΦΟΥϹ ΑΥΤΟΥ τοὺϲ ΥΙΟΥϹ ᾿ΙϹΡΑΗΛ. καὶ 24
ἰδών τινα ἀδικούμενον ἠμύνατο καὶ ἐποίησεν ἐκδίκησιν τῷ
καταπονουμένῳ ΠΑΤΑΞΑϹ ΤΟΝ ΑΙΓΥΠΤΙΟΝ. ἐνόμιζεν δὲ συ- 25
νιέναι τοὺς ἀδελφοὺς ὅτι ὁ θεὸς διὰ χειρὸς αὐτοῦ δίδωσιν
σωτηρίαν αὐτοῖς, οἱ δὲ οὐ συνῆκαν. τῇ τε ἐπιούσῃ ἡμέρᾳ 26
ὤφθη αὐτοῖς μαχομένοις καὶ συνήλλασσεν αὐτοὺς εἰς εἰρήνην εἰπών ῎Ανδρες, ἀδελφοί ἐστε· ἵνα τί ἀδικεῖτε ἀλλήλους;
ὁ δὲ ἀΔΙΚΩΝ ΤΟΝ ΠΛΗϹΙΟΝ ἀπώσατο αὐτὸν εἰπών Τίϲ ϹΕ 27
ΚΑΤΕϹΤΗϹΕΝ ἄΡΧΟΝΤΑ καὶ ΔΙΚΑϹΤΗΝ ἐπ᾿ ΗΜΩΝ; ΜΗ ἀΝΕ- 28
ΛΕΙΝ ΜΕ ϹΥ θέλειϲ ὃΝ ΤΡΟΠΟΝ ἀΝΕΙΛΕϹ ἐχθὲϲ ΤΟΝ ΑΙ-
ΓΥΠΤΙΟΝ; ἔΦΥΓΕΝ ΔΕ ΜωυϹῆϹ ἐν τῷ λόγῳ τούτῳ, 29
καὶ ἐγένετο πάροικος ἐν γῇ Μαδιάμ, οὗ ἐγέννησεν υἱοὺς
δύο. Καὶ πληρωθέντων ἐτῶν τεσσεράκοντα ὤφθη ΑΥΤῼ 30
ἐν τῇ ἐρήμῳ τοῦ ΟΡΟΥϹ Σινὰ ἄγγελος ἐν φλογὶ πυρὸς
Βάτου· ὁ δὲ Μωυσῆς ἰδὼν .ἐθαύμασεν τὸ ὅραμα· προσερ- 31
χομένου δὲ αὐτοῦ κατανοῆσαι ἐγένετο φωνὴ Κυρίου ᾿Εγώ 32

15 καὶ κατέβη   38 ἡμῖν

ὁ θεὸϲ τῶν πατέρων ϲογ, ὁ θεὸϲ Ἀβραὰμ καὶ Ἰϲαὰκ
καὶ Ἰακώβ. ἔντρομος δὲ γενόμενος Μωυσῆς οὐκ ἐτόλμα
33 κατανοῆσαι. εἶπεν Δὲ αγτῷ ὁ κγριοϲ Λγϲον τὸ γπό-
Δημα τῶν ποΔῶν ϲογ, ὁ ΓὰΡ τόποϲ ἐφ' ᾧ ἕϲτηκαϲ Γῆ
34 ἁΓία ἐϲτίν. ἰΔὼν εἶΔον τὴν κάκωϲιν τογ λαογ μογ
τογ ἐν ΑἰΓγπτῳ, καὶ τογ ϲτεναΓμογ αγτογ ἥκογϲα,
καὶ κατέβην ἐξελέϲθαι αγτογϲ· καὶ νγν Δεγρο ἀποϲτεί-
35 λω ϲε εἰϲ ΑἴΓγπτον. Τοῦτον τὸν Μωυσῆν, ὃν ἠρνήσαντο
εἰπόντες Τίϲ ϲὲ κατέϲτηϲεν ἄρχοντα καὶ Δικαϲτήν,
τοῦτον ὁ θεὸς καὶ ἄρχοντα καὶ λυτρωτὴν ἀπέσταλκεν σὺν χει-
36 ρὶ ἀγγέλου τοῦ ὀφθέντος αὐτῷ ἐν τῇ βάτῳ. οὗτος ἐξήγαγεν
αὐτοὺς ποιήσας τέρατα καὶ ϲημεῖα ἐν τῇ ΑἰΓγπτῳ καὶ ἐν
Ἐρυθρᾷ Θαλάσσῃ καὶ ἐν τῇ ἐρήμῳ ἔτη τεϲϲεράκοντα.
37 οὗτός ἐϲτιν ὁ Μωυσῆς ὁ εἴπας τοῖς υἱοῖς Ἰσραὴλ Προφήτην γμῖν ἀναϲτήϲει ὁ θεὸϲ ἐκ τῶν ἀΔελφῶν γμῶν
38 ὡϲ ἐμέ. οὗτός ἐϲτιν ὁ γενόμενος ἐν τῇ ἐκκλησίᾳ ἐν τῇ
ἐρήμῳ μετὰ τοῦ ἀγγέλου τοῦ λαλοῦντος αὐτῷ ἐν τῷ ὄρει
Σινᾶ καὶ τῶν πατέρων ἡμῶν, ὃς ἐδέξατο λόγια ζῶντα δοῦναι
39 ⌜ὑμῖν⌝, ᾧ οὐκ ἠθέλησαν ὑπήκοοι γενέσθαι οἱ πατέρες ἡμῶν
ἀλλὰ ἀπώσαντο καὶ ἐϲτράφηϲαν ἐν ταῖς καρδίαις αὐτῶν
40 εἰϲ ΑἴΓγπτον, εἰπόντες τῷ Ἀαρών Ποίηϲον ἡμῖν
θεογϲ οἳ προπορεγϲονται ἡμῶν· ὁ γὰρ Μωγϲῆϲ
οὗτοϲ, ὃϲ ἐξήΓαΓεν ἡμᾶϲ ἐκ Γῆϲ ΑἰΓγπτογ, ογκ οἴ-
41 Δαμεν τί ἐΓένετο αγτῷ. καὶ ἐμοσχοποίηϲαν ἐν ταῖς
ἡμέραις ἐκείναις καὶ ἀνήΓαΓον θγϲίαν τῷ εἰδώλῳ, καὶ εὐ-
42 φραίνοντο ἐν τοῖς ἔργοις τῶν χειρῶν αὐτῶν. ἔϲτρεψεν δὲ
ὁ θεὸς καὶ παρέδωκεν αὐτοὺς λατρεύειν τῇ ϲτρατιᾷ τογ
ογρανογ, καθὼς γέγραπται ἐν Βίβλῳ τῶν προφητῶν
Μὴ ϲφάΓια καὶ θγϲίαϲ προϲηνέΓκατέ μοι
ἔτη τεϲϲεράκοντα ἐν τῇ ἐρήμῳ, οἶκοϲ Ἰϲραήλ;
43 καὶ ἀνελάβετε τὴν ϲκηνὴν τογ Μολόχ
καὶ τὸ ἄϲτρον τογ θεογ Ῥομφά,
τογϲ τγπογϲ ογϲ ἐποιήϲατε προσκυνεῖν αὐτοῖς.
καὶ μετοικιῶ γμᾶϲ ἐπέκεινα Βαβυλῶνος.

P.   2

Ἡ σκηνὴ τοῦ μαρτυρίου ἦν τοῖς πατράσιν ἡμῶν ἐν τῇ 44
ἐρήμῳ, καθὼς διετάξατο ὁ λαλῶν τῷ Μωυϲῇ ποιῆϲαι
αὐτὴν κατὰ τὸν τύπον ὃν ἑωράκει, ἣν καὶ εἰσήγαγον 45
διαδεξάμενοι οἱ πατέρες ἡμῶν μετὰ Ἰησοῦ ἐν τῇ κατα-
ϲχέϲει τῶν ἐθνῶν ὧν ἐξῶσεν ὁ θεὸς ἀπὸ προσώπου τῶν
πατέρων ἡμῶν ἕως τῶν ἡμερῶν Δαυείδ· ὃς εὗρεν χάριν 46
ἐνώπιον τοῦ θεοῦ καὶ ᾐτήσατο εὑρεῖν ϲκήνωμα τῷ
⌜θεῷ⌝ Ἰακώβ. Ϲολομῶν δὲ οἰκοδόμηϲεν αὐτῷ οἶκον. 47
ἀλλ' οὐχ ὁ ὕψιστος ἐν χειροποιήτοις κατοικεῖ· καθὼς ὁ 48
προφήτης λέγει
    Ὁ οὐρανός μοι θρόνος,   49
  ⌜καὶ ἡ⌝ γῆ ὑποπόδιον τῶν ποδῶν μου·
  ποῖον οἶκον οἰκοδομήϲετέ μοι, λέγει Κύριος,
  ἢ τίς τόπος τῆϲ καταπαύϲεώϲ μου;
    οὐχὶ ἡ χείρ μου ἐποίηϲεν ταῦτα πάντα ; 50
Ϲκληροτράχηλοι καὶ ἀπερίτμητοι ⌜καρδίαιϲ⌝ καὶ τοῖϲ 51
ὠϲίν, ὑμεῖς ἀεὶ τῷ πνεύματι τῷ ἁγίῳ ἀντιπίπτετε, ὡς
οἱ πατέρες ὑμῶν καὶ ὑμεῖς. τίνα τῶν προφητῶν οὐκ ἐδίωξαν 52
οἱ πατέρες ὑμῶν ; καὶ ἀπέκτειναν τοὺς προκαταγγείλαντας
περὶ τῆς ἐλεύσεως τοῦ δικαίου οὗ νῦν ὑμεῖς προδόται καὶ
φονεῖς ἐγένεσθε, οἵτινες ἐλάβετε τὸν νόμον εἰς διαταγὰς 53
ἀγγέλων, καὶ οὐκ ἐφυλάξατε.   Ἀκούοντες δὲ 54
ταῦτα διεπρίοντο ταῖς καρδίαις αὐτῶν καὶ ἔβρυχον τοὺς
ὀδόντας ἐπ' αὐτόν. ὑπάρχων δὲ πλήρης πνεύματος ἁγίου 55
ἀτενίσας εἰς τὸν οὐρανὸν εἶδεν δόξαν θεοῦ καὶ Ἰησοῦν ἑστῶτα
ἐκ δεξιῶν τοῦ θεοῦ, καὶ εἶπεν Ἰδοὺ θεωρῶ τοὺς οὐρανοὺς 56
διηνοιγμένους καὶ τὸν υἱὸν τοῦ ἀνθρώπου ἐκ δεξιῶν ἑστῶτα
τοῦ θεοῦ. κράξαντες δὲ φωνῇ μεγάλῃ συνέσχον τὰ ὦτα 57
αὐτῶν, καὶ ὥρμησαν ὁμοθυμαδὸν ἐπ' αὐτόν, καὶ ἐκβαλόντες 58
ἔξω τῆς πόλεως ἐλιθοβόλουν. καὶ οἱ μάρτυρες ἀπέθεντο τὰ
ἱμάτια αὐτῶν παρὰ τοὺς πόδας νεανίου καλουμένου Ϲαύλου.
καὶ ἐλιθοβόλουν τὸν Ϲτέφανον ἐπικαλούμενον καὶ λέγοντα 59
Κύριε Ἰησοῦ, δέξαι τὸ πνεῦμά μου. θεὶς δὲ τὰ γόνατα 60

46 †...†   49 ἡ δὲ

ἔκραξεν φωνῇ μεγάλῃ Κύριε, μὴ στήσῃς αὐτοῖς ταύτην τὴν
1 ἁμαρτίαν· καὶ τοῦτο εἰπὼν ἐκοιμήθη. Σαῦλος
δὲ ἦν συνευδοκῶν τῇ ἀναιρέσει αὐτοῦ.

Ἐγένετο δὲ ἐν ἐκείνῃ τῇ ἡμέρᾳ διωγμὸς μέγας ἐπὶ τὴν
ἐκκλησίαν τὴν ἐν Ἱεροσολύμοις· πάντες [δὲ] διεσπάρησαν
κατὰ τὰς χώρας τῆς Ἰουδαίας καὶ Σαμαρίας πλὴν τῶν
2 ἀποστόλων. συνεκόμισαν δὲ τὸν Στέφανον ἄνδρες εὐλα-
3 βεῖς καὶ ἐποίησαν κοπετὸν μέγαν ἐπ' αὐτῷ. Σαῦλος δὲ
ἐλυμαίνετο τὴν ἐκκλησίαν κατὰ τοὺς οἴκους εἰσπορευόμενος, σύρων τε ἄνδρας καὶ γυναῖκας παρεδίδου εἰς φυλακήν.

4 Οἱ μὲν οὖν διασπαρέντες διῆλθον εὐαγγελιζόμενοι τὸν
5 λόγον. Φίλιππος δὲ κατελθὼν εἰς τὴν πόλιν τῆς Σαμα-
6 ρίας ἐκήρυσσεν αὐτοῖς τὸν χριστόν. προσεῖχον δὲ οἱ ὄχλοι
τοῖς λεγομένοις ὑπὸ τοῦ Φιλίππου ὁμοθυμαδὸν ἐν τῷ
7 ἀκούειν αὐτοὺς καὶ βλέπειν τὰ σημεῖα ἃ ἐποίει· πολλοὶ
γὰρ τῶν ἐχόντων πνεύματα ἀκάθαρτα βοῶντα φωνῇ μεγάλῃ ἐξήρχοντο, πολλοὶ δὲ παραλελυμένοι καὶ χωλοὶ
8 ἐθεραπεύθησαν· ἐγένετο δὲ πολλὴ χαρὰ ἐν τῇ πόλει
9 ἐκείνῃ. Ἀνὴρ δέ τις ὀνόματι Σίμων προυπῆρχεν
ἐν τῇ πόλει μαγεύων καὶ ἐξιστάνων τὸ ἔθνος τῆς Σαμαρίας,
10 λέγων εἶναί τινα ἑαυτὸν μέγαν, ᾧ προσεῖχον πάντες ἀπὸ
μικροῦ ἕως μεγάλου λέγοντες Οὗτός ἐστιν ἡ Δύναμις τοῦ
11 θεοῦ ἡ καλουμένη Μεγάλη. προσεῖχον δὲ αὐτῷ διὰ τὸ
12 ἱκανῷ χρόνῳ ταῖς μαγίαις ἐξεστακέναι αὐτούς. ὅτε δὲ
ἐπίστευσαν τῷ Φιλίππῳ εὐαγγελιζομένῳ περὶ τῆς βασιλείας τοῦ θεοῦ καὶ τοῦ ὀνόματος Ἰησοῦ Χριστοῦ, ἐβαπτί-
13 ζοντο ἄνδρες τε καὶ γυναῖκες. ὁ δὲ Σίμων καὶ αὐτὸς ἐπίστευσεν, καὶ βαπτισθεὶς ἦν προσκαρτερῶν τῷ Φιλίππῳ,
θεωρῶν τε σημεῖα καὶ δυνάμεις μεγάλας γινομένας ἐξί-
14 στατο. Ἀκούσαντες δὲ οἱ ἐν Ἱεροσολύμοις
ἀπόστολοι ὅτι δέδεκται ἡ Σαμαρία τὸν λόγον τοῦ θεοῦ
15 ἀπέστειλαν πρὸς αὐτοὺς Πέτρον καὶ Ἰωάνην, οἵτινες κατα-

51 καρδίας 2—2

βάντες προσηύξαντο περὶ αὐτῶν ὅπως λάβωσιν πνεῦμα
ἅγιον· οὐδέπω γὰρ ἦν ἐπ᾽ οὐδενὶ αὐτῶν ἐπιπεπτωκός, μόνον 16
δὲ βεβαπτισμένοι ὑπῆρχον εἰς τὸ ὄνομα τοῦ κυρίου Ἰησοῦ.
τότε ἐπετίθεσαν τὰς χεῖρας ἐπ᾽ αὐτούς, καὶ ἐλάμβανον 17
πνεῦμα ἅγιον. Ἰδὼν δὲ ὁ Σίμων ὅτι διὰ τῆς ἐπιθέσεως τῶν 18
χειρῶν τῶν ἀποστόλων δίδοται τὸ πνεῦμα προσήνεγκεν
αὐτοῖς χρήματα λέγων Δότε κἀμοὶ τὴν ἐξουσίαν ταύτην 19
ἵνα ᾧ ἐὰν ἐπιθῶ τὰς χεῖρας λαμβάνῃ πνεῦμα ἅγιον. Πέ- 20
τρος δὲ εἶπεν πρὸς αὐτόν Τὸ ἀργύριόν σου σὺν σοὶ εἴη
εἰς ἀπώλειαν, ὅτι τὴν δωρεὰν τοῦ θεοῦ ἐνόμισας διὰ χρημά-.
των κτᾶσθαι. οὐκ ἔστιν σοι μερὶς οὐδὲ κλῆρος ἐν τῷ λόγῳ 21
τούτῳ, ἡ γὰρ καρδία σου ΟΫ́Κ ΕΣΤΙΝ ΕΫ́ΘΕΙΑ ΕΝΑΝΤΙ ΤΟΫ́
ΘΕΟΫ́. μετανόησον οὖν ἀπὸ τῆς κακίας σου ταύτης, καὶ 22
δεήθητι τοῦ κυρίου εἰ ἄρα ἀφεθήσεταί σοι ἡ ἐπίνοια τῆς
καρδίας σου· εἰς γὰρ ΧΟΛΉΝ ΠΙΚΡΊΑΣ καὶ ϹΫ́ΝΔΕϹΜΟΝ ἀΔΙ- 23
ΚΊΑϹ ὁρῶ σε ὄντα. ἀποκριθεὶς δὲ ὁ Σίμων εἶπεν Δεήθητε 24
ὑμεῖς ὑπὲρ ἐμοῦ πρὸς τὸν κύριον ὅπως μηδὲν ἐπέλθῃ ἐπ᾽ ἐμὲ
ὧν εἰρήκατε. Οἱ μὲν οὖν διαμαρτυράμενοι καὶ 25
λαλήσαντες τὸν λόγον τοῦ κυρίου ὑπέστρεφον εἰς Ἱεροσόλυμα, πολλάς τε κώμας τῶν Σαμαρειτῶν εὐηγγελίζοντο.

Ἄγγελος δὲ Κυρίου ἐλάλησεν πρὸς Φίλιππον λέγων 26
Ἀνάστηθι καὶ πορεύου κατὰ μεσημβρίαν ἐπὶ τὴν ὁδὸν τὴν
καταβαίνουσαν ἀπὸ Ἰερουσαλὴμ εἰς Γάζαν· αὕτη ἐστὶν
ἔρημος. καὶ ἀναστὰς ἐπορεύθη, καὶ ἰδοὺ ἀνὴρ Αἰθίοψ 27
εὐνοῦχος δυνάστης Κανδάκης βασιλίσσης Αἰθιόπων, ὃς ἦν
ἐπὶ πάσης τῆς γάζης αὐτῆς, [ὃς] ἐληλύθει προσκυνήσων εἰς
Ἰερουσαλήμ, ἦν δὲ ὑποστρέφων καὶ καθήμενος ἐπὶ τοῦ 28
ἅρματος αὐτοῦ καὶ ἀνεγίνωσκεν τὸν προφήτην Ἠσαίαν.
εἶπεν δὲ τὸ πνεῦμα τῷ Φιλίππῳ Πρόσελθε καὶ κολλήθητι 29
τῷ ἅρματι τούτῳ. προσδραμὼν δὲ ὁ Φίλιππος ἤκουσεν 30
αὐτοῦ ἀναγινώσκοντος Ἠσαίαν τὸν προφήτην, καὶ εἶπεν
Ἆρά γε γινώσκεις ἃ ἀναγινώσκεις; ὁ δὲ εἶπεν Πῶς γὰρ 31

ἂν δυναίμην ἐὰν μή τις ὁδηγήσει με; παρεκάλεσέν τε τὸν
32 Φίλιππον ἀναβάντα καθίσαι σὺν αὐτῷ. ἡ δὲ περιοχὴ τῆς
γραφῆς ἣν ἀνεγίνωσκεν ἦν αὕτη
'Ωc πρόΒατοΝ ἐπὶ cφαγὴΝ ἤχθη,
καὶ ὡc ἀмΝὸc ἐΝαΝτίοΝ τοΥ ⌜κείροΝτοc⌝ αΥτὸΝ
ἄφωΝοc,
οΥτωc οΥκ ἀΝοίγει τὸ cτόмα αΥτοΥ.
33   ᾽ΕΝ τῇ ταπειΝώcει ἡ κρίcιc αΥτοΥ ἤρθη·
τὴΝ γεΝεὰΝ αΥτοΥ τίc διηγήcεται;
ὅτι αἴρεται ἀπὸ τᾶc γᾶc ἡ ζωὴ αΥτοΥ.
34 ἀποκριθεὶς δὲ ὁ εὐνοῦχος τῷ Φιλίππῳ εἶπεν Δέομαί σου,
περὶ τίνος ὁ προφήτης λέγει τοῦτο; περὶ ἑαυτοῦ ἢ περὶ
35 ἑτέρου τινός; ἀνοίξας δὲ ὁ Φίλιππος τὸ στόμα αὐτοῦ καὶ
ἀρξάμενος ἀπὸ τῆς γραφῆς ταύτης εὐηγγελίσατο αὐτῷ τὸν
36 Ἰησοῦν. ὡς δὲ ἐπορεύοντο κατὰ τὴν ὁδόν, ἦλθον ἐπί τι
ὕδωρ, καί φησιν ὁ εὐνοῦχος Ἰδοὺ ὕδωρ· τί κωλύει με
38 βαπτισθῆναι; καὶ ἐκέλευσεν στῆναι τὸ ἅρμα, καὶ κατέβησαν ἀμφότεροι εἰς τὸ ὕδωρ ὅ τε Φίλιππος καὶ ὁ εὐνοῦχος,
39 καὶ ἐβάπτισεν αὐτόν. ὅτε δὲ ἀνέβησαν ἐκ τοῦ ὕδατος,
πνεῦμα Κυρίου ἥρπασεν τὸν Φίλιππον, καὶ οὐκ εἶδεν αὐτὸν
οὐκέτι ὁ εὐνοῦχος, ἐπορεύετο γὰρ τὴν ὁδὸν αὐτοῦ χαίρων.
40 Φίλιππος δὲ εὑρέθη εἰς Ἄζωτον, καὶ διερχόμενος εὐηγγελίζετο τὰς πόλεις πάσας ἕως τοῦ ἐλθεῖν αὐτὸν εἰς Καισαρίαν.

1   Ὁ δὲ Σαῦλος, ἔτι ἐνπνέων ἀπειλῆς καὶ φόνου εἰς τοὺς
2 μαθητὰς τοῦ κυρίου, προσελθὼν τῷ ἀρχιερεῖ ᾐτήσατο
παρ᾽ αὐτοῦ ἐπιστολὰς εἰς Δαμασκὸν πρὸς τὰς συναγωγάς,
ὅπως ἐάν τινας εὕρῃ τῆς ὁδοῦ ὄντας, ἄνδρας τε καὶ γυναῖ-
3 κας, δεδεμένους ἀγάγῃ εἰς Ἰερουσαλήμ.   Ἐν δὲ
τῷ πορεύεσθαι ἐγένετο αὐτὸν ἐγγίζειν τῇ Δαμασκῷ, ἐξέ-
4 φνης τε αὐτὸν περιήστραψεν φῶς ἐκ τοῦ οὐρανοῦ, καὶ πεσὼν

ἐπὶ τὴν γῆν ἤκουσεν φωνὴν λέγουσαν αὐτῷ Σαούλ Σαούλ,
τί με διώκεις; εἶπεν δέ Τίς εἶ, κύριε; ὁ δέ Ἐγώ εἰμι 5
Ἰησοῦς ὃν σὺ διώκεις· ἀλλὰ ἀνάστηθι καὶ εἴσελθε εἰς τὴν 6
πόλιν, καὶ λαληθήσεταί σοι ὅτι σε δεῖ ποιεῖν. οἱ δὲ 7
ἄνδρες οἱ συνοδεύοντες αὐτῷ ἱστήκεισαν ἐνεοί, ἀκούοντες
μὲν τῆς φωνῆς μηδένα δὲ θεωροῦντες. ἠγέρθη δὲ Σαῦλος 8
ἀπὸ τῆς γῆς, ἀνεῳγμένων δὲ τῶν ὀφθαλμῶν αὐτοῦ οὐδὲν
ἔβλεπεν· χειραγωγοῦντες δὲ αὐτὸν εἰσήγαγον εἰς Δαμασκόν. καὶ ἦν ἡμέρας τρεῖς μὴ βλέπων, καὶ οὐκ ἔφαγεν 9
οὐδὲ ἔπιεν.
    Ἦν δέ τις μαθητὴς ἐν Δαμασκῷ ὀνόματι Ἀνανίας, 10
καὶ εἶπεν πρὸς αὐτὸν ἐν ὁράματι ὁ κύριος Ἀνανία. ὁ δὲ
εἶπεν Ἰδοὺ ἐγώ, κύριε. ὁ δὲ κύριος πρὸς αὐτόν ⌜Ἀνάστα⌝ 11
πορεύθητι ἐπὶ τὴν ῥύμην τὴν καλουμένην Εὐθεῖαν καὶ ζή-
τησον ἐν οἰκίᾳ Ἰούδα Σαῦλον ὀνόματι Ταρσέα, ἰδοὺ γὰρ
προσεύχεται, καὶ εἶδεν ἄνδρα [ἐν ὁράματι] Ἀνανίαν ὀνό- 12
ματι εἰσελθόντα καὶ ἐπιθέντα αὐτῷ [τὰς] χεῖρας ὅπως ἀνα-
βλέψῃ. ἀπεκρίθη δὲ Ἀνανίας Κύριε, ἤκουσα ἀπὸ πολλῶν 13
περὶ τοῦ ἀνδρὸς τούτου, ὅσα κακὰ τοῖς ἁγίοις σου ἐποίησεν
ἐν Ἰερουσαλήμ· καὶ ὧδε ἔχει ἐξουσίαν παρὰ τῶν ἀρχιερέων 14
δῆσαι πάντας τοὺς ἐπικαλουμένους τὸ ὄνομά σου. εἶπεν 15
δὲ πρὸς αὐτὸν ὁ κύριος Πορεύου, ὅτι σκεῦος ἐκλογῆς ἐστίν
μοι οὗτος τοῦ βαστάσαι τὸ ὄνομά μου ἐνώπιον [τῶν] ἐθνῶν
τε καὶ βασιλέων υἱῶν τε Ἰσραήλ, ἐγὼ γὰρ ὑποδείξω αὐτῷ 16
ὅσα δεῖ αὐτὸν ὑπὲρ τοῦ ὀνόματός μου παθεῖν. Ἀπῆλθεν 17
δὲ Ἀνανίας καὶ εἰσῆλθεν εἰς τὴν οἰκίαν, καὶ ἐπιθεὶς ἐπ' αὐτὸν
τὰς χεῖρας εἶπεν Σαοὺλ ἀδελφέ, ὁ κύριος ἀπέσταλκέν με,
Ἰησοῦς ὁ ὀφθείς σοι ἐν τῇ ὁδῷ ᾗ ἤρχου, ὅπως ἀναβλέψῃς
καὶ πλησθῇς πνεύματος ἁγίου. καὶ εὐθέως ἀπέπεσαν αὐ- 18
τοῦ ἀπὸ τῶν ὀφθαλμῶν ὡς λεπίδες, ἀνέβλεψέν τε, καὶ ἀναστὰς ἐβαπτίσθη, καὶ λαβὼν τροφὴν ἐνισχύθη. 19
    Ἐγένετο δὲ μετὰ τῶν ἐν Δαμασκῷ μαθητῶν ἡμέρας
τινάς, καὶ εὐθέως ἐν ταῖς συναγωγαῖς ἐκήρυσσεν τὸν Ἰησοῦν 20

11 Ἀναστὰς

21 ὅτι οὗτός ἐστιν ὁ υἱὸς τοῦ θεοῦ. ἐξίσταντο δὲ πάντες οἱ
ἀκούοντες καὶ ἔλεγον Οὐχ οὗτός ἐστιν ὁ πορθήσας ἐν
Ἰερουσαλὴμ τοὺς ἐπικαλουμένους τὸ ὄνομα τοῦτο, καὶ ὧδε
εἰς τοῦτο ἐληλύθει ἵνα δεδεμένους αὐτοὺς ἀγάγῃ ἐπὶ τοὺς
22 ἀρχιερεῖς; Σαῦλος δὲ μᾶλλον ἐνεδυναμοῦτο καὶ συνέχυννεν
Ἰουδαίους τοὺς κατοικοῦντας ἐν Δαμασκῷ, συνβιβάζων ὅτι
23 οὗτός ἐστιν ὁ χριστός. Ὡς δὲ ἐπληροῦντο ἡμέραι ἱκαναί, συνεβουλεύσαντο οἱ Ἰουδαῖοι ἀνελεῖν αὐτόν·
24 ἐγνώσθη δὲ τῷ Σαύλῳ ἡ ἐπιβουλὴ αὐτῶν. παρετηροῦντο
δὲ καὶ τὰς πύλας ἡμέρας τε καὶ νυκτὸς ὅπως αὐτὸν ἀνέλω-
25 σιν· λαβόντες δὲ οἱ μαθηταὶ αὐτοῦ νυκτὸς διὰ τοῦ τείχους
26 καθῆκαν αὐτὸν χαλάσαντες ἐν σφυρίδι. Παραγενόμενος δὲ εἰς Ἰερουσαλὴμ ἐπείραζεν κολλᾶσθαι τοῖς
μαθηταῖς· καὶ πάντες ἐφοβοῦντο αὐτόν, μὴ πιστεύοντες
27 ὅτι ἐστὶν μαθητής. Βαρνάβας δὲ ἐπιλαβόμενος αὐτὸν ἤγαγεν πρὸς τοὺς ἀποστόλους, καὶ διηγήσατο αὐτοῖς πῶς ἐν
τῇ ὁδῷ εἶδεν τὸν κύριον καὶ ὅτι ἐλάλησεν αὐτῷ, καὶ πῶς ἐν
28 Δαμασκῷ ἐπαρρησιάσατο ἐν τῷ ὀνόματι Ἰησοῦ. καὶ ἦν
μετ' αὐτῶν εἰσπορευόμενος καὶ ἐκπορευόμενος εἰς Ἰερου-
29 σαλήμ, παρρησιαζόμενος ἐν τῷ ὀνόματι τοῦ κυρίου, ἐλάλει
τε καὶ συνεζήτει πρὸς τοὺς Ἑλληνιστάς· οἱ δὲ ἐπεχείρουν
30 ἀνελεῖν αὐτόν. ἐπιγνόντες δὲ οἱ ἀδελφοὶ κατήγαγον αὐτὸν
εἰς Καισαρίαν καὶ ἐξαπέστειλαν αὐτὸν εἰς Ταρσόν.
31 Ἡ μὲν οὖν ἐκκλησία καθ' ὅλης τῆς Ἰουδαίας καὶ Γαλιλαίας καὶ Σαμαρίας εἶχεν εἰρήνην οἰκοδομουμένη, καὶ
πορευομένη τῷ φόβῳ τοῦ κυρίου καὶ τῇ παρακλήσει τοῦ
ἁγίου πνεύματος ἐπληθύνετο.

32 ΕΓΕΝΕΤΟ ΔΕ ΠΕΤΡΟΝ διερχόμενον διὰ πάντων
κατελθεῖν καὶ πρὸς τοὺς ἁγίους τοὺς κατοικοῦντας Λύδδα.
33 εὗρεν δὲ ἐκεῖ ἄνθρωπόν τινα ὀνόματι Αἰνέαν ἐξ ἐτῶν ὀκτὼ

κατακείμενον ἐπὶ κραβάττου, ὃς ἦν παραλελυμένος. καὶ 34
εἶπεν αὐτῷ ὁ Πέτρος Αἰνέα, ἰαταί σε Ἰησοῦς Χριστός·
ἀνάστηθι καὶ στρῶσον σεαυτῷ· καὶ εὐθέως ἀνέστη. καὶ 35
εἶδαν αὐτὸν πάντες οἱ κατοικοῦντες Λύδδα καὶ τὸν Σαρῶνα,
οἵτινες ἐπέστρεψαν ἐπὶ τὸν κύριον.

Ἐν Ἰόππῃ δέ τις ἦν μαθήτρια ὀνόματι Ταβειθά, ἣ 36
διερμηνευομένη λέγεται Δορκάς· αὕτη ἦν πλήρης ἔργων
ἀγαθῶν καὶ ἐλεημοσυνῶν ὧν ἐποίει. ἐγένετο δὲ ἐν ταῖς 37
ἡμέραις ἐκείναις ἀσθενήσασαν αὐτὴν ἀποθανεῖν· λούσαντες
δὲ ἔθηκαν ᵀ ἐν ὑπερῴῳ. ἐγγὺς δὲ οὔσης Λύδδας τῇ Ἰόππῃ 38
οἱ μαθηταὶ ἀκούσαντες ὅτι Πέτρος ἐστὶν ἐν αὐτῇ ἀπέστειλαν δύο ἄνδρας πρὸς αὐτὸν παρακαλοῦντες Μὴ ὀκνήσῃς
διελθεῖν ἕως ἡμῶν· ἀναστὰς δὲ Πέτρος συνῆλθεν αὐτοῖς· 39
ὃν παραγενόμενον ἀνήγαγον εἰς τὸ ὑπερῷον, καὶ παρέστησαν αὐτῷ πᾶσαι αἱ χῆραι κλαίουσαι καὶ ἐπιδεικνύμεναι
χιτῶνας καὶ ἱμάτια ὅσα ἐποίει μετ᾽ αὐτῶν οὖσα ἡ Δορκάς.
ἐκβαλὼν δὲ ἔξω πάντας ὁ Πέτρος καὶ θεὶς τὰ γόνατα 40
προσηύξατο, καὶ ἐπιστρέψας πρὸς τὸ σῶμα εἶπεν Ταβειθά,
ἀνάστηθι. ἡ δὲ ἤνοιξεν τοὺς ὀφθαλμοὺς αὐτῆς, καὶ ἰδοῦσα
τὸν Πέτρον ἀνεκάθισεν. δοὺς δὲ αὐτῇ χεῖρα ἀνέστησεν 41
αὐτήν, φωνήσας δὲ τοὺς ἁγίους καὶ τὰς χήρας παρέστησεν
αὐτὴν ζῶσαν. γνωστὸν δὲ ἐγένετο καθ᾽ ὅλης Ἰόππης, καὶ 42
ἐπίστευσαν πολλοὶ ἐπὶ τὸν κύριον. Ἐγένετο δὲ ἡμέρας 43
ἱκανὰς μεῖναι ἐν Ἰόππῃ παρά τινι Σίμωνι βυρσεῖ.

Ἀνὴρ δέ τις ἐν Καισαρίᾳ ὀνόματι Κορνήλιος, ἑκατον- 1
τάρχης ἐκ σπείρης τῆς καλουμένης Ἰταλικῆς, εὐσεβὴς καὶ 2
φοβούμενος τὸν θεὸν σὺν παντὶ τῷ οἴκῳ αὐτοῦ, ποιῶν ἐλεημοσύνας πολλὰς τῷ λαῷ καὶ δεόμενος τοῦ θεοῦ διὰ παντός,
εἶδεν ἐν ὁράματι φανερῶς ὡσεὶ περὶ ὥραν ἐνάτην τῆς ἡμέ- 3
ρας ἄγγελον τοῦ θεοῦ εἰσελθόντα πρὸς αὐτὸν καὶ εἰπόντα
αὐτῷ Κορνήλιε. ὁ δὲ ἀτενίσας αὐτῷ καὶ ἔμφοβος γενό- 4
μενος εἶπεν Τί ἐστιν, κύριε; εἶπεν δὲ αὐτῷ Αἱ προσευ-

37 αὐτὴν

χαί σου καὶ αἱ ἐλεημοσύναι σου ἀνέβησαν εἰς μνημόσυνον
5 ἔμπροσθεν τοῦ θεοῦ· καὶ νῦν πέμψον ἄνδρας εἰς Ἰόππην
6 καὶ μετάπεμψαι Σίμωνά τινα ὃς ἐπικαλεῖται Πέτρος· οὗτος
ξενίζεται παρά τινι Σίμωνι βυρσεῖ, ᾧ ἐστὶν οἰκία παρὰ θά-
7 λασσαν. ὡς δὲ ἀπῆλθεν ὁ ἄγγελος ὁ λαλῶν αὐτῷ, φωνήσας
δύο τῶν οἰκετῶν καὶ στρατιώτην εὐσεβῆ τῶν προσκαρτερούν-
8 των αὐτῷ καὶ ἐξηγησάμενος ἅπαντα αὐτοῖς ἀπέστειλεν
9 αὐτοὺς εἰς τὴν Ἰόππην. Τῇ δὲ ἐπαύριον ὁδοι-
πορούντων ἐκείνων καὶ τῇ πόλει ἐγγιζόντων ἀνέβη Πέτρος
10 ἐπὶ τὸ δῶμα προσεύξασθαι περὶ ὥραν ἕκτην. ἐγένετο δὲ
πρόσπεινος καὶ ἤθελεν γεύσασθαι· παρασκευαζόντων δὲ
11 αὐτῶν ἐγένετο ἐπ᾽ αὐτὸν ἔκστασις, καὶ θεωρεῖ τὸν οὐρανὸν
ἀνεῳγμένον καὶ καταβαῖνον σκεῦός τι ὡς ὀθόνην μεγάλην
12 τέσσαρσιν ἀρχαῖς καθιέμενον ἐπὶ τῆς γῆς, ἐν ᾧ ὑπῆρχεν
πάντα τὰ τετράποδα καὶ ἑρπετὰ τῆς γῆς καὶ πετεινὰ τοῦ
13 οὐρανοῦ. καὶ ἐγένετο φωνὴ πρὸς αὐτόν Ἀναστάς, Πέτρε,
14 θῦσον καὶ φάγε. ὁ δὲ Πέτρος εἶπεν Μηδαμῶς, κύριε, ὅτι
15 οὐδέποτε ἔφαγον πᾶν κοινὸν καὶ ἀκάθαρτον. καὶ φωνὴ
πάλιν ἐκ δευτέρου πρὸς αὐτόν Ἃ ὁ θεὸς ἐκαθάρισεν σὺ μὴ
16 κοίνου. τοῦτο δὲ ἐγένετο ἐπὶ τρίς, καὶ εὐθὺς ἀνελήμφθη τὸ
17 σκεῦος εἰς τὸν οὐρανόν. Ὡς δὲ ἐν ἑαυτῷ διηπόρει ὁ Πέτρος τί ἂν εἴη τὸ ὅραμα ὃ εἶδεν, ἰδοὺ οἱ ἄνδρες
οἱ ἀπεσταλμένοι ὑπὸ τοῦ Κορνηλίου διερωτήσαντες τὴν
18 οἰκίαν τοῦ Σίμωνος ἐπέστησαν ἐπὶ τὸν πυλῶνα, καὶ φωνή-
σαντες ⌜ἐπύθοντο⌝ εἰ Σίμων ὁ ἐπικαλούμενος Πέτρος ἐν-
19 θάδε ξενίζεται. Τοῦ δὲ Πέτρου διενθυμυμένου περὶ τοῦ
ὁράματος εἶπεν τὸ πνεῦμα ᵀ Ἰδοὺ ἄνδρες ⌜δύο⌝ ζητοῦντές σε·
20 ἀλλὰ ἀναστὰς κατάβηθι καὶ πορεύου σὺν αὐτοῖς μηδὲν
21 διακρινόμενος, ὅτι ἐγὼ ἀπέσταλκα αὐτούς. καταβὰς δὲ Πέτρος πρὸς τοὺς ἄνδρας εἶπεν Ἰδοὺ ἐγώ εἰμι ὃν ζητεῖτε· τίς
22 ἡ αἰτία δι᾽ ἣν πάρεστε; οἱ δὲ εἶπαν Κορνήλιος ἑκατοντάρχης, ἀνὴρ δίκαιος καὶ φοβούμενος τὸν θεὸν μαρτυρού-
μενός τε ὑπὸ ὅλου τοῦ ἔθνους τῶν Ἰουδαίων, ἐχρηματίσθη

18 ἐπυνθάνοντο   19 αὐτῷ | [τρεῖς]

ὑπὸ ἀγγέλου ἁγίου μεταπέμψασθαί σε εἰς τὸν οἶκον αὐτοῦ
καὶ ἀκοῦσαι ῥήματα παρὰ σοῦ. εἰσκαλεσάμενος οὖν αὐτοὺς 23
ἐξένισεν. Τῇ δὲ ἐπαύριον ἀναστὰς ἐξῆλθεν σὺν
αὐτοῖς, καί τινες τῶν ἀδελφῶν τῶν ἀπὸ Ἰόππης συνῆλθαν αὐτῷ. τῇ δὲ ἐπαύριον εἰσῆλθεν εἰς τὴν Καισαρίαν· 24
ὁ δὲ Κορνήλιος ἦν προσδοκῶν αὐτοὺς συνκαλεσάμενος τοὺς
συγγενεῖς αὐτοῦ καὶ τοὺς ἀναγκαίους φίλους. Ὡς δὲ ἐγέ- 25
νετο τοῦ εἰσελθεῖν τὸν Πέτρον, συναντήσας αὐτῷ ὁ Κορνήλιος πεσὼν ἐπὶ τοὺς πόδας προσεκύνησεν. ὁ δὲ Πέτρος 26
ἤγειρεν αὐτὸν λέγων Ἀνάστηθι· καὶ ἐγὼ αὐτὸς ἄνθρωπός
εἰμι. καὶ συνομιλῶν αὐτῷ εἰσῆλθεν, καὶ εὑρίσκει συνελη- 27
λυθότας πολλούς, ἔφη τε πρὸς αὐτούς Ὑμεῖς ἐπίστασθε 28
ὡς ἀθέμιτόν ἐστιν ἀνδρὶ Ἰουδαίῳ κολλᾶσθαι ἢ προσέρχεσθαι ἀλλοφύλῳ· κἀμοὶ ὁ θεὸς ἔδειξεν μηδένα κοινὸν ἢ
ἀκάθαρτον λέγειν ἄνθρωπον· διὸ καὶ ἀναντιρήτως ἦλθον 29
μεταπεμφθείς. πυνθάνομαι οὖν τίνι λόγῳ μετεπέμψασθέ
με. καὶ ὁ Κορνήλιος ἔφη Ἀπὸ τετάρτης ἡμέρας μέχρι 30
ταύτης τῆς ὥρας ἤμην τὴν ἐνάτην προσευχόμενος ἐν τῷ
οἴκῳ μου, καὶ ἰδοὺ ἀνὴρ ἔστη ἐνώπιόν μου ἐν ἐσθῆτι λαμ-
πρᾷ καί φησι Κορνήλιε, εἰσηκούσθη σου ἡ προσευχὴ καὶ 31
αἱ ἐλεημοσύναι σου ἐμνήσθησαν ἐνώπιον τοῦ θεοῦ· πέμψον 32
οὖν εἰς Ἰόππην καὶ μετακάλεσαι Σίμωνα ὃς ἐπικαλεῖται
Πέτρος· οὗτος ξενίζεται ἐν οἰκίᾳ Σίμωνος βυρσέως παρὰ
θάλασσαν. ἐξαυτῆς οὖν ἔπεμψα πρὸς σέ, σύ τε καλῶς 33
ἐποίησας παραγενόμενος. νῦν οὖν πάντες ἡμεῖς ἐνώπιον
τοῦ θεοῦ πάρεσμεν ἀκοῦσαι πάντα τὰ προστεταγμένα
σοι ὑπὸ τοῦ κυρίου. ἀνοίξας δὲ Πέτρος τὸ στόμα εἶπεν 34
Ἐπ' ἀληθείας καταλαμβάνομαι ὅτι ΟΥΚ ΕϹΤΙΝ ΠΡΟϹΩΠΟ-
ΛΗΜΠΤΗϹ ὁ ΘΕΟϹ, ἀλλ' ἐν παντὶ ἔθνει ὁ φοβούμενος αὐ- 35
τὸν καὶ ἐργαζόμενος δικαιοσύνην δεκτὸς αὐτῷ ἐστίν. ΤΟΝ 36
ΛΟΓΟΝ ⌐ἀπέϹΤΕΙΛΕΝ τοῖς υἱοῖς ἸϹΡΑΗΛ ΕΥΑΓΓΕΛΙΖΟΜΕΝΟϹ
ΕΙΡΗΝΗΝ διὰ ἸηϹΟΥ ΧΡΙϹΤΟΥ· ΟΥΤΟϹ ἐστιν πάντων κύριος.
ὑμεῖς οἴδατε τὸ⌐ γενόμενον ῥῆμα καθ' ὅλης τῆς Ἰουδαίας, 37

36,37 ὃν ἀπέστειλεν......Χριστοῦ (οὗτος......κύριος) ὑμεῖς οἴδατε, τὸ

ἀρξάμενος ἀπὸ τῆς Γαλιλαίας μετὰ τὸ βάπτισμα ὃ ἐκήρυ-
38 ξεν Ἰωάνης, Ἰησοῦν τὸν ἀπὸ Ναζαρέθ, ὡς ἔχρισεν αὐτὸν
ὁ θεὸς πνεΎματι ἁγίῳ καὶ δυνάμει, ὃς διῆλθεν εὐεργετῶν
καὶ ἰώμενος πάντας τοὺς καταδυναστευομένους ὑπὸ τοῦ
39 διαβόλου, ὅτι ὁ θεὸς ἦν μετ᾽ αὐτοῦ· καὶ ἡμεῖς μάρτυρες
πάντων ὧν ἐποίησεν ἔν τε τῇ χώρᾳ τῶν Ἰουδαίων καὶ
Ἰερουσαλήμ· ὃν καὶ ἀνεῖλαν ΚΡΕΜΑϹΑΝΤΕϹ ἐπὶ ξΎλοΥ.
40 τοῦτον ὁ θεὸς ἤγειρεν τῇ τρίτῃ ἡμέρᾳ καὶ ἔδωκεν αὐτὸν
41 ἐμφανῆ γενέσθαι, οὐ παντὶ τῷ λαῷ ἀλλὰ μάρτυσι τοῖς
προκεχειροτονημένοις ὑπὸ τοῦ θεοῦ, ἡμῖν, οἵτινες συνεφά-
γομεν καὶ συνεπίομεν αὐτῷ μετὰ τὸ ἀναστῆναι αὐτὸν ἐκ
42 νεκρῶν· καὶ παρήγγειλεν ἡμῖν κηρύξαι τῷ λαῷ καὶ δια-
μαρτύρασθαι ὅτι οὗτός ἐστιν ὁ ὡρισμένος ὑπὸ τοῦ θεοῦ
43 κριτὴς ζώντων καὶ νεκρῶν. τούτῳ πάντες οἱ προφῆται
μαρτυροῦσιν, ἄφεσιν ἁμαρτιῶν λαβεῖν διὰ τοῦ ὀνόματος
44 αὐτοῦ πάντα τὸν πιστεύοντα εἰς αὐτόν. Ἔτι
λαλοῦντος τοῦ Πέτρου τὰ ῥήματα ταῦτα ἐπέπεσε τὸ πνεῦμα
45 τὸ ἅγιον ἐπὶ πάντας τοὺς ἀκούοντας τὸν λόγον. καὶ
ἐξέστησαν οἱ ἐκ περιτομῆς πιστοὶ ⌐οἳ⌐ συνῆλθαν τῷ Πέτρῳ,
ὅτι καὶ ἐπὶ τὰ ἔθνη ἡ δωρεὰ τοῦ πνεύματος τοῦ ἁγίου ἐκκέ-
46 χυται· ἤκουον γὰρ αὐτῶν λαλούντων γλώσσαις καὶ μεγα-
47 λυνόντων τὸν θεόν. τότε ἀπεκρίθη Πέτρος Μήτι τὸ ὕδωρ
δύναται κωλῦσαί τις τοῦ μὴ βαπτισθῆναι τούτους οἵτινες
48 τὸ πνεῦμα τὸ ἅγιον ἔλαβον ὡς καὶ ἡμεῖς; προσέταξεν
δὲ αὐτοὺς ἐν τῷ ὀνόματι Ἰησοῦ Χριστοῦ βαπτισθῆναι.
τότε ἠρώτησαν αὐτὸν ἐπιμεῖναι ἡμέρας τινάς.
1 Ἤκουσαν δὲ οἱ ἀπόστολοι καὶ οἱ ἀδελφοὶ οἱ ὄντες κατὰ
τὴν Ἰουδαίαν ὅτι καὶ τὰ ἔθνη ἐδέξαντο τὸν λόγον τοῦ θεοῦ.
2 Ὅτε δὲ ἀνέβη Πέτρος εἰς Ἰερουσαλήμ, διεκρίνοντο πρὸς
3 αὐτὸν οἱ ἐκ περιτομῆς λέγοντες ὅτι ⌐εἰσῆλθεν πρὸς ἄνδρας
4 ἀκροβυστίαν ἔχοντας καὶ συνέφαγεν⌐ αὐτοῖς. ἀρξάμενος
5 δὲ Πέτρος ἐξετίθετο αὐτοῖς καθεξῆς λέγων Ἐγὼ ἤμην ἐν
πόλει Ἰόππῃ προσευχόμενος καὶ εἶδον ἐν ἐκστάσει ὅραμα,

45 ὅσοι   3 Εἰσῆλθες πρὸς......καὶ συνέφαγες

καταβαῖνον σκεῦός τι ὡς ὀθόνην μεγάλην τέσσαρσιν ἀρχαῖς
καθιεμένην ἐκ τοῦ οὐρανοῦ, καὶ ἦλθεν ἄχρι ἐμοῦ· εἰς ἣν 6
ἀτενίσας κατενόουν καὶ εἶδον τὰ τετράποδα τῆς γῆς καὶ
τὰ θηρία καὶ τὰ ἑρπετὰ καὶ τὰ πετεινὰ τοῦ οὐρανοῦ· ἤκουσα 7
δὲ καὶ φωνῆς λεγούσης μοι Ἀναστάς, Πέτρε, θῦσον καὶ
φάγε. εἶπον δέ Μηδαμῶς, κύριε, ὅτι κοινὸν ἢ ἀκάθαρτον 8
οὐδέποτε εἰσῆλθεν εἰς τὸ στόμα μου. ἀπεκρίθη δὲ ⌜ἐκ δευ- 9
τέρου φωνὴ⌝¹ ἐκ τοῦ οὐρανοῦ ᵟΑ ὁ θεὸς ἐκαθάρισεν σὺ μὴ
κοίνου. τοῦτο δὲ ἐγένετο ἐπὶ τρίς, καὶ ἀνεσπάσθη πάλιν 10
ἅπαντα εἰς τὸν οὐρανόν. καὶ ἰδοὺ ἐξαυτῆς τρεῖς ἄνδρες 11
ἐπέστησαν ἐπὶ τὴν οἰκίαν ἐν ᾗ ⌜ἦμεν⌝, ἀπεσταλμένοι ἀπὸ
Καισαρίας πρός με. εἶπεν δὲ τὸ πνεῦμά μοι συνελθεῖν 12
αὐτοῖς μηδὲν διακρίναντα. ἦλθον δὲ σὺν ἐμοὶ καὶ οἱ ἓξ
ἀδελφοὶ οὗτοι, καὶ εἰσήλθομεν εἰς τὸν οἶκον τοῦ ἀνδρός.
ἀπήγγειλεν δὲ ἡμῖν πῶς εἶδεν τὸν ἄγγελον ἐν τῷ οἴκῳ αὐτοῦ 13
σταθέντα καὶ εἰπόντα Ἀπόστειλον εἰς Ἰόππην καὶ μετάπεμψαι Σίμωνα τὸν ἐπικαλούμενον Πέτρον, ὃς λαλήσει 14
ῥήματα πρὸς σὲ ἐν οἷς σωθήσῃ σὺ καὶ πᾶς ὁ οἶκός σου.
ἐν δὲ τῷ ἄρξασθαί με λαλεῖν ἐπέπεσεν τὸ πνεῦμα τὸ ἅγιον 15
ἐπ᾽ αὐτοὺς ὥσπερ καὶ ἐφ᾽ ἡμᾶς ἐν ἀρχῇ. ἐμνήσθην δὲ τοῦ 16
ῥήματος τοῦ κυρίου ὡς ἔλεγεν Ἰωάνης μὲν ἐβάπτισεν
ὕδατι ὑμεῖς δὲ βαπτισθήσεσθε ἐν πνεύματι ἁγίῳ. εἰ οὖν 17
τὴν ἴσην δωρεὰν ἔδωκεν αὐτοῖς ὁ θεὸς ὡς καὶ ἡμῖν πιστεύ-
σασιν ἐπὶ τὸν κύριον Ἰησοῦν Χριστόν, ἐγὼ τίς ἤμην δυνατὸς
κωλῦσαι τὸν θεόν; ἀκούσαντες δὲ ταῦτα ἡσύχασαν καὶ 18
ἐδόξασαν τὸν θεὸν λέγοντες Ἄρα καὶ τοῖς ἔθνεσιν ὁ θεὸς
τὴν μετάνοιαν εἰς ζωὴν ἔδωκεν.

Οἱ μὲν οὖν διασπαρέντες ἀπὸ τῆς θλίψεως τῆς γενομέ- 19
νης ἐπὶ Στεφάνῳ διῆλθον ἕως Φοινίκης καὶ Κύπρου καὶ
Ἀντιοχείας, μηδενὶ λαλοῦντες τὸν λόγον εἰ μὴ μόνον Ἰουδαίοις. Ἦσαν δέ τινες ἐξ αὐτῶν ἄνδρες Κύπριοι καὶ 20
Κυρηναῖοι, οἵτινες ἐλθόντες εἰς Ἀντιόχειαν ἐλάλουν καὶ

9 φωνὴ ἐκ δευτέρου   11 ἤμην

πρὸς τοὺς Ἑλληνιστάς, εὐαγγελιζόμενοι τὸν κύριον Ἰησοῦν.
21 καὶ ἦν χεὶρ Κυρίου μετ' αὐτῶν, πολύς τε ἀριθμὸς ὁ πιστεύ-
22 σας ἐπέστρεψεν ἐπὶ τὸν κύριον. Ἠκούσθη δὲ ὁ λόγος εἰς
τὰ ὦτα τῆς ἐκκλησίας τῆς οὔσης ἐν Ἰερουσαλὴμ περὶ
23 αὐτῶν, καὶ ἐξαπέστειλαν Βαρνάβαν ἕως Ἀντιοχείας· ὃς
παραγενόμενος καὶ ἰδὼν τὴν χάριν τὴν τοῦ θεοῦ ἐχάρη
καὶ παρεκάλει πάντας τῇ προθέσει τῆς καρδίας προσμένειν
24 [ἐν] τῷ κυρίῳ, ὅτι ἦν ἀνὴρ ἀγαθὸς καὶ πλήρης πνεύματος ἁγίου καὶ πίστεως. καὶ προσετέθη ὄχλος ἱκανὸς τῷ
25 κυρίῳ. ἐξῆλθεν δὲ εἰς Ταρσὸν ἀναζητῆσαι Σαῦλον, καὶ
26 εὑρὼν ἤγαγεν εἰς Ἀντιόχειαν. ἐγένετο δὲ αὐτοῖς καὶ ἐνιαυτὸν ὅλον συναχθῆναι ἐν τῇ ἐκκλησίᾳ καὶ διδάξαι ὄχλον
ἱκανόν, χρηματίσαι τε πρώτως ἐν Ἀντιοχείᾳ τοὺς μαθητὰς
Χριστιανούς.

27 ΕΝ ΤΑΥΤΑΙΣ ΔΕ ΤΑΙΣ ΗΜΕΡΑΙΣ κατῆλθον ἀπὸ
28 Ἰεροσολύμων προφῆται εἰς Ἀντιόχειαν· ἀναστὰς δὲ εἷς ἐξ
αὐτῶν ὀνόματι Ἄγαβος ⌈ἐσήμαινεν⌉ διὰ τοῦ πνεύματος λιμὸν
μεγάλην μέλλειν ἔσεσθαι ἐφ' ὅλην τὴν οἰκουμένην· ἥτις
29 ἐγένετο ἐπὶ Κλαυδίου. τῶν δὲ μαθητῶν καθὼς εὐπορεῖτό τις
ὥρισαν ἕκαστος αὐτῶν εἰς διακονίαν πέμψαι τοῖς κατοικοῦσιν
30 ἐν τῇ Ἰουδαίᾳ ἀδελφοῖς· ὃ καὶ ἐποίησαν ἀποστείλαντες
πρὸς τοὺς πρεσβυτέρους διὰ χειρὸς Βαρνάβα καὶ Σαύλου.
1 Κατ' ἐκεῖνον δὲ τὸν καιρὸν ἐπέβαλεν Ἡρῴδης ὁ βασιλεὺς τὰς χεῖρας κακῶσαί τινας τῶν ἀπὸ τῆς ἐκκλη-
2 σίας. ἀνεῖλεν δὲ Ἰάκωβον τὸν ἀδελφὸν Ἰωάνου μαχαίρῃ.
3 ἰδὼν δὲ ὅτι ἀρεστόν ἐστιν τοῖς Ἰουδαίοις προσέθετο συλ-
λαβεῖν καὶ Πέτρον, (ἦσαν δὲ ἡμέραι τῶν ἀζύμων,)
4 ὃν καὶ πιάσας ἔθετο εἰς φυλακήν, παραδοὺς τέσσαρσιν
τετραδίοις στρατιωτῶν φυλάσσειν αὐτόν, βουλόμενος μετὰ
5 τὸ πάσχα ἀναγαγεῖν αὐτὸν τῷ λαῷ. ὁ μὲν οὖν Πέτρος

28 ἐσήμανεν

ἐτηρεῖτο ἐν τῇ φυλακῇ· προσευχὴ δὲ ἦν ἐκτενῶς γινομένη
ὑπὸ τῆς ἐκκλησίας πρὸς τὸν θεὸν περὶ αὐτοῦ. Ὅτε δὲ 6
ἤμελλεν ⌐προσαγαγεῖν⌐ αὐτὸν ὁ Ἡρῴδης, τῇ νυκτὶ ἐκείνῃ ἦν
ὁ Πέτρος κοιμώμενος μεταξὺ δύο στρατιωτῶν δεδεμένος
ἁλύσεσιν δυσίν, φύλακές τε πρὸ τῆς θύρας ἐτήρουν τὴν
φυλακήν. καὶ ἰδοὺ ἄγγελος Κυρίου ἐπέστη, καὶ φῶς ἔλαμ- 7
ψεν ἐν τῷ οἰκήματι· πατάξας δὲ τὴν πλευρὰν τοῦ Πέτρου
ἤγειρεν αὐτὸν λέγων Ἀνάστα ἐν τάχει· καὶ ἐξέπεσαν
αὐτοῦ αἱ ἁλύσεις ἐκ τῶν χειρῶν. εἶπεν δὲ ὁ ἄγγελος 8
πρὸς αὐτόν Ζῶσαι καὶ ὑπόδησαι τὰ σανδάλιά σου· ἐποίησεν δὲ οὕτως. καὶ λέγει αὐτῷ Περιβαλοῦ τὸ ἱμάτιόν σου
καὶ ἀκολούθει μοι· καὶ ἐξελθὼν ἠκολούθει, καὶ οὐκ ᾔδει 9
ὅτι ἀληθές ἐστιν τὸ γινόμενον διὰ τοῦ ἀγγέλου, ἐδόκει δὲ
ὅραμα βλέπειν. διελθόντες δὲ πρώτην φυλακὴν καὶ δευτέ- 10
ραν ἦλθαν ἐπὶ τὴν πύλην τὴν σιδηρᾶν τὴν φέρουσαν εἰς
τὴν πόλιν, ἥτις αὐτομάτη ἠνοίγη αὐτοῖς, καὶ ἐξελθόντες
προῆλθον ῥύμην μίαν, καὶ εὐθέως ἀπέστη ὁ ἄγγελος
ἀπ᾽ αὐτοῦ. καὶ ὁ Πέτρος ἐν ἑαυτῷ γενόμενος εἶπεν Νῦν 11
οἶδα ἀληθῶς ὅτι ἐξαπέστειλεν ⌐ὁ κύριος⌐ τὸν ἄγγελον αὐτοῦ καὶ ἐξείλατό με ἐκ χειρὸς Ἡρῴδου καὶ πάσης τῆς
προσδοκίας τοῦ λαοῦ τῶν Ἰουδαίων. συνιδών τε ἦλθεν ἐπὶ 12
τὴν οἰκίαν τῆς Μαρίας τῆς μητρὸς Ἰωάνου τοῦ ἐπικαλουμένου
Μάρκου, οὗ ἦσαν ἱκανοὶ συνηθροισμένοι καὶ προσευχόμενοι.
κρούσαντος δὲ αὐτοῦ τὴν θύραν τοῦ πυλῶνος ⌐προσῆλθε⌐ 13
παιδίσκη ὑπακοῦσαι ὀνόματι Ῥόδη, καὶ ἐπιγνοῦσα τὴν 14
φωνὴν τοῦ Πέτρου ἀπὸ τῆς χαρᾶς οὐκ ἤνοιξεν τὸν πυλῶνα,
εἰσδραμοῦσα δὲ ἀπήγγειλεν ἑστάναι τὸν Πέτρον πρὸ τοῦ
πυλῶνος. οἱ δὲ πρὸς αὐτὴν εἶπαν Μαίνῃ. ἡ δὲ διισχυρί- 15
ζετο οὕτως ἔχειν. οἱ δὲ ⌐ἔλεγον⌐ Ὁ ἄγγελός ἐστιν αὐτοῦ.
ὁ δὲ Πέτρος ἐπέμενεν κρούων· ἀνοίξαντες δὲ εἶδαν αὐτὸν καὶ 16
ἐξέστησαν. κατασείσας δὲ αὐτοῖς τῇ χειρὶ σιγᾷν διηγή- 17
σατο αὐτοῖς πῶς ὁ κύριος αὐτὸν ἐξήγαγεν ἐκ τῆς φυλακῆς,
εἶπέν τε Ἀπαγγείλατε Ἰακώβῳ καὶ τοῖς ἀδελφοῖς ταῦτα.

6 προαγαγεῖν   11 Κύριος   13 προῆλθε   15 εἶπαν

18 καὶ ἐξελθὼν ἐπορεύθη εἰς ἕτερον τόπον. Γενομένης δὲ ἡμέρας ἦν τάραχος οὐκ ὀλίγος ἐν τοῖς στρατιώταις, τί ἄρα ὁ
19 Πέτρος ἐγένετο. Ἡρῴδης δὲ ἐπιζητήσας αὐτὸν καὶ μὴ εὑρὼν
ἀνακρίνας τοὺς φύλακας ἐκέλευσεν ἀπαχθῆναι, καὶ κατελθὼν
20 ἀπὸ τῆς Ἰουδαίας εἰς Καισαρίαν διέτριβεν.   Ἦν
δὲ θυμομαχῶν Τυρίοις καὶ Σιδωνίοις· ὁμοθυμαδὸν δὲ πα-
ρῆσαν πρὸς αὐτόν, καὶ πείσαντες Βλάστον τὸν ἐπὶ τοῦ
κοιτῶνος τοῦ βασιλέως ᾐτοῦντο εἰρήνην διὰ τὸ τρέφεσθαι
21 αὐτῶν τὴν χώραν ἀπὸ τῆς βασιλικῆς. τακτῇ δὲ ἡμέρᾳ
[ὁ] Ἡρῴδης ἐνδυσάμενος ἐσθῆτα βασιλικὴν καθίσας ἐπὶ
22 τοῦ βήματος ἐδημηγόρει πρὸς αὐτούς· ὁ δὲ δῆμος ἐπεφώνει
23 Θεοῦ φωνὴ καὶ οὐκ ἀνθρώπου. παραχρῆμα δὲ ἐπάταξεν αὐτὸν ἄγγελος Κυρίου ἀνθ᾽ ὧν οὐκ ἔδωκεν τὴν δόξαν τῷ θεῷ,
24 καὶ γενόμενος σκωληκόβρωτος ἐξέψυξεν.   Ὁ δὲ
λόγος τοῦ ⌜κυρίου⌝ ηὔξανεν καὶ ἐπληθύνετο.
25 Βαρνάβας δὲ καὶ Σαῦλος ὑπέστρεψαν ⌜εἰς Ἰερουσαλὴμ
πληρώσαντες τὴν⌝ διακονίαν, συνπαραλαβόντες Ἰωάνην τὸν
ἐπικληθέντα Μάρκον.

1 Ἦσαν δὲ ἐν Ἀντιοχείᾳ κατὰ τὴν οὖσαν ἐκκλησίαν προφῆται καὶ διδάσκαλοι ὅ τε Βαρνάβας καὶ Συμεὼν ὁ καλούμενος Νίγερ, καὶ Λούκιος ὁ Κυρηναῖος, Μαναήν τε Ἡρῴδου
2 τοῦ τετραάρχου σύντροφος καὶ Σαῦλος.   Λειτουργούντων
δὲ αὐτῶν τῷ κυρίῳ καὶ νηστευόντων εἶπεν τὸ πνεῦμα τὸ
ἅγιον Ἀφορίσατε δή μοι τὸν Βαρνάβαν καὶ Σαῦλον εἰς τὸ
3 ἔργον ὃ προσκέκλημαι αὐτούς. τότε νηστεύσαντες καὶ προσευξάμενοι καὶ ἐπιθέντες τὰς χεῖρας αὐτοῖς ἀπέλυσαν.
4 Αὐτοὶ μὲν οὖν ἐκπεμφθέντες ὑπὸ τοῦ ἁγίου πνεύματος
κατῆλθον εἰς Σελευκίαν, ἐκεῖθέν τε ἀπέπλευσαν εἰς Κύπρον,
5 καὶ γενόμενοι ἐν Σαλαμῖνι κατήγγελλον τὸν λόγον τοῦ θεοῦ ἐν ταῖς συναγωγαῖς τῶν Ἰουδαίων· εἶχον δὲ καὶ Ἰωάν-
6 νην ὑπηρέτην.   Διελθόντες δὲ ὅλην τὴν νῆσον
ἄχρι Πάφου εὗρον ἄνδρα τινὰ μάγον ψευδοπροφήτην Ἰου-

24 θεοῦ   25 †ἐξ Ἰερουσαλὴμ πληρώσαντες τὴν†

δαῖον ᾧ ὄνομα Βαριησοῦς, ὃς ἦν σὺν τῷ ἀνθυπάτῳ Σεργίῳ 7
Παύλῳ, ἀνδρὶ συνετῷ. οὗτος προσκαλεσάμενος Βαρνάβαν
καὶ Σαῦλον ἐπεζήτησεν ἀκοῦσαι τὸν λόγον τοῦ θεοῦ· ἀν- 8
θίστατο δὲ αὐτοῖς Ἐλύμας ὁ μάγος, οὕτως γὰρ μεθερμη-
νεύεται τὸ ὄνομα αὐτοῦ, ζητῶν διαστρέψαι τὸν ἀνθύπατον
ἀπὸ τῆς πίστεως. Σαῦλος δέ, ὁ καὶ Παῦλος, πλησθεὶς 9
πνεύματος ἁγίου ἀτενίσας εἰς αὐτὸν εἶπεν Ὦ πλήρης παν- 10
τὸς δόλου καὶ πάσης ῥᾳδιουργίας, υἱὲ διαβόλου, ἐχθρὲ
πάσης δικαιοσύνης, οὐ παύσῃ διαστρέφων τὰς ὁδοὺς ͵τοῦ
κυρίου͵ τὰς εὐθείας; καὶ νῦν ἰδοὺ χεὶρ Κυρίου ἐπὶ σέ, καὶ 11
ἔσῃ τυφλὸς μὴ βλέπων τὸν ἥλιον ἄχρι καιροῦ. ͵παρα-
χρῆμα δὲ͵ ἔπεσεν ἐπ᾽ αὐτὸν ἀχλὺς καὶ σκότος, καὶ περιάγων
ἐζήτει χειραγωγούς. τότε ἰδὼν ὁ ἀνθύπατος τὸ γεγονὸς ἐπί- 12
στευσεν ἐκπληττόμενος ἐπὶ τῇ διδαχῇ τοῦ κυρίου.

Ἀναχθέντες δὲ ἀπὸ τῆς Πάφου οἱ περὶ Παῦλον ἦλθον 13
εἰς Πέργην τῆς Παμφυλίας· Ἰωάνης δὲ ἀποχωρήσας
ἀπ᾽ αὐτῶν ὑπέστρεψεν εἰς Ἱεροσόλυμα. αὐτοὶ δὲ διελ- 14
θόντες ἀπὸ τῆς Πέργης παρεγένοντο εἰς Ἀντιόχειαν τὴν
Πισιδίαν, καὶ ἐλθόντες εἰς τὴν συναγωγὴν τῇ ἡμέρᾳ τῶν
σαββάτων ἐκάθισαν. μετὰ δὲ τὴν ἀνάγνωσιν τοῦ νόμου 15
καὶ τῶν προφητῶν ἀπέστειλαν οἱ ἀρχισυνάγωγοι πρὸς αὐτοὺς λέγοντες Ἄνδρες ἀδελφοί, εἴ τις ἔστιν ἐν ὑμῖν λόγος
παρακλήσεως πρὸς τὸν λαόν, λέγετε. ἀναστὰς δὲ Παῦλος 16
καὶ κατασείσας τῇ χειρὶ εἶπεν Ἄνδρες Ἰσραηλεῖται καὶ οἱ
φοβούμενοι τὸν θεόν, ἀκούσατε. Ὁ θεὸς τοῦ λαοῦ τούτου 17
Ἰσραὴλ ἐξελέξατο τοὺς πατέρας ἡμῶν, καὶ τὸν λαὸν ὕψωσεν
ἐν τῇ παροικίᾳ ἐν γῇ Αἰγύπτου, καὶ μετὰ βραχίονος
ὑψηλοῦ ἐξήγαγεν αὐτοὺς ἐξ αὐτῆς, ͵καί, ὡς τεσσερακον- 18
ταετῆ χρόνον ἐτροποφόρησεν αὐτοὺς ἐν τῇ ἐρήμῳ,
καθελὼν͵ ἔθνη ἑπτὰ ἐν γῇ Χαναὰν κατεκληρο- 19
νόμησεν τὴν γῆν αὐτῶν ὡς ἔτεσι τετρακοσίοις καὶ πεντή- 20
κοντα. καὶ μετὰ ταῦτα ἔδωκεν κριτὰς ἕως Σαμουὴλ προφήτου. κἀκεῖθεν ᾐτήσαντο βασιλέα, καὶ ἔδωκεν αὐτοῖς 21

10 Κυρίου   11 παραχρῆμά τε   18 καὶ ὡς......ἐρήμῳ, καὶ καθελὼν

ὁ θεὸς τὸν Σαοὺλ υἱὸν Κείς, ἄνδρα ἐκ φυλῆς Βενιαμείν, ἔτη
22 τεσσεράκοντα· καὶ μεταστήσας αὐτὸν ἤγειρεν τὸν Δαυεὶδ
αὐτοῖς εἰς βασιλέα, ᾧ καὶ εἶπεν μαρτυρήσας Εὗρον
Δαγεὶδ τὸν τοῦ Ἰεσσαί, [ἄνδρα] κατὰ τὴν καρδίαν μου,
23 ὃς ποιήσει πάντα τὰ θελήματά μου. τούτου ὁ θεὸς ἀπὸ
τοῦ σπέρματος κατ' ἐπαγγελίαν ἤγαγεν τῷ Ἰσραὴλ σωτῆρα
24 Ἰησοῦν, προκηρύξαντος Ἰωάνου πρὸ προσώπου τῆς εἰσόδου
25 αὐτοῦ βάπτισμα μετανοίας παντὶ τῷ λαῷ Ἰσραήλ. ὡς δὲ
ἐπλήρου Ἰωάνης τὸν δρόμον, ἔλεγεν Τί ἐμὲ ὑπονοεῖτε
⌜εἶναι⌝; οὐκ⌝ εἰμὶ ἐγώ· ἀλλ' ἰδοὺ ἔρχεται μετ' ἐμὲ οὗ οὐκ εἰμὶ
26 ἄξιος τὸ ὑπόδημα τῶν ποδῶν λῦσαι. Ἄνδρες ἀδελφοί, υἱοὶ
γένους Ἀβραὰμ καὶ οἱ ἐν ὑμῖν φοβούμενοι τὸν θεόν, ἡμῖν
27 ὁ λόγος τῆς σωτηρίας ταύτης ἐξαπεστάλη. οἱ γὰρ κατοικοῦντες ἐν Ἰερουσαλὴμ καὶ οἱ ἄρχοντες αὐτῶν τοῦτον
ἀγνοήσαντες καὶ τὰς φωνὰς τῶν προφητῶν τὰς κατὰ πᾶν
28 σάββατον ἀναγινωσκομένας κρίναντες ἐπλήρωσαν, καὶ
μηδεμίαν αἰτίαν θανάτου εὑρόντες ⌜ᾐτήσαντο⌝ Πειλᾶτον
29 ἀναιρεθῆναι αὐτόν· ὡς δὲ ἐτέλεσαν πάντα τὰ ⌜περὶ αὐτοῦ
γεγραμμένα⌝, καθελόντες ἀπὸ τοῦ ξύλου ἔθηκαν εἰς μνη-
30 μεῖον. ὁ δὲ θεὸς ἤγειρεν αὐτὸν ἐκ νεκρῶν· ὃς ὤφθη ἐπὶ
31 ἡμέρας πλείους τοῖς συναναβᾶσιν αὐτῷ ἀπὸ τῆς Γαλιλαίας
εἰς Ἰερουσαλήμ, οἵτινες [νῦν] εἰσὶ μάρτυρες αὐτοῦ πρὸς τὸν
32 λαόν. καὶ ἡμεῖς ὑμᾶς εὐαγγελιζόμεθα τὴν πρὸς τοὺς
33 πατέρας ἐπαγγελίαν γενομένην ὅτι ταύτην ὁ θεὸς ἐκπεπλή-
ρωκεν τοῖς τέκνοις ⌜ἡμῶν⌝ ἀναστήσας Ἰησοῦν, ὡς καὶ ἐν τῷ
ψαλμῷ γέγραπται τῷ δευτέρῳ Υἱός μου εἶ σύ, ἐγὼ
34 σήμερον γεγέννηκά σε. ὅτι δὲ ἀνέστησεν αὐτὸν ἐκ
νεκρῶν μηκέτι μέλλοντα ὑποστρέφειν εἰς διαφθοράν, οὕτως εἴρηκεν ὅτι Δώσω ὑμῖν τὰ ὅσια Δαγεὶδ τὰ πιστά.
35 διότι καὶ ἐν ἑτέρῳ λέγει Οὐ δώσεις τὸν ὅσιόν σου
36 ἰδεῖν διαφθοράν· Δαγεὶδ μὲν γὰρ ἰδίᾳ γενεᾷ ὑπηρετή-
σας τῇ τοῦ θεοῦ βουλῇ ἐκοιμήθη καὶ προσετέθη πρὸς
37 τοὺς πατέρας αὐτοῦ καὶ εἶδεν διαφθοράν, ὃν δὲ ὁ θεὸς

25 εἶναι, οὐκ   28 ᾔτησαν τὸν   29 γεγραμμένα περὶ αὐτοῦ   33 †...†

ἤγειρεν οὐκ εἶδεν διαφθοράν.   Γνωστὸν οὖν ἔστω ὑμῖν, 38
ἄνδρες ἀδελφοί, ὅτι διὰ τούτου ὑμῖν ἄφεσις ἁμαρτιῶν καταγ-
γέλλεται, καὶ ἀπὸ πάντων ὧν οὐκ ἠδυνήθητε ἐν νόμῳ 39
Μωυσέως δικαιωθῆναι ἐν τούτῳ πᾶς ὁ πιστεύων δικαιοῦται.
βλέπετε οὖν μὴ ἐπέλθῃ τὸ εἰρημένον ἐν τοῖς προφήταις   40
Ἴλετε, οἱ καταφρονηταί, καὶ θαγμάсατε καὶ ἀφα- 41
       νίсθητε,
ὅτι ἔργον ἐργάzομαι ἐγὼ ἐν ταῖс ἡμέραιс ὑμῶν,
ἔργον ὃ οὐ μὴ πιστεύсητε ἐάν τιс ἐκλιηγῆται
       ὑμῖν.
ᵋἘξιόντων δὲ αὐτῶν παρεκάλουν εἰς τὸ μεταξὺ σάββατον 42
λαληθῆναι αὐτοῖς τὰ ῥήματα ταῦτα.¹   λυθείσης δὲ τῆς 43
συναγωγῆς ἠκολούθησαν πολλοὶ τῶν Ἰουδαίων καὶ τῶν
σεβομένων προσηλύτων τῷ Παύλῳ καὶ τῷ Βαρνάβᾳ, οἵτινες
προσλαλοῦντες αὐτοῖς ἔπειθον αὐτοὺς προσμένειν τῇ χάριτι
τοῦ θεοῦ.   Τῷ ᵋδὲᵌ ᵋἐρχομένῳᵌ σαββάτῳ σχε- 44
δὸν πᾶσα ἡ πόλις συνήχθη ἀκοῦσαι τὸν λόγον τοῦ ᵋθεοῦᵌ.
ἰδόντες δὲ οἱ Ἰουδαῖοι τοὺς ὄχλους ἐπλήσθησαν ζήλου καὶ 45
ἀντέλεγον τοῖς ὑπὸ Παύλου λαλουμένοις βλασφημοῦντες.
παρρησιασάμενοί τε ὁ Παῦλος καὶ ὁ Βαρνάβας εἶπαν 46
Ὑμῖν ἦν ἀναγκαῖον πρῶτον λαληθῆναι τὸν λόγον τοῦ θεοῦ·
ᵋἐπειδὴᵌ ἀπωθεῖσθε αὐτὸν καὶ οὐκ ἀξίους κρίνετε ἑαυτοὺς
τῆς αἰωνίου ζωῆς, ἰδοὺ στρεφόμεθα εἰς τὰ ἔθνη· οὕτω γὰρ 47
ἐντέταλται ἡμῖν ὁ κύριος
Τέθεικά сε εἰс φῶс ἐθνῶν
τοῦ εἶναί сε εἰс сωτηρίαν ἕωс ἐσχάτου τῆс γῆс.
ἀκούοντα δὲ τὰ ἔθνη ἔχαιρον καὶ ἐδόξαζον τὸν λόγον τοῦ 48
ᵋθεοῦᵌ, καὶ ἐπίστευσαν ὅσοι ἦσαν τεταγμένοι εἰς ζωὴν
αἰώνιον· διεφέρετο δὲ ὁ λόγος τοῦ κυρίου δι᾽ ὅλης τῆς 49
χώρας. οἱ δὲ Ἰουδαῖοι παρώτρυναν τὰς σεβομένας γυναῖ- 50
κας τὰς εὐσχήμονας καὶ τοὺς πρώτους τῆς πόλεως καὶ
ἐπήγειραν διωγμὸν ἐπὶ τὸν Παῦλον καὶ Βαρνάβαν, καὶ
ἐξέβαλον αὐτοὺς ἀπὸ τῶν ὁρίων αὐτῶν. οἱ δὲ ἐκτιναξάμε- 51

.42 †...†   44 τε | ἐχομένῳ | κυρίου   46 ἐπεὶ δὲ   48 κυρίου

νοι τὸν κονιορτὸν τῶν ποδῶν ἐπ' αὐτοὺς ἦλθον εἰς Ἰκόνιον,
52 ⌜οἵ τε⌝ μαθηταὶ ἐπληροῦντο χαρᾶς καὶ πνεύματος ἁγίου.
1 Ἐγένετο δὲ ἐν Ἰκονίῳ κατὰ τὸ αὐτὸ εἰσελθεῖν αὐτοὺς
εἰς τὴν συναγωγὴν τῶν Ἰουδαίων καὶ λαλῆσαι οὕτως ὥστε
2 πιστεῦσαι Ἰουδαίων τε καὶ Ἑλλήνων πολὺ πλῆθος. οἱ δὲ
ἀπειθήσαντες Ἰουδαῖοι ἐπήγειραν καὶ ἐκάκωσαν τὰς ψυχὰς
3 τῶν ἐθνῶν κατὰ τῶν ἀδελφῶν. ἱκανὸν μὲν οὖν χρόνον
διέτριψαν παρρησιαζόμενοι ἐπὶ τῷ κυρίῳ τῷ μαρτυροῦντι
τῷ λόγῳ τῆς χάριτος αὐτοῦ, διδόντι σημεῖα καὶ τέρατα
4 γίνεσθαι διὰ τῶν χειρῶν αὐτῶν. ἐσχίσθη δὲ τὸ πλῆθος
τῆς πόλεως, καὶ οἱ μὲν ἦσαν σὺν τοῖς Ἰουδαίοις οἱ δὲ σὺν
5 τοῖς ἀποστόλοις. ὡς δὲ ἐγένετο ὁρμὴ τῶν ἐθνῶν τε καὶ
Ἰουδαίων σὺν τοῖς ἄρχουσιν αὐτῶν ὑβρίσαι καὶ λιθοβολῆ-
6 σαι αὐτούς, συνιδόντες κατέφυγον εἰς τὰς πόλεις τῆς Λυ-
7 καονίας Λύστραν καὶ Δέρβην καὶ τὴν περίχωρον, κἀκεῖ
8 εὐαγγελιζόμενοι ἦσαν. Καί τις ἀνὴρ ἀδύνατος
ἐν Λύστροις τοῖς ποσὶν ἐκάθητο, χωλὸς ἐκ κοιλίας μητρὸς
9 αὐτοῦ, ὃς οὐδέποτε περιεπάτησεν. οὗτος ἤκουεν τοῦ Παύλου λαλοῦντος· ὃς ἀτενίσας αὐτῷ καὶ ἰδὼν ὅτι ἔχει πίστιν
10 τοῦ σωθῆναι εἶπεν μεγάλῃ φωνῇ Ἀνάστηθι ἐπὶ τοὺς πό-
11 δας σου ὀρθός· καὶ ἥλατο καὶ περιεπάτει. οἵ τε ὄχλοι
ἰδόντες ὃ ἐποίησεν Παῦλος ἐπῆραν τὴν φωνὴν αὐτῶν Λυ-
καονιστὶ λέγοντες Οἱ θεοὶ ὁμοιωθέντες ἀνθρώποις κατέ-
12 βησαν πρὸς ἡμᾶς, ἐκάλουν τε τὸν Βαρνάβαν Δία, τὸν δὲ
Παῦλον Ἑρμῆν ἐπειδὴ αὐτὸς ἦν ὁ ἡγούμενος τοῦ λόγου.
13 ὅ τε ἱερεὺς τοῦ Διὸς τοῦ ὄντος πρὸ τῆς πόλεως ταύρους
καὶ στέμματα ἐπὶ τοὺς πυλῶνας ἐνέγκας σὺν τοῖς ὄχλοις
14 ἤθελεν θύειν. ἀκούσαντες δὲ οἱ ἀπόστολοι Βαρνάβας καὶ
Παῦλος, διαρρήξαντες τὰ ἱμάτια ⌜ἑαυτῶν⌝ ἐξεπήδησαν
15 εἰς τὸν ὄχλον, κράζοντες καὶ λέγοντες Ἄνδρες, τί ταῦτα
ποιεῖτε; καὶ ἡμεῖς ὁμοιοπαθεῖς ἐσμὲν ὑμῖν ἄνθρωποι, εὐαγγελιζόμενοι ὑμᾶς ἀπὸ τούτων τῶν ματαίων ἐπιστρέφειν ἐπὶ
θεὸν ζῶντα ὋϹ ἘΠΟΊΗϹΕΝ ΤῸΝ ΟΥ̓ΡΑΝῸΝ ΚΑῚ ΤῊΝ ΓΗ͂Ν

52 οἱ δὲ 14 αὐτῶν

καὶ τὴν θάλασσαν καὶ πάντα τὰ ἐν αὐτοῖς· ὃς ἐν ταῖς 16
παρῳχημέναις γενεαῖς εἴασεν πάντα τὰ ἔθνη πορεύεσθαι
ταῖς ὁδοῖς αὐτῶν· καίτοι οὐκ ἀμάρτυρον αὐτὸν ἀφῆκεν 17
ἀγαθουργῶν, οὐρανόθεν ὑμῖν ὑετοὺς διδοὺς καὶ καιροὺς
καρποφόρους, ἐμπιπλῶν τροφῆς καὶ εὐφροσύνης τὰς καρδίας ὑμῶν. καὶ ταῦτα λέγοντες μόλις κατέπαυσαν τοὺς 18
ὄχλους τοῦ μὴ θύειν αὐτοῖς. Ἐπῆλθαν δὲ ἀπὸ 19
Ἀντιοχείας καὶ Ἰκονίου Ἰουδαῖοι, καὶ πείσαντες τοὺς ὄχλους
καὶ λιθάσαντες τὸν Παῦλον ἔσυρον ἔξω τῆς πόλεως, νομί-
ζοντες αὐτὸν τεθνηκέναι. κυκλωσάντων δὲ τῶν μαθητῶν 20
αὐτὸν ἀναστὰς εἰσῆλθεν εἰς τὴν πόλιν. καὶ τῇ ἐπαύριον
ἐξῆλθεν σὺν τῷ Βαρνάβᾳ εἰς Δέρβην. εὐαγγελισάμενοί 21
τε τὴν πόλιν ἐκείνην καὶ μαθητεύσαντες ἱκανοὺς ὑπέστρεψαν εἰς τὴν Λύστραν καὶ εἰς Ἰκόνιον καὶ [εἰς] Ἀντιόχειαν,
ἐπιστηρίζοντες τὰς ψυχὰς τῶν μαθητῶν, παρακαλοῦντες 22
ἐμμένειν τῇ πίστει καὶ ὅτι διὰ πολλῶν θλίψεων δεῖ ἡμᾶς
εἰσελθεῖν εἰς τὴν βασιλείαν τοῦ θεοῦ. χειροτονήσαντες δὲ 23
αὐτοῖς κατ᾽ ἐκκλησίαν πρεσβυτέρους προσευξάμενοι μετὰ
νηστειῶν παρέθεντο αὐτοὺς τῷ κυρίῳ εἰς ὃν πεπιστεύκει-
σαν. καὶ διελθόντες τὴν Πισιδίαν ἦλθαν εἰς τὴν Παμ- 24
φυλίαν, καὶ λαλήσαντες ⌜ἐν Πέργῃ⌝ τὸν λόγον κατέβησαν 25
εἰς Ἀτταλίαν, κἀκεῖθεν ἀπέπλευσαν εἰς Ἀντιόχειαν, ὅθεν 26
ἦσαν παραδεδομένοι τῇ χάριτι τοῦ θεοῦ εἰς τὸ ἔργον ὃ
ἐπλήρωσαν. Παραγενόμενοι δὲ καὶ συναγαγόντες τὴν 27
ἐκκλησίαν ἀνήγγελλον ὅσα ἐποίησεν ὁ θεὸς μετ᾽ αὐτῶν
καὶ ὅτι ἤνοιξεν τοῖς ἔθνεσιν θύραν πίστεως. διέτριβον δὲ 28
χρόνον οὐκ ὀλίγον σὺν τοῖς μαθηταῖς.

ΚΑΙ ΤΙΝΕΣ ΚΑΤΕΛΘΟΝΤΕΣ ἀπὸ τῆς Ἰουδαίας 1
ἐδίδασκον τοὺς ἀδελφοὺς ὅτι Ἐὰν μὴ περιτμηθῆτε τῷ
ἔθει τῷ Μωυσέως, οὐ δύνασθε σωθῆναι. γενομένης δὲ 2

25 εἰς τὴν Πέργην

στάσεως καὶ ζητήσεως οὐκ ὀλίγης τῷ Παύλῳ καὶ τῷ Βαρνάβᾳ πρὸς αὐτοὺς ἔταξαν ἀναβαίνειν Παῦλον καὶ Βαρνάβαν καί τινας ἄλλους ἐξ αὐτῶν πρὸς τοὺς ἀποστόλους
καὶ πρεσβυτέρους εἰς Ἰερουσαλὴμ περὶ τοῦ ζητήματος
3 τούτου.   Οἱ μὲν οὖν προπεμφθέντες ὑπὸ τῆς
ἐκκλησίας διήρχοντο τήν τε Φοινίκην καὶ Σαμαρίαν ἐκδιη-
γούμενοι τὴν ἐπιστροφὴν τῶν ἐθνῶν, καὶ ἐποίουν χαρὰν
4 μεγάλην πᾶσι τοῖς ἀδελφοῖς. παραγενόμενοι δὲ εἰς Ἱεροσόλυμα παρεδέχθησαν ἀπὸ τῆς ἐκκλησίας καὶ τῶν ἀποστόλων καὶ τῶν πρεσβυτέρων, ἀνήγγειλάν τε ὅσα ὁ θεὸς
5 ἐποίησεν μετ᾽ αὐτῶν.   Ἐξανέστησαν δέ τινες τῶν ἀπὸ τῆς
αἱρέσεως τῶν Φαρισαίων πεπιστευκότες, λέγοντες ὅτι δεῖ
περιτέμνειν αὐτοὺς παραγγέλλειν τε τηρεῖν τὸν νόμον
Μωυσέως.
6   Συνήχθησάν τε οἱ ἀπόστολοι καὶ οἱ πρεσβίτεροι ἰδεῖν
7 περὶ τοῦ λόγου τούτου.   Πολλῆς δὲ ζητήσεως γενομένης
ἀναστὰς Πέτρος εἶπεν πρὸς αὐτούς Ἄνδρες ἀδελφοί, ὑμεῖς
ἐπίστασθε ὅτι ἀφ᾽ ἡμερῶν ἀρχαίων ἐν ὑμῖν ἐξελέξατο
ὁ θεὸς διὰ τοῦ στόματός μου ἀκοῦσαι τὰ ἔθνη τὸν λόγον
8 τοῦ εὐαγγελίου καὶ πιστεῦσαι, καὶ ὁ καρδιογνώστης θεὸς
ἐμαρτύρησεν αὐτοῖς δοὺς τὸ πνεῦμα τὸ ἅγιον καθὼς
9 καὶ ἡμῖν, καὶ ⌐οὐθὲν⌐ διέκρινεν μεταξὺ ἡμῶν τε καὶ αὐτῶν,
10 τῇ πίστει καθαρίσας τὰς καρδίας αὐτῶν.   νῦν οὖν τί πειράζετε τὸν θεόν, ἐπιθεῖναι ζυγὸν ἐπὶ τὸν τράχηλον τῶν
μαθητῶν ὃν οὔτε οἱ πατέρες ἡμῶν οὔτε ἡμεῖς ἰσχύσαμεν
11 βαστάσαι; ἀλλὰ διὰ τῆς χάριτος τοῦ κυρίου Ἰησοῦ πιστεύο-
12 μεν σωθῆναι καθ᾽ ὃν τρόπον κἀκεῖνοι.   Ἐσίγησεν δὲ πᾶν
τὸ πλῆθος, καὶ ἤκουον Βαρνάβα καὶ Παύλου ἐξηγουμένων
ὅσα ἐποίησεν ὁ θεὸς σημεῖα καὶ τέρατα ἐν τοῖς ἔθνεσιν
13 δι᾽ αὐτῶν.   Μετὰ δὲ τὸ σιγῆσαι αὐτοὺς ἀπεκρίθη Ἰάκωβος
14 λέγων Ἄνδρες ἀδελφοί, ἀκούσατέ μου.   Συμεὼν ἐξηγή-
σατο καθὼς πρῶτον ὁ θεὸς ἐπεσκέψατο λαβεῖν ἐξ ἐθνῶν
15 λαὸν τῷ ὀνόματι αὐτοῦ.   καὶ τούτῳ συμφωνοῦσιν οἱ λόγοι

9 οὐδὲν

τῶν προφητῶν, καθὼς γέγραπται

Μετὰ ταῦτα ἀναστρέψω 16
καὶ ἀνοικοδομήϲω τὴν ϲκηνὴν Δαγεὶδ τὴν πε-
πτωκγῖαν
καὶ τὰ κατεϲτραμμένα αγτῆϲ ἀνοικοδομήϲω
καὶ ἀνορθώϲω αγτήν,
ὅπωϲ ἂν ἐκζητήϲωϲιν οἱ κατάλοιποι τῶν ἀνθρώ- 17
πων τὸν κγριον,
καὶ πάντα τὰ ἔθνη ἐφ᾽ ογϲ ἐπικέκληται τὸ ὄνομά
μογ ἐπ᾽ αγτογϲ,
λέγει Κγριοϲ ποιῶν ταγτα γνωϲτὰ ἀπ᾽ αἰῶνοϲ. 18
διὸ ἐγὼ κρίνω μὴ παρενοχλεῖν τοῖς ἀπὸ τῶν ἐθνῶν ἐπιστρέ- 19
φουσιν ἐπὶ τὸν θεόν, ἀλλὰ ἐπιστεῖλαι αὐτοῖς τοῦ ἀπέχεσθαι 20
τῶν ἀλισγημάτων τῶν εἰδώλων καὶ τῆς πορνείας καὶ πνικτοῦ
καὶ τοῦ αἵματος· Μωυσῆς γὰρ ἐκ γενεῶν ἀρχαίων κατὰ πόλιν 21
τοὺς κηρύσσοντας αὐτὸν ἔχει ἐν ταῖς συναγωγαῖς κατὰ πᾶν
σάββατον ἀναγινωσκόμενος. Τότε ἔδοξε τοῖς 22
ἀποστόλοις καὶ τοῖς πρεσβυτέροις σὺν ὅλῃ τῇ ἐκκλησίᾳ
ἐκλεξαμένους ἄνδρας ἐξ αὐτῶν πέμψαι εἰς Ἀντιόχειαν σὺν
τῷ Παύλῳ καὶ Βαρνάβᾳ, Ἰούδαν τὸν καλούμενον Βαρσαββᾶν καὶ Σίλαν, ἄνδρας ἡγουμένους ἐν τοῖς ἀδελφοῖς, γρά- 23
ψαντες διὰ χειρὸς αὐτῶν Οἱ ἀπόστολοι καὶ οἱ πρεσβύτεροι
ἀδελφοὶ τοῖς κατὰ τὴν Ἀντιόχειαν καὶ Συρίαν καὶ Κιλικίαν
ἀδελφοῖς τοῖς ἐξ ἐθνῶν χαίρειν. Ἐπειδὴ ἠκούσαμεν ὅτι 24
τινὲς ἐξ ἡμῶν ἐτάραξαν ὑμᾶς λόγοις ἀνασκευάζοντες τὰς
ψυχὰς ὑμῶν, οἷς οὐ διεστειλάμεθα, ἔδοξεν ἡμῖν γενομένοις 25
ὁμοθυμαδὸν ⌜ἐκλεξαμένοις⌝ ἄνδρας πέμψαι πρὸς ὑμᾶς σὺν
τοῖς ἀγαπητοῖς ἡμῶν Βαρνάβᾳ καὶ Παύλῳ, ἀνθρώποις 26
παραδεδωκόσι τὰς ψυχὰς αὐτῶν ὑπὲρ τοῦ ὀνόματος τοῦ
κυρίου ἡμῶν Ἰησοῦ Χριστοῦ. ἀπεστάλκαμεν οὖν Ἰούδαν 27
καὶ Σίλαν, καὶ αὐτοὺς διὰ λόγου ἀπαγγέλλοντας τὰ αὐτά.
ἔδοξεν γὰρ τῷ πνεύματι τῷ ἁγίῳ καὶ ἡμῖν μηδὲν πλέον ἐπι- 28

25 ἐκλεξαμένους

τίθεσθαι ὑμῖν βάρος πλὴν τούτων τῶν ἐπάναγκες, ἀπέχεσθαι
29 εἰδωλοθύτων καὶ αἵματος καὶ πνικτῶν καὶ πορνείας· ἐξ ὧν
διατηροῦντες ἑαυτοὺς εὖ πράξετε. Ἔρρωσθε.
30 Οἱ μὲν οὖν ἀπολυθέντες κατῆλθον εἰς Ἀντιόχειαν, καὶ
31 συναγαγόντες τὸ πλῆθος ἐπέδωκαν τὴν ἐπιστολήν· ἀνα-
32 γνόντες δὲ ἐχάρησαν ἐπὶ τῇ παρακλήσει. Ἰούδας τε καὶ
Σίλας, καὶ αὐτοὶ προφῆται ὄντες, διὰ λόγου πολλοῦ πα-
33 ρεκάλεσαν τοὺς ἀδελφοὺς καὶ ἐπεστήριξαν· ποιήσαντες
δὲ χρόνον ἀπελύθησαν μετ᾽ εἰρήνης ἀπὸ τῶν ἀδελφῶν
35 πρὸς τοὺς ἀποστείλαντας αὐτούς. Παῦλος δὲ
καὶ Βαρνάβας διέτριβον ἐν Ἀντιοχείᾳ διδάσκοντες καὶ
εὐαγγελιζόμενοι μετὰ καὶ ἑτέρων πολλῶν τὸν λόγον τοῦ
κυρίου.

36 Μετὰ δέ τινας ἡμέρας εἶπεν πρὸς Βαρνάβαν Παῦλος
Ἐπιστρέψαντες δὴ ἐπισκεψώμεθα τοὺς ἀδελφοὺς κατὰ πόλιν πᾶσαν ἐν αἷς κατηγγείλαμεν τὸν λόγον τοῦ κυρίου, πῶς
37 ἔχουσιν. Βαρνάβας δὲ ἐβούλετο συνπαραλαβεῖν καὶ τὸν
38 Ἰωάνην τὸν καλούμενον Μάρκον· Παῦλος δὲ ἠξίου, τὸν ἀπο-
στάντα ἀπ᾽ αὐτῶν ἀπὸ Παμφυλίας καὶ μὴ συνελθόντα
39 αὐτοῖς εἰς τὸ ἔργον, μὴ συνπαραλαμβάνειν τοῦτον. ἐγένετο
δὲ παροξυσμὸς ὥστε ἀποχωρισθῆναι αὐτοὺς ἀπ᾽ ἀλλήλων,
τόν τε Βαρνάβαν παραλαβόντα τὸν Μάρκον ἐκπλεῦσαι εἰς
40 Κύπρον. Παῦλος δὲ ἐπιλεξάμενος Σίλαν ἐξῆλθεν παρα-
41 δοθεὶς τῇ χάριτι τοῦ κυρίου ὑπὸ τῶν ἀδελφῶν, διήρχετο
δὲ τὴν Συρίαν καὶ [τὴν] Κιλικίαν ἐπιστηρίζων τὰς ἐκκλη-
1 σίας. Κατήντησεν δὲ καὶ εἰς Δέρβην καὶ εἰς
Λύστραν. καὶ ἰδοὺ μαθητής τις ἦν ἐκεῖ ὀνόματι Τιμόθεος,
2 υἱὸς γυναικὸς Ἰουδαίας πιστῆς πατρὸς δὲ Ἕλληνος, ὃς
ἐμαρτυρεῖτο ὑπὸ τῶν ἐν Λύστροις καὶ Ἰκονίῳ ἀδελφῶν·
3 τοῦτον ἠθέλησεν ὁ Παῦλος σὺν αὐτῷ ἐξελθεῖν, καὶ λαβὼν
περιέτεμεν αὐτὸν διὰ τοὺς Ἰουδαίους τοὺς ὄντας ἐν τοῖς
τύποις ἐκείνοις, ᾔδεισαν γὰρ ἅπαντες ὅτι Ἕλλην ὁ

πατὴρ αὐτοῦ ὑπῆρχεν. Ὡς δὲ διεπορεύοντο τὰς πόλεις, 4
παρεδίδοσαν αὐτοῖς φυλάσσειν τὰ δόγματα τὰ κεκριμένα
ὑπὸ τῶν ἀποστόλων καὶ πρεσβυτέρων τῶν ἐν Ἱεροσολύμοις. Αἱ μὲν οὖν ἐκκλησίαι ἐστερεοῦντο τῇ 5
πίστει καὶ ἐπερίσσευον τῷ ἀριθμῷ καθ᾽ ἡμέραν.

Διῆλθον δὲ τὴν Φρυγίαν καὶ Γαλατικὴν χώραν, κωλυ- 6
θέντες ὑπὸ τοῦ ἁγίου πνεύματος λαλῆσαι τὸν λόγον ἐν τῇ
Ἀσίᾳ, ἐλθόντες δὲ κατὰ τὴν Μυσίαν ἐπείραζον εἰς τὴν 7
Βιθυνίαν πορευθῆναι καὶ οὐκ εἴασεν αὐτοὺς τὸ πνεῦμα
Ἰησοῦ· παρελθόντες δὲ τὴν Μυσίαν κατέβησαν εἰς Τρῳάδα. 8
καὶ ὅραμα διὰ νυκτὸς τῷ Παύλῳ ὤφθη, ἀνὴρ Μακεδών 9
τις ἦν ἑστὼς καὶ παρακαλῶν αὐτὸν καὶ λέγων Διαβὰς
εἰς Μακεδονίαν βοήθησον ἡμῖν. ὡς δὲ τὸ ὅραμα εἶδεν, 10
εὐθέως ἐζητήσαμεν ἐξελθεῖν εἰς Μακεδονίαν, συνβιβάζοντες
ὅτι προσκέκληται ἡμᾶς ὁ θεὸς εὐαγγελίσασθαι αὐτούς.

Ἀναχθέντες οὖν ἀπὸ Τρῳάδος εὐθυδρομήσαμεν εἰς Σαμο- 11
θράκην, τῇ δὲ ἐπιούσῃ εἰς Νέαν Πόλιν, κἀκεῖθεν εἰς Φιλίπ- 12
πους, ἥτις ἐστὶν ⌜πρώτη τῆς μερίδος⌝ Μακεδονίας πόλις,
κολωνία. Ἦμεν δὲ ἐν ταύτῃ τῇ πόλει δια-
τρίβοντες ἡμέρας τινάς. τῇ τε ἡμέρᾳ τῶν σαββάτων ἐξήλ- 13
θομεν ἔξω τῆς πύλης· παρὰ ποταμὸν οὗ ἐνομίζομεν προσευχὴν εἶναι, καὶ καθίσαντες ἐλαλοῦμεν ταῖς συνελθούσαις
γυναιξίν. καί τις γυνὴ ὀνόματι Λυδία, πορφυρόπωλις 14
πόλεως Θυατείρων σεβομένη τὸν θεόν, ἤκουεν, ἧς ὁ κύριος διήνοιξεν τὴν καρδίαν προσέχειν τοῖς λαλουμένοις ὑπὸ
Παύλου. ὡς δὲ ἐβαπτίσθη καὶ ὁ οἶκος αὐτῆς, παρεκάλε- 15
σεν λέγουσα Εἰ κεκρίκατέ με πιστὴν τῷ κυρίῳ εἶναι,
εἰσελθόντες εἰς τὸν οἶκόν μου μένετε· καὶ παρεβιάσατο
ἡμᾶς. Ἐγένετο δὲ πορευομένων ἡμῶν εἰς τὴν 16
προσευχὴν παιδίσκην τινὰ ἔχουσαν πνεῦμα πύθωνα ὑπαν-
τῆσαι ἡμῖν, ἥτις ἐργασίαν πολλὴν παρεῖχεν τοῖς κυρίοις
αὐτῆς μαντευομένη· αὕτη κατακολουθοῦσα [τῷ] Παύλῳ καὶ 17
ἡμῖν ἔκραζεν λέγουσα Οὗτοι οἱ ἄνθρωποι δοῦλοι τοῦ θεοῦ·

12 †...†

τοῦ ὑψίστου εἰσίν, οἵτινες καταγγέλλουσιν ὑμῖν ὁδὸν σωτη-
18 ρίας. τοῦτο δὲ ἐποίει ἐπὶ πολλὰς ἡμέρας. διαπονηθεὶς
δὲ Παῦλος καὶ ἐπιστρέψας τῷ πνεύματι εἶπεν Παραγ-
γέλλω σοι ἐν ὀνόματι Ἰησοῦ Χριστοῦ ἐξελθεῖν ἀπ᾽ αὐτῆς·
19 καὶ ἐξῆλθεν αὐτῇ τῇ ὥρᾳ. ⌜Ἰδόντες δὲ⌝ οἱ κύριοι αὐτῆς ὅτι
ἐξῆλθεν ἡ ἐλπὶς τῆς ἐργασίας αὐτῶν ἐπιλαβόμενοι τὸν
Παῦλον καὶ τὸν Σίλαν εἵλκυσαν εἰς τὴν ἀγορὰν ἐπὶ τοὺς
20 ἄρχοντας, καὶ προσαγαγόντες αὐτοὺς τοῖς στρατηγοῖς εἶπαν
Οὗτοι οἱ ἄνθρωποι ἐκταράσσουσιν ἡμῶν τὴν πόλιν Ἰουδαῖοι
21 ὑπάρχοντες, καὶ καταγγέλλουσιν ἔθη ἃ οὐκ ἔξεστιν ἡμῖν
22 παραδέχεσθαι οὐδὲ ποιεῖν Ῥωμαίοις οὖσιν. καὶ συνεπέστη
ὁ ὄχλος κατ᾽ αὐτῶν, καὶ οἱ στρατηγοὶ περιρήξαντες αὐτῶν
23 τὰ ἱμάτια ἐκέλευον ῥαβδίζειν, ⌜πολλὰς δὲ⌝ ἐπιθέντες αὐτοῖς
πληγὰς ἔβαλον εἰς φυλακήν, παραγγείλαντες τῷ δεσμοφύ-
24 λακι ἀσφαλῶς τηρεῖν αὐτούς· ὃς παραγγελίαν τοιαύτην
λαβὼν ἔβαλεν αὐτοὺς εἰς τὴν ἐσωτέραν φυλακὴν καὶ τοὺς
25 πόδας ἠσφαλίσατο αὐτῶν εἰς τὸ ξύλον. Κατὰ δὲ τὸ μεσο-
νύκτιον Παῦλος καὶ Σίλας προσευχόμενοι ὕμνουν τὸν θεόν,
26 ἐπηκροῶντο δὲ αὐτῶν οἱ δέσμιοι· ἄφνω δὲ σεισμὸς ἐγένετο
μέγας ὥστε σαλευθῆναι τὰ θεμέλια τοῦ δεσμωτηρίου, ἠνεῴ-
χθησαν δὲ [παραχρῆμα] αἱ θύραι πᾶσαι, καὶ πάντων τὰ
27 δεσμὰ ἀνέθη. ἔξυπνος δὲ γενόμενος ὁ δεσμοφύλαξ καὶ
ἰδὼν ἀνεῳγμένας τὰς θύρας τῆς φυλακῆς σπασάμενος τὴν
μάχαιραν ἤμελλεν ἑαυτὸν ἀναιρεῖν, νομίζων ἐκπεφευγέναι
28 τοὺς δεσμίους. ἐφώνησεν δὲ Παῦλος μεγάλῃ φωνῇ λέγων
Μηδὲν πράξῃς σεαυτῷ κακόν, ἅπαντες γάρ ἐσμεν ἐνθάδε.
29 αἰτήσας δὲ φῶτα εἰσεπήδησεν, καὶ ἔντρομος γενόμενος προσ-
30 έπεσεν τῷ Παύλῳ καὶ Σίλα, καὶ προαγαγὼν αὐτοὺς ἔξω
31 ἔφη Κύριοι, τί με δεῖ ποιεῖν ἵνα σωθῶ; οἱ δὲ εἶπαν
Πίστευσον ἐπὶ τὸν κύριον Ἰησοῦν, καὶ σωθήσῃ σὺ καὶ
32 ὁ οἶκός σου. καὶ ἐλάλησαν αὐτῷ τὸν λόγον τοῦ ⌜θεοῦ⌝ σὺν
33 πᾶσι τοῖς ἐν τῇ οἰκίᾳ αὐτοῦ. καὶ παραλαβὼν αὐτοὺς ἐν
ἐκείνῃ τῇ ὥρᾳ τῆς νυκτὸς ἔλουσεν ἀπὸ τῶν πληγῶν, καὶ

19 Καὶ ἰδόντες   23 πολλάς τε   32 κυρίου

ἐβαπτίσθη αὐτὸς καὶ οἱ αὐτοῦ ἅπαντες παραχρῆμα, ἀναγα- 34
γών τε αὐτοὺς εἰς τὸν οἶκον παρέθηκεν τράπεζαν, καὶ ἠγαλλιάσατο πανοικεὶ πεπιστευκὼς τῷ θεῷ. Ἡμέρας δὲ γενομέ- 35
νης ἀπέστειλαν οἱ στρατηγοὶ τοὺς ῥαβδούχους λέγοντες
Ἀπόλυσον τοὺς ἀνθρώπους ἐκείνους. ἀπήγγειλεν δὲ ὁ δε- 36
σμοφύλαξ τοὺς λόγους πρὸς τὸν Παῦλον, ὅτι Ἀπέσταλ-
καν οἱ στρατηγοὶ ἵνα ἀπολυθῆτε· νῦν οὖν ἐξελθόντες πορεύ-
εσθε ἐν εἰρήνῃ. ὁ δὲ Παῦλος ἔφη πρὸς αὐτούς Δείραντες 37
ἡμᾶς δημοσίᾳ ἀκατακρίτους, ἀνθρώπους Ῥωμαίους ὑπάρ-
χοντας, ἔβαλαν εἰς φυλακήν· καὶ νῦν λάθρᾳ ἡμᾶς ἐκβάλλουσιν; οὐ γάρ, ἀλλὰ ἐλθόντες αὐτοὶ ἡμᾶς ἐξαγαγέτωσαν.
ἀπήγγειλαν δὲ τοῖς στρατηγοῖς οἱ ῥαβδοῦχοι τὰ ῥήματα 38
ταῦτα· ἐφοβήθησαν δὲ ἀκούσαντες ὅτι Ῥωμαῖοί εἰσιν, καὶ 39
ἐλθόντες παρεκάλεσαν αὐτούς, καὶ ἐξαγαγόντες ἠρώτων
ἀπελθεῖν ἀπὸ τῆς πόλεως. ἐξελθόντες δὲ ἀπὸ τῆς φυλακῆς 40
εἰσῆλθον πρὸς τὴν Λυδίαν, καὶ ἰδόντες παρεκάλεσαν τοὺς
ἀδελφοὺς καὶ ἐξῆλθαν.
Διοδεύσαντες δὲ τὴν Ἀμφίπολιν καὶ τὴν Ἀπολλωνίαν 1
ἦλθον εἰς Θεσσαλονίκην, ὅπου ἦν συναγωγὴ τῶν Ἰουδαίων.
κατὰ δὲ τὸ εἰωθὸς τῷ Παύλῳ εἰσῆλθεν πρὸς αὐτοὺς καὶ ἐπὶ 2
σάββατα τρία διελέξατο αὐτοῖς ἀπὸ τῶν γραφῶν, διανοί- 3
γων καὶ παρατιθέμενος ὅτι τὸν χριστὸν ἔδει παθεῖν καὶ
ἀναστῆναι ἐκ νεκρῶν, καὶ ὅτι οὗτός ἐστιν ⌐ὁ χριστός, ὁ
Ἰησοῦς⌐ ὃν ἐγὼ καταγγέλλω ὑμῖν. καί τινες ἐξ αὐτῶν 4
ἐπείσθησαν καὶ προσεκληρώθησαν τῷ Παύλῳ καὶ [τῷ] Σίλᾳ,
τῶν τε σεβομένων Ἑλλήνων πλῆθος πολὺ γυναικῶν τε
τῶν πρώτων οὐκ ὀλίγαι. Ζηλώσαντες δὲ οἱ Ἰουδαῖοι καὶ 5
προσλαβόμενοι τῶν ἀγοραίων ἄνδρας τινὰς πονηροὺς καὶ
ὀχλοποιήσαντες ἐθορύβουν τὴν πόλιν, καὶ ἐπιστάντες τῇ
οἰκίᾳ Ἰάσονος ἐζήτουν αὐτοὺς προαγαγεῖν εἰς τὸν δῆμον·
μὴ εὑρόντες δὲ αὐτοὺς ἔσυρον Ἰάσονα καί τινας ἀδελφοὺς 6
ἐπὶ τοὺς πολιτάρχας, βοῶντες ὅτι Οἱ τὴν οἰκουμένην
ἀναστατώσαντες οὗτοι καὶ ἐνθάδε πάρεισιν, οὓς ὑποδέ- 7

3 Χριστὸς Ἰησοῦς

δεκται 'Ιάσων· καὶ οὗτοι πάντες ἀπέναντι τῶν δογμάτων
Καίσαρος πράσσουσι, βασιλέα ἕτερον λέγοντες εἶναι 'Ιη-
8 σοῦν. ἐτάραξαν δὲ τὸν ὄχλον καὶ τοὺς πολιτάρχας ἀκούον-
9 τας ταῦτα, καὶ λαβόντες τὸ ἱκανὸν παρὰ τοῦ 'Ιάσονος καὶ
10 τῶν λοιπῶν ἀπέλυσαν αὐτούς. Οἱ δὲ ἀδελφοὶ
εὐθέως διὰ νυκτὸς ἐξέπεμψαν τόν τε Παῦλον καὶ τὸν Σίλαν
εἰς Βέροιαν, οἵτινες παραγενόμενοι εἰς τὴν συναγωγὴν τῶν
11 'Ιουδαίων ἀπῄεσαν· οὗτοι δὲ ἦσαν εὐγενέστεροι τῶν ἐν Θεσ-
σαλονίκῃ, οἵτινες ἐδέξαντο τὸν λόγον μετὰ πάσης προ-
θυμίας, [τὸ] καθ' ἡμέραν ἀνακρίνοντες τὰς γραφὰς εἰ ἔχοι
12 ταῦτα οὕτως. πολλοὶ μὲν οὖν ἐξ αὐτῶν ἐπίστευσαν, καὶ
τῶν Ἑλληνίδων γυναικῶν τῶν εὐσχημόνων καὶ ἀνδρῶν
13 οὐκ ὀλίγοι. Ὡς δὲ ἔγνωσαν οἱ ἀπὸ τῆς Θεσσαλονίκης
'Ιουδαῖοι ὅτι καὶ ἐν τῇ Βεροίᾳ κατηγγέλη ὑπὸ τοῦ Παύλου
ὁ λόγος τοῦ θεοῦ, ἦλθον κἀκεῖ σαλεύοντες καὶ ταράσσοντες
14 τοὺς ὄχλους. εὐθέως δὲ τότε τὸν Παῦλον ἐξαπέστειλαν οἱ
ἀδελφοὶ πορεύεσθαι ἕως ἐπὶ τὴν θάλασσαν· ὑπέμεινάν τε
15 ὅ τε Σίλας καὶ ὁ Τιμόθεος ἐκεῖ. οἱ δὲ καθιστάνοντες τὸν
Παῦλον ἤγαγον ἕως Ἀθηνῶν, καὶ λαβόντες ἐντολὴν πρὸς
τὸν Σίλαν καὶ τὸν Τιμόθεον ἵνα ὡς τάχιστα ἔλθωσιν πρὸς
αὐτὸν ἐξῄεσαν.
16 Ἐν δὲ ταῖς Ἀθήναις ἐκδεχομένου αὐτοὺς τοῦ Παύλου,
παρωξύνετο τὸ πνεῦμα αὐτοῦ ἐν αὐτῷ θεωροῦντος κατείδω-
17 λον οὖσαν τὴν πόλιν. διελέγετο μὲν οὖν ἐν τῇ συναγωγῇ
τοῖς 'Ιουδαίοις καὶ τοῖς σεβομένοις καὶ ἐν τῇ ἀγορᾷ κατὰ
18 πᾶσαν ἡμέραν πρὸς τοὺς παρατυγχάνοντας. τινὲς δὲ καὶ
τῶν Ἐπικουρίων καὶ Στωικῶν φιλοσόφων συνέβαλλον
αὐτῷ, καί τινες ἔλεγον Τί ἂν θέλοι ὁ σπερμολόγος οὗτος
λέγειν; οἱ δέ Ξένων δαιμονίων δοκεῖ καταγγελεὺς εἶναι·
19 ὅτι τὸν 'Ιησοῦν καὶ τὴν ἀνάστασιν εὐηγγελίζετο. ἐπιλαβόμενοι δὲ αὐτοῦ ἐπὶ τὸν Ἄρειον Πάγον ἤγαγον, λέγοντες
Δυνάμεθα γνῶναι τίς ἡ καινὴ αὕτη [ἡ] ὑπὸ σοῦ λαλουμένη
20 διδαχή; ξενίζοντα γάρ τινα εἰσφέρεις εἰς τὰς ἀκοὰς ἡμῶν·

βουλόμεθα οὖν γνῶναί τίνα θέλει ταῦτα εἶναι. Ἀθηναῖοι ₂₁ δὲ πάντες καὶ οἱ ἐπιδημοῦντες ξένοι εἰς οὐδὲν ἕτερον ηὐκαίρουν ἢ λέγειν τι ἢ ἀκούειν τι καινότερον. σταθεὶς δὲ ₂₂ Παῦλος ἐν μέσῳ τοῦ Ἀρείου Πάγου ἔφη Ἄνδρες Ἀθηναῖοι, κατὰ πάντα ὡς δεισιδαιμονεστέρους ὑμᾶς θεωρῶ· διερχόμενος γὰρ καὶ ἀναθεωρῶν τὰ σεβάσματα ὑμῶν εὗρον ₂₃ καὶ βωμὸν ἐν ᾧ ἐπεγέγραπτο ΑΓΝΩΣΤΩ ΘΕΩ. ὃ οὖν ἀγνοοῦντες εὐσεβεῖτε, τοῦτο ἐγὼ καταγγέλλω ὑμῖν. ὁ ₂₄ θεὸς ὁ ποιήσας τὸν κόσμον καὶ πάντα τὰ ἐν αὐτῷ, οὗτος οὐρανοῦ καὶ γῆς ὑπάρχων κύριος οὐκ ἐν χειροποιήτοις ναοῖς κατοικεῖ οὐδὲ ὑπὸ χειρῶν ἀνθρωπίνων θερα- ₂₅ πεύεται προσδεόμενός τινος, αὐτὸς διδοὺς πᾶσι ζωὴν καὶ πνοὴν καὶ τὰ πάντα· ἐποίησέν τε ἐξ ἑνὸς πᾶν ἔθνος ἀν- ₂₆ θρώπων κατοικεῖν ἐπὶ παντὸς προσώπου τῆς γῆς, ὁρίσας προστεταγμένους καιροὺς καὶ τὰς ὁροθεσίας τῆς κατοικίας αὐτῶν, ζητεῖν τὸν θεὸν εἰ ἄρα γε ψηλαφήσειαν αὐτὸν καὶ εὕροιεν, καί γε οὐ μακρὰν ἀπὸ ἑνὸς ἑκάστου ἡμῶν ὑπάρ- ₂₇ χοντα. ἐν αὐτῷ γὰρ ζῶμεν καὶ κινούμεθα καὶ ἐσμέν, ὡς ₂₈ καί τινες τῶν καθ᾽ ⸢ὑμᾶς⸥ ποιητῶν εἰρήκασιν

Τοῦ γὰρ καὶ γένος ἐσμέν.

γένος οὖν ὑπάρχοντες τοῦ θεοῦ οὐκ ὀφείλομεν νομίζειν ₂₉ χρυσῷ ἢ ἀργύρῳ ἢ λίθῳ, χαράγματι τέχνης καὶ ἐνθυμήσεως ἀνθρώπου, τὸ θεῖον εἶναι ὅμοιον. τοὺς μὲν οὖν χρόνους ₃₀ τῆς ἀγνοίας ὑπεριδὼν ὁ θεὸς τὰ νῦν ἀπαγγέλλει τοῖς ἀνθρώποις πάντας πανταχοῦ μετανοεῖν, καθότι ἔστησεν ἡμέραν ₃₁ ἐν ᾗ μέλλει κρίνειν τὴν οἰκουμένην ἐν δικαιοσύνῃ ἐν ἀνδρὶ ᾧ ὥρισεν, πίστιν παρασχὼν πᾶσιν ἀναστήσας αὐτὸν ἐκ νεκρῶν. ἀκούσαντες δὲ ἀνάστασιν νεκρῶν οἱ ₃₂ μὲν ἐχλεύαζον οἱ δὲ εἶπαν Ἀκουσόμεθά σου περὶ τούτου καὶ πάλιν. οὕτως ὁ Παῦλος ἐξῆλθεν ἐκ μέσου αὐτῶν· ₃₃ τινὲς δὲ ἄνδρες κολληθέντες αὐτῷ ἐπίστευσαν, ἐν οἷς καὶ ₃₄ Διονύσιος [ὁ] Ἀρεοπαγίτης καὶ γυνὴ ὀνόματι Δάμαρις καὶ ἕτεροι σὺν αὐτοῖς.

28 ἡμᾶς

1 Μετὰ ταῦτα χωρισθεὶς ἐκ τῶν Ἀθηνῶν ἦλθεν εἰς Κό-
2 ρινθον. καὶ εὑρών τινα Ἰουδαῖον ὀνόματι Ἀκύλαν, Ποντικὸν τῷ γένει, προσφάτως ἐληλυθότα ἀπὸ τῆς Ἰταλίας καὶ
Πρίσκιλλαν γυναῖκα αὐτοῦ διὰ τὸ διατεταχέναι Κλαύδιον
χωρίζεσθαι πάντας τοὺς Ἰουδαίους ἀπὸ τῆς Ῥώμης, προσ-
3 ῆλθεν αὐτοῖς, καὶ διὰ τὸ ὁμότεχνον εἶναι ἔμενεν παρ' αὐτοῖς καὶ ⌜ἠργάζοντο⌝, ἦσαν γὰρ σκηνοποιοὶ τῇ τέχνῃ.
4 διελέγετο δὲ ἐν τῇ συναγωγῇ κατὰ πᾶν σάββατον, ἔπειθέν
5 τε Ἰουδαίους καὶ Ἕλληνας.   Ὡς δὲ κατῆλθον
ἀπὸ τῆς Μακεδονίας ὅ τε Σίλας καὶ ὁ Τιμόθεος, συνείχετο
τῷ λόγῳ ὁ Παῦλος, διαμαρτυρόμενος τοῖς Ἰουδαίοις εἶναι
6 τὸν χριστὸν Ἰησοῦν. ἀντιτασσομένων δὲ αὐτῶν καὶ βλα-
σφημούντων ἐκτιναξάμενος τὰ ἱμάτια εἶπεν πρὸς αὐτούς
Τὸ αἷμα ὑμῶν ἐπὶ τὴν κεφαλὴν ὑμῶν· καθαρὸς ⌜ἐγώ· ἀπὸ⌝
7 τοῦ νῦν εἰς τὰ ἔθνη πορεύσομαι. καὶ μεταβὰς ἐκεῖθεν
ἦλθεν εἰς οἰκίαν τινὸς ὀνόματι Τιτίου Ἰούστου σεβομέ-
νου τὸν θεόν, οὗ ἡ οἰκία ἦν συνομοροῦσα τῇ συναγωγῇ.
8 Κρίσπος δὲ ὁ ἀρχισυνάγωγος ἐπίστευσεν τῷ κυρίῳ σὺν
ὅλῳ τῷ οἴκῳ αὐτοῦ, καὶ πολλοὶ τῶν Κορινθίων ἀκούοντες
9 ἐπίστευον καὶ ἐβαπτίζοντο. Εἶπεν δὲ ὁ κύριος ἐν νυκτὶ
δι' ὁράματος τῷ Παύλῳ Μὴ φοβοῦ, ἀλλὰ λάλει καὶ μὴ
10 σιωπήσῃς, Διότι ἐγώ εἰμι μετὰ σοῦ καὶ οὐδεὶς ἐπιθήσεταί
σοι τοῦ κακῶσαί σε, διότι λαός ἐστί μοι πολὺς ἐν τῇ πόλει
11 ταύτῃ. Ἐκάθισεν δὲ ἐνιαυτὸν καὶ μῆνας ἓξ διδάσκων ἐν
12 αὐτοῖς τὸν λόγον τοῦ θεοῦ.   Γαλλίωνος δὲ ἀνθυπάτου ὄντος τῆς Ἀχαίας κατεπέστησαν ⌜οἱ Ἰουδαῖοι ὁμοθυ-
13 μαδὸν⌝ τῷ Παύλῳ καὶ ἤγαγον αὐτὸν ἐπὶ τὸ βῆμα, λέγοντες
ὅτι Παρὰ τὸν νόμον ἀναπείθει οὗτος τοὺς ἀνθρώπους
14 σέβεσθαι τὸν θεόν. μέλλοντος δὲ τοῦ Παύλου ἀνοίγειν
τὸ στόμα εἶπεν ὁ Γαλλίων πρὸς τοὺς Ἰουδαίους Εἰ μὲν
ἦν ἀδίκημά τι ἢ ῥᾳδιούργημα πονηρόν, ὦ Ἰουδαῖοι, κατὰ
15 λόγον ἂν ἀνεσχόμην ὑμῶν· εἰ δὲ ζητήματά ἐστιν περὶ
λόγου καὶ ὀνομάτων καὶ νόμου τοῦ καθ' ὑμᾶς, ὄψεσθε αὐτοί·

3 ἠργάζετο   6 ἐγὼ ἀπό   12 ὁμοθυμαδὸν οἱ Ἰουδαῖοι

κριτὴς ἐγὼ τούτων οὐ βούλομαι εἶναι. καὶ ἀπήλασεν 16
αὐτοὺς ἀπὸ τοῦ βήματος. ἐπιλαβόμενοι δὲ πάντες Σωσθέ- 17
νην τὸν ἀρχισυνάγωγον ἔτυπτον ἔμπροσθεν τοῦ βήματος·
καὶ οὐδὲν τούτων τῷ Γαλλίωνι ἔμελεν.   Ὁ δὲ 18
Παῦλος ἔτι προσμείνας ἡμέρας ἱκανὰς τοῖς ἀδελφοῖς ἀποταξάμενος ἐξέπλει εἰς τὴν Συρίαν, καὶ σὺν αὐτῷ Πρίσκιλλα
καὶ Ἀκύλας, κειράμενος ἐν Κενχρεαῖς τὴν κεφαλήν, εἶχεν
γὰρ εὐχήν. κατήντησαν δὲ εἰς Ἔφεσον, κἀκείνους κατέ- 19
λιπεν αὐτοῦ, αὐτὸς δὲ εἰσελθὼν εἰς τὴν συναγωγὴν· διελέξατο τοῖς Ἰουδαίοις. ἐρωτώντων δὲ αὐτῶν ἐπὶ πλείονα 20
χρόνον μεῖναι οὐκ ἐπένευσεν, ἀλλὰ ἀποταξάμενος καὶ εἰπών 21
Πάλιν ἀνακάμψω πρὸς ὑμᾶς τοῦ θεοῦ θέλοντος   ἀνήχθη
ἀπὸ τῆς Ἐφέσου, καὶ κατελθὼν εἰς Καισαρίαν, ἀναβὰς 22
καὶ ἀσπασάμενος τὴν ἐκκλησίαν, κατέβη εἰς Ἀντιόχειαν,
καὶ ποιήσας χρόνον τινὰ ἐξῆλθεν, διερχόμενος καθεξῆς 23
τὴν Γαλατικὴν χώραν καὶ Φρυγίαν, στηρίζων πάντας τοὺς
μαθητάς.

Ἰουδαῖος δέ τις Ἀπολλὼς ὀνόματι, Ἀλεξανδρεὺς τῷ 24
γένει, ἀνὴρ λόγιος, κατήντησεν εἰς Ἔφεσον, δυνατὸς ὢν ἐν
ταῖς γραφαῖς. οὗτος ἦν κατηχημένος τὴν ὁδὸν ⌜τοῦ κυρίου⌝, 25
καὶ ζέων τῷ πνεύματι ἐλάλει καὶ ἐδίδασκεν ἀκριβῶς τὰ περὶ
τοῦ Ἰησοῦ, ἐπιστάμενος μόνον τὸ βάπτισμα Ἰωάνου. οὗτός 26
τε ἤρξατο παρρησιάζεσθαι ἐν τῇ συναγωγῇ· ἀκούσαντες
δὲ αὐτοῦ Πρίσκιλλα καὶ Ἀκύλας προσελάβοντο αὐτὸν καὶ
ἀκριβέστερον αὐτῷ ἐξέθεντο τὴν ὁδὸν τοῦ θεοῦ. βουλο- 27
μένου δὲ αὐτοῦ διελθεῖν εἰς τὴν Ἀχαίαν προτρεψάμενοι
οἱ ἀδελφοὶ ἔγραψαν τοῖς μαθηταῖς ἀποδέξασθαι αὐτόν·
ὃς παραγενόμενος συνεβάλετο πολὺ τοῖς πεπιστευκόσιν
διὰ τῆς χάριτος· εὐτόνως γὰρ τοῖς Ἰουδαίοις διακατηλέγ- 28
χετο δημοσίᾳ ἐπιδεικνὺς διὰ τῶν γραφῶν εἶναι τὸν χριστὸν
Ἰησοῦν.   Ἐγένετο δὲ ἐν τῷ τὸν Ἀπολλὼ εἶναι

25 Κυρίου

ἐν Κορίνθῳ Παῦλον διελθόντα τὰ ἀνωτερικὰ μέρη ἐλθεῖν
2 εἰς Ἔφεσον καὶ εὑρεῖν τινὰς μαθητάς, εἶπέν τε πρὸς αὐτούς
Εἰ πνεῦμα ἅγιον ἐλάβετε πιστεύσαντες ; οἱ δὲ πρὸς αὐτόν
3 Ἀλλ᾽ οὐδ᾽ εἰ πνεῦμα ἅγιον ἔστιν ἠκούσαμεν. ⌜εἶπέν τε⌝ Εἰς
τί οὖν ἐβαπτίσθητε ; οἱ δὲ εἶπαν Εἰς τὸ Ἰωάνου βάπτισμα.
4 εἶπεν δὲ Παῦλος Ἰωάνης ἐβάπτισεν βάπτισμα μετανοίας,
τῷ λαῷ λέγων εἰς τὸν ἐρχόμενον μετ᾽ αὐτὸν ἵνα πιστεύσω-
5 σιν, τοῦτ᾽ ἔστιν εἰς τὸν Ἰησοῦν. ἀκούσαντες δὲ ἐβαπτίσθη-
6 σαν εἰς τὸ ὄνομα τοῦ κυρίου Ἰησοῦ· καὶ ἐπιθέντος αὐτοῖς
τοῦ Παύλου χεῖρας ἦλθε τὸ πνεῦμα τὸ ἅγιον ἐπ᾽ αὐτούς,
7 ἐλάλουν τε γλώσσαις καὶ ἐπροφήτευον. ἦσαν δὲ οἱ πάντες
8 ἄνδρες ὡσεὶ δώδεκα. Εἰσελθὼν δὲ εἰς τὴν συναγωγὴν ἐπαρρησιάζετο ἐπὶ μῆνας τρεῖς διαλεγόμενος καὶ
9 πείθων περὶ τῆς βασιλείας τοῦ θεοῦ. ὡς δέ τινες ἐσκλη-
ρύνοντο καὶ ἠπείθουν κακολογοῦντες τὴν ὁδὸν ἐνώπιον τοῦ
πλήθους, ἀποστὰς ἀπ᾽ αὐτῶν ἀφώρισεν τοὺς μαθητάς,
10 καθ᾽ ἡμέραν διαλεγόμενος ἐν τῇ σχολῇ Τυράννου. τοῦτο
δὲ ἐγένετο ἐπὶ ἔτη δύο, ὥστε πάντας τοὺς κατοικοῦντας τὴν
Ἀσίαν ἀκοῦσαι τὸν λόγον τοῦ κυρίου, Ἰουδαίους τε καὶ
11 Ἕλληνας. Δυνάμεις τε οὐ τὰς τυχούσας ὁ θεὸς
12 ἐποίει διὰ τῶν χειρῶν Παύλου, ὥστε καὶ ἐπὶ τοὺς ἀσθενοῦν-
τας ἀποφέρεσθαι ἀπὸ τοῦ χρωτὸς αὐτοῦ σουδάρια ἢ σιμικίν-
θια καὶ ἀπαλλάσσεσθαι ἀπ᾽ αὐτῶν τὰς νόσους, τά τε πνεύ-
13 ματα τὰ πονηρὰ ἐκπορεύεσθαι. Ἐπεχείρησαν δέ τινες καὶ
τῶν περιερχομένων Ἰουδαίων ἐξορκιστῶν ὀνομάζειν ἐπὶ τοὺς
ἔχοντας τὰ πνεύματα τὰ πονηρὰ τὸ ὄνομα τοῦ κυρίου Ἰησοῦ
λέγοντες Ὁρκίζω ὑμᾶς τὸν Ἰησοῦν ὃν Παῦλος κηρύσσει.
14 ἦσαν δέ τινος Σκευᾶ Ἰουδαίου ἀρχιερέως ἑπτὰ υἱοὶ τοῦτο
15 ποιοῦντες. ἀποκριθὲν δὲ τὸ πνεῦμα τὸ πονηρὸν εἶπεν αὐτοῖς Τὸν [μὲν] Ἰησοῦν γινώσκω καὶ τὸν Παῦλον ἐπίστα-
16 μαι, ὑμεῖς δὲ τίνες ἐστέ ; καὶ ἐφαλόμενος ὁ ἄνθρωπος

3 ὁ δὲ εἶπεν

ἐπ᾽ αὐτοὺς ἐν ᾧ ἦν τὸ πνεῦμα τὸ πονηρὸν κατακυριεύσας ἀμφοτέρων ἴσχυσεν κατ᾽ αὐτῶν, ὥστε γυμνοὺς καὶ τετραυματισμένους ἐκφυγεῖν ἐκ τοῦ οἴκου ἐκείνου. τοῦτο δὲ 17 ἐγένετο γνωστὸν πᾶσιν Ἰουδαίοις τε καὶ Ἕλλησιν τοῖς κατοικοῦσιν τὴν Ἔφεσον, καὶ ἐπέπεσεν φόβος ἐπὶ πάντας αὐτούς, καὶ ἐμεγαλύνετο τὸ ὄνομα τοῦ κυρίου Ἰησοῦ. πολλοί τε τῶν πεπιστευκότων ἤρχοντο ἐξομολογούμενοι καὶ 18 ἀναγγέλλοντες τὰς πράξεις αὐτῶν. ἱκανοὶ δὲ τῶν τὰ πε- 19 ρίεργα πραξάντων συνενέγκαντες τὰς βίβλους κατέκαιον ἐνώπιον πάντων· καὶ συνεψήφισαν τὰς τιμὰς αὐτῶν καὶ εὗρον ἀργυρίου μυριάδας πέντε. Οὕτως κατὰ κράτος τοῦ 20 κυρίου ὁ λόγος ηὔξανεν καὶ ἴσχυεν.

ΩΣ ΔΕ ΕΠΛΗΡΩΘΗ ταῦτα, ἔθετο ὁ Παῦλος ἐν τῷ 21 πνεύματι διελθὼν τὴν Μακεδονίαν καὶ Ἀχαίαν πορεύεσθαι εἰς Ἰεροσόλυμα, εἰπὼν ὅτι Μετὰ τὸ γενέσθαι με ἐκεῖ δεῖ με καὶ Ῥώμην ἰδεῖν. ἀποστείλας δὲ εἰς τὴν Μακεδονίαν 22 δύο τῶν διακονούντων αὐτῷ, Τιμόθεον καὶ Ἔραστον, αὐτὸς ἐπέσχεν χρόνον εἰς τὴν Ἀσίαν. Ἐγένετο δὲ 23 κατὰ τὸν καιρὸν ἐκεῖνον τάραχος οὐκ ὀλίγος περὶ τῆς ὁδοῦ. Δημήτριος γάρ τις ὀνόματι, ἀργυροκόπος, ποιῶν ναοὺς 24 [ἀργυροῦς] Ἀρτέμιδος παρείχετο τοῖς τεχνίταις οὐκ ὀλίγην ἐργασίαν, οὓς συναθροίσας καὶ τοὺς περὶ τὰ τοιαῦτα ἐργά- 25 τας εἶπεν Ἄνδρες, ἐπίστασθε ὅτι ἐκ ταύτης τῆς ἐργασίας ἡ εὐπορία ἡμῖν ἐστίν, καὶ θεωρεῖτε καὶ ἀκούετε ὅτι οὐ μόνον 26 Ἐφέσου ἀλλὰ σχεδὸν πάσης τῆς Ἀσίας ὁ Παῦλος οὗτος πείσας μετέστησεν ἱκανὸν ὄχλον, λέγων ὅτι οὐκ εἰσὶν θεοὶ οἱ διὰ χειρῶν γινόμενοι. οὐ μόνον δὲ τοῦτο κινδυνεύει 27 ἡμῖν τὸ μέρος εἰς ἀπελεγμὸν ἐλθεῖν, ἀλλὰ καὶ τὸ τῆς μεγάλης θεᾶς Ἀρτέμιδος ἱερὸν εἰς οὐθὲν λογισθῆναι, μέλλειν

34 ὡς | κράζοντες

τε καὶ καθαιρεῖσθαι τῆς μεγαλειότητος αὐτῆς, ἣν ὅλη
28 [ἡ] Ἀσία καὶ [ἡ] οἰκουμένη σέβεται. ἀκούσαντες δὲ καὶ
γενόμενοι πλήρεις θυμοῦ ἔκραζον λέγοντες Μεγάλη ἡ
29 Ἄρτεμις Ἐφεσίων. καὶ ἐπλήσθη ἡ πόλις τῆς συγχύσεως,
ὥρμησάν τε ὁμοθυμαδὸν εἰς τὸ θέατρον συναρπάσαντες
Γαῖον καὶ Ἀρίσταρχον Μακεδόνας, συνεκδήμους Παύλου.
30 Παύλου δὲ βουλομένου εἰσελθεῖν εἰς τὸν δῆμον οὐκ εἴων
31 αὐτὸν οἱ μαθηταί· τινὲς δὲ καὶ τῶν Ἀσιαρχῶν, ὄντες αὐτῷ
φίλοι, πέμψαντες πρὸς αὐτὸν παρεκάλουν μὴ δοῦναι ἑαυ-
32 τὸν εἰς τὸ θέατρον. ἄλλοι μὲν οὖν ἄλλο τι ἔκραζον, ἦν
γὰρ ἡ ἐκκλησία συνκεχυμένη, καὶ οἱ πλείους οὐκ ᾔδεισαν
33 τίνος ἕνεκα συνεληλύθεισαν. ἐκ δὲ τοῦ ὄχλου συνεβίβασαν Ἀλέξανδρον προβαλόντων αὐτὸν τῶν Ἰουδαίων, ὁ δὲ
Ἀλέξανδρος κατασείσας τὴν χεῖρα ἤθελεν ἀπολογεῖσθαι
34 τῷ δήμῳ. ἐπιγνόντες δὲ ὅτι Ἰουδαῖός ἐστιν φωνὴ ἐγένετο
μία ἐκ πάντων ⌜ὡσεὶ⌝ ἐπὶ ὥρας δύο ⌜κραζόντων⌝ Μεγάλη ἡ
35 Ἄρτεμις Ἐφεσίων⌝. καταστείλας δὲ τὸν ὄχλον ὁ γραμματεύς φησιν Ἄνδρες Ἐφέσιοι, τίς γάρ ἐστιν ἀνθρώπων
ὃς οὐ γινώσκει τὴν Ἐφεσίων πόλιν νεωκόρον οὖσαν τῆς
36 μεγάλης Ἀρτέμιδος καὶ τοῦ διοπετοῦς; ἀναντιρήτων οὖν
ὄντων τούτων δέον ἐστὶν ὑμᾶς κατεσταλμένους ὑπάρχειν
37 καὶ μηδὲν προπετὲς πράσσειν. ἠγάγετε γὰρ τοὺς ἄνδρας
τούτους οὔτε ἱεροσύλους οὔτε βλασφημοῦντας τὴν θεὸν
38 ἡμῶν. εἰ μὲν οὖν Δημήτριος καὶ οἱ σὺν αὐτῷ τεχνῖται
ἔχουσιν πρός τινα λόγον, ἀγοραῖοι ἄγονται καὶ ἀνθύπατοί
39 εἰσιν, ἐγκαλείτωσαν ἀλλήλοις. εἰ δέ τι περαιτέρω ἐπιζη-
40 τεῖτε, ἐν τῇ ἐννόμῳ ἐκκλησίᾳ ἐπιλυθήσεται. καὶ γὰρ
κινδυνεύομεν ἐγκαλεῖσθαι στάσεως ⌜περὶ τῆς σήμερον μηδενὸς αἰτίου ὑπάρχοντος, περὶ οὗ οὐ δυνησόμεθα ἀποδοῦναι
41 λόγον περὶ τῆς συστροφῆς ταύτης⌝. καὶ ταῦτα εἰπὼν ἀπέ-
λυσεν τὴν ἐκκλησίαν.
1 Μετὰ δὲ τὸ παύσασθαι τὸν θόρυβον μεταπεμψάμενος

34 Μεγάλη ἡ Ἄρτεμις Ἐφεσίων   40 †...†

ὁ Παῦλος τοὺς μαθητὰς καὶ παρακαλέσας ἀσπασάμενος
ἐξῆλθεν πορεύεσθαι εἰς Μακεδονίαν. διελθὼν δὲ τὰ μέρη 2
ἐκεῖνα καὶ παρακαλέσας αὐτοὺς λόγῳ πολλῷ ἦλθεν εἰς τὴν
Ἑλλάδα, ποιήσας τε μῆνας τρεῖς γενομένης ἐπιβουλῆς 3
αὐτῷ ὑπὸ τῶν Ἰουδαίων μέλλοντι ἀνάγεσθαι εἰς τὴν Συρίαν
ἐγένετο γνώμης τοῦ ὑποστρέφειν διὰ Μακεδονίας. συνεί- 4
πετο δὲ αὐτῷ Σώπατρος Πύρρου Βεροιαῖος, Θεσσαλονι-
κέων δὲ Ἀρίσταρχος καὶ Σέκουνδος καὶ Γαῖος Δερβαῖος καὶ
Τιμόθεος, Ἀσιανοὶ δὲ Τύχικος καὶ Τρόφιμος· οὗτοι δὲ 5
⌜προσελθόντες⌝ ἔμενον ἡμᾶς ἐν Τρῳάδι· ἡμεῖς δὲ ἐξεπλεύσα- 6
μεν μετὰ τὰς ἡμέρας τῶν ἀζύμων ἀπὸ Φιλίππων, καὶ ἤλθομεν πρὸς αὐτοὺς εἰς τὴν Τρῳάδα ἄχρι ἡμερῶν πέντε, οὗ
διετρίψαμεν ἡμέρας ἑπτά. Ἐν δὲ τῇ μιᾷ τῶν 7
σαββάτων συνηγμένων ἡμῶν κλάσαι ἄρτον ὁ Παῦλος διελέγετο αὐτοῖς, μέλλων ἐξιέναι τῇ ἐπαύριον, παρέτεινέν τε
τὸν λόγον μέχρι μεσονυκτίου. ἦσαν δὲ λαμπάδες ἱκαναὶ 8
ἐν τῷ ὑπερῴῳ οὗ ἦμεν συνηγμένοι· καθεζόμενος δέ τις 9
νεανίας ὀνόματι Εὔτυχος ἐπὶ τῆς θυρίδος, καταφερόμενος
ὕπνῳ βαθεῖ διαλεγομένου τοῦ ⌜Παύλου ἐπὶ πλεῖον, κατε-
νεχθεὶς⌝ ἀπὸ τοῦ ὕπνου ἔπεσεν ἀπὸ τοῦ τριστέγου κάτω καὶ
ἤρθη νεκρός. καταβὰς δὲ ὁ Παῦλος ἐπέπεσεν αὐτῷ καὶ 10
συνπεριλαβὼν εἶπεν ⌜Μὴ θορυβεῖσθε⌝, ἡ γὰρ ψυχὴ αὐτοῦ
ἐν αὐτῷ ἐστιν. ἀναβὰς δὲ [καὶ] κλάσας τὸν ἄρτον καὶ 11
γευσάμενος ἐφ' ἱκανόν τε ὁμιλήσας ἄχρι αὐγῆς οὕτως
ἐξῆλθεν. ἤγαγον δὲ τὸν παῖδα ζῶντα, καὶ παρεκλήθησαν 12
οὐ μετρίως. Ἡμεῖς δὲ ⌜προελθόντες⌝ ἐπὶ τὸ 13
πλοῖον ἀνήχθημεν ἐπὶ τὴν Ἆσσον, ἐκεῖθεν μέλλοντες ἀνα-
λαμβάνειν τὸν Παῦλον, οὕτως γὰρ διατεταγμένος ἦν μέλλων αὐτὸς πεζεύειν. ὡς δὲ συνέβαλλεν ἡμῖν εἰς τὴν Ἆσσον, 14
ἀναλαβόντες αὐτὸν ἤλθομεν εἰς Μιτυλήνην, κἀκεῖθεν ἀπο- 15
πλεύσαντες τῇ ἐπιούσῃ κατηντήσαμεν ἄντικρυς Χίου, τῇ
δὲ ⌜ἑτέρᾳ⌝ παρεβάλομεν εἰς Σάμον, τῇ δὲ ἐχομένῃ ἤλθομεν
εἰς Μίλητον· κεκρίκει γὰρ ὁ Παῦλος παραπλεῦσαι τὴν 16

5 προελθόντες   9 Παύλου, ἐπὶ πλεῖον κατενεχθεὶς   10 μὴ θορυβεῖσθαι

Ἔφεσον, ὅπως μὴ γένηται αὐτῷ χρονοτριβῆσαι ἐν τῇ Ἀσίᾳ,
ἔσπευδεν γὰρ εἰ δυνατὸν εἴη αὐτῷ τὴν ἡμέραν τῆς πεντηκοστῆς γενέσθαι εἰς Ἱεροσόλυμα.

17 Ἀπὸ δὲ τῆς Μιλήτου πέμψας εἰς Ἔφεσον μετεκαλέ-
18 σατο τοὺς πρεσβυτέρους ͵τῆς ἐκκλησίας. ὡς δὲ παρεγένοντο
πρὸς αὐτὸν εἶπεν αὐτοῖς Ὑμεῖς ἐπίστασθε ἀπὸ πρώτης
ἡμέρας ἀφ᾽ ἧς ἐπέβην εἰς τὴν Ἀσίαν πῶς μεθ᾽ ὑμῶν τὸν
19 πάντα χρόνον ἐγενόμην, δουλεύων τῷ κυρίῳ μετὰ πάσης
ταπεινοφροσύνης καὶ δακρύων καὶ πειρασμῶν τῶν συμβάν-
20 των μοι ἐν ταῖς ἐπιβουλαῖς τῶν Ἰουδαίων· ὡς οὐδὲν ὑπεστειλάμην τῶν συμφερόντων τοῦ μὴ ἀναγγεῖλαι ὑμῖν καὶ
21 διδάξαι ὑμᾶς δημοσίᾳ καὶ κατ᾽ οἴκους, διαμαρτυρόμενος
Ἰουδαίοις τε καὶ Ἕλλησιν τὴν εἰς θεὸν μετάνοιαν καὶ
22 πίστιν εἰς τὸν κύριον ἡμῶν Ἰησοῦν⌐. καὶ νῦν ἰδοὺ δεδεμένος ἐγὼ τῷ πνεύματι πορεύομαι εἰς Ἱερουσαλήμ, τὰ ἐν
23 αὐτῇ συναντήσοντα ἐμοὶ μὴ εἰδώς, πλὴν ὅτι τὸ πνεῦμα τὸ
ἅγιον κατὰ πόλιν διαμαρτύρεταί μοι λέγον ὅτι δεσμὰ καὶ
24 θλίψεις με μένουσιν· ἀλλ᾽ οὐδενὸς λόγου ποιοῦμαι τὴν
ψυχὴν τιμίαν ἐμαυτῷ ὡς ⌐τελειώσω⌐ τὸν δρόμον μου καὶ
τὴν διακονίαν ἣν ἔλαβον παρὰ τοῦ κυρίου Ἰησοῦ, διαμαρ-
25 τύρασθαι τὸ εὐαγγέλιον τῆς χάριτος τοῦ θεοῦ. καὶ νῦν
ἰδοὺ ἐγὼ οἶδα ὅτι οὐκέτι ὄψεσθε τὸ πρόσωπόν μου ὑμεῖς
26 πάντες ἐν οἷς διῆλθον κηρύσσων τὴν βασιλείαν· διότι μαρτύρομαι ὑμῖν ἐν τῇ σήμερον ἡμέρᾳ ὅτι καθαρός εἰμι ἀπὸ
27 τοῦ αἵματος πάντων, οὐ γὰρ ὑπεστειλάμην τοῦ μὴ ἀναγ-
28 γεῖλαι πᾶσαν τὴν βουλὴν τοῦ θεοῦ ὑμῖν. προσέχετε ἑαυτοῖς καὶ παντὶ τῷ ποιμνίῳ, ἐν ᾧ ὑμᾶς τὸ πνεῦμα τὸ ἅγιον
ἔθετο ἐπισκόπους, ποιμαίνειν ΤΗΝ ἘΚΚΛΗΣΊΑΝ ΤΟΥ̑ ΘΕΟΥ̑,
29 ῊΝ ΠΕΡΙΕΠΟΙΉΣΑΤΟ διὰ τοῦ αἵματος τοῦ ⌐ἰδίου⌐. ἐγὼ
οἶδα ὅτι εἰσελεύσονται μετὰ τὴν ἄφιξίν μου λύκοι βαρεῖς
30 εἰς ὑμᾶς μὴ φειδόμενοι τοῦ ποιμνίου, καὶ ἐξ ὑμῶν [αὐτῶν]
ἀναστήσονται ἄνδρες λαλοῦντες διεστραμμένα τοῦ ἀπο-
31 σπᾶν τοὺς μαθητὰς ὀπίσω ἑαυτῶν· διὸ γρηγορεῖτε, μνημο-

13 προσελθόντες   15 ἑσπέρᾳ   21 Χριστόν   24 τελειῶσαι   28 †...†

4—2

νεύοντες ὅτι τριετίαν νύκτα καὶ ἡμέραν οὐκ ἐπαυσάμην μετὰ
δακρύων νουθετῶν ἕνα ἕκαστον. καὶ τὰ νῦν παρατίθεμαι 32
ὑμᾶς τῷ ⌜κυρίῳ⌝ καὶ τῷ λόγῳ τῆς χάριτος αὐτοῦ τῷ δυναμένῳ
οἰκοδομῆσαι καὶ δοῦναι τὴν κληρονομίαν ἐν τοῖς ἡγια-
cμένοιc πᾶcιν. ἀργυρίου ἢ χρυσίου ἢ ἱματισμοῦ οὐδενὸς 33
ἐπεθύμησα· αὐτοὶ γινώσκετε ὅτι ταῖς χρείαις μου καὶ τοῖς 34
οὖσι μετ᾽ ἐμοῦ ὑπηρέτησαν αἱ χεῖρες αὗται. πάντα ὑπέδειξα 35
ὑμῖν ὅτι οὕτως κοπιῶντας δεῖ ἀντιλαμβάνεσθαι τῶν ἀσθε-
νούντων, μνημονεύειν τε τῶν λόγων τοῦ κυρίου Ἰησοῦ ὅτι
αὐτὸς εἶπεν Μακάριόν ἐστιν μᾶλλον διδόναι ἢ λαμβάνειν.
καὶ ταῦτα εἰπὼν θεὶς τὰ γόνατα αὐτοῦ σὺν πᾶσιν αὐτοῖς 36
προσηύξατο. ἱκανὸς δὲ κλαυθμὸς ἐγένετο πάντων, καὶ 37
ἐπιπεσόντες ἐπὶ τὸν τράχηλον τοῦ Παύλου κατεφίλουν
αὐτόν, ὀδυνώμενοι μάλιστα ἐπὶ τῷ λόγῳ ᾧ εἰρήκει ὅτι 38
οὐκέτι μέλλουσιν τὸ πρόσωπον αὐτοῦ θεωρεῖν. προέπεμ-
πον δὲ αὐτὸν εἰς τὸ πλοῖον.

Ὡς δὲ ἐγένετο ἀναχθῆναι ⌜ἡμᾶς⌝ ἀποσπασθέντας ἀπ᾽ αὐ- 1
τῶν,⌝ εὐθυδρομήσαντες ἤλθομεν εἰς τὴν Κῶ, τῇ δὲ ἑξῆς εἰς
τὴν Ῥόδον, κἀκεῖθεν εἰς Πάταρα· καὶ εὑρόντες πλοῖον 2
διαπερῶν εἰς Φοινίκην ἐπιβάντες ἀνήχθημεν. ἀναφάναντες 3
δὲ τὴν Κύπρον καὶ καταλιπόντες αὐτὴν εὐώνυμον ἐπλέομεν
εἰς Συρίαν, καὶ κατήλθομεν εἰς Τύρον, ἐκεῖσε γὰρ τὸ πλοῖον
ἦν ἀποφορτιζόμενον τὸν γόμον. ἀνευρόντες δὲ τοὺς μαθη- 4
τὰς ἐπεμείναμεν αὐτοῦ ἡμέρας ἑπτά, οἵτινες τῷ Παύλῳ
ἔλεγον διὰ τοῦ πνεύματος μὴ ἐπιβαίνειν εἰς Ἱεροσόλυμα.
ὅτε δὲ ἐγένετο ⌜ἐξαρτίσαι ἡμᾶς⌝ τὰς ἡμέρας, ἐξελθόντες 5
ἐπορευόμεθα προπεμπόντων ἡμᾶς πάντων σὺν γυναιξὶ καὶ
τέκνοις ἕως ἔξω τῆς πόλεως, καὶ θέντες τὰ γόνατα ἐπὶ
τὸν αἰγιαλὸν προσευξάμενοι ἀπησπασάμεθα ἀλλήλους, καὶ 6
ἐνέβημεν εἰς τὸ πλοῖον, ἐκεῖνοι δὲ ὑπέστρεψαν εἰς τὰ
ἴδια.   Ἡμεῖς δὲ τὸν πλοῦν διανύσαντες ἀπὸ 7
Τύρου κατηντήσαμεν εἰς Πτολεμαΐδα, καὶ ἀσπασάμενοι
τοὺς ἀδελφοὺς ἐμείναμεν ἡμέραν μίαν παρ᾽ αὐτοῖς. τῇ δὲ 8

32 θεῷ   1 ἡμᾶς, ἀποσπασθέντες ἀπ᾽ αὐτῶν

ἐπαύριον ἐξελθόντες ἤλθαμεν εἰς Καισαρίαν, καὶ εἰσελθόντες εἰς τὸν οἶκον Φιλίππου τοῦ εὐαγγελιστοῦ ὄντος ἐκ
9 τῶν ἑπτὰ ἐμείναμεν παρ᾽ αὐτῷ. τούτῳ δὲ ἦσαν θυγατέρες
10 τέσσαρες παρθένοι προφητεύουσαι. Ἐπιμενόντων δὲ ἡμέρας πλείους κατῆλθέν τις ἀπὸ τῆς Ἰουδαίας προφήτης
11 ὀνόματι Ἄγαβος, καὶ ἐλθὼν πρὸς ἡμᾶς καὶ ἄρας τὴν ζώνην
τοῦ Παύλου δήσας ἑαυτοῦ τοὺς πόδας καὶ τὰς χεῖρας εἶπεν
Τάδε λέγει τὸ πνεῦμα τὸ ἅγιον Τὸν ἄνδρα οὗ ἐστὶν ἡ
ζώνη αὕτη οὕτως δήσουσιν ἐν Ἰερουσαλὴμ οἱ Ἰουδαῖοι καὶ
12 παραδώσουσιν εἰς χεῖρας ἐθνῶν. ὡς δὲ ἠκούσαμεν ταῦτα,
παρεκαλοῦμεν ἡμεῖς τε καὶ οἱ ἐντόπιοι τοῦ μὴ ἀναβαίνειν
13 αὐτὸν εἰς Ἰερουσαλήμ. τότε ἀπεκρίθη [ὁ] Παῦλος Τί
ποιεῖτε κλαίοντες καὶ συνθρύπτοντές μου τὴν καρδίαν; ἐγὼ
γὰρ οὐ μόνον δεθῆναι ἀλλὰ καὶ ἀποθανεῖν εἰς Ἰερουσαλὴμ
14 ἑτοίμως ἔχω ὑπὲρ τοῦ ὀνόματος τοῦ κυρίου Ἰησοῦ. μὴ
πειθομένου δὲ αὐτοῦ ἡσυχάσαμεν εἰπόντες Τοῦ κυρίου τὸ
θέλημα γινέσθω.

15 Μετὰ δὲ τὰς ἡμέρας ταύτας ἐπισκευασάμενοι ἀνεβαίνο-
16 μεν εἰς Ἰεροσόλυμα· συνῆλθον δὲ καὶ τῶν μαθητῶν ἀπὸ
Καισαρίας σὺν ἡμῖν, ἄγοντες παρ᾽ ᾧ ξενισθῶμεν Μνάσωνί
17 τινι Κυπρίῳ, ἀρχαίῳ μαθητῇ. Γενομένων δὲ ἡμῶν εἰς
18 Ἰεροσόλυμα ἀσμένως ἀπεδέξαντο ἡμᾶς οἱ ἀδελφοί. τῇ δὲ
ἐπιούσῃ εἰσῄει ὁ Παῦλος σὺν ἡμῖν πρὸς Ἰάκωβον, πάντες
19 τε παρεγένοντο οἱ πρεσβύτεροι. καὶ ἀσπασάμενος αὐτοὺς
ἐξηγεῖτο καθ᾽ ἓν ἕκαστον ὧν ἐποίησεν ὁ θεὸς ἐν τοῖς ἔθνεσιν
20 διὰ τῆς διακονίας αὐτοῦ. οἱ δὲ ἀκούσαντες ἐδόξαζον τὸν
θεόν, εἶπάν τε αὐτῷ Θεωρεῖς, ἀδελφέ, πόσαι μυριάδες
εἰσὶν ἐν τοῖς Ἰουδαίοις τῶν πεπιστευκότων, καὶ πάντες
21 ζηλωταὶ τοῦ νόμου ὑπάρχουσιν· κατηχήθησαν δὲ περὶ σοῦ
ὅτι ἀποστασίαν διδάσκεις ἀπὸ Μωυσέως τοὺς κατὰ τὰ ἔθνη
πάντας Ἰουδαίους, λέγων μὴ περιτέμνειν αὐτοὺς τὰ τέκνα
22 μηδὲ τοῖς ἔθεσιν περιπατεῖν. τί οὖν ἐστίν; πάντως ἀκού-

5 ἡμᾶς ἐξαρτίσαι

σονται ὅτι ἐλήλυθας. τοῦτο οὖν ποίησον ὅ σοι λέγομεν· 23
εἰσὶν ἡμῖν ἄνδρες τέσσαρες εὐχὴν ἔχοντες ⌜ἀφ'⌝ ἑαυτῶν·
τούτους παραλαβὼν ἁγνίσθητι σὺν αὐτοῖς καὶ δαπάνησον 24
ἐπ' αὐτοῖς ἵνα ξυρήσονται τὴν κεφαλήν, καὶ γνώσονται
πάντες ὅτι ὧν κατήχηνται περὶ σοῦ οὐδὲν ἔστιν, ἀλλὰ
στοιχεῖς καὶ αὐτὸς φυλάσσων τὸν νόμον. περὶ δὲ τῶν 25
πεπιστευκότων ἐθνῶν ἡμεῖς ⌜ἀπεστείλαμεν⌝ κρίναντες φυλάσσεσθαι αὐτοὺς τό τε εἰδωλόθυτον καὶ αἷμα καὶ πνικτὸν
καὶ πορνείαν. τότε ὁ Παῦλος παραλαβὼν τοὺς ἄνδρας τῇ 26
ἐχομένῃ ἡμέρᾳ σὺν αὐτοῖς ἁγνισθεὶς εἰσῄει εἰς τὸ ἱερόν,
διαγγέλλων τὴν ἐκπλήρωσιν ΤѠΝ ΗΜΕΡѠΝ ΤΟΥ ἉΓΝΙΣΜΟΥ
ἕως οὗ προσηνέχθη ὑπὲρ ἑνὸς ἑκάστου αὐτῶν ἡ προσφορά.

Ὡς δὲ ἔμελλον αἱ ἑπτὰ ἡμέραι συντελεῖσθαι, οἱ ἀπὸ 27
τῆς Ἀσίας Ἰουδαῖοι θεασάμενοι αὐτὸν ἐν τῷ ἱερῷ συνέχεον
πάντα τὸν ὄχλον καὶ ἐπέβαλαν ἐπ' αὐτὸν τὰς χεῖρας, κρά- 28
ζοντες Ἄνδρες Ἰσραηλεῖται, βοηθεῖτε· οὗτός ἐστιν ὁ
ἄνθρωπος ὁ κατὰ τοῦ λαοῦ καὶ τοῦ νόμου καὶ τοῦ τόπου
τούτου πάντας πανταχῇ διδάσκων, ἔτι τε καὶ Ἕλληνας
εἰσήγαγεν εἰς τὸ ἱερὸν καὶ κεκοίνωκεν τὸν ἅγιον τόπον
τοῦτον. ἦσαν γὰρ προεωρακότες Τρόφιμον τὸν Ἐφέσιον 29
ἐν τῇ πόλει σὺν αὐτῷ, ὃν ἐνόμιζον ὅτι εἰς τὸ ἱερὸν εἰσήγαγεν ὁ Παῦλος. ἐκινήθη τε ἡ πόλις ὅλη καὶ ἐγένετο συν- 30
δρομὴ τοῦ λαοῦ, καὶ ἐπιλαβόμενοι τοῦ Παύλου εἷλκον
αὐτὸν ἔξω τοῦ ἱεροῦ, καὶ εὐθέως ἐκλείσθησαν αἱ θύραι.
Ζητούντων τε αὐτὸν ἀποκτεῖναι ἀνέβη φάσις τῷ χιλιάρχῳ 31
τῆς σπείρης ὅτι ὅλη συνχύννεται Ἰερουσαλήμ, ὃς ἐξαυτῆς 32
⌜παραλαβὼν⌝ στρατιώτας καὶ ἑκατοντάρχας κατέδραμεν
ἐπ' αὐτούς, οἱ δὲ ἰδόντες τὸν χιλίαρχον καὶ τοὺς στρατιώτας ἐπαύσαντο τύπτοντες τὸν Παῦλον. τότε ἐγγίσας ὁ 33
χιλίαρχος ἐπελάβετο αὐτοῦ καὶ ἐκέλευσε δεθῆναι ἁλύσεσι
δυσί, καὶ ἐπυνθάνετο τίς εἴη καὶ τί ἐστιν πεποιηκώς· ἄλλοι 34
δὲ ἄλλο τι ἐπεφώνουν ἐν τῷ ὄχλῳ· μὴ δυναμένου δὲ αὐτοῦ
γνῶναι τὸ ἀσφαλὲς διὰ τὸν θόρυβον ἐκέλευσεν ἄγεσθαι

23 ἐφ'   25 ἐπεστείλαμεν   32 λαβών

35 αὐτὸν εἰς τὴν παρεμβολήν. ὅτε δὲ ἐγένετο ἐπὶ τοὺς ἀναβαθμούς, συνέβη βαστάζεσθαι αὐτὸν ὑπὸ τῶν στρατιωτῶν
36 διὰ τὴν βίαν τοῦ ὄχλου, ἠκολούθει γὰρ τὸ πλῆθος τοῦ λαοῦ
37 κράζοντες Αἶρε αὐτόν. Μέλλων τε εἰσάγε-
σθαι εἰς τὴν παρεμβολὴν ὁ Παῦλος λέγει τῷ χιλιάρχῳ
Εἰ ἔξεστίν μοι εἰπεῖν τι πρὸς σέ; ὁ δὲ ἔφη Ἑλληνιστὶ
38 γινώσκεις; οὐκ ἄρα σὺ εἶ ὁ Αἰγύπτιος ὁ πρὸ τούτων τῶν
ἡμερῶν ἀναστατώσας καὶ ἐξαγαγὼν εἰς τὴν ἔρημον τοὺς
39 τετρακισχιλίους ἄνδρας τῶν σικαρίων; εἶπεν δὲ ὁ Παῦλος
Ἐγὼ ἄνθρωπος μέν εἰμι Ἰουδαῖος, Ταρσεὺς τῆς Κιλικίας,
οὐκ ἀσήμου πόλεως πολίτης· δέομαι δέ σου, ἐπίτρεψόν μοι
40 λαλῆσαι πρὸς τὸν λαόν. ἐπιτρέψαντος δὲ αὐτοῦ ὁ Παῦλος
ἑστὼς ἐπὶ τῶν ἀναβαθμῶν κατέσεισε τῇ χειρὶ τῷ λαῷ,
πολλῆς δὲ ⌜σιγῆς γενομένης⌝ προσεφώνησεν τῇ Ἑβραΐδι
1 διαλέκτῳ λέγων Ἄνδρες ἀδελφοὶ καὶ πατέρες, ἀκούσατέ
2 μου τῆς πρὸς ὑμᾶς νυνὶ ἀπολογίας.— ἀκούσαντες δὲ ὅτι
τῇ Ἑβραΐδι διαλέκτῳ προσεφώνει αὐτοῖς μᾶλλον παρέσχον
3 ἡσυχίαν. καί φησιν— Ἐγώ εἰμι ἀνὴρ Ἰουδαῖος, γεγεννημένος ἐν Ταρσῷ τῆς Κιλικίας, ἀνατεθραμμένος δὲ ἐν τῇ πόλει
ταύτῃ παρὰ τοὺς πόδας Γαμαλιήλ, πεπαιδευμένος κατὰ
ἀκρίβειαν τοῦ πατρῴου νόμου, ζηλωτὴς ὑπάρχων τοῦ θεοῦ
4 καθὼς πάντες ὑμεῖς ἐστὲ σήμερον, ὃς ταύτην τὴν ὁδὸν
ἐδίωξα ἄχρι θανάτου, δεσμεύων καὶ παραδιδοὺς εἰς φυλακὰς
5 ἄνδρας τε καὶ γυναῖκας, ὡς καὶ ὁ ἀρχιερεὺς μαρτυρεῖ μοι
καὶ πᾶν τὸ πρεσβυτέριον· παρ' ὧν καὶ ἐπιστολὰς δεξάμε-
νος πρὸς τοὺς ἀδελφοὺς εἰς Δαμασκὸν ἐπορευόμην ἄξων
καὶ τοὺς ἐκεῖσε ὄντας δεδεμένους εἰς Ἰερουσαλὴμ ἵνα τιμω-
6 ρηθῶσιν. Ἐγένετο δέ μοι πορευομένῳ καὶ ἐγγίζοντι τῇ
Δαμασκῷ περὶ μεσημβρίαν ἐξαίφνης ἐκ τοῦ οὐρανοῦ περια-
7 στράψαι φῶς ἱκανὸν περὶ ἐμέ, ἔπεσά τε εἰς τὸ ἔδαφος καὶ
ἤκουσα φωνῆς λεγούσης μοι Σαοὺλ Σαούλ, τί με διώκεις;
8 ἐγὼ δὲ ἀπεκρίθην Τίς εἶ, κύριε; εἶπέν τε πρὸς ἐμέ
9 Ἐγώ εἰμι Ἰησοῦς ὁ Ναζωραῖος ὃν σὺ διώκεις. οἱ δὲ σὺν

40 γενομένης σιγῆς

ἐμοὶ ὄντες τὸ μὲν φῶς ἐθεάσαντο τὴν δὲ φωνὴν οὐκ ἤκουσαν
τοῦ λαλοῦντός μοι. εἶπον δέ Τί ποιήσω, κύριε; ὁ δὲ κύ- 10
ριος εἶπεν πρός με Ἀναστὰς πορεύου εἰς Δαμασκόν, κἀκεῖ
σοι λαληθήσεται περὶ πάντων ὧν τέτακταί σοι ποιῆσαι. ὡς 11
δὲ ⌜οὐκ ἐνέβλεπον⌝ ἀπὸ τῆς δόξης τοῦ φωτὸς ἐκείνου, χειρα-
γωγούμενος ὑπὸ τῶν συνόντων μοι ἦλθον εἰς Δαμασκόν.
Ἀνανίας δέ τις ἀνὴρ εὐλαβὴς κατὰ τὸν νόμον, μαρτυρούμε- 12
νος ὑπὸ πάντων τῶν κατοικούντων Ἰουδαίων, ἐλθὼν πρὸς 13
ἐμὲ καὶ ἐπιστὰς εἶπέν μοι Σαοὺλ ἀδελφέ, ἀνάβλεψον·
κἀγὼ αὐτῇ τῇ ὥρᾳ ἀνέβλεψα εἰς αὐτόν. ὁ δὲ εἶπεν Ὁ 14
θεὸς τῶν πατέρων ἡμῶν προεχειρίσατό σε γνῶναι τὸ θέλημα
αὐτοῦ καὶ ἰδεῖν τὸν δίκαιον καὶ ἀκοῦσαι φωνὴν ἐκ τοῦ στόματος αὐτοῦ, ὅτι ἔσῃ μάρτυς αὐτῷ πρὸς πάντας ἀνθρώπους 15
ὧν ἑώρακας καὶ ἤκουσας. καὶ νῦν τί μέλλεις; ἀναστὰς 16
βάπτισαι καὶ ἀπόλουσαι τὰς ἁμαρτίας σου ἐπικαλεσάμενος
τὸ ὄνομα αὐτοῦ. Ἐγένετο δέ μοι ὑποστρέψαντι εἰς Ἰερου- 17
σαλὴμ καὶ προσευχομένου μου ἐν τῷ ἱερῷ γενέσθαι με ἐν
ἐκστάσει καὶ ἰδεῖν αὐτὸν λέγοντά μοι Σπεῦσον καὶ ἔξελθε 18
ἐν τάχει ἐξ Ἰερουσαλήμ, διότι οὐ παραδέξονταί σου μαρ-
τυρίαν περὶ ἐμοῦ. κἀγὼ εἶπον Κύριε, αὐτοὶ ἐπίστανται 19
ὅτι ἐγὼ ἤμην φυλακίζων καὶ δέρων κατὰ τὰς συναγωγὰς
τοὺς πιστεύοντας ἐπὶ σέ· καὶ ὅτε ἐξεχύννετο τὸ αἷμα Στε- 20
φάνου τοῦ μάρτυρός σου, καὶ αὐτὸς ἤμην ἐφεστὼς καὶ
συνευδοκῶν καὶ φυλάσσων τὰ ἱμάτια τῶν ἀναιρούντων
αὐτόν. καὶ εἶπεν πρός με Πορεύου, ὅτι ἐγὼ εἰς ἔθνη 21
μακρὰν ⌜ἐξαποστελῶ⌝ σε.   Ἤκουον δὲ αὐτοῦ 22
ἄχρι τούτου τοῦ λόγου καὶ ἐπῆραν τὴν φωνὴν αὐτῶν λέγοντες Αἶρε ἀπὸ τῆς γῆς τὸν τοιοῦτον, οὐ γὰρ καθῆκεν
αὐτὸν ζῆν. κραυγαζόντων τε αὐτῶν καὶ ῥιπτούντων τὰ 23
ἱμάτια καὶ κονιορτὸν βαλλόντων εἰς τὸν ἀέρα ἐκέλευσεν 24
ὁ χιλίαρχος εἰσάγεσθαι αὐτὸν εἰς τὴν παρεμβολήν, εἴπας
μάστιξιν ἀνετάζεσθαι αὐτὸν ἵνα ἐπιγνῷ δι᾽ ἣν αἰτίαν οὕτως ἐπεφώνουν αὐτῷ. ὡς δὲ προέτειναν αὐτὸν τοῖς ἱμᾶσιν 25

11 οὐδὲν ἔβλεπον   21 ἀποστελῶ

εἶπεν πρὸς τὸν ἐστῶτα ἑκατόνταρχον ὁ Παῦλος Εἰ ἄνθρωπον Ῥωμαῖον καὶ ἀκατάκριτον ἔξεστιν ὑμῖν μαστίζειν;
26 ἀκούσας δὲ ὁ ἑκατοντάρχης προσελθὼν τῷ χιλιάρχῳ ἀπήγγειλεν λέγων Τί μέλλεις ποιεῖν; ὁ γὰρ ἄνθρωπος οὗτος
27 Ῥωμαῖός ἐστιν. προσελθὼν δὲ ὁ χιλίαρχος εἶπεν αὐτῷ
28 Λέγε μοι, σὺ Ῥωμαῖος εἶ; ὁ δὲ ἔφη Ναί. ἀπεκρίθη δὲ
ὁ χιλίαρχος Ἐγὼ πολλοῦ κεφαλαίου τὴν πολιτείαν ταύτην
ἐκτησάμην. ὁ δὲ Παῦλος ἔφη Ἐγὼ δὲ καὶ γεγέννημαι.
29 εὐθέως οὖν ἀπέστησαν ἀπ᾽ αὐτοῦ οἱ μέλλοντες αὐτὸν ἀνε-
τάζειν· καὶ ὁ χιλίαρχος δὲ ἐφοβήθη ἐπιγνοὺς ὅτι Ῥωμαῖός
ἐστιν καὶ ὅτι αὐτὸν ἦν δεδεκώς.
30 Τῇ δὲ ἐπαύριον βουλόμενος γνῶναι τὸ ἀσφαλὲς τὸ τί
κατηγορεῖται ὑπὸ τῶν Ἰουδαίων ἔλυσεν αὐτόν, καὶ ἐκέλευσεν συνελθεῖν τοὺς ἀρχιερεῖς καὶ πᾶν τὸ συνέδριον, καὶ
1 καταγαγὼν τὸν Παῦλον ἔστησεν εἰς αὐτούς. ἀτενίσας δὲ
⌜Παῦλος τῷ συνεδρίῳ⌝ εἶπεν Ἄνδρες ἀδελφοί, ἐγὼ πάσῃ
συνειδήσει ἀγαθῇ πεπολίτευμαι τῷ θεῷ ἄχρι ταύτης τῆς
2 ἡμέρας. ὁ δὲ ἀρχιερεὺς Ἀνανίας ἐπέταξεν τοῖς παρεστῶ-
3 σιν αὐτῷ τύπτειν αὐτοῦ τὸ στόμα. τότε ὁ Παῦλος πρὸς
αὐτὸν εἶπεν Τύπτειν σε μέλλει ὁ θεός, τοῖχε κεκονιαμένε·
καὶ σὺ κάθῃ κρίνων με κατὰ τὸν νόμον, καὶ παρανομῶν κε-
4 λεύεις με τύπτεσθαι; οἱ δὲ παρεστῶτες εἶπαν Τὸν ἀρχι-
5 ερέα τοῦ θεοῦ λοιδορεῖς; ἔφη τε ὁ Παῦλος Οὐκ ᾔδειν,
ἀδελφοί, ὅτι ἐστὶν ἀρχιερεύς· γέγραπται γὰρ ὅτι Ἄρχοντα
6 τοῦ λαοῦ σου οὐκ ἐρεῖς κακῶς. Γνοὺς δὲ ὁ Παῦλος
ὅτι τὸ ἓν μέρος ἐστὶν Σαδδουκαίων τὸ δὲ ἕτερον Φαρισαίων
ἔκραζεν ἐν τῷ συνεδρίῳ Ἄνδρες ἀδελφοί, ἐγὼ Φαρισαῖός
εἰμι, υἱὸς Φαρισαίων· περὶ ἐλπίδος καὶ ἀναστάσεως νεκρῶν
7 ⌜κρίνομαι. τοῦτο δὲ αὐτοῦ ⌜λαλοῦντος⌝ ⌜ἐγένετο⌝ στάσις
τῶν Φαρισαίων καὶ Σαδδουκαίων, καὶ ἐσχίσθη τὸ πλῆθος.
8 Σαδδουκαῖοι ⌜ γὰρ λέγουσιν μὴ εἶναι ἀνάστασιν μήτε ἄγγελον μήτε πνεῦμα, Φαρισαῖοι δὲ ὁμολογοῦσιν τὰ ἀμφό-
9 τερα. ἐγένετο δὲ κραυγὴ μεγάλη, καὶ ἀναστάντες τινὲς

τῶν γραμματέων τοῦ μέρους τῶν Φαρισαίων διεμάχοντο
λέγοντες Οὐδὲν κακὸν εὑρίσκομεν ἐν τῷ ἀνθρώπῳ τούτῳ·
εἰ δὲ πνεῦμα ἐλάλησεν αὐτῷ ἢ ἄγγελος—. Πολλῆς δὲ 10
γινομένης στάσεως φοβηθεὶς ὁ χιλίαρχος μὴ διασπασθῇ
ὁ Παῦλος ὑπ᾽ αὐτῶν ἐκέλευσεν τὸ στράτευμα καταβὰν
ἁρπάσαι αὐτὸν ἐκ μέσου αὐτῶν, ἄγειν ᵀ εἰς τὴν παρεμβολήν. Τῇ δὲ ἐπιούσῃ νυκτὶ ἐπιστὰς αὐτῷ ὁ κύριος 11
εἶπεν Θάρσει, ὡς γὰρ διεμαρτύρω τὰ περὶ ἐμοῦ εἰς Ἰερουσαλὴμ οὕτω σε δεῖ καὶ εἰς Ῥώμην μαρτυρῆσαι. Γε- 12
νομένης ⌐δὲ⌐ ἡμέρας ποιήσαντες συστροφὴν οἱ Ἰουδαῖοι
ἀνεθεμάτισαν ἑαυτοὺς λέγοντες μήτε φαγεῖν μήτε πεῖν
ἕως οὗ ἀποκτείνωσιν τὸν Παῦλον. ἦσαν δὲ πλείους 13
τεσσεράκοντα οἱ ταύτην τὴν συνωμοσίαν ποιησάμενοι·
οἵτινες προσελθόντες τοῖς ἀρχιερεῦσιν καὶ τοῖς πρεσβυτέ- 14
ροις εἶπαν Ἀναθέματι ἀνεθεματίσαμεν ἑαυτοὺς μηδενὸς
γεύσασθαι ἕως οὗ ἀποκτείνωμεν τὸν Παῦλον. νῦν οὖν 15
ὑμεῖς ἐμφανίσατε τῷ χιλιάρχῳ σὺν τῷ συνεδρίῳ ὅπως
καταγάγῃ αὐτὸν εἰς ὑμᾶς ὡς μέλλοντας διαγινώσκειν
ἀκριβέστερον τὰ περὶ αὐτοῦ· ἡμεῖς δὲ πρὸ τοῦ ἐγγίσαι
αὐτὸν ἕτοιμοί ἐσμεν τοῦ ἀνελεῖν αὐτόν. Ἀκούσας δὲ ὁ υἱὸς 16
τῆς ἀδελφῆς Παύλου τὴν ἐνέδραν παραγενόμενος καὶ
εἰσελθὼν εἰς τὴν παρεμβολὴν ἀπήγγειλεν τῷ Παύλῳ.
προσκαλεσάμενος δὲ ὁ Παῦλος ἕνα τῶν ἑκατονταρχῶν 17
ἔφη Τὸν νεανίαν τοῦτον ἄπαγε πρὸς τὸν χιλίαρχον, ἔχει
γὰρ ἀπαγγεῖλαί τι αὐτῷ. ὁ μὲν οὖν παραλαβὼν αὐτὸν 18
ἤγαγεν πρὸς τὸν χιλίαρχον καί φησιν Ὁ δέσμιος Παῦλος
προσκαλεσάμενός με ἠρώτησεν τοῦτον τὸν ⌐νεανίαν⌐ ἀγα-
γεῖν πρὸς σέ, ἔχοντά τι λαλῆσαί σοι. ἐπιλαβόμενος δὲ 19
τῆς χειρὸς αὐτοῦ ὁ χιλίαρχος καὶ ἀναχωρήσας κατ᾽ ἰδίαν
ἐπυνθάνετο Τί ἐστιν ὃ ἔχεις ἀπαγγεῖλαί μοι; εἶπεν δὲ 20
ὅτι Οἱ Ἰουδαῖοι συνέθεντο τοῦ ἐρωτῆσαί σε ὅπως αὔριον
τὸν Παῦλον καταγάγῃς εἰς τὸ συνέδριον ὡς μέλλων τι
ἀκριβέστερον πυνθάνεσθαι περὶ αὐτοῦ· σὺ οὖν μὴ πεισθῇς 21

10 τε   12 τε   18 νεανίσκον

αὐτοῖς, ἐνεδρεύουσιν γὰρ αὐτὸν ἐξ αὐτῶν ἄνδρες πλείους
τεσσεράκοντα, οἵτινες ἀνεθεμάτισαν ἑαυτοὺς μήτε φαγεῖν
μήτε πεῖν ἕως οὗ ἀνέλωσιν αὐτόν, καὶ νῦν εἰσὶν ἕτοιμοι
22 προσδεχόμενοι τὴν ἀπὸ σοῦ ἐπαγγελίαν. ὁ μὲν οὖν χιλίαρχος ἀπέλυσε τὸν νεανίσκον παραγγείλας μηδενὶ ἐκλαλῆ-
23 σαι ὅτι ταῦτα ἐνεφάνισας πρὸς ἐμέ. Καὶ προσκαλεσάμενός
τινας δύο τῶν ἑκατονταρχῶν εἶπεν Ἑτοιμάσατε στρατιώτας διακοσίους ὅπως πορευθῶσιν ἕως Καισαρίας, καὶ ἱππεῖς
ἑβδομήκοντα καὶ δεξιολάβους διακοσίους, ἀπὸ τρίτης ὥρας
24 τῆς νυκτός, κτήνη τε παραστῆσαι ἵνα ἐπιβιβάσαντες τὸν
25 Παῦλον διασώσωσι πρὸς Φήλικα τὸν ἡγεμόνα, γράψας
26 ἐπιστολὴν ἔχουσαν τὸν τύπον τοῦτον Κλαύδιος Λυσίας
27 τῷ κρατίστῳ ἡγεμόνι Φήλικι χαίρειν. Τὸν ἄνδρα τοῦτον
συλλημφθέντα ὑπὸ τῶν Ἰουδαίων καὶ μέλλοντα ἀναιρεῖσθαι
ὑπ᾽ αὐτῶν ἐπιστὰς σὺν τῷ στρατεύματι ἐξειλάμην, μαθὼν
28 ὅτι Ῥωμαῖός ἐστιν, βουλόμενός τε ἐπιγνῶναι τὴν αἰτίαν
δι᾽ ἣν ἐνεκάλουν αὐτῷ [κατήγαγον εἰς τὸ συνέδριον αὐτῶν]·
29 ὃν εὗρον ἐγκαλούμενον περὶ ζητημάτων τοῦ νόμου αὐτῶν,
30 μηδὲν δὲ ἄξιον θανάτου ἢ δεσμῶν ἔχοντα ἔγκλημα. μηνυθείσης δέ μοι ἐπιβουλῆς εἰς τὸν ἄνδρα ἔσεσθαι ἐξαυτῆς
ἔπεμψα πρὸς σέ, παραγγείλας καὶ τοῖς κατηγόροις λέγειν
31 πρὸς αὐτὸν ἐπὶ σοῦ.   Οἱ μὲν οὖν στρατιῶται
κατὰ τὸ διατεταγμένον αὐτοῖς ἀναλαβόντες τὸν Παῦλον
32 ἤγαγον διὰ νυκτὸς εἰς τὴν Ἀντιπατρίδα· τῇ δὲ ἐπαύριον
ἐάσαντες τοὺς ἱππεῖς ἀπέρχεσθαι σὺν αὐτῷ ὑπέστρεψαν
33 εἰς τὴν παρεμβολήν· οἵτινες εἰσελθόντες εἰς τὴν Καισαρίαν
καὶ ἀναδόντες τὴν ἐπιστολὴν τῷ ἡγεμόνι παρέστησαν καὶ
34 τὸν Παῦλον αὐτῷ. ἀναγνοὺς δὲ καὶ ἐπερωτήσας ἐκ ποίας
35 ἐπαρχείας ἐστὶν καὶ πυθόμενος ὅτι ἀπὸ Κιλικίας Διακού-
σομαί σου, ἔφη, ὅταν καὶ οἱ κατήγοροί σου παραγένωνται·
κελεύσας ἐν τῷ πραιτωρίῳ ⌐τοῦ⌐ Ἡρῴδου φυλάσσεσθαι
αὐτόν.
1 Μετὰ δὲ πέντε ἡμέρας κατέβη ὁ ἀρχιερεὺς Ἀνανίας

35 τῷ

μετὰ πρεσβυτέρων τινῶν καὶ ῥήτορος Τερτύλλου τινός,
οἵτινες ἐνεφάνισαν τῷ ἡγεμόνι κατὰ τοῦ Παύλου. κλη- 2
θέντος δὲ [αὐτοῦ] ἤρξατο κατηγορεῖν ὁ Τέρτυλλος λέγων Πολλῆς εἰρήνης τυγχάνοντες διὰ σοῦ καὶ διορθωμάτων
γινομένων τῷ ἔθνει τούτῳ διὰ τῆς σῆς προνοίας πάντη τε 3
καὶ πανταχοῦ ἀποδεχόμεθα, κράτιστε Φῆλιξ, μετὰ πάσης
εὐχαριστίας. ἵνα δὲ μὴ ἐπὶ πλεῖόν σε ἐνκόπτω, παρακαλῶ 4
ἀκοῦσαί σε ἡμῶν συντόμως τῇ σῇ ἐπιεικίᾳ. εὑρόντες γὰρ 5
τὸν ἄνδρα τοῦτον λοιμὸν καὶ κινοῦντα στάσεις πᾶσι τοῖς
Ἰουδαίοις τοῖς κατὰ τὴν οἰκουμένην πρωτοστάτην τε τῆς
τῶν Ναζωραίων αἱρέσεως, ὃς καὶ τὸ ἱερὸν ἐπείρασεν βεβη- 6
λῶσαι, ὃν καὶ ἐκρατήσαμεν, παρ' οὗ δυνήσῃ αὐτὸς ἀνα- 8
κρίνας περὶ πάντων τούτων ἐπιγνῶναι ὧν ἡμεῖς κατηγοροῦ-
μεν αὐτοῦ. συνεπέθεντο δὲ καὶ οἱ Ἰουδαῖοι φάσκοντες 9
ταῦτα οὕτως ἔχειν. Ἀπεκρίθη τε ὁ Παῦλος νεύσαντος αὐτῷ 10
τοῦ ἡγεμόνος λέγειν Ἐκ πολλῶν ἐτῶν ὄντα σε κριτὴν τῷ
ἔθνει τούτῳ ἐπιστάμενος εὐθύμως τὰ περὶ ἐμαυτοῦ ἀπολο-
γοῦμαι, δυναμένου σου ἐπιγνῶναι, ὅτι οὐ πλείους εἰσίν μοι 11
ἡμέραι δώδεκα ἀφ' ἧς ἀνέβην προσκυνήσων εἰς Ἰερουσαλήμ, καὶ οὔτε ἐν τῷ ἱερῷ εὗρόν με πρός τινα διαλεγό- 12
μενον ἢ ἐπίστασιν ποιοῦντα ὄχλου οὔτε ἐν ταῖς συναγωγαῖς
οὔτε κατὰ τὴν πόλιν, οὐδὲ παραστῆσαι δύνανταί σοι περὶ 13
ὧν νυνὶ κατηγοροῦσίν μου. ὁμολογῶ δὲ τοῦτό σοι ὅτι 14
κατὰ τὴν ὁδὸν ἣν λέγουσιν αἵρεσιν οὕτως λατρεύω τῷ πατρῴῳ θεῷ, πιστεύων πᾶσι τοῖς κατὰ τὸν νόμον καὶ τοῖς
ἐν τοῖς προφήταις γεγραμμένοις, ἐλπίδα ἔχων εἰς τὸν θεόν, ἣν 15
καὶ αὐτοὶ οὗτοι προσδέχονται, ἀνάστασιν μέλλειν ἔσεσθαι
δικαίων τε καὶ ἀδίκων· ἐν τούτῳ καὶ αὐτὸς ἀσκῶ ἀπρόσ- 16
κοπον συνείδησιν ἔχειν πρὸς τὸν θεὸν καὶ τοὺς ἀνθρώπους
διὰ παντός. δι' ἐτῶν δὲ πλειόνων ἐλεημοσύνας ποιήσων εἰς 17
τὸ ἔθνος μου παρεγενόμην καὶ προσφοράς, ἐν αἷς εὗρόν με 18
ἡγνισμένον ἐν τῷ ἱερῷ, οὐ μετὰ ὄχλου οὐδὲ μετὰ θορύβου,
τινὲς δὲ ἀπὸ τῆς Ἀσίας Ἰουδαῖοι, οὓς ἔδει ἐπὶ σοῦ παρεῖναι 19

20 καὶ κατηγορεῖν εἴ τι ἔχοιεν πρὸς ἐμέ,– ἢ αὐτοὶ οὗτοι εἰπά-
21 τωσαν τί εὗρον ἀδίκημα στάντος μου ἐπὶ τοῦ συνεδρίου ἢ
περὶ μιᾶς ταύτης φωνῆς ἧς ἐκέκραξα ἐν αὐτοῖς ἑστὼς ὅτι
Περὶ ἀναστάσεως νεκρῶν ἐγὼ κρίνομαι σήμερον ἐφ' ὑμῶν.
22 Ἀνεβάλετο δὲ αὐτοὺς ὁ Φῆλιξ, ἀκριβέστερον εἰδὼς τὰ
περὶ τῆς ὁδοῦ, εἴπας "Οταν Λυσίας ὁ χιλίαρχος καταβῇ
23 διαγνώσομαι τὰ καθ' ὑμᾶς· διαταξάμενος τῷ ἑκατοντάρχῃ τηρεῖσθαι αὐτὸν ἔχειν τε ἄνεσιν καὶ μηδένα κωλύειν
24 τῶν ἰδίων αὐτοῦ ὑπηρετεῖν αὐτῷ.   Μετὰ δὲ
ἡμέρας τινὰς παραγενόμενος ὁ Φῆλιξ σὺν Δρουσίλλῃ τῇ
ἰδίᾳ γυναικὶ οὔσῃ Ἰουδαίᾳ μετεπέμψατο τὸν Παῦλον καὶ
25 ἤκουσεν αὐτοῦ περὶ τῆς εἰς Χριστὸν Ἰησοῦν πίστεως. διαλεγομένου δὲ αὐτοῦ περὶ δικαιοσύνης καὶ ἐγκρατείας καὶ τοῦ
κρίματος τοῦ μέλλοντος ἔμφοβος γενόμενος ὁ Φῆλιξ ἀπεκρίθη Τὸ νῦν ἔχον πορεύου, καιρὸν δὲ μεταλαβὼν μετακαλέσο-
26 μαί σε· ἅμα καὶ ἐλπίζων ὅτι χρήματα δοθήσεται [αὐτῷ]
ὑπὸ τοῦ Παύλου· διὸ καὶ πυκνότερον αὐτὸν μεταπεμπόμενος
27 ὡμίλει αὐτῷ.   Διετίας δὲ πληρωθείσης ἔλαβεν
διάδοχον ὁ Φῆλιξ Πόρκιον Φῆστον· θέλων τε χάριτα καταθέσθαι τοῖς Ἰουδαίοις ὁ Φῆλιξ κατέλιπε τὸν Παῦλον δεδεμένον.

1   Φῆστος οὖν ἐπιβὰς τῇ ⌜ἐπαρχείᾳ⌝ μετὰ τρεῖς ἡμέρας
2 ἀνέβη εἰς Ἱεροσόλυμα ἀπὸ Καισαρίας, ἐνεφάνισάν τε αὐτῷ
οἱ ἀρχιερεῖς καὶ οἱ πρῶτοι τῶν Ἰουδαίων κατὰ τοῦ Παύλου,
3 καὶ παρεκάλουν αὐτὸν αἰτούμενοι χάριν κατ' αὐτοῦ ὅπως
μεταπέμψηται αὐτὸν εἰς Ἰερουσαλήμ, ἐνέδραν ποιοῦντες
4 ἀνελεῖν αὐτὸν κατὰ τὴν ὁδόν. ὁ μὲν οὖν Φῆστος ἀπεκρίθη
τηρεῖσθαι τὸν Παῦλον εἰς Καισαρίαν, ἑαυτὸν δὲ μέλλειν
5 ἐν τάχει ἐκπορεύεσθαι· Οἱ οὖν ἐν ὑμῖν, φησίν, δυνατοὶ
συνκαταβάντες εἴ τί ἐστιν ἐν τῷ ἀνδρὶ ἄτοπον κατηγορεί-
6 τωσαν αὐτοῦ.   Διατρίψας δὲ ἐν αὐτοῖς ἡμέρας
οὐ πλείους ὀκτὼ ἢ δέκα, καταβὰς εἰς Καισαρίαν, τῇ
ἐπαύριον καθίσας ἐπὶ τοῦ βήματος ἐκέλευσεν τὸν Παῦλον

1 ἐπαρχείῳ

ἀχθῆναι. παραγενομένου δὲ αὐτοῦ περιέστησαν αὐτὸν οἱ 7
ἀπὸ Ἱεροσολύμων καταβεβηκότες Ἰουδαῖοι, πολλὰ καὶ
βαρέα αἰτιώματα καταφέροντες ἃ οὐκ ἴσχυον ἀποδεῖξαι,
τοῦ Παύλου ἀπολογουμένου ὅτι Οὔτε εἰς τὸν νόμον τῶν 8
Ἰουδαίων οὔτε εἰς τὸ ἱερὸν οὔτε εἰς Καίσαρά τι ἥμαρτον.
ὁ Φῆστος δὲ θέλων τοῖς Ἰουδαίοις χάριν καταθέσθαι ἀπο- 9
κριθεὶς τῷ Παύλῳ εἶπεν Θέλεις εἰς Ἱεροσόλυμα ἀναβὰς
ἐκεῖ περὶ τούτων κριθῆναι ἐπ᾽ ἐμοῦ; εἶπεν δὲ ὁ Παῦλος 10
Ἑστὼς ἐπὶ τοῦ βήματος Καίσαρός εἰμι, οὗ με δεῖ κρίνεσθαι.
Ἰουδαίους οὐδὲν ἠδίκηκα, ὡς καὶ σὺ κάλλιον ἐπιγινώσκεις.
εἰ μὲν οὖν ἀδικῶ καὶ ἄξιον θανάτου πέπραχά τι, οὐ παραι- 11
τοῦμαι τὸ ἀποθανεῖν· εἰ δὲ οὐδέν ἐστιν ὧν οὗτοι κατηγοροῦσίν
μου, οὐδείς με δύναται αὐτοῖς χαρίσασθαι· Καίσαρα ἐπικαλοῦμαι. τότε ὁ Φῆστος συνλαλήσας μετὰ τοῦ συμβουλίου 12
ἀπεκρίθη Καίσαρα ἐπικέκλησαι, ἐπὶ Καίσαρα πορεύσῃ.

Ἡμερῶν δὲ διαγενομένων τινῶν Ἀγρίππας ὁ βασιλεὺς 13
καὶ Βερνίκη κατήντησαν εἰς Καισαρίαν ⌜ἀσπασάμενοι⌝ τὸν
Φῆστον. ὡς δὲ πλείους ἡμέρας διέτριβον ἐκεῖ, ὁ Φῆστος 14
τῷ βασιλεῖ ἀνέθετο τὰ κατὰ τὸν Παῦλον λέγων Ἀνήρ
τίς ἐστιν καταλελιμμένος ὑπὸ Φήλικος δέσμιος, περὶ οὗ 15
γενομένου μου εἰς Ἱεροσόλυμα ἐνεφάνισαν οἱ ἀρχιερεῖς
καὶ οἱ πρεσβύτεροι τῶν Ἰουδαίων, αἰτούμενοι κατ᾽ αὐτοῦ
καταδίκην· πρὸς οὓς ἀπεκρίθην ὅτι οὐκ ἔστιν ἔθος Ῥω- 16
μαίοις χαρίζεσθαί τινα ἄνθρωπον πρὶν ἢ ὁ κατηγορού-
μενος κατὰ πρόσωπον ἔχοι τοὺς κατηγόρους τόπον ⌜τε⌝
ἀπολογίας λάβοι περὶ τοῦ ἐγκλήματος. συνελθόντων οὖν 17
ἐνθάδε ἀναβολὴν μηδεμίαν ποιησάμενος τῇ ἑξῆς καθίσας
ἐπὶ τοῦ βήματος ἐκέλευσα ἀχθῆναι τὸν ἄνδρα· περὶ οὗ 18
σταθέντες οἱ κατήγοροι οὐδεμίαν αἰτίαν ἔφερον ὧν ἐγὼ
ὑπενόουν ⌜πονηρῶν⌝, ζητήματα δέ τινα περὶ τῆς ἰδίας δεισι- 19
δαιμονίας εἶχον πρὸς αὐτὸν καὶ περί τινος Ἰησοῦ τεθνηκό-
τος, ὃν ἔφασκεν ὁ Παῦλος ζῆν. ἀπορούμενος δὲ ἐγὼ τὴν 20
περὶ τούτων ζήτησιν ἔλεγον εἰ βούλοιτο πορεύεσθαι εἰς

21 Ἱεροσόλυμα κἀκεῖ κρίνεσθαι περὶ τούτων. τοῦ δὲ Παύλου
ἐπικαλεσαμένου τηρηθῆναι αὐτὸν εἰς τὴν τοῦ Σεβαστοῦ
διάγνωσιν, ἐκέλευσα τηρεῖσθαι αὐτὸν ἕως οὗ ἀναπέμψω αὐ-
22 τὸν πρὸς Καίσαρα. Ἀγρίππας δὲ πρὸς τὸν Φῆστον Ἐβουλόμην καὶ αὐτὸς τοῦ ἀνθρώπου ἀκοῦσαι. Αὔριον, φησίν,
23 ἀκούσῃ αὐτοῦ.   Τῇ οὖν ἐπαύριον ἐλθόντος τοῦ
Ἀγρίππα καὶ τῆς Βερνίκης μετὰ πολλῆς φαντασίας καὶ
εἰσελθόντων εἰς τὸ ἀκροατήριον σύν τε χιλιάρχοις καὶ
ἀνδράσιν τοῖς κατ᾽ ἐξοχὴν τῆς πόλεως καὶ κελεύσαντος τοῦ
24 Φήστου ἤχθη ὁ Παῦλος. καί φησιν ὁ Φῆστος Ἀγρίππα
βασιλεῦ καὶ πάντες οἱ συνπαρόντες ἡμῖν ἄνδρες, θεωρεῖτε
τοῦτον περὶ οὗ ἅπαν τὸ πλῆθος τῶν Ἰουδαίων ⌜ἐνέτυχέν⌝ μοι
ἔν τε Ἱεροσολύμοις καὶ ἐνθάδε, βοῶντες μὴ δεῖν αὐτὸν ζῆν
25 μηκέτι. ἐγὼ δὲ κατελαβόμην μηδὲν ἄξιον αὐτὸν θανάτου
πεπραχέναι, αὐτοῦ δὲ τούτου ἐπικαλεσαμένου τὸν Σεβαστὸν
26 ἔκρινα πέμπειν. περὶ οὗ ἀσφαλές τι γράψαι τῷ κυρίῳ
οὐκ ἔχω· διὸ προήγαγον αὐτὸν ἐφ᾽ ὑμῶν καὶ μάλιστα ἐπὶ
σοῦ, βασιλεῦ Ἀγρίππα, ὅπως τῆς ἀνακρίσεως γενομένης
27 σχῶ τί γράψω· ἄλογον γάρ μοι δοκεῖ πέμποντα δέσμιον
1 μὴ καὶ τὰς κατ᾽ αὐτοῦ αἰτίας σημᾶναι. Ἀγρίππας δὲ πρὸς
τὸν Παῦλον ἔφη Ἐπιτρέπεταί σοι ⌜ὑπὲρ⌝ σεαυτοῦ λέγειν.
2 τότε ὁ Παῦλος ἐκτείνας τὴν χεῖρα ἀπελογεῖτο Περὶ πάντων ὧν ἐγκαλοῦμαι ὑπὸ Ἰουδαίων, βασιλεῦ Ἀγρίππα,
ἥγημαι ἐμαυτὸν μακάριον ἐπὶ σοῦ μέλλων σήμερον ἀπολο-
3 γεῖσθαι, μάλιστα γνώστην ὄντα σε πάντων τῶν κατὰ
Ἰουδαίους ἐθῶν τε καὶ ζητημάτων· διὸ δέομαι μακροθύμως
4 ἀκοῦσαί μου. Τὴν μὲν οὖν βίωσίν μου ἐκ νεότητος τὴν
ἀπ᾽ ἀρχῆς γενομένην ἐν τῷ ἔθνει μου ἔν τε Ἱεροσολύμοις
5 ἴσασι πάντες Ἰουδαῖοι, προγινώσκοντές με ἄνωθεν, ἐὰν
θέλωσι μαρτυρεῖν, ὅτι κατὰ τὴν ἀκριβεστάτην αἵρεσιν τῆς
6 ἡμετέρας θρησκείας ἔζησα Φαρισαῖος. καὶ νῦν ἐπ᾽ ἐλπίδι
τῆς εἰς τοὺς πατέρας ἡμῶν ἐπαγγελίας γενομένης ὑπὸ
7 τοῦ θεοῦ ἕστηκα κρινόμενος, εἰς ἣν τὸ δωδεκάφυλον ἡμῶν

24 ἐνέτυχόν   1 περὶ

ἐν ἐκτενείᾳ νύκτα καὶ ἡμέραν λατρεῦον ἐλπίζει ⌐καταν-
τῆσαι⌐· περὶ ἧς ἐλπίδος ἐγκαλοῦμαι ὑπὸ Ἰουδαίων, βασι-
λεῦ· τί ἄπιστον κρίνεται παρ᾽ ὑμῖν εἰ ὁ θεὸς νεκροὺς 8
ἐγείρει; Ἐγὼ μὲν οὖν ἔδοξα ἐμαυτῷ πρὸς τὸ ὄνομα 9 .
Ἰησοῦ τοῦ Ναζωραίου δεῖν πολλὰ ἐναντία πρᾶξαι· ὃ καὶ 10
ἐποίησα ἐν Ἱεροσολύμοις, καὶ ⌐πολλούς τε⌐ τῶν ἁγίων ἐγὼ
ἐν φυλακαῖς κατέκλεισα τὴν παρὰ τῶν ἀρχιερέων ἐξουσίαν
λαβών, ἀναιρουμένων τε αὐτῶν κατήνεγκα ψῆφον, καὶ 11
κατὰ πάσας τὰς συναγωγὰς πολλάκις τιμωρῶν αὐτοὺς
ἠνάγκαζον βλασφημεῖν, περισσῶς τε ἐμμαινόμενος αὐτοῖς
ἐδίωκον ἕως καὶ εἰς τὰς ἔξω πόλεις. Ἐν οἷς πορευόμενος 12
εἰς τὴν Δαμασκὸν μετ᾽ ἐξουσίας καὶ ἐπιτροπῆς τῆς τῶν
ἀρχιερέων ἡμέρας μέσης κατὰ τὴν ὁδὸν εἶδον, βασιλεῦ, 13
οὐρανόθεν ὑπὲρ τὴν λαμπρότητα τοῦ ἡλίου περιλάμψαν με
φῶς καὶ τοὺς σὺν ἐμοὶ πορευομένους· πάντων τε καταπε- 14
σόντων ἡμῶν εἰς τὴν γῆν ἤκουσα φωνὴν λέγουσαν πρός
με τῇ Ἑβραΐδι διαλέκτῳ   Σαούλ Σαούλ, τί με διώκεις;
σκληρόν σοι πρὸς κέντρα λακτίζειν. ἐγὼ δὲ εἶπα Τίς εἶ, 15
κύριε; ὁ δὲ κύριος εἶπεν Ἐγώ εἰμι Ἰησοῦς ὃν σὺ διώκεις·
ἀλλὰ ἀνάστηθι καὶ ϲΤΗΘΙ ἐπὶ τοΥϲ πόΔαϲ ϲοΥ· εἰς τοῦτο 16
γὰρ ὤφθην σοι, προχειρίσασθαί σε ὑπηρέτην καὶ μάρτυρα ὧν
τε εἶδές με ὧν τε ὀφθήσομαί σοι, ἐξαιροΥμενόϲ ϲε ἐκ 17
τοῦ λαοῦ καὶ ἐκ τῶν ἐθνῶν, εἰϲ οΫϲ ἐγὼ ἀποϲτέλλω
ϲε ἀνοῖξαι ὀφθαλμοΫϲ αὐτῶν, τοῦ ἐπιστρέψαι ἀπὸ ϲκό- 18
τοΥϲ εἰϲ φῶϲ καὶ τῆς ἐξουσίας τοῦ Σατανᾶ ἐπὶ τὸν θεόν,
τοῦ λαβεῖν αὐτοὺς ἄφεσιν ἁμαρτιῶν καὶ κλῆρον ἐν τοῖς
ἡγιασμένοις πίστει τῇ εἰς ἐμέ. Ὅθεν, βασιλεῦ Ἀγρίππα, 19
οὐκ ἐγενόμην ἀπειθὴς τῇ οὐρανίῳ ὀπτασίᾳ, ἀλλὰ τοῖς ἐν 20
Δαμασκῷ πρῶτόν τε καὶ Ἱεροσολύμοις, πᾶσάν τε τὴν χώραν τῆς Ἰουδαίας, καὶ τοῖς ἔθνεσιν ἀπήγγελλον μετανοεῖν
καὶ ἐπιστρέφειν ἐπὶ τὸν· θεόν, ἄξια τῆς μετανοίας ἔργα
πράσσοντας. ἕνεκα τούτων με Ἰουδαῖοι συλλαβόμενοι ἐν 21
τῷ ἱερῷ ἐπειρῶντο διαχειρίσασθαι. ἐπικουρίας οὖν τυχὼν 22

7 καταντήσειν   10 πολλούς

τῆς ἀπὸ τοῦ θεοῦ ἄχρι τῆς ἡμέρας ταύτης ἔστηκα μαρτυρόμενος μικρῷ τε καὶ μεγάλῳ, οὐδὲν ἐκτὸς λέγων ὧν τε οἱ προ-
23 φῆται ἐλάλησαν μελλόντων γίνεσθαι καὶ Μωυσῆς, εἰ παθητὸς ὁ χριστός, εἰ πρῶτος ἐξ ἀναστάσεως νεκρῶν φῶς μέλλει
24 καταγγέλλειν τῷ τε λαῷ καὶ τοῖς ἔθνεσιν.   Ταῦτα δὲ αὐτοῦ ἀπολογουμένου ὁ Φῆστος μεγάλῃ τῇ φωνῇ φησίν Μαίνῃ, Παῦλε· τὰ πολλά σε γράμματα εἰς μανίαν
25 περιτρέπει. ὁ δὲ Παῦλος Οὐ μαίνομαι, φησίν, κράτιστε
Φῆστε, ἀλλὰ ἀληθείας καὶ σωφροσύνης ῥήματα ἀποφθέγ-
26 γομαι. ἐπίσταται γὰρ περὶ τούτων ὁ βασιλεύς, πρὸς ὃν ᵀ
παρρησιαζόμενος λαλῶ· λανθάνειν γὰρ ⌜αὐτὸν⌝ τούτων οὐ
πείθομαι οὐθέν, οὐ γάρ ἐστιν ἐν γωνίᾳ πεπραγμένον τοῦτο.
27 πιστεύεις, βασιλεῦ Ἀγρίππα, τοῖς προφήταις; οἶδα ὅτι
28 πιστεύεις. ὁ δὲ Ἀγρίππας πρὸς τὸν Παῦλον Ἐν ὀλίγῳ
29 ⌜με πείθεις Χριστιανὸν ποιῆσαι⌝. ὁ δὲ Παῦλος Εὐξαίμην
ἂν τῷ θεῷ καὶ ἐν ὀλίγῳ καὶ ἐν μεγάλῳ οὐ μόνον σὲ
ἀλλὰ καὶ πάντας τοὺς ἀκούοντάς μου σήμερον γενέσθαι
τοιούτους ὁποῖος καὶ ἐγώ εἰμι παρεκτὸς τῶν δεσμῶν τού-
30 των.   Ἀνέστη τε ὁ βασιλεὺς καὶ ὁ ἡγεμὼν ἥ
31 τε Βερνίκη καὶ οἱ συνκαθήμενοι αὐτοῖς, καὶ ἀναχωρήσαν-
τες ἐλάλουν πρὸς ἀλλήλους·λέγοντες ὅτι Οὐδὲν θανάτου
32 ἢ δεσμῶν ⌜ἄξιον⌝ πράσσει ὁ ἄνθρωπος οὗτος. Ἀγρίππας
δὲ τῷ Φήστῳ ἔφη Ἀπολελύσθαι ἐδύνατο ὁ ἄνθρωπος
οὗτος εἰ μὴ ἐπεκέκλητο Καίσαρα.

1   Ὡς δὲ ἐκρίθη τοῦ ἀποπλεῖν ἡμᾶς εἰς τὴν Ἰταλίαν,
παρεδίδουν τόν τε Παῦλον καί τινας ἑτέρους δεσμώτας
2 ἑκατοντάρχῃ ὀνόματι Ἰουλίῳ σπείρης Σεβαστῆς. ἐπιβάντες δὲ πλοίῳ Ἀδραμυντηνῷ μέλλοντι πλεῖν εἰς τοὺς κατὰ
τὴν Ἀσίαν τόπους ἀνήχθημεν, ὄντος σὺν ἡμῖν Ἀριστάρχου
3 Μακεδόνος Θεσσαλονικέως· τῇ τε ἑτέρᾳ κατήχθημεν εἰς
Σιδῶνα, φιλανθρώπως τε ὁ Ἰούλιος τῷ Παύλῳ χρησάμενος
ἐπέτρεψεν πρὸς τοὺς φίλους πορευθέντι ἐπιμελείας τυχεῖν.

26 καὶ | αὐτόν τι   28 †...†   31 ἄξιόν τι
P.   5

κἀκεῖθεν ἀναχθέντες ὑπεπλεύσαμεν τὴν Κύπρον διὰ τὸ 4
τοὺς ἀνέμους εἶναι ἐναντίους, τό τε πέλαγος τὸ κατὰ τὴν 5
Κιλικίαν καὶ Παμφυλίαν διαπλεύσαντες κατήλθαμεν εἰς
Μύρρα τῆς Λυκίας. Κἀκεῖ εὑρὼν ὁ ἑκατοντάρχης πλοῖον 6
Ἀλεξανδρινὸν πλέον εἰς τὴν Ἰταλίαν ἐνεβίβασεν ἡμᾶς εἰς
αὐτό. ἐν ἱκαναῖς δὲ ἡμέραις βραδυπλοοῦντες καὶ μόλις 7
γενόμενοι κατὰ τὴν Κνίδον, μὴ προσεῶντος ἡμᾶς τοῦ ἀνέ-
μου, ὑπεπλεύσαμεν τὴν Κρήτην κατὰ Σαλμώνην, μόλις τε 8
παραλεγόμενοι αὐτὴν ἤλθομεν εἰς τόπον τινὰ καλούμενον
Καλοὺς Λιμένας, ᾧ ἐγγὺς ἦν πόλις Λασέα.   Ἱκα- 9
νοῦ δὲ χρόνου διαγενομένου καὶ ὄντος ἤδη ἐπισφαλοῦς
τοῦ πλοὸς διὰ τὸ καὶ τὴν νηστείαν ἤδη παρεληλυθέναι,
παρῄνει ὁ Παῦλος λέγων αὐτοῖς Ἄνδρες, θεωρῶ ὅτι μετὰ 10
ὕβρεως καὶ πολλῆς ζημίας οὐ μόνον τοῦ φορτίου καὶ
τοῦ πλοίου ἀλλὰ καὶ τῶν ψυχῶν ἡμῶν μέλλειν ἔσεσθαι
τὸν πλοῦν. ὁ δὲ ἑκατοντάρχης τῷ κυβερνήτῃ καὶ τῷ 11
ναυκλήρῳ μᾶλλον ἐπείθετο ἢ τοῖς ὑπὸ Παύλου λεγομένοις.
ἀνευθέτου δὲ τοῦ λιμένος ὑπάρχοντος πρὸς παραχειμασίαν 12
οἱ πλείονες ἔθεντο βουλὴν ἀναχθῆναι ἐκεῖθεν, εἴ πως δύναιντο καταντήσαντες εἰς Φοίνικα παραχειμάσαι, λιμένα
τῆς Κρήτης βλέποντα κατὰ λίβα καὶ κατὰ χῶρον. Ὑπο- 13
πνεύσαντος δὲ νότου δόξαντες τῆς προθέσεως κεκρατηκέναι
ἄραντες ἆσσον παρελέγοντο τὴν Κρήτην. μετ᾽ οὐ πολὺ 14
δὲ ἔβαλεν κατ᾽ αὐτῆς ἄνεμος τυφωνικὸς ὁ καλούμενος
Εὐρακύλων· συναρπασθέντος δὲ τοῦ πλοίου καὶ μὴ δυναμέ- 15
νου ἀντοφθαλμεῖν· τῷ ἀνέμῳ ἐπιδόντες ἐφερόμεθα. νησίον 16
δέ τι ὑποδραμόντες καλούμενον Καῦδα ἰσχύσαμεν μόλις
περικρατεῖς γενέσθαι ˙ τῆς σκάφης, ἣν ἄραντες βοηθείαις 17
ἐχρῶντο ὑποζωννύντες τὸ πλοῖον· φοβούμενοί τε μὴ εἰς τὴν
Σύρτιν ἐκπέσωσιν, χαλάσαντες τὸ σκεῦος, οὕτως ἐφέροντο.
σφοδρῶς δὲ χειμαζομένων ἡμῶν τῇ ἑξῆς ἐκβολὴν ἐποιοῦντο, 18
καὶ τῇ τρίτῃ αὐτόχειρες τὴν σκευὴν τοῦ πλοίου ἔριψαν. 19
μήτε δὲ ἡλίου μήτε ἄστρων ἐπιφαινόντων ἐπὶ πλείονας 20

ἡμέρας, χειμῶνός τε οὐκ ὀλίγου ἐπικειμένου, λοιπὸν περιη-
21 ρεῖτο ἐλπὶς πᾶσα τοῦ σώζεσθαι ἡμᾶς. Πολλῆς τε ἀσιτίας
ὑπαρχούσης τότε σταθεὶς ὁ Παῦλος ἐν μέσῳ αὐτῶν εἶπεν
Ἔδει μέν, ὦ ἄνδρες, πειθαρχήσαντάς μοι μὴ ἀνάγεσθαι
ἀπὸ τῆς Κρήτης κερδῆσαί τε τὴν ὕβριν ταύτην καὶ τὴν
22 ζημίαν. καὶ τὰ νῦν παραινῶ ὑμᾶς εὐθυμεῖν, ἀποβολὴ γὰρ
23 ψυχῆς οὐδεμία ἔσται ἐξ ὑμῶν πλὴν τοῦ πλοίου· παρέστη
γάρ μοι ταύτῃ τῇ νυκτὶ τοῦ θεοῦ οὗ εἰμί, ᾧ καὶ λατρεύω,
24 ἄγγελος λέγων Μὴ φοβοῦ, Παῦλε· Καίσαρί σε δεῖ παρα-
στῆναι, καὶ ἰδοὺ κεχάρισταί σοι ὁ θεὸς πάντας τοὺς πλέον-
25 τας μετὰ σοῦ. διὸ εὐθυμεῖτε, ἄνδρες· πιστεύω γὰρ τῷ θεῷ
26 ὅτι οὕτως ἔσται καθ᾽ ὃν τρόπον λελάληταί μοι. εἰς νῆσον
27 δέ τινα δεῖ ἡμᾶς ἐκπεσεῖν. Ὡς δὲ τεσσαρεσκαι-
δεκάτη νὺξ ἐγένετο διαφερομένων ἡμῶν ἐν τῷ Ἀδρίᾳ, κατὰ
μέσον τῆς νυκτὸς ὑπενόουν οἱ ναῦται ⌈προσάγειν⌉ τινὰ αὐτοῖς
28 χώραν. καὶ βολίσαντες εὗρον ὀργυιὰς εἴκοσι, βραχὺ δὲ
διαστήσαντες καὶ πάλιν βολίσαντες εὗρον ὀργυιὰς δεκα-
29 πέντε· φοβούμενοί τε μή που κατὰ τραχεῖς τόπους ἐκπέ-
σωμεν ἐκ πρύμνης ῥίψαντες ἀγκύρας τέσσαρας ηὔχοντο
30 ἡμέραν γενέσθαι. Τῶν δὲ ναυτῶν ζητούντων φυγεῖν ἐκ
τοῦ πλοίου καὶ χαλασάντων τὴν σκάφην εἰς τὴν θάλασσαν
προφάσει ὡς ἐκ πρῴρης ἀγκύρας μελλόντων ἐκτείνειν,
31 εἶπεν ὁ Παῦλος τῷ ἑκατοντάρχῃ καὶ τοῖς στρατιώταις
Ἐὰν μὴ οὗτοι μείνωσιν ἐν τῷ πλοίῳ, ὑμεῖς σωθῆναι οὐ
32 δύνασθε. τότε ἀπέκοψαν οἱ στρατιῶται τὰ σχοινία τῆς
33 σκάφης καὶ εἴασαν αὐτὴν ἐκπεσεῖν. Ἄχρι δὲ οὗ ἡμέρα
ἤμελλεν γίνεσθαι παρεκάλει ὁ Παῦλος ἅπαντας μεταλαβεῖν τροφῆς λέγων Τεσσαρεσκαιδεκάτην σήμερον ἡμέραν
προσδοκῶντες ἄσιτοι διατελεῖτε, μηθὲν προσλαβόμενοι·
34 διὸ παρακαλῶ ὑμᾶς μεταλαβεῖν τροφῆς, τοῦτο γὰρ πρὸς
τῆς ὑμετέρας σωτηρίας ὑπάρχει· οὐδενὸς γὰρ ὑμῶν θρὶξ
35 ἀπὸ τῆς κεφαλῆς ἀπολεῖται. εἴπας δὲ ταῦτα καὶ λαβὼν

27 προσαχεῖν

ἄρτον εὐχαρίστησεν τῷ θεῷ ἐνώπιον πάντων καὶ κλάσας
ἤρξατο ἐσθίειν. εὔθυμοι δὲ γενόμενοι πάντες καὶ αὐτοὶ 36
προσελάβοντο τροφῆς. ἤμεθα δὲ αἱ πᾶσαι ψυχαὶ ἐν τῷ 37
πλοίῳ ⌜ὡς⌝ ἑβδομήκοντα ἕξ. κορεσθέντες δὲ τροφῆς ἐκού- 38
φιζον τὸ πλοῖον ἐκβαλλόμενοι τὸν σῖτον εἰς τὴν θάλασσαν.
Ὅτε δὲ ἡμέρα ἐγένετο, τὴν γῆν οὐκ ἐπεγίνωσκον, κόλπον 39
δέ τινα κατενόουν ἔχοντα αἰγιαλὸν εἰς ὃν ἐβουλεύοντο εἰ
δύναιντο ⌜ἐκσῶσαι⌝ τὸ πλοῖον. καὶ τὰς ἀγκύρας περιελόν- 40
τες εἴων εἰς τὴν θάλασσαν, ἅμα ἀνέντες τὰς ζευκτηρίας τῶν
πηδαλίων, καὶ ἐπάραντες τὸν ἀρτέμωνα τῇ πνεούσῃ κατεῖχον εἰς τὸν αἰγιαλόν. περιπεσόντες δὲ εἰς τόπον διθά- 41
λασσον ἐπέκειλαν τὴν ναῦν, καὶ ἡ μὲν πρῷρα ἐρείσασα
ἔμεινεν ἀσάλευτος, ἡ δὲ πρύμνα ἐλύετο ὑπὸ τῆς βίας.
Τῶν δὲ στρατιωτῶν βουλὴ ἐγένετο ἵνα τοὺς δεσμώτας 42
ἀποκτείνωσιν, μή τις ἐκκολυμβήσας διαφύγῃ· ὁ δὲ ἑκατόν- 43
ταρχης βουλόμενος διασῶσαι τὸν Παῦλον ἐκώλυσεν αὐτοὺς
τοῦ βουλήματος, ἐκέλευσέν τε τοὺς δυναμένους κολυμβᾶν
ἀπορίψαντας πρώτους ἐπὶ τὴν γῆν ἐξιέναι, καὶ τοὺς λοι- 44
ποὺς οὓς μὲν ἐπὶ σανίσιν οὓς δὲ ἐπί τινων τῶν ἀπὸ τοῦ
πλοίου· καὶ οὕτως ἐγένετο πάντας διασωθῆναι ἐπὶ τὴν γῆν.

Καὶ διασωθέντες τότε ἐπέγνωμεν ὅτι Μελιτήνη ἡ 1
νῆσος καλεῖται. οἵ τε βάρβαροι παρεῖχαν οὐ τὴν τυχοῦ- 2
σαν φιλανθρωπίαν ἡμῖν, ἅψαντες γὰρ πυρὰν προσελάβοντο
πάντας ἡμᾶς διὰ τὸν ὑετὸν τὸν ἐφεστῶτα καὶ διὰ τὸ ψύχος.
συστρέψαντος δὲ τοῦ Παύλου φρυγάνων τι πλῆθος καὶ 3
ἐπιθέντος ἐπὶ τὴν πυράν, ἔχιδνα ἀπὸ τῆς θέρμης ἐξελθοῦσα
καθῆψε τῆς χειρὸς αὐτοῦ. ὡς δὲ εἶδαν οἱ βάρβαροι κρεμά- 4
μενον τὸ θηρίον ἐκ τῆς χειρὸς αὐτοῦ, πρὸς ἀλλήλους ἔλεγον
Πάντως φονεύς ἐστιν ὁ ἄνθρωπος οὗτος ὃν διασωθέντα ἐκ
τῆς θαλάσσης ἡ δίκη ζῆν οὐκ εἴασεν. ὁ μὲν οὖν ἀποτινά- 5
ξας τὸ θηρίον εἰς τὸ πῦρ ἔπαθεν οὐδὲν κακόν· οἱ δὲ προσε- 6
δόκων αὐτὸν μέλλειν πίμπρασθαι ἢ καταπίπτειν ἄφνω
νεκρόν. ἐπὶ πολὺ δὲ αὐτῶν προσδοκώντων καὶ θεωρούντων

37 διακόσιαι   39 ἐξῶσαι

μηδὲν ἄτοπον εἰς αὐτὸν γινόμενον, μεταβαλόμενοι ἔλεγον
7 αὐτὸν εἶναι θεόν. Ἐν δὲ τοῖς περὶ τὸν τόπον
ἐκεῖνον ὑπῆρχεν χωρία τῷ πρώτῳ τῆς νήσου ὀνόματι Ποπλίῳ, ὃς ἀναδεξάμενος ἡμᾶς ⌐ἡμέρας τρεῖς⌐ φιλοφρόνως
8 ἐξένισεν. ἐγένετο δὲ τὸν πατέρα τοῦ Ποπλίου πυρετοῖς
καὶ δυσεντερίῳ συνεχόμενον κατακεῖσθαι, πρὸς ὃν ὁ Παῦλος
εἰσελθὼν καὶ προσευξάμενος ἐπιθεὶς τὰς χεῖρας αὐτῷ ἰάσατο
9 αὐτόν. τούτου δὲ γενομένου [καὶ] οἱ λοιποὶ οἱ ἐν τῇ νήσῳ
10 ἔχοντες ἀσθενείας προσήρχοντο καὶ ἐθεραπεύοντο, οἳ καὶ
πολλαῖς τιμαῖς ἐτίμησαν ἡμᾶς καὶ ἀναγομένοις ἐπέθεντο
τὰ πρὸς τὰς χρείας.
11 Μετὰ δὲ τρεῖς μῆνας ἀνήχθημεν ἐν πλοίῳ παρακεχει-
μακότι ἐν τῇ νήσῳ Ἀλεξανδρινῷ, παρασήμῳ Διοσκούροις.
12 καὶ καταχθέντες εἰς Συρακούσας ἐπεμείναμεν ἡμέρας
13 τρεῖς, ὅθεν περιελόντες κατηντήσαμεν εἰς Ῥήγιον. καὶ
μετὰ μίαν ἡμέραν ἐπιγενομένου νότου δευτεραῖοι ἤλθο-
14 μεν εἰς Ποτιόλους, οὗ εὑρόντες ἀδελφοὺς παρεκλήθημεν
παρ᾽ αὐτοῖς ἐπιμεῖναι ἡμέρας ἑπτά· καὶ οὕτως εἰς τὴν Ῥώ-
15 μην ἤλθαμεν. κἀκεῖθεν οἱ ἀδελφοὶ ἀκούσαντες τὰ περὶ
ἡμῶν ἦλθαν εἰς ἀπάντησιν ἡμῖν ἄχρι Ἀππίου Φόρου καὶ
Τριῶν Ταβερνῶν, οὓς ἰδὼν ὁ Παῦλος εὐχαριστήσας τῷ θεῷ
16 ἔλαβε θάρσος. Ὅτε δὲ εἰσήλθαμεν εἰς Ῥώμην,
ἐπετράπη τῷ Παύλῳ μένειν καθ᾽ ἑαυτὸν σὺν τῷ φυλάσ-
σοντι αὐτὸν στρατιώτῃ.

17 Ἐγένετο δὲ μετὰ ἡμέρας τρεῖς συνκαλέσασθαι αὐτὸν
τοὺς ὄντας τῶν Ἰουδαίων πρώτους· συνελθόντων δὲ αὐτῶν
ἔλεγεν πρὸς αὐτούς Ἐγώ, ἄνδρες ἀδελφοί, οὐδὲν ἐναντίον
ποιήσας τῷ λαῷ ἢ τοῖς ἔθεσι τοῖς πατρῴοις δέσμιος ἐξ
Ἰεροσολύμων παρεδόθην εἰς τὰς χεῖρας τῶν Ῥωμαίων,
18 οἵτινες ἀνακρίναντές με ἐβούλοντο ἀπολῦσαι διὰ τὸ μηδε-
19 μίαν αἰτίαν θανάτου ὑπάρχειν ἐν ἐμοί· ἀντιλεγόντων δὲ
τῶν Ἰουδαίων ἠναγκάσθην ἐπικαλέσασθαι Καίσαρα, οὐχ ὡς

7 τρεῖς ἡμέρας

τοῦ ἔθνους μου ἔχων τι κατηγορεῖν. διὰ ταύτην οὖν τὴν 20
αἰτίαν παρεκάλεσα ὑμᾶς ἰδεῖν καὶ προσλαλῆσαι, εἵνεκεν
γὰρ τῆς ἐλπίδος τοῦ Ἰσραὴλ τὴν ἅλυσιν ταύτην περίκειμαι.
οἱ δὲ πρὸς αὐτὸν εἶπαν Ἡμεῖς οὔτε γράμματα περὶ σοῦ 21
ἐδεξάμεθα ἀπὸ τῆς Ἰουδαίας, οὔτε παραγενόμενός τις τῶν
ἀδελφῶν ἀπήγγειλεν ἢ ἐλάλησέν τι περὶ σοῦ πονηρόν.
ἀξιοῦμεν δὲ παρὰ σοῦ ἀκοῦσαι ἃ φρονεῖς, περὶ μὲν γὰρ 22
τῆς αἱρέσεως ταύτης γνωστὸν ἡμῖν ἐστιν ὅτι πανταχοῦ
ἀντιλέγεται.   Ταξάμενοι δὲ αὐτῷ ἡμέραν ἦλθαν 23
πρὸς αὐτὸν εἰς τὴν ξενίαν πλείονες, οἷς ἐξετίθετο διαμαρτυρόμενος τὴν βασιλείαν τοῦ θεοῦ πείθων τε αὐτοὺς περὶ τοῦ
Ἰησοῦ ἀπό τε τοῦ νόμου Μωυσέως καὶ τῶν προφητῶν ἀπὸ
πρωὶ ἕως ἑσπέρας. Καὶ οἱ μὲν ἐπείθοντο τοῖς λεγομένοις 24
οἱ δὲ ἠπίστουν, ἀσύμφωνοι δὲ ὄντες πρὸς ἀλλήλους 25
ἀπελύοντο, εἰπόντος τοῦ Παύλου ῥῆμα ἓν ὅτι Καλῶς
τὸ πνεῦμα τὸ ἅγιον ἐλάλησεν διὰ Ἠσαίου τοῦ προφήτου
πρὸς τοὺς πατέρας ὑμῶν λέγων   26
  Πορεύθητι πρὸς τὸν λαὸν τοῦτον καὶ εἰπόν
  Ἀκοῇ ἀκούσετε καὶ οὐ μὴ συνῆτε,
    καὶ βλέποντες βλέψετε καὶ οὐ μὴ ἴδητε·
  ἐπαχύνθη γὰρ ἡ καρδία τοῦ λαοῦ τούτου,   27
    καὶ τοῖς ὠσὶν βαρέως ἤκουσαν,
      καὶ τοὺς ὀφθαλμοὺς αὐτῶν ἐκάμμυσαν·
  μή ποτε ἴδωσιν τοῖς ὀφθαλμοῖς
    καὶ τοῖς ὠσὶν ἀκούσωσιν
  καὶ τῇ καρδίᾳ συνῶσιν καὶ ἐπιστρέψωσιν,
    καὶ ἰάσομαι αὐτούς.
γνωστὸν οὖν ὑμῖν ἔστω ὅτι τοῖς ἔθνεσιν ἀπεστάλη τοῦτο 28
τὸ σωτήριον τοῦ θεοῦ· αὐτοὶ καὶ ἀκούσονται.
  Ἐνέμεινεν δὲ διετίαν ὅλην ἐν ἰδίῳ μισθώματι, καὶ ἀπε- 30
δέχετο πάντας τοὺς εἰσπορευομένους πρὸς αὐτόν, κηρύσσων 31
τὴν βασιλείαν τοῦ θεοῦ καὶ διδάσκων τὰ περὶ τοῦ κυρίου
Ἰησοῦ Χριστοῦ μετὰ πάσης παρρησίας ἀκωλύτως.

NOTES.

LIST OF BOOKS CHIEFLY CONSULTED.

Referred to as	
A.	The Acts, by Dean Alford. Sixth edition, 1871.
A. V.	The Authorized Version of 1611.
B.	Bengelii Gnomon Novi Testamenti, originally published 1742.
Baum.	Die Apostelgeschichte, by Dr M. Baumgarten. 2nd edition, 1859.
Bruder.	Concordantia Novi Testamenti Græci, by D. H. Bruder. Leipzig, 1880.
C. & H.	Conybeare and Howson, Life and Epistles of St Paul, 2 vol. 1875.
Cook.	The Acts, by Canon Cook, 1880.
de W.	Kurze Erklärung der Apostelgeschichte von Dr W. M. L. de Wette, 4th edition, revised and largely increased by F. Overbeck. Leipzig, 1870.
Eder.	Edersheim, A., Life and Times of Jesus the Messiah. 2 vol. London, 1883.
F.	The Life and Work of St Paul, by Canon Farrar, Popular Edition, 1884.
H.	A Commentary on the Acts, by W. G. Humphry, B.D. 2nd edition, 1854.
La.	Der Apostel Geschichten in Lange's Bibelwerk as revised by Dr G. V. Lechler. Leipzig, 1881.
Lumby.	The Acts, by Prof. J. R. Lumby. Cambridge, 1885.
M.	Die Apostelgeschichte in Meyer's Kommentar, 5th edition, revised by Dr H. H. Wendt. Göttingen, 1880.
N.	Geschichte der Pflanzung und Leitung der christlichen Kirche von Dr August Neander. Gotha, 1862.
R. V.	The Revised Version of the New Testament, 1880.
LXX.	Vetus Testamentum Græce juxta LXX. Interpretes. Textum Vaticanum Romanum edidit Constantinus Tischendorf. 2nd edition, 1856.
Smith.	The Voyage and Shipwreck of St Paul, by James Smith of Jordanhill. 2nd edition, 1856.
T. R.	The Textus Receptus, the text of the second Elzevir edition, Leyden, 1633, founded on a collation of the third edition of Stephanus, 1550, with the editions of Beza : it is the text which practically underlies the Authorized Version.
W.	The Acts, by Bishop Wordsworth. New Edition, 1860.
W. & H.	The New Testament in Greek, by Dr Westcott and Dr Hort, 2 vol. 1881.
V.	The Vulgate or Latin version of Jerome, circ. 383.

THE
ACTS OF THE APOSTLES.

CHAPTER I.

1. τὸν μὲν πρῶτον λόγον] 'The Gospel according to
St Luke', which also commences with a formal inscription
to Theophilus, Luke i. 1—4.

λόγος ('treatise' A. and R.V.) is a very general term
applied to any 'narrative' or 'account'. Plato contrasts it
with μῦθος 'a (fictitious) tale', *Phaedo* 61 B ποιεῖν μύθους,
ἀλλ' οὐ λόγους. The phrase λόγον ἐποιησάμην is more simple
and less formal than the ἱστορίης ἀπόδειξις of Herod. I. 1,
or the ξυνέγραψε of Thuc. I. 1.

πρῶτον by a natural inaccuracy = πρότερον. μέν has
nothing formally to answer to it: Luke glides impercept-
ibly into 'the second narrative'.

ὦ Θεόφιλε] Luke i. 4 κράτιστε Θεόφιλε; from the epithet κράτιστε which is applied to Felix twice, xxiii. 26, xxiv.
3, and to Festus xxvi. 25, it has been inferred that Theophilus held some high official position.

ὧν] by attraction for ἅ, a very frequent idiom, cf. e.g.
iii. 21 ὧν ἐλάλησεν, iii. 25 ἧς διέθετο, vii. 17 ἧς ὡμολόγησεν.

ἤρξατο ποιεῖν] The work which Jesus '*began*' on earth
is regarded as *continued* by the Apostles with the aid of
Jesus in heaven. Luke marks his second narrative as a
natural and necessary sequel to his first.

Others say that the use of ἄρχεσθαι with the inf. (which
occurs 28 times in Luke) is only a slightly more 'vivid and M.
dramatic' way of putting the simple verb: but a careful
examination of the passages (e.g. Luke iii. 8, xi. 29; Acts
ii. 4, xi. 4, xi. 15, xviii. 26) will shew that, although ἄρχο-
μαι is not always emphatic as here, where the context
throws emphasis upon it, yet it never entirely loses its
meaning or degenerates into a mere auxiliary verb.

2. ἄχρι ἧς ἡμ.] by attraction for ἄ. τῆς ἡμέρας ᾖ. Cf. ver. 22, ἕως τῆς ἡμέρας ἧς.

ἐξελέξατο] a word frequently used of the 'choosing' of the Apostles, e.g. Luke vi. 13 ἐκλεξάμενος ἀπ' αὐτῶν δώδεκα: also of the 'choosing' of Israel, xiii. 17 n.: and Christians are often called 'chosen', ἐκλεκτοί.

3. παρέστησεν...] e. g. on the mountain in Galilee, Matt. xxviii. 16, to the eleven as they sat at meat, Mark xvi. 14, at the sea of Tiberias, John xxi. 1—23.

παθεῖν] So absolutely of 'the passion' xvii. 3, xxvi. 23.

τεκμηρίοις] 'infallible proofs' A.V., 'proofs' R.V.   τεκμήριον is defined as ἀναγκαῖον σημεῖον Arist. *Rhet.* I. 2. 16.

δι' ἡμ. τεσσεράκοντα] The length of time is given here only. At the flood 'it rained upon the earth forty days', Gen. vii. 4; Moses was in the mount forty days, Ex. xxiv. 18; Jesus fasted forty days, Matt. iv. 2.

ὀπτανόμενος] 'being seen' A.V.; but R.V. rightly 'appearing'. The word only occurs here in N.T., and seems to describe 'transitory appearances attended with miracu-
II. lous circumstances', cf. the use of ὀπτασία 'a vision' xxvi. 19; Luke i. 22, xxiv. 23.

τῆς βασ. τοῦ θεοῦ] This phrase occurs 33 times in Luke, 15 times in Mark, but Matt. almost always has ἡ βασ. τῶν οὐρανῶν. It represents that kingdom which the Messiah was sent to establish. The meaning attached to it has naturally varied with the belief held as to the person and purpose of the Messiah. The Jews looked for a restoration of their empire as it had been in the days of David. The same feeling was entertained by the first disciples, cf. ver. 6, Matt. xx. 21, and only gradually disappeared. On the other hand, in their widest sense, the words may include (1) the spiritual kingdom which our Lord came to establish upon earth, (2) His kingdom in heaven.

4. συναλιζόμενος] 'being assembled together with them' A. and R.V. The marg. gives 'eating with them' and V. *convescens*, but this derivation of the word from ἄλς, 'salt', is without authority, and probably due to a comparison of passages such as Luke xxiv. 41; John xxi. 12, where the risen Jesus is described as 'eating' with His disciples.

παρήγγειλεν...] Cf. carefully Luke xxiv. 49. The 'promise of the Father' is the Holy Spirit, cf. ii. 33. τοῦ πατρός is the subjective gen.; the Father gives the promise: on the other hand ii. 33 τοῦ πνεύματος is the objective gen.; it is that to which the promise refers.

ἐπαγγελία is regularly used in N.T. of 'divine promises' (cf. ii. 39, vii. 17, xiii. 23) which are not promises made under an agreement (ὑπόσχεσις) but voluntary offers; ἐπαγγέλλεσθαι=*ultro offerre.*

ἣν ἠκούσατέ μου] R.V. 'which, *said he*, ye heard from me'. Transition to direct speech, cf. Luke v. 14.

5. Ἰωάνης μὲν...] John's own words are ἐγὼ μὲν βαπτίζω ὑμᾶς ἐν ὕδατι...αὐτὸς ὑμ. βαπτίσει ἐν πν. ἁγ. καὶ πυρί (Matt. iii. 11).

οὐ μετά...] At Pentecost (see ch. ii.), 10 days after the Ascension. In the Church Calendar Ascension Day is the 40th day after Easter, and Whitsunday the 10th day after Ascension Day.

6. οἱ μὲν οὖν...] 'So then they (the eleven) having come together...'. At this point the regular narrative of the Acts begins, viz. with an account of the Ascension. οὖν connects it with the brief Introduction and Summary of vv. 1—4, which in its turn connects the Acts with the Gospel.

R.V. rightly here commences a fresh paragraph.

κύριε] κύριος = (1) 'having strength', 'power', (2) 'master', 'lord', *dominus;* frequently applied to men, e.g. xvi. 30; Matt. xxi. 30 ἐγώ, κύριε, 'I go, Sir'; to an angel x. 4; but especially in LXX. to God, cf. Gen. ii. 15 κύριος ὁ θεός 'the Lord God', and Acts ii. 34 εἶπεν Κύριος τῷ κυρίῳ μου: it is used in prayer to the Father, e.g. i. 24, iv. 29 ; it is however especially applied in N.T. to Jesus 'the Master', cf. xix. 5, 10, 13, 17; and in prayer to Him, vii. 59.

εἰ] The use of εἰ after phrases like οὐκ οἶδα in classical Gk. = 'whether' is well known. Hence its use in N.T. to express a direct question in the form of a doubt which the utterer desires to have solved, cf. vii. 1, xix. 2, xxi. 37, xxii. 25 ; Matt. xii. 10; Luke xiii. 23.

ἐν τῷ χρόνῳ τούτῳ] Emphatic. 'Is it *now* that thou dost re-establish?' The resurrection of Jesus and His subsequent words about 'the kingdom of God' (ver. 3) had re-kindled their hopes of the immediate re-establishment of an earthly Jewish empire.

7. χρόνους ἢ καιρούς] Usually distinguished as 'periods' and 'points (i.e. critical moments) of time'. The distinction cannot however be maintained, cf. καιρούς (xvii. 26) of long periods of national existence, and the common phrase ὁ νῦν κ. = 'the present life': see too iii. 19, 21 n.

χρόνος = 'time', 'period of time' merely; καιρός, 'a period
of time' not with reference to its length, but regarded as
fixed upon, marked out, or adapted for some end.

ἔθετο...] An absolute monarch may 'place' certain
affairs 'in the hands of his ministers': òthers he may
'place within (or 'subject to') his own personal authority':
these latter he would be said τίθεσθαι ἐν τῇ ἰδ. ἐξουσίᾳ. The
phrase is an emphatic one, ἰδίᾳ being as much stronger
than ἑαυτοῦ as *proprius* than *suus*, and ἐξουσία expresses
full and uncontrolled authority (cf. v. 4).

8. καὶ ἔσεσθε...τῆς γῆς] The Acts themselves form the
best commentary on these words, and the words themselves might be given as the best summary of the Acts.

We have first the preaching of the gospel 'in Jerusalem'
until the martyrdom of Stephen; then the dispersion
throughout Judaea and Samaria, viii. 1; Philip going down
to Samaria, viii. 5; and afterwards Peter and John, viii. 14;
then the conversion of Paul 'the Apostle of the Gentiles' and the vision of Peter; finally a full account of the
missionary labours of Paul and others, culminating in
the establishment of the gospel in the capital of the
world.

μάρτυρες] 'witnesses': *doctrinâ et sanguine*, B. Notice
the first duty of an Apostle and cf. iv. 33, x. 39, xiii.
31.

9. ὑπέλαβεν] 'received him' so that He seemed to be
supported by it. ὄχημα βασιλικόν, Chrysostom.

10. ἀτενίζοντες] A. and R. V. 'looking stedfastly'. The
word (from α intensive and τείνω) occurs 10 times in the Acts
and describes a somewhat strained, earnest gaze, cf. iii. 4,
12, vi. 15, vii. 55.

εἰς τὸν οὐρανὸν] Notice the quiet emphasis of these
words four times repeated.

ὡς...ἦσαν, καὶ ἰδοὺ] Cf. Luke vii. 12 ὡς ἤγγισε...καὶ ἰδού.
The simplest method of representing two events as happening together is to place them side by side, and this method,
very common in Homer, is fairly frequent in classical
Gk, e.g. Plat. *Symp.* 220 c, ἤδη μεσημβρία ἦν καὶ ἄνθρωποι
ἠσθάνοντο, 'it was midday *when* they began to notice'. Cf.
too iii. 2 n.; Mark xv. 25 ἦν ὥρα τρίτη καὶ ἐσταύρωσαν αὐτόν,
and the use of *atque* in *simul atque*. Hence even where a
temporal particle, e.g. ὡς, is used we often find, as here, a

pleonastic καί added to mark that the two events happened exactly together.

ἄνδρες] Cf. Luke xxiv. 4 : so too an 'angel' is called 'a man' x. 30. Cf. xi. 13.

11. οὕτως...ὅν τρόπον] Emphatic repetition.

12. Ἐλαιῶνος] 'Olivet', V. *Olivetum*, 'the olive-garden' (cf. ἀμπελών); only here, usually τὸ ὄρος τῶν ἐλαιῶν. The Mt of Olives is a ridge about one mile long, running N. and S., on the E. of Jerusalem, separated from it by the narrow ravine of the Kidron.

σαββάτου...] Cf. Ex. xvi. 29, ' abide ye every man in his place, let no man go out of his place on the seventh day'. This special command had been made by the Rabbis the basis of a general rule fixing the distance which might be lawfully traversed on the Sabbath at ' 2000 cubits' (about six furlongs), the space kept between the ark and the people in the wilderness Josh. iii. 4, the distance to which the suburbs of a Levitical city extended, Numb. xxxv. 5, and the traditional distance which separated the tabernacle from the furthest part of the camp.

εἶχον is not = ἀπεῖχον: the distance is regarded as a quality *possessed* by the mountain. Many consider that Luke here describes the Ascension as taking place at some spot on the Mt of Olives distant a sabbath day's journey from Jerusalem, and the present Church of the Ascension is on the central peak of the mountain, which is at about that distance. But this view does not agree with Luke xxiv. 50 where it is said that ' Jesus led them out to over against (ἕως πρός) Bethany', which is a village on the E. slope of the Mt of Olives '*fifteen* furlongs' (John xi. 18) from Jerusalem. Probably therefore Luke here gives the distance of the Mt of Olives from Jerusalem for the information of his Gentile readers and does not fix the exact spot of the Ascension, which took place amid ' the wild uplands which overhang Bethany, in a seclusion which would perhaps nowhere else be found so near the stir of a mighty city '. *B. W. A.*

Stanley, Sinai and Pal. c. 3.

13. τὸ ὑπερῷον] Possibly the ἀνώγεον μέγα of Mark xiv: 15, Luke xxii. 12, where the Last Supper took place. The ὑπερῷον in a house was a large room suitable for gatherings, cf. xx. 8.

ὅ τε Πέτρος...] The following table gives the four lists of the Apostles to be found in the N. T.

Matthew x. 2.	Mark iii. 16.	Luke vi. 14.	Acts i. 13.
	Simon	Peter	
Andrew	James	Andrew	John
James	John	James	James
John	Andrew	John	Andrew
	Phi	lip	
Bartholomew	Bartholomew	Bartholomew	Thomas
Thomas	Matthew	Matthew	Bartholomew
Matthew	Thomas	Thomas	Matthew
	James ὁ	τοῦ 'Αλφαίου	
	Thad|daeus	Simon	ὁ Ζηλωτής
	Simon	ὁ Καναναῖος	'Judas	of James'
	Ju|das Isca|riot		Vacant

In each list the twelve names fall into three groups of four,
each group headed by the same name. The first two groups
are identical in their composition. In the third it is necessary to identify Thaddaeus (or Lebbaeus, for the readings
vary) with 'Judas of James'. For the use of double
names cf. ver. 23 n.

ὁ ζηλωτής] The Greek equivalent of the Chaldee Κανα-
ναῖος (not Χαναναῖος = 'inhabitant of Canaan'). Simon
belonged to the sect of the Zealots who were noted for their
fierce advocacy of the Mosaic ritual, and who assume so
prominent a position in the siege of Jerusalem.

Meri-
vale,
c. 59.

'Ι. 'Ιακώβου] A. V. ' brother of James', assuming that he
is 'Ιούδας ἀδελφὸς 'Ιακώβου of Jude i. 1. R. V. rightly gives
the natural rendering ' son of James'. He is referred to as
' Judas not Iscariot' John xiv. 22. Nothing else is known
of him.

14. ὁμοθυμαδὸν] Eleven times in the Acts: not elsewhere in N. T. except Rom. xv. 6.

σὺν γυναιξὶν καὶ M.] 'with women and (noteworthy
among them) Mary'. Such women might be Mary Magda-
lene, Joanna, Susanna, Luke viii. 2, ' Mary the mother of

James and Joses', and Salome the 'mother of Zebedee's children', Matt. xxvii. 56.

τοῖς ἀδελφοῖς] Cf. Matt. xii. 46; Mark iii. 31; Luke viii. 19, 'his mother and his brethren'; mentioned with 'his mother' and 'his sisters', and their names given 'James and Joses and Simon and Judas' Matt. xiii. 56; Mark vi. 3; 'his brethren' John vii. 9; 'James the Lord's brother' Gal. i. 19.

The fact that they are *invariably* termed ἀδελφοί, and so often mentioned, as here, with 'his mother', seems to make it certain that they were actually His brethren the sons of Mary. No other meaning can naturally be given to the words.

A strong desire however to make Jesus the only son of 'the Virgin' has given rise to many theories, of which the two chief are:

(1) A theory advanced first by Jerome A.D. 383 that they were 'cousins' of Jesus. To assign such a meaning to ἀδελφός is distinctly contrary to its biblical usage (its application to a 'nephew' Gen. xxix. 15 being exceptional, and its frequent metaphorical use, e.g. i. 15, being quite distinct). The theory is built upon a series of assumptions of which the first is that Mary had a sister also called Mary (a most improbable view and only supported by a very doubtful punctuation of John xix. 25), and that this Mary is identical with 'Mary the mother of James and Joses', Matt. xxvii. 56. It is sufficiently disproved by Lightfoot. *Excursus ad Gal.*

(2) A theory held in very early times and strongly advocated by Epiphanius bishop of Constantia A.D. 367, that they were the sons of Joseph by a former wife. According to Epiphanius Joseph was eighty years old when betrothed to Mary. This theory being purely suppositional admits no proof or disproof. It is advocated by Lightfoot who refers to the fact that the dying Jesus commended His mother to John (John xix. 26, 27) who took her 'unto his own home', as a 'fatal objection' to her having had sons of her own. *Lightfoot. Gal.* ed. 2, p. 264.

15. ἐν ταῖς ἡμ. ταύταις] i.e. between the Ascension and Pentecost.

ὀνομάτων] A. V. 'names'; R. V. rightly 'persons'. For this Hebrew use cf. Numb. i. 2, 18, 20; Rev. iii. 4.

ἐπὶ τὸ αὐτό] of place 'gathered together', cf. ii. 1, iii. 44; Luke xvii. 35.

16. ἄνδρες...] The clear and telling argument of this speech is so obscured in both A. and R.V. that it needs careful attention.

In it Peter brings forward a Messianic prophecy to shew (1) that a certain event in the past was necessary, viz. the betrayal of Jesus by an Apostle, (2) that thereby a necessary duty is imposed upon them in the present, viz. the selection of a successor. This connection is emphatically marked by the prominent ἔδει the first word of the speech, and the equally prominent δεῖ (ver. 21) the first word of the second half.

With regard to the first division of his speech the method Peter adopts is not to give the prophecy first and the corresponding facts afterwards, but to give the facts first and the prophecy afterwards.

(*a*) He states that the prophecy had to be fulfilled which was spoken concerning Judas, and argues that its application must be to Judas *because* Judas was an Apostle. (It will be seen that the prophecy refers to one who held an 'overseership', so that the fact of Judas being an Apostle is the proof of its reference to him.)

(*β*) He then proceeds (v. 18) further to prepare the way for the quotation of the prophecy by referring to another remarkable fact, viz. the purchase by Judas of a field and (i) his suicide in that field, (ii) the consequent pollution of the field, which became 'a field of blood' and uninhabitable.

Then he brings forward the prophecy which accurately tallies with these facts, (*β*) (i) as invoking a curse on the betrayer, (ii) as referring to an ἔπαυλις he possessed (=χωρίον ὃ ἐκτήσατο) which is to be desolate and uninhabitable, and (*a*) as mentioning the betrayer as holding an 'overseership'.

ἔδει] 'It was *necessary*'. Throughout the Acts Jesus is regarded as the Messiah whom the Jewish scriptures foretold. The circumstances of His life and death must therefore *necessarily* fulfil the prophetic passages of Scripture. It is the constant endeavour of the Apostles to shew that the life and works of Jesus do accurately correspond with these prophecies.

τὴν γραφὴν] 'the passage of scripture', i. e. the one he is about to quote, ver. 20. A. V. wrongly refers in margin to Ps. xli. 9.

Light-foot, *Gal.* iii. 22.

'The singular γραφή in the N. T. always means a *particular passage* of Scripture'.

ἦν προεῖπε...]   The Psalmist spoke of his own troubles, but through his instrumentality (διά) the Holy Spirit fore-told the sufferings and betrayal of the Messiah.

τοῦ γεν. ὁδηγοῦ] Cf. Matt. xxvi. 47.

17. ὅτι] 'that', 'in that', 'seeing that', 'because'. H. gives ὅτι = 'although'—a typical instance of mistrans-lation intended to save, and in fact ruining, the sense.

κλῆρον] (1) 'a lot', (2) 'a thing assigned by lot', (3) 'allotment', 'portion'. Hence *clerus* = 'the clergy'.

18. οὗτος μὲν οὖν...Αἵματος] Marked off in R. V. as a parenthesis, (and so in the text,) and generally regarded as inserted by the historian. But it has been rightly re-marked that (1) such an insertion of a historical notice is   A. M. La. unnatural, (2) the use of μὲν οὖν (a formula of transition = 'so then') to introduce a parenthesis is unknown, (3) the whole verse is rhetorical not narrative in style, cf. οὗτος, μισθοῦ τῆς ἀδικίας, ἐλάκησε μέσος, and beyond all (4) the words are absolutely necessary to Peter's argument.

On the other hand in ver. 19 τῇ διαλέκτῳ αὐτῶν and τοῦτ' ἔστιν Χωρίον Αἵματος are clearly explanations inserted—perhaps awkwardly but very naturally—by Luke writing in Greek for Greek readers who would not have understood the word Ἀκελδαμάχ.

ἐκτήσατο χ...] ' acquired (i. e. made a κτῆμα or posses-sion) a field from the reward of his guilt', i.e. from the ' 30 pieces of silver' which the chief priests had 'covenanted' to give him, cf. Matt. xxvi. 14—16, and xxvii. 3—8, where the account given differs considerably from that given here. Attempts to reconcile the two passages by translating ἐκτή-σατο ' gave occasion to the purchase of' involve a perversion of the plain meaning of the Greek.

πρηνὴς...] 'having fallen face-foremost'. The words indicate suicide by jumping or falling from a height of some sort, and the suicide is clearly referred to as connected with the field. Matt. has ἀπελθὼν ἀπήγξατο.

ἐλάκησεν, from λάσκω, always of *sound*, is here used of bursting accompanied with sound, cf. *frango, fragor*; ' crack'.

19. τῇ διαλέκτῳ αὐτῶν] inserted by Luke from the point of view of himself and Theophilus who used Greek.

διάλεκτος, from διαλέγεσθαι, ' to converse', = 'language' not ' dialect', cf. ii. 6, xxi. 40.

Χωρίον Αἵματος] Matt. has ἀγρὸς αἵματος, adding that its former name was ὁ ἀγ. τοῦ κεραμέως.

20. γενηθήτω...] Ps. lxix. 25:

γενηθήτω ἡ ἔπαυλις αὐτῶν ἠρημωμένη
καὶ ἐν τοῖς σκηνώμασιν αὐτῶν μὴ ἔστω ὁ κατοικῶν.

David and his kingdom are types of the Son of David and His kingdom. Hence words used of his own enemies by David are applied to the enemies of the Messiah, or referred specially to one such enemy as here. 'The 69th Psalm is often quoted in St Matt. and St John and seems to have been regarded as peculiarly prophetic of the Messiah'.

**H.
So M.
with
Chrys.**

ἔπαυλις] Clearly parallel to χωρίον.

τὴν ἐπισκοπὴν...] Ps. cix. 8. For ἐπισκοπήν A. V. gives the derived word 'Bishoprick', but R. V. 'office' and in the margin 'overseership'.

21. ᾧ εἰσῆλθεν κ. ἐξ. ἐφ' ἡμᾶς]=*versabatur inter nos*, of habitual daily intercourse, cf. ix. 28; Ps. cxxi. 8; 1 Sam. xxix. 6; John x. 9.

22. τοῦ βαπτ. Ἰωάνου] which immediately preceded the public ministry of Jesus, cf. Luke iii.

τούτων] Deictic, and emphatic by position.

23. ἔστησαν] i.e. the whole company did so.

Ἰωσὴφ...] Nothing is known of either.

Joseph's regular name (cf. καλούμενον) was Joseph Barsabbas, i.e. son of Sabbas, it being common thus to distinguish men by adding the name of the father, cf. Matt. xvi. 17 Simon Barjona, Acts xiii. 6 Barjesus. To this name was often added an additional name, a sort of 'surname' (cf. ἐπεκλήθη), sometimes expressing some personal characteristic (cf. iv. 36 Ἰωσὴφ ὁ ἐπικληθεὶς Βαρνάβας, i. e. 'son of consolation'; x. 5 Σίμωνα ὃς ἐπικαλεῖται Πέτρος, i. e. 'the rock'), frequently Latin in form, for use no doubt in dealing with non-Jews, and often similar in sound to the Hebrew name, as here Joseph Justus; cf. xiii. 9 Saul, Paul.

**v. F.
c. 19, s.f.**

Ματθίαν] Short for Mattathias (= Theodorus), a common Jewish name.

. 24. καρδιογνῶστα] Emphatic. He 'who knows the heart' must judge right. The same adj. applied to God xv. 8.

ἀνάδειξον] 'appoint', cf. Luke x. 1, ἀνέδειξεν ὁ κύριος ἑτέρους ἑβδομήκοντα.

25. εἰς τὸν τόπον τὸν ἴδιον] Euphemism. The phrase is a strong antithesis to τὸν τόπον...ἀποστολῆς; he was chosen for the place of an Apostle, he had chosen his own place for himself. In Numb. xxiv. 25 'Balaam returned to his place' (τὸν τόπον αὐτοῦ) was interpreted by the Rabbis of Gehenna.

Not only is the adj. ἴδιος a strong one, cf. i. 7 n., but it is emphasized by its position, as always, when the adj. is thus placed after the noun and preceded by the article, cf. ii. 20 ἡμέραν τὴν μεγάλην καὶ ἐπιφανῆ, ii. 40 τῆς γενεᾶς τῆς σκολιᾶς ταύτης, vi. 13 τοῦ τόπου τοῦ ἁγίου, xi. 23 τὴν χάριν τὴν τοῦ θ., xiii. 10 τὰς ὁδοὺς τὰς εὐθείας.

26. ἔδωκαν κλήρους] 'cast lots'; αὐτοῖς, ethic dat. 'for them'. Decision by lots is very frequent in O.T. The scape-goat was chosen from two by lot Lev. xvi. 7—10, Moses ordained (Numb. xxxiv. 13) that the inheritance of the 12 tribes should be assigned by lot, and Joshua so assigned it, Josh. xiv. 2, xviii. 6—an instance which would naturally be considered here in filling up the number of the *twelve* Apostles, who represent the *twelve* tribes (cf. Luke xxii. 30).

The two names would be written on small tablets and cast into a vessel (or 'the lap', cf. Prov. xvi. 33) and then shaken (cf. πάλλω, πάλος) until one fell (ἔπεσεν) out.

συνκατεψηφίσθη] The word is exactly = συγκαταριθμέω, 'reckon in along with', 'number with': ψῆφοι, *calculi*, were regularly used in counting. Cf. συνεψήφισαν, xix. 19.

CHAPTER II.

1. ἐν τῷ συνπληροῦσθαι...] lit. 'on the day of P. being fulfilled'. Pentecost was a festal day looked forward to as *completing* the period of harvest: hence, when it arrives, it can be spoken of as 'being fulfilled', 'filled up', 'added to the now full tale of days'.

Cf. Luke ix. 51 ἐν τῷ συμπληροῦσθαι τὰς ἡμέρας τῆς ἀναλήψεως αὐτοῦ, καὶ αὐτὸς...ἐστήριξε, i.e. simultaneously with the days of his taking up being completed (filled up to the proper number) he set his face......

τῆς πεντηκοστῆς] A feast, as its name implies, held on the *fiftieth* day from the second day of the Passover, on which day a sheaf of the *firstfruits* was 'waved' before the Lord, whereas at Pentecost a sacrifice was made for the *completion* of the harvest, cf. Lev. xxiii. 15—21. The Passover, Pentecost, and the Feast of Tabernacles were the three great feasts of the year, on which all males were 'to appear before the Lord in the place that he shall choose', Deut. xvi. 16. It is also called the 'feast of weeks', from

the 'numbering seven weeks'. Whitsunday, on which the
sending of the Holy Spirit is commemorated, is the 10th
day after Ascension day, and so 50 days from the day when
'Christ our passover was sacrificed for us'.

πάντες] All the believers in Jesus.

2. ὥσπερ] Note that it is not 'the sound of a blast'
but 'of as it were a blast': so too ὡσεὶ πυρός.

3. διαμεριζόμεναι] Not 'cloven' as A.V. (for the word
is not an adj., but a present part.) but 'distributing themselves', i.e. one to each, a meaning which is necessary to
account for the *singular* verb ἐκάθισεν, the nom. to which
is γλῶσσα, which can be naturally supplied after the γλῶσσαι have been referred to as 'distributing themselves', but
not otherwise. V. has *dispertitae*, and cf. διεμέριζον ver. 45.

For the resting of a flame on the head as a sign of
divine favour cf. Virg. *Aen.* II. 683,

> *Ecce levis summo de vertice visus Iuli*
> *Fundere lumen apex.*

So too Ov. *Fast.* VI. 635 *flammeus apex*, and Hom. *Il.* XVIII.
214.

4. λαλεῖν ἑτέραις γλώσσαις] 'to speak with tongues
different to their own', for ἕτερος expresses something different (cf. ver. 13), not merely, like ἄλλος, something
additional.

With regard to this event nothing is known but what
Luke tells us. From his words it is clear (1) that he
describes the speakers speaking in languages they did not
know before, and the hearers *understanding* them, vv. 8 and
11, (2) that the event is described as exceptional and
accompanied by great excitement, ver. 13, (3) that it is
connected not with teaching but with praise and adoration, ver. 11. Compare x. 46—48 where 'speaking with
tongues' is also spoken of as an exceptional event and
connected with 'glorifying God', and xix. 6 where it is
again exceptional and distinguished from 'prophesying'
or preaching.

'Speaking with tongues' seems to have been used as a
regular form of worship in the Corinthian Church. St Paul
describes the practice at length 1 Cor. xiv., but it is clear
that as in use there it differed from what is described
here, for he dwells on the fact that the utterances could
not be understood without an interpreter: he also distinctly
deprecates the practice: he speaks of it as inferior to preaching (προφητεύειν) and adds ver. 19 'I would rather speak
five words with my understanding (τῷ νοΐ), that I might

instruct others also, than ten thousand words in a tongue
(ἐν γλώσσῃ)'.

Mark xvi. 17, where to 'speak with new (καιναῖς)
tongues' is promised by Jesus, is a doubtful passage, and
the reading καιναῖς is also extremely uncertain.

ἀποφθέγγεσθαι] *eloqui:* expresses eager impassioned
utterance, cf. ver. 14 and xxvi. 25, the only other passages
where it is found in N.T. Lucian (*Paras.* 4) uses it of the
'ring' of a vessel when struck.

5. κατοικοῦντες] 'dwelling' A. and R. V. The word
certainly usually describes *residence* in a place, cf. iv. 16,
vii. 2, 4, ix. 22, 32, but should here perhaps be taken in
a fairly wide sense, to include those who were ' dwelling' in
Jerusalem temporarily for the feast, as well as those who
had returned to reside there, either hoping for 'the
consolation of Israel', like Simeon (Luke ii. 25 ἄνθρωπος
εὐλαβής), or desiring to die and be buried in the Holy City.

6. γενομένης δὲ τῆς φωνῆς] A. V. 'when this was
noised abroad', which would require φήμης, 'a rumour',
'report': R.V. rightly 'when this sound was heard', referring
to the ἦχος of ver. 2; cf. φωνή, of the sound of the wind,
John iii. 8; of an instrument, 1 Cor. xiv. 7, 8, 10.

συνεχύθη] *mente confusa est.* V.

7. Γαλιλαῖοι] All the Apostles and many of the disciples came from Galilee, the chief scene of Jesus' labours.
The word is used here in its simple geographical sense: as
Galilaeans their natural language was Aramaic, not the language of any of the nations about to be named.

There is no trace of contempt in the word here, although
Galilee was looked down upon (cf. John vii. 52), nor is
there any reference to the Galilaean 'accent' (cf. Mark
xiv. 70), for διάλεκτος is not='dialect', cf. i. 19 n. The
contemptuous application of *Galilaei* by Julian to the Christians is of course wholly distinct from the use of the word
here.

Gibbon,
c. 23.

9. Πάρθοι...] i.e. Jews who had settled and become
naturalized in those districts. They were known as ' Jews
of the dispersion' (διασπορά); cf. too xxi. 21 τοὺς κατὰ τὰ ἔθνη
Ἰουδαίους. They may be divided into four divisions :

(1) The *Eastern* or *Babylonian,* originating in the
carrying away of the ten tribes by Shalmaneser B.c. 721,
2 Kings xviii. 11, and of Judah and Benjamin under Nebu-
chadnezzar B.c. 588, 2 Kings xxiv.

(2) The *Syrian,* due to the removal of Jewish colonists
by Seleucus Nicator (B.c. 312—280) from Babylon to the

west. Antiochus the Great also removed 2000 Jewish families from Judaea to Lydia and Phrygia.

Meri-
vale,
c. 28
and 29.
(3) The *Egyptian*, due to the Jewish settlements established in Alexandria by Alexander and Ptolemy I., where
at the Christian era Jews formed two-fifths of the population. Cf. xviii. 24 n.

(4) The *Roman* Jews brought to Rome by Pompey after
his occupation of Jerusalem B. c. 63 and settled in the trans-
Tiberine region.

The text corresponds to these four historical and geographical divisions : (1) Πάρθοι...Μεσοποταμίαν, (2) Ἰουδαίαν
...Παμφυλίαν, (3) Αἴγυπτον...Κυρήνην, (4) οἱ ἐπι. Ῥωμαῖοι.

The Cretes and Arabians are mentioned last—somewhat
awkwardly—as not falling into any group.

Πάρθοι] Put first as most important : their empire at
this time extended from India to the Tigris.

Μῆδοι] A name strictly applied to a people of Western
Asia, who were merged with the Persians into one powerful
empire by Cyrus the Great (B.C. 559). They were subdued
by Alexander the Great, and after his death soon absorbed
by the Parthians. The Greek writers use the word vaguely
= 'Persians', ' the inhabitants of the Persian kingdom '.

Ἐλαμεῖται] 'inhabitants of Elam', a district S. of Assyria and E. of Persia, with Susa (Shushan) for its capital.

Μεσοποταμίαν] Between the Euphrates and Tigris.

Ἰουδαίαν] Clearly not Judaea as distinguished from
Samaria (cf. i. 8) but the 'land of the Jews ', i.e. Palestine
and perhaps some part of Syria. It is naturally placed at
the head of the second group with which it is geographically
connected.

Cappadocia extends from Mt Taurus northward to
Pontus, which extends to the Euxine ; Phrygia lies inland
W. of Cappadocia ; Pamphylia on the S. coast E. of Cilicia.

τὴν Ἀσίαν] As throughout the Acts = the Roman province of Asia comprising Mysia, Lydia and Caria, with
Ephesus for its capital.

10. τὰ μέρη...] The singularly fertile district to the W.
of the Greater Syrtis known as the Cyrenaic Pentapolis,
the modern Tripoli. ' Simon a Cyrenian' is mentioned
Matt. xxvi. 73.

ἐπιδημοῦντες] Used generally of *temporary* stay in a
foreign place, cf. xvii. 21 οἱ ἐπι. ξένοι. The word is not however here contrasted with κατοικοῦντες (ver. 5), but seems
added to shew that Ῥωμαῖοι is used in a geographical sense

='from Rome', and not, as often, in a political sense
='Roman citizens', cf. xvi. 21, 37, 38.

'Ιουδαῖοί τε καὶ προσήλυτοι] In apposition with and So A.
defining *all* the preceding proper names, and not merely M. La.
'Ρωμαῖοι. This would have been perfectly clear had it not
been for the addition of the 'Cretes and Arabians', apparently as a sort of afterthought, to what was already a
complete and symmetrical list.

προσήλυτος (from προσέρχεσθαι='one who joins') is
used in LXX. to render the Hebrew word for which A. V.
gives 'stranger', e.g. Ex. xx. 10 ὁ προσ. ὁ παροικῶν ἐν σοί.
Instances in the O. T. are Uriah the Hittite and Araunah
the Jebusite. Matt. xxiii. 15 refers to the zeal shewn for
'making proselytes'; cf. Hor. *Sat.* i. 4. 142 *ac veluti te* |
Judaei cogemus in hanc concedere turbam. For the number
of Jews and Jewish proselytes in Italy cf. Tac. *Ann.* ii. 85,
who refers to a decree made by Tiberius (A. D. 19) *ut quattuor
millia libertini generis ea superstitione infecta...in insulam
Sardiniam veherentur ..ceteri cederent Italia.* The division
into Proselytes of the Gate, who were not bound by circumcision and the other special laws of the Mosaic code, and
Proselytes of Righteousness, who were circumcised and
carried out the full Judaic ritual, seems later than this
period.

12. διηποροῦντο, διαχλευάζοντες] Cf. x. 17 n.

13. γλεύκους] A. and R. V. 'new wine', somewhat un-
wisely, as Pentecost came *before* the vintage. From Lucian
Ep. Sat. xxii. it is clear that it is raw young wine with fer-
mentation still going on, indigestible and intoxicating,
served to poor guests, while the rich man drinks οἶνος
ἀνθοσμίας. Cf. too Job xxxii. 19 ἀσκὸς γλεύκους ζέων δεδεμένος. The use of the word clearly implies contempt, cf. Juv.
iii. 292 *cujus aceto...tumes?* where *aceto* is contemptuous

14. σταθεὶς δὲ...] Peter's object is to explain and
justify what has occurred, his whole argument being from
the fulfilment of prophecy. Signs and wonders were to
accompany the coming of Messiah, and the speaking with
tongues is one of these signs. Moreover that Jesus is Messiah is shewn by His works (ver. 22) and especially by His
death and resurrection, which exactly fulfil the words of
David.

σταθεὶς, ἐπῆρεν τὴν φωνήν, ἀπεφθέγξατο] These introductory words mark the importance of the speech. This
pictorial use of σταθεὶς is a marked peculiarity of Luke,
being used by no other writer in N. T. Cf. Luke xviii. 11, 40,
xix. 8; Acts v. 20, xvii. 22, xxvii. 21.

τοῦτο] explained by οὐ γὰρ... below : 'this, namely that these men are not...'.

15. οὗτοι] Deictic.

ὥρα τρίτη] The Jews, like the Romans, divided the time between sunrise and sunset into 12 equal parts, which would vary in length according to the time of year. At the equinoxes the 'third hour' would be 9 a.m. It was the first hour of prayer, and the time of the offering of the morning sacrifice in the Temple. 'Before it no pious Jew might eat or drink'.

A. and
so W.

16. τοῦτό ἐστιν τὸ εἰρημένον...] i.e. 'this, which is happening, is identical with' or 'the fulfilment of what was spoken...'.

The quotation is from Joel ii. 28—32 and closely follows the LXX.

17. ἐν ταῖς ἐσχάταις ἡμ.] Joel has merely μετὰ ταῦτα, but himself proceeds to define the time as ἡμέραις ἐκείναις and ἡμ. Κυρίου (Joel ii. 29, 31), and so Peter, interpreting the prophecy as foretelling Messiah's kingdom, naturally substitutes for μετὰ ταῦτα the well-known phrase 'the last days', which is frequently used to indicate the time of Messiah's coming (e.g. Is. ii. 2 ; Micah iv. 1), and which Peter would naturally use of the time when he was speaking, for the Apostles regarded themselves as living 'in the last days' and looked forward to the coming of Christ in glory in the near future. (Cf. Heb. i. 2 ἐπ' ἐσχάτων τῶν ἡμ. τούτων.)

ὁράσεις] 'visions': this word, for which Luke always employs ὅραμα, indicates something clearer than 'a dream'. Matt. xvii. 9 describes the appearance (ὤφθησαν) of Moses and Elias at the transfiguration as ὅραμα, cf. vii. 31 where the 'burning bush' is ὅραμα : its clearness is marked x. 3 ἐν ὁράματι φανερῶς. On the other hand it may occur to a person 'in an ecstasy', xi. 5, or 'in the night', xvi. 9, xviii. 9; and xii. 9 it is marked as something which the beholder knows to be unreal.

18. τοὺς δούλους μου] A. V. in Joel, following the Hebrew, has 'the servants and the handmaids', i. e. actual servants. Peter here follows LXX.

19. The words ἄνω and σημεῖα κάτω are not in LXX. and seem to be introduced to make the antithesis between what should happen in heaven and on earth clearer. In heaven there are to be τέρατα, 'marvels', 'prodigies', such as changes in the sun, on earth σημεῖα, 'signs', events which symbolize some great change. The next words illustrate these τέρατα and σημεῖα in inverse order (*per Chiasmum*), and therefore αἷμα καὶ πῦρ... must be taken as = 'bloodshed and devastation by fire', and not 'bloody and fiery appearances'. Cf. the prediction by Jesus, Matt. xxiv. 6, 29, of wars on earth and portents in heaven.

20. ἡμ. Κυρίου...] The second coming of Messiah in glory. For the adj. emphatic by position cf. i. 25 n. ἐπιφανῇ (in the Heb. 'terrible'; A. and R.V. 'notable'; V. *manifestus*) describes a day which will be 'clearly visible' to all in its occurrences and meaning.

For ἐπιφάνεια used of 'the second coming', cf. 2 Thess. ii. 8; 1 Tim. vi. 14. We use the term 'Epiphany' of the 'manifestation' to the Gentiles: cf. Collect for the Epiphany 'O God, who by the leading of a star didst manifest thy only-begotten Son to the Gentiles'.

22. Ἰησοῦν τὸν Ναζωραῖον] The names applied to our Lord in the Acts deserve careful study.

(1) *Jesus* is His name as a man. It is an ordinary name, and is the Gk form of Joshua (cf. vii. 45 'brought in with Jesus'), which is contracted from Jehoshua = 'the help of Jehovah' or 'Saviour', cf. Matt. i. 21.

'*Jesus of Nazareth*' is used when reference is made to Jesus as a man needing thus to be identified (cf. carefully John xviii. 5, 7, xix. 19; Acts vi. 14, xxvi. 9, and the very interesting instance xxii. 8 with note). In the absence of surnames this addition of their birthplace is one of the best known methods of identifying individuals.

In the healing of the impotent man, iii. 6 and iv. 10, Paul twice speaks of 'Jesus Christ of Nazareth', thus (1) clearly identifying the person, (2) giving Him the title in virtue of which the act of healing is performed.

(2) *Christ*, ὁ χριστός, 'the anointed one', is a rendering of the word 'Messiah' (cf. John i. 41), the name applied by the Jews to the Great Deliverer whom the Prophets foretold. He is described as 'the anointed one' because priests and kings were anointed, and He was to be *the* Priest and *the* King. The descent of the Holy Spirit at His baptism is regarded as the 'anointing' of Jesus, cf. Luke iv. 18; Is. lxi. 1; Acts x. 38 ἔχρισεν αὐτὸν ὁ θεὸς πνεύματι ἁγίῳ.

(3) *Jesus Christ* has not in the Acts yet become a mere name, but involves a statement, viz. the identity of the man Jesus with Messiah; 'Jesus Messiah' may be compared as an appellation with '*Caesar Imperator*'. To prove the claim of the man Jesus to the title 'Christ' is one main purpose of the Acts. As ascribing the title Messiah to Him the name 'Jesus Christ' is very frequently assigned to our Lord when authority, power, or dignity is

ascribed to Him, e.g. ii. 38, iv. 10 'in the name of Jesus Christ', ix. 34 'Jesus Christ healeth thee'.

The following passages afford instances of the use of χριστός as applied to Jesus:—

ii. 36 χριστὸν ἐποίησεν ὁ θεὸς τοῦτον τὸν ᾿Ιησ., 'made Jesus (to be) Messiah'.

iii. 20 τὸν...χριστὸν ᾿Ιησοῦν = 'the...Messiah' and then is added in explanation 'Jesus'; so too v. 42.

xvii. 3 οὗτός ἐστιν ὁ χριστὸς ὁ ᾿Ιησοῦς, 'this man is the Messiah even Jesus'.

xviii. 5 διαμαρτυρόμενος εἶναι τὸν χριστὸν ᾿Ιησοῦν, 'that the Messiah is Jesus'; so too xviii. 28.

In xxiv. 24 τῆς εἰς Χριστὸν ᾿Ιησοῦν πίστεως is somewhat doubtfully supported and probably wrong, being contrary to the entire usage of the Acts.

ἀποδεδειγμένον] A. and R.V. 'approved'. The word is a strong one, 'clearly shewn', 'pointed out specially', 'apart from others', cf. 1 Cor. iv. 9: it also, while thus expressing clearness, suggests certainty, cf. xxv. 7.

ἀπὸ τοῦ θεοῦ] *divinitus;* not 'by', but 'from God', from whom he received His mission and authority; cf. Gal. i. 1 οὐκ ἀπ' ἀνθρώπων. Notice how Peter marks the *divine* origin of the mission of Jesus by emphatic repetition of ὁ θεός, τοῦ θ., ὁ θεός (vv. 22—24), ὁ θεός, τοῦ θεοῦ (vv. 32, 33), ὁ θεός (ver. 36).

δυνάμεσι, τέρασι, σημείοις] The same acts viewed in different lights, (1) as indicating *power* in the person doing them, (2) as exciting *wonder* in the persons seeing them, (3) as being *signs* from which inferences can be drawn.

23. τοῦτον] recalls attention with emphasis to the person described, a very frequent use.

βουλῇ] 'will', 'purpose', 'counsel'; cf. Hom. *Il.* I. 5 Διὸς δ' ἐτελείετο βουλή.

προγνώσει] '*praescientiâ*' V., 'foreknowledge' A. and R.V. The death of Jesus is described as willed and known beforehand by God, and for that reason alone possible.

διὰ χειρὸς ἀνόμων] through the instrumentality of lawless men, i.e. the Roman soldiers. The Jews did not actually crucify Jesus, although they caused His crucifixion.

προσπήξαντες] A graphic and realistic word, used designedly.

ἀνείλατε] 'made away with', 'destroyed'; a word very frequent in the Acts of putting to a *violent* or *unjust* death, cf. v. 33, vii. 28, ix. 23, 29, x. 39, and ἀναίρεσις viii. 1; Luke xxii. 2.

24. λύσας τὰς...] The 'pangs of death' had 'laid See M. here.
hold' of Jesus (cf. κρατεῖσθαι, and its use iii. 11, xxiv. 6;
Luke viii. 54); from this 'hold' God had 'loosed' Him.
For pain or disease described as 'confining', 'holding prisoner', cf. xxviii. 8 δυσεντερίῳ συνεχόμενον; Plat. *Rep.* 574 A
ὠδῖσι συνέχεσθαι.

The phrase ὠδ. θανάτου is from LXX. Psalm xviii. 4,
cxvi. 3 περιεσχόν με ὠδῖνες θανάτου, where the Hebrew however gives 'snares' or 'traps of death', death being compared to a hunter. Having regard to the sense of λύσας
and κρατεῖσθαι, and to the fact that Peter was not speaking
in Greek but to Jews, it is not improbable that he used the
word 'snares' and that Luke has replaced it by the well-
known LXX. rendering.

25. προορώμην...] Almost verbatim from LXX. Psalm
xvi. 8—11. Peter argues that the words of David could not
all have been spoken of himself alone, especially ver. 27, and
should rather be regarded as applicable (cf. λέγει εἰς αὐτόν)
to Messiah in His hour of trouble: he therefore interprets
them of Messiah, who is regarded as uttering them as an
expression of His trust in Jehovah, even when 'held' by
the 'pangs of death'.

προορώμην = 'I saw before me', i.e. present: A.V. gives
'foresaw', obscuring the sense. κύριον = Jehovah.

ἐκ δεξιῶν] In the position of a defender: the advocate M.
stood at his client's *right* hand, cf. Psalm cix. 31.

26. ἔτι δὲ καὶ] Emphatic. 'Nay more my flesh (i.e.
my actual body) shall dwell awhile (i.e. in the grave) supported upon hope (ἐπ' ἐλπίδι)'.

For κατασκηνώσει, 'pitch a tent', 'rest', 'dwell awhile',
cf. Matt. xiii. 32 'the birds of the air come and lodge (κατα-
σκηνοῦν)', John i. 14 ὁ λόγος σάρξ ἐγένετο καὶ ἐσκήνωσεν ἐν
ἡμῖν.

27. εἰς ᾅδην] *Constructio praegnans.* A.V. has 'in
hell', R.V. 'in Hades', i.e. 'the unseen world'. ᾅδης represents the Hebrew *sheol*, 'the grave' (e.g. Gen. xxxvii. 35),
a very negative word, 'the place not of the living but of
the dead'. It is often used *locally* as the opposite of
'heaven', e.g. Job xi. 8, and cf. Matt. xi. 23; Luke x. 15.
Neither it, nor ᾅδης, denotes a place of punishment; even in
Luke xvi. 23 'in hell (ἐν τῷ ᾅδῃ) he lift up his eyes', the
marked addition of the words ὑπάρχων ἐν βασάνοις shews
that the idea of torment is in no way involved in the word.
'Death' and 'Hades' are strictly parallel terms: he who
'is dead' is 'in Hades': the word is used four times in
Rev., and always with θάνατος, 'death'.

The 'in Hades' of R.V. is not a translation but a mere transliteration, and does not to an ordinary reader convey the simple meaning of the Greek, viz. 'in the grave', while to an educated reader it is useless.

From this passage are derived the words of the Apostles' Creed ' He descended into hell'. The English word 'hell' is derived from 'helan', to hide. The bad sense which attaches to it is partly due to its having been employed not only as a rendering of ᾅδης but also of γέεννα, e. g. Matt. v. 22.

28. ὁδοὺς ζωῆς] i.e. as applied by Peter to Jesus, His rising from the dead: so too the next words describe His ascension and position in heaven enjoying the presence of Jehovah.

29. ἄνδρες ἀδελφοί] The addition of the word ἄνδρες in addressing an audience is respectful and therefore necessary in any speech that is in any way formal, cf. the well-known ἄνδρες δικασταί, 'Αθηναῖοι, &c., and cf. i. 11, ii. 14, ii. 22, vii. 2. It may often be rendered 'men', but in the present phrase we are compelled to omit it and translate 'brethren', thus losing the distinction between this more formal phrase and the affectionate ἀδελφοί of iii. 17 and the Pauline epistles.

ἐξόν sc. ἐστί. ' I may speak freely to you about David', for you are Israelites and know (1) the facts of his death and burial, (2) his hopes and predictions about his descendant, the Messiah.

πατριάρχου] Usually applied to Abraham, or the twelve sons of Jacob (cf. vii. 8) as the great 'original fathers' of the race. Here to David as head of the family from which Messiah was to come.

τὸ μνῆμα αὐτοῦ...] Cf. 1 Kings ii. 10; Neh. iii. 16. The sepulchre is said to have been opened and robbed by Hyrcanus B.C. 134 and again by Herod.

Jos. *Ant.* vii. 15. 3.

30. ὑπάρχων] Strictly 'to be originally', 'in the beginning', 'to start with'; hence τὰ ὑπάρχοντα, 'property', iv. 32, and often in Luke, and ὑπάρξεις ii. 45. It is a favourite word with Luke (never found in Matt., Mark, or John), and though perhaps never quite losing its strict meaning, it becomes often almost= 'to be', e.g. vii. 55. Hence the use of προυπῆρχεν viii. 9 when the sense of ' before' has to be clearly expressed.

ὅρκῳ...] Cf. 2 Sam. vii. 16 with Ps. cxxxii. 11.

καθίσαι] Active, ' set', ' cause to sit'. There is no acc. after it, for the words ' from the fruit of his loins' practically contain the object of the verb, viz. 'a son', 'descendant'.

32. τοῦτον τὸν 'I.] Emphatic, bringing home and summing up the argument. 'David foretold that Messiah should rise from the dead: this man Jesus (cf. ver. 22) God did raise from the dead : therefore Jesus is Messiah'.

οὗ = ' of which fact'.

33. τῇ δεξιᾷ] 'by the right hand' : dat. of instrument. Throughout Peter emphasizes the action of God. The renderings 'at' or 'to the right hand' are impossible, but Bengel's *dextra Dei exaltatus est ad dextram Dei* is a fair deduction from the Greek, especially when compared with ver. 34.

οὖν] 'therefore', 'and so' : God's raising Him to heaven is the natural sequel to His raising Him from the grave.

τήν τε...λαβών] i.e. having received the Holy Spirit which had been promised, cf. i. 4.

ἐξέχεεν, referring to ver. 17. τοῦτο δ...i. e. the phenomenon, which you have just witnessed, which was an 'outpouring of the Holy Spirit'.

34. οὐ γὰρ...] *Dilemma. Propheta loquitur aut de se aut de Messia. Non de se v.* 29, *ergo de Messia.* B.

κάθου ἐκ δεξιῶν μου] Cf. Matt. xx. 21. 'Be thou a Lumby. sharer of my throne and power. This is a common Eastern expression'.

κάθου is conversational and late Gk for the classical κάθησο imperative of κάθημαι.

35. ἕως ἂν θῶ...] Indicating complete subjugation, cf. Josh. x. 24.

36. ἀσφαλῶς οὖν...] Summary of the argument introduced emphatically by ἀσφαλῶς.

αὐτὸν...τοῦτον τὸν 'I.] 'him...even this Jesus', a strong assertion (for the second time, cf. ver. 32) of the identity of Messiah and the man Jesus, introducing also the powerful contrast between Messiah whom God glorified and Jesus ' whom you crucified'.

ὃν ὑμεῖς ἐσταυρώσατε] Note the position of these words. *Aculeus in fine*, B.; cf. κατενύγησαν.

37. κατενύγησαν] They felt the sting of his words, felt *compunction* (*compungo*). The same metaphor in the famous description of Pericles' oratory—τὸ κέντρον ἐγκατ- Eupol.
Dem. 6. έλιπε τοῖς ἀκροωμένοις.

38. βαπτισθήτω...] In accordance with the command of Jesus, Matt. xxviii. 19. The same phrase is used x. 48, and βαπτ. εἰς τὸ ὄνομα τοῦ κυρίου Ἰησ. viii. 16, xix. 5. Luke does not give the *form* of words used in baptism by the Apostles, but merely states the *fact* that they baptized those who acknowledged Jesus as Messiah or as Lord.

The Church has made the words of Jesus (βαπτίζοντες εἰς τὸ ὄνομα τοῦ πατρὸς καὶ τοῦ υἱοῦ καὶ τοῦ ἁγίου πνεύματος) into a baptismal formula: 'I baptize thee in the name of the Father, and of the Son, and of the Holy Ghost'.

εἰς ἄφεσιν] of the object or aim of the baptism.

τὴν δωρεὰν τοῦ...] The Holy Spirit is itself the gift, cf. viii. 17 n.

39. ἡ ἐπαγγελία] The promise contained in the passage quoted from Joel, ver. 18.

πᾶσι τοῖς εἰς μακρὰν...] i.e. to the whole heathen world, cf. ver. 21, a verse which Paul (Rom. x. 13) quotes as proving that there is to be no distinction between Jew and Gentile; cf. Eph. ii. 13, where he speaks of the Gentiles as οἵ ποτε ὄντες μακράν.

A. La. The command of Jesus (Matt. xxviii. 19) is clear, 'Go and teach all nations' (πάντα τὰ ἔθνη); and Messiah's kingdom was generally expected to be universal: Peter expresses this belief, but (cf. ch. x.) it had not yet been revealed to him that the Gentiles *as such*, i.e. without becoming proselytes to Judaism, were to be included in it.

40. διεμαρτύρατο] A. and R. V. 'testified', and so throughout the Acts. In classical Gk μαρτυρέω = 'I am a witness', 'testify'; μαρτύρομαι, = 'I call to witness' (often invoking God), 'I protest', and this distinction is maintained in N.T., cf. n. on μαρτύρομαι xx. 26. It seems unreasonable therefore to translate διαμαρτύρομαι 'testify'.

L. & Scott, s.v. Its exact sense is 'to protest solemnly', especially in the case of falsehood or wrong, and it is accurately used in the Acts of the witness borne by the Apostles to Jesus, viewed as a *protest* against the *false* view of Him held by those they are addressing, cf. x. 42, xviii. 5, xx. 21. Cf. also its use in Luke xvi. 28 of a *warning, protesting* message; Acts xx. 23 of a *warning* spiritual voice. In 1 Tim. v. 21, διαμαρτύρομαι ἐνώπιον τοῦ θεοῦ, it is distinctly 'I protest solemnly', 'I conjure you': so too 2 Tim. ii. 14, iv. 1.

σκολιᾶς] *pravus;* opposite of εὐθύς (xiii. 10), *rectus*

41, 42, 43. οἱ μὲν οὖν......ἦσαν δὲ......ἐγίνετο δὲ...] 'So then they indeed......and were......but fear fell'.

The use of μὲν οὖν should be carefully noticed: it is a formula of transition very frequent in the Acts. οὖν connects with what precedes; μὲν points forward to an anti-

thesis to follow. Here μὲν οὖν introduces a brief statement
of the immediate effect of Peter's speech and prepares the
way for the general account of the condition of the Church
given in vv. 43—47.

The statement introduced by μὲν οὖν need not consist of
only one clause, but may consist of several clauses *parallel*
to or *subordinate* to the first clause; such clauses may be
introduced by δέ (as for instance the clause ἦσαν δὲ…here),
and it is therefore important not to confuse these with the
real *antithesis* to the μὲν clause, which must be discovered
by attention to the sense. It is by no means necessary that
the first δέ which follows it should be the antithesis to μέν.

Simple instances of the use of μὲν οὖν are v. 41, viii.
4, 25, ix. 31, xi. 19, xvi. 5. Instances where several
clauses intervene between the μὲν clause and the clause
with the antithetical δὲ are xii. 5, xiii. 4, xiv. 3, and the
very important xvii. 17, in all of which R.V. is entirely at
fault; also xxiii. 31, xxv. 4.

42. τῇ κοινωνίᾳ] 'fellowship', i.e. in daily intercourse
and also in mutual sharing of goods, cf. ver. 44, and the use
of κοινωνία = 'contribution', Rom. xv. 26; Heb. xiii. 16.

τῇ κλάσει τοῦ ἄρτου] 'the breaking of bread', R.V.
The 'breaking of bread' at common meals, which was
practised by the other believers, cf. ver. 46, is mentioned as
the third point in which these new converts observed the
same practices.

At a meal he who presided first blessed and then broke
bread, cf. Luke xxiv. 30; Acts xxvii. 35. This act Jesus
had performed (Matt. xxvi. 26 λαβὼν ἄρτον εὐλογήσας ἔκλασε,
Luke xxii. 19 λ. ἄ. εὐχαριστήσας ἔκλασε) during[1] the Last
Supper, and had by a solemn command added to it a special significance. Thenceforth with the disciples that special significance attached to the 'breaking of bread' at
their common meals. It so attaches to the 'breaking of
bread' in the Holy Communion. At first, however, "and
for some time till abuses put an end to the practice (cf.
1 Cor. x. xi.), the Holy Communion was inseparably con- A. and
nected with the ἀγάπαι or 'love-feasts' of the Christians and so B.

---

[1] Matt. xxvi. 26 says 'while they were eating'. Edersheim
describing the Paschal ritual says that the 'Head of the Company'
would at the commencement of the meal "break one of the un-
leavened cakes, of which half was put aside for after supper and
called the *Aphikomon* or 'after-dish'." The Aphikomon is again
broken and eaten at the close of the meal in connection with the
third cup, or 'cup of blessing'. Although this custom only commenced when the Paschal Lamb ceased to be offered, Edersheim
considers that the 'breaking of bread' by Jesus *during* the meal is
to be connected with it. II. 510.

unknown as a separate ordinance". Cf. ver. 46 κλῶντες
...ἄρτον, μετελάμβανον τροφῆς, and xx. 7, xxvii. 35.

To simply explain τῇ κλάσει τοῦ ἄρτου as = 'The Holy
Communion , is to pervert the plain meaning of words,
and to mar the picture of family life, which the text places
before us as the ideal of the early believers.

Before τῇ κλάσει T.R. has καί, which does not alter the
sense: in the text the four things are put in two pairs.

ταῖς προσευχαῖς] For the regular hours of prayer cf.
iii. 1 n.

Vv. 43—47. A brief general description of the position
of the Church (1) as regarded by the people with a certain
'fear' due to the wonders wrought by the Apostles, (2) as
being a brotherhood or 'single family' living in common
and regarding all they had as belonging to the common
stock, (3) as increasing in numbers.

So B.
Baum.
M.

44. ἐπὶ τὸ αὐτό] of place, 'being together', cf. ver. 47,
and i. 15.

εἶχον ἄπαντα κοινά...] The text clearly describes the
early believers as treating individual property as subject to
the claims of all members of the community; cf. iv. 32.
It may be remarked, however, that (1) the rule was not
absolute even at first, cf. v. 4, and the special mention of the
'alms' of Dorcas ix. 36 ; (2) it is nowhere mentioned except
in the church at Jerusalem.

45. κτήματα] landed property; ὑπάρξεις, other property.
For the sense cf. Luke xii. 33 πωλήσατε τὰ ὑπάρχοντα ὑμῶν
καὶ δότε ἐλεημοσύνην.

αὐτά] 'them', i.e. the price received for them.

Herm.
ad Vig.,
p. 820.

καθότι ἄν...εἶχεν] Cf. iv. 35.   καθότι = 'just as'; καθότι
ἄν is more indefinite, 'non certo quodam tempore, sed quo-
tiescunque occasio ita ferret'.

46. κατ' οἶκον] 'at home', opposed to ἐν τῷ ἱερῷ, cf.
v. 42.

ἀφελότητι] The adj. ἀφελής = 'simple', 'blunt',
'straightforward', e.g. Dem. 1489, 10 ἀφελὴς καὶ παρρησίας
μεστός (ἀ priv. and φελλεύς, 'stony ground').

47. τοὺς σωζομένους] A.V. wrongly, 'such as should
be saved': R.V. rightly, 'those that were being saved', i.e.
those who joined the new Church (cf. σώθητε ver. 40), and
so came to be on the road to salvation.

CHAPTER III.

1. ἐπὶ τὸ αὐτό] T.R. reads τῇ ἐκκλησίᾳ after καθ᾽ Text
ἡμέραν, and begins the next sentence with ἐπὶ τὸ αὐτὸ δὲ ℵABCD.
Πέτρος....

Πέτρος καὶ Ἰωάνης] Frequently mentioned together:
as partners Luke v. 10; sent to prepare the Passover Luke
xxii. 8; running to the sepulchre John xx. 2—5. See too
Acts viii. 10.

ἀνέβαινον] The temple stood probably on Mt Zion, Smith's
the 'holy hill' (Ps. ii. 6), to the E. of Jerusalem. *Dict.*,
s.v. Jeru-

ἐπὶ τὴν ὥραν...] 'for', i.e. to be there at that hour. τὴν salem.
ἐνάτην: the adj. is often thus added after the noun to
make clear or definite some point as to which there might
otherwise be doubt, cf. ver. 2 τὴν λεγομένην.
There were three hours of prayer, the 3rd, the 6th, and
the 9th the time of the evening sacrifice, cf. Dan. vi. 10;
Ps. lv. 17.

2. καί τις ἀνὴρ...] A. and R.V. wrongly place a full
stop before καί: the sentence is 'they were going up...and
a lame man was being carried', cf. i. 10 n.

τὴν θύραν τὴν...] Not named elsewhere. It is perhaps
the gate of Nicanor on the E. side of the outermost court
of the temple looking towards Kidron, which Josephus, B. J.
after describing the other nine gates overlaid with gold and v. 5.
silver, describes as μία ἡ ἔξωθεν τοῦ νεὼ Κορινθίου χαλκοῦ,
πολὺ τῇ τιμῇ τὰς καταργύρους καὶ τὰς περιχρύσους ὑπεράγουσα. M. I.a.

τοῦ αἰτεῖν] gen. of purpose, or the thing aimed at: very
common, cf. ix. 15 τοῦ βαστάσαι, xx. 30 τοῦ ἀποσπᾶν.

ἐλεημοσύνην] 'that which is given in pity' (ἔλεος).
Hence our word 'alms'; Germ. *Almosen*.

3. ἠρώτα...] '*in me benefac tibi*' is a form of asking
alms quoted from the Rabbis. M.

5. ἐπεῖχεν] sc. τὸν νοῦν; cf. Luke vii. 14 ἐπέχων, πῶς
'when he marked how', 1 Tim. iv. 16 ἔπεχε σεαυτῷ. In
classical Gk much more frequently προσέχω.

6. ἐν τῷ ὀνόματι...] 'in the name...': the healing power
is *in* that name, and so *by* it the power is exercised. So
Luke ix. 49 ἐν τῷ ὀνόματί σου ἐκβάλλοντα δαιμόνια; x. 17
τὰ δαιμόνια ὑποτάσσεται ἡμῖν ἐν τῷ ὀν. σου, and Acts iv. 7,
10, ix. 27, xvi. 18.
For ἐν cf. ἐν τίνι iv. 9 n.

The 'name of Jesus' is a phrase frequent in the Acts. It should be borne in mind that in Hebrew 'name' often does not "mean a definite appellation but denotes office, rank, dignity. The 'Name of God' in the O. T. denotes the Divine Presence or the Divine Majesty, more especially as the object of adoration and praise. To praise the *name*, to bless the *name*, to fear the *name* of God are frequent expressions. Gesenius defines the 'name of God' (*Thes.* p. 1432) as '*Deus quatenus ab hominibus invocatur, celebratur*.'"

Light. ad Phil. ii. 9.

In the Acts the 'name of Jesus' comprehends the idea of His person, power, and dignity as acknowledged to be Messiah and Lord; it sums up the cause which the Apostles advocated; hence such expressions as ὑπὲρ τοῦ ὀνόματος ἀτιμασθῆναι v. 41, παθεῖν ix. 16, παραδεδωκόσι τὰς ψυχὰς ὑπὲρ τοῦ ὀνόματος τοῦ κυρίου ἡμῶν Ἰησ. Χρ. xv. 26.

7. παραχρῆμα] A strong word. 'Parallel to' or 'along with the act', i.e. of Peter's taking him by the hand; 'then and there'. The word occurs ten times in Luke, six times in the Acts, twice in Matt., and nowhere else in N. T.

αἱ βάσεις] 'things to go upon', 'feet', as in Plat. *Tim.* 92 A.

τὰ σφυδρά (T. R. σφυρά) 'ankle-bones', '*tali*'. *Proprie locutus est medicus Lucas.* B.

8. ἐξαλλόμενος] 'leaping *up*'. Cf. Is. xxxv. 6, 'Then shall the lame man leap as a hart'.

ἔστη] one single act; περιεπάτει, 'kept walking about'.

10. ἐπεγίνωσκον] A. V. 'knew'; R. V. rightly 'took knowledge of'. The word indicates the direction of the perceptive powers *towards* an object, often producing consequent recognition. Cf. iv. 13, xii. 14, xix. 34, xxvii. 39.

θάμβους] amazement mingled with awe, cf. Luke iv. 36, v. 9 θάμβος περιέσχεν αὐτόν. So often in classical Gk, e.g. *Od.* iii. 372 θάμβος δ' ἔλε πάντας ἰδόντας.

ἐκστάσεως] The condition of one who is no longer in his ordinary state of mind. Like the frequent ἐξίστασθαι (cf. ii. 7, 12) it often describes amazement, as here, and Mark v. 42. But x. 10, xi. 5, xxii. 17 = 'a trance'.

ἐπὶ τῷ συμβ.] ἐπὶ with the dat. is very frequently used of that which is the *ground* or *foundation upon* which some feeling or act is based. Here the miracle is the ground of their amazement.

Cf. iii. 12 θαυμάζειν ἐπὶ τούτῳ; iii. 16 ἐπὶ τῇ πίστει, resting on faith as the foundation; iv. 9 ἀνακρινόμεθα ἐπ' εὐεργεσίᾳ, of the subject-matter of the inquiry; λαλεῖν ἐπὶ τῷ

ὀνόματι making the name the basis of the preaching, and
v. 28, 40, xv. 31, xx. 38.

11. κρατοῦντος...τὸν II.] 'holding', and so naturally
with acc. Where the sense of 'winning', 'gaining possession of' prevails the gen. is more common, cf. xxvii. 13,
and Soph. *O. C.* 1380 τοὺς σοὺς θρόνους κρατοῦσιν with 1385
γῆς ἐμφυλίου κρατῆσαι.

ἐπὶ τῇ στοᾷ...] Solomon's porch was on the E. of the
temple. It was said to be an original work of Solomon
which had survived from the former temple. Jos.*Ant.* xx. 9. 7.

ὁ λαὸς...ἔκθαμβοι] Construction according to the sense.
Cf. v. 16 πλῆθος...φέροντες, vi. 7 ὄχλος...ὑπήκουον, xi. 1
ἔθνη...ἐδέξαντο.

12. ἀπεκρίνατο] 'answered', i.e. not any expressed
question, but their obvious desire for information, cf. v. 8
ἀπεκρίθη, where Sapphira had probably come desiring information about her husband; cf. too x. 46; Luke iii. 16; and
Matt. xi. 25.

ἡμῖν] Emphatic by position, and so parallel to ἰδίᾳ:
'Why gaze on *us?* It is not by *our own* power...'.

δυνάμει] *causa effectiva; εὐσεβείᾳ, causa meritoria.* M.

πεποιηκόσιν τοῦ περιπατεῖν] The gen. of purpose with
the inf. (cf. iii. 2 n.) becomes increasingly frequent in later
Gk, and the idea of purpose passes often, as here, into
that of result : or rather it may be said that the gen. gives
the *contents* of the action described by the verb, cf. xxvii. 1
ἐκρίθη τοῦ ἀποπλεῖν where the gen. gives the contents of the
decision (cf. xx. 3 ἐγένετο γνώμης τοῦ ὑποστρέφειν, where τοῦ
ὑπ. gives the contents of the γνώμη : 'the determination'
was 'to return'), and vii. 19 ἐκάκωσε...τοῦ ποιεῖν, where the
gen. gives the act in which the κάκωσις consisted. Cf. also
ix. 1 n.

13. ὁ θεὸς...] Ex. iii. 6; Matt. xxii. 32; Acts vii. 32.
For ὁ θ. τῶν πατέρων cf. v. 30; 1 Chron. xii. 17.

ἐδόξασεν] 'glorified', i.e. by means of the miracle just
wrought, which was wrought through faith in Jesus (ver.
16) and set forth His 'glory'; and this is no cause for
wonder, Peter urges, but is in accordance with Jehovah's
clear declaration of Jesus as Messiah, as shewn in raising
Him from the dead (ver. 15) and receiving Him into
heaven (ver. 21). So La. M.

τὸν παῖδα] R. V. 'his Servant', adding in margin 'or
Child', and so throughout the Acts. The phrase 'servant
of Jehovah' is specially applied to Messiah in the second
part of Isaiah. Cf. Is. xlii. 1—7, xlix. 1—9, lii. 13—liii. Baum. and Cheyne, *Is.* ed. 2, Essay 4.

12. Cf. too Matt. xii. 18, where Is. xlii. 1 'Behold my servant (παῖς) whom I have chosen' is referred to Jesus. The term παῖς θ. is also frequently applied to Israel, cf. Luke i. 54 Ἰσραὴλ παιδὸς αὐτοῦ; it is used of David, Luke i. 69; Acts iv. 25. The term for 'Son of God' is υἱὸς θεοῦ. The Apostles do not call themselves παῖδες θ. but δοῦλοι θ., cf. iv. 29; Tit. i. 1, Παῦλος δοῦλος θ.

M.

ὑμεῖς μὲν...] Nothing formally answers to μέν. The real antithesis is ver. 15, ὃν ὁ θεὸς ἤγειρεν. Cf. the strong opposition throughout, ὁ θεὸς...ὑμεῖς μὲν...ὑμεῖς δὲ...ὁ θεός.

ἠρνήσασθε] 'denied', i. e. that he was Messiah, Luke xxiii. 2; John xix. 15. ἠρνήσατο is the word used by all four Evangelists of Peter's 'denial'.

Baum.

κρίναντος] Luke xxiii. 13—22.

ἐκείνου] Not αὐτοῦ, and so pointing the antithesis between *them* and *him*.

M.

14. τὸν ἅγιον καὶ δίκ.] Strong contrast to ἄνδρα φονέα. For τὸν ἅγ. cf. Luke iv. 39, ὁ ἅγ. τοῦ θεοῦ, and ὁ ἅγιος Ἰσραήλ is applied continually to Jehovah in Isaiah, e. g. xliii. 3. Jesus is also called ὁ δίκαιος vii. 52, xxii. 14.

ἄνδρα φονέα] Luke xxiii. 18, 19.

χαρισθῆναι] The word indicates 'to grant as a favour', not as a matter of right or justice: it is used accurately here and xxv. 11, xxvii. 24.

15. τὸν ἀρχηγὸν τῆς ζ.] A. and R.V. 'Prince of life', and in margin 'Author'. For ἀρχηγός applied to Jesus cf. v. 31, ἀρχ. καὶ σωτῆρα; Heb. ii. 10 ἀρχ. τῆς σωτηρίας; xii. 2 τῆς πίστεως ἀρχ. καὶ τελειωτὴν Ἰησοῦν.
In classical Gk the word is used='founder' of a race (Soph. *O. C.* 60) or city (Plat. *Tim.* 21 ε), and also='a general', Aesch. *Ag.* 259; Thuc. I. 132 Ἑλλήνων ἀρχ. of Pausanias.
It seems here (and v. 31) rather to mean 'Prince' or 'Leader of life', i. e. he who leads to life and salvation: the idea seems that of a chief who leads his followers to win life. The words are in strong contrast to ἀπεκτείνατε.

16. τῇ πίστει τοῦ ὀν.] For ὄνομα cf. iii. 6 n. τοῦ ὀν. is the objective gen. The name of Jesus is that *to* which their belief is directed: they believe that He is Messiah and so has power to heal. Observe the emphatic repetition of πίστις and τὸ ὄνομα.

ἡ πίστις ἡ δι' αὐτοῦ] 'the faith which comes through Him': Jesus gives the faith, and is also the object of it.

ὁλοκληρίαν] Cf. Plat. *Tim.* 44 c ὁλόκληρος ὑγίης τε παντελῶς. ταύτην: deictic.

17. καὶ νῦν] Favourite particles of transition in speeches in the Acts; cf. vii. 34, x. 5, xxii. 16. So too καὶ τὰ νῦν iv. 29, v. 38, xx. 32, xxvii. 22. καὶ νῦν, ἰδού not only connects a new statement with what precedes, but gives marked emphasis to it, cf. xiii. 11, xx. 22.

ἀδελφοί] Much more affectionate than ἄνδρες ἀδ., cf. ii. 29 n. *Appellatio comitatis et misericordiae plena.* B.

κατὰ ἄγνοιαν] Luke xxiii. 34.

18. , πάντων τῶν π.] Luke xxiv. 27; Acts x. 43. That Jesus is the Messiah, to whom all prophecy points, is the argument of all speeches addressed to Jews in the Acts.

παθεῖν τὸν χριστὸν] 'that the Messiah should suffer'; cf. xvii. 3 and xxvi. 23, εἰ παθητὸς ὁ χρ. To Peter's hearers the words would be an immense paradox. They looked for a triumphant Messiah: a crucified Messiah was an idea they could not reconcile with their hopes, a 'stumblingblock' as Paul calls it 1 Cor. i. 23 Χριστὸν ἐσταυρωμένον, 'Ιουδαίοις σκάνδαλον. Cf. too Peter's own use of τὰ τοῦ Χρ. παθήματα 1 Pet. iv. 13, v. 1. In all these cases no version can reproduce the force the words originally had. *(margin: Cheyne, Is. Essay 5.)*

19. μετανοήσατε...] Change of mind is to produce change of attitude. They are to 'turn' from sin (cf. ver. 26) and look 'towards (i.e. keep before them as their object) the blotting out of their sins'. Cf. ἐπιστρέφειν ἐπὶ τὸν κύριον ix. 35, xi. 21; ἐπὶ τὸν θεὸν xiv. 15, xv. 19, xxvi. 20; εἰς φῶς xxvi. 18; absolutely xxviii. 27; Luke xxii. 32.

ἐξαλιφθῆναι] 'blotted out', and so commonly in classical Gk, e.g. Dem. 791, 12 ἐξαλήλιπται τὸ ὄφλημα. Lit. = 'smear out', of obliterating the writing on a wax tablet.

20. ὅπως ἄν...] 'in order that so'; R.V. 'that so'. ὅπως ἄν differs from ὅπως in making the end spoken of somewhat more conditional or dependent upon something else happening; here it gives the sense 'repent that so (i.e. when you have repented) times &c.' The words convey the idea that the 'times of refreshing' can only follow the repentance. Cf. carefully xv. 17, and Luke ii. 35 ὅπως ἄν ἀποκαλυφθῶσιν. *(margin: Jelf, Gk Gram. § 810.)*

καιροὶ ἀναψ.] These words are defined by the words which follow (καὶ ἀποστείλῃ...) as referring to the second coming of Messiah in glory. This was the παράκλησις τοῦ 'Ισραήλ Luke ii. 25.

τὸν προκεχειρισμένον...] 'him who was appointed (or 'elected') for you as Messiah, even Jesus'. For προχει-ρίζεσθαι cf. xxii. 14, xxvi. 16.

Text   T. R. reads Ἰησοῦν Χρ.—an excellent specimen of ignorant
NBDEP.   correction.

21. οὐρανὸν μὲν] The acc. *before* the verb. Take away δεῖ, and the statement is ὃν οὐρανὸς μὲν δέξεται.... Nothing formally answers to μὲν, but the real antithesis is clear. Jesus shall remain in *heaven* 'until the restoration of all things', then He shall return in glory to *earth*.

χρόνων ἀποκατ.] The same as the καιροὶ ἀναψύξεως. The phrase describes the period of Messiah's reign in glory, II. cf. i. 6 n. 'The word ἀποκατάστασις is applied by Josephus to the return from captivity, and by Philo to the restitution of inheritances in the year of jubilee'. The phrase 'restora-tion of all things' seems to have been used specially with reference to the Messianic time, cf. Matt. xvii. 11 Ἠλίας μὲν ἔρχεται καὶ ἀποκαταστήσει πάντα.

ὧν] with χρόνων; the words ἀποκατ. πάντων form a single idea, and if the reference were to them ἧς would be needed.

διὰ στόματος] as the channel or instrument through which God's words were communicated.

22. Μωυσῆς μὲν] Peter justifies his reference to 'all the prophets' (1) by quoting from Moses, the greatest of them, (2) by referring to 'the prophets from Samuel' who also all (καὶ πάντες) foretold Messiah. The same division into 'Moses' and 'all the prophets' is made xxvi. 22; Luke xxiv. 27.

προφήτην] Quoted again vii. 37; taken with slight variations from LXX. Deut. xviii. 15—19. For προφήτην cf. xi. 27 n.

ὡς ἐμέ] A. and R.V. 'like me', but R.V. in margin 'as he raised up me', which is the only rendering the Gk will bear.

For Moses as a type of Christ cf. Stephen's speech chap. vii. The Jews regarded him as the greatest of the prophets (cf. Deut. xxxiv. 10), with whom alone 'the Lord spake face to face, as a man speaketh to his friend', Ex. xxxiii. 11.

αὐτοῦ] Emphatic. ἀκούσεσθε, 'hear' with the combined idea of 'hearken', 'obey', cf. iv. 19 θεοῦ ἀκούειν.

23. ἐξολεθρ.] LXX., following the Hebrew, ἐγὼ ἐκδικήσω ἐξ αὐτοῦ, 'I will require it of him', i.e. exact punishment from him. For this Peter substitutes a phrase very common M. (e.g. Gen. xvii. 14) in LXX. 'that soul shall be cut off (ἐξολεθρ.) from his people', which indicates (1) separation from among the chosen people, (2) sentence of death.

24. ἀπὸ Σ. καὶ τῶν καθ.] 'from S. and those that succeeded him', a slightly inaccurate but very clear expression = 'all the series of prophets beginning with S.' For the absence of prophecy before Samuel cf. 1 Sam. iii. 1: it is in his time that we first hear of the 'schools of the prophets'.

25. ὑμεῖς…ὑμῖν πρῶτον] The emphatic position of these words marks the argument. 'You are the…therefore to you first…'.

διαθήκης] Cf. vii. 8 n. For the covenant cf. Gen. xii. 1—3. The quotation is from Gen. xxii. 18. In Gal. iii. 16 the words τῷ σπέρματί σου are definitely referred to Christ. 'In Him the race was summed up. In Him it fulfilled its purpose and became a blessing to the whole earth'. Lightfoot, *ad loc.*

26. πρῶτον] *Praevium indicium de vocatione gentium.* B. It must not however be supposed that Peter as yet had a complete idea of the universality of Messiah's kingdom. Like the Jews generally he believed that other nations would share its blessings, but he was as yet ignorant that they could do so otherwise than by accepting Judaism.

ἀναστήσας] as in ver. 22.

ἐν τῷ……] 'the turning away each of you' is that *in* which the blessing has its place of action.

CHAPTER IV.

1. οἱ ἀρχ.] v. 24 n.

ὁ στρατ. τοῦ ἱεροῦ] The temple was guarded by 24 bands of Levites, one band being on duty at a time. The commanders of these bands are the στρατηγοί of Luke xxii. 4 τοῖς ἀρχιερεῦσι καὶ στρατηγοῖς, and some think that ὁ στρατ. here = 'the commander of the band then on duty', but from the prominent position assigned him v. 24 it is perhaps better to regard him as the captain of the whole body.

καὶ οἱ Σαδδ.] Naturally 'sore troubled', because they denied a resurrection, cf. Matt. xxii. 23 Σαδδ. λέγοντες μὴ εἶναι ἀνάστασιν; Acts xxiii. 8. They were the opponents of the Pharisees (1) as denying that an oral law had been given to Moses in addition to the written law, (2) as denying a resurrection because it is not mentioned in the written law.

2. ἐν τῷ Ἰησ.] 'in', i.e. in the person, or in the case of Jesus. *Unico exemplo refutabantur penitus.* B.

4. ἐγενήθη] i.e. the total number of believers *was made* by this addition about 5000.

5. συναχθῆναι...] i.e. a meeting of the Sanhedrin. Little is known of it, except that it numbered 70 or 72 members. The Rabbis referred its institution to Numb. xi. 16, 17, but its Gk name (συνέδριον) shews its late origin. It may be the same as the γερουσία τῶν Ἰουδαίων 2 Macc. i. 10, iv. 44, xi. 27.

Before it Jesus was brought, cf. Matt. xxvi. 3; Mark xiv. 53, and Luke xxii. 66, where it is also called τὸ πρεσβυτέριον τοῦ λαοῦ; its members are described as 'chief priests' (=οἱ ἄρχοντες here), 'elders' and 'scribes'—*qui conspicui erant imperio, consilio, doctrina.* B.

τοὺς γραμματεῖς] *Sopherim*, 'writers'. A body of men who rise into importance during the Captivity, probably owing to the growing necessity of carefully preserving the sacred writings. Ezra (vii. 12) was 'a scribe of the law of the God of heaven'. Gradually, as Hebrew ceased to be the language of daily life, they became the expounders of scripture. The comments and expositions of their great teachers or 'Rabbis' were handed down by 'tradition', and began to be treated as more authoritative than the original text, the plain sense of which they frequently altered, cf. Matt. xxiii. These 'traditions' were, subsequently to the Christian era, embodied in the Talmud. At this time the scribes were practically the religious teachers of the Jews.

6. καὶ "Αννας] R.V. rightly supplies 'was there'. He was high-priest A.D. 7—14, and was then deposed by the Roman governor. Five of his sons became high-priests. Caiaphas was his son-in-law and legally high-priest at this time, having held the office A.D. 25—37. The influence of Hannas was clearly great among the Jews: Jesus was led away 'to Hannas first', John xviii. 13; he was to them still 'the high-priest' though no longer legally so. Luke (iii. 2) mentions both 'Hannas and Caiaphas' as being the high-priests, the one being so in the opinion of the Jews, the other by Roman law.

Of John and Alexander nothing is known, but no doubt they were prominent members of the 'kindred of Hannas' (γένος ἀρχιερατικόν), which is clearly described as forming a considerable portion of the Sanhedrin.

II. W.   **7. ἐν τῷ μέσῳ]** The council sat in a semicircle.

ἐν ποίᾳ...] Cf. iii. 6 n. Luke represents the Sanhedrin as ignorant, or ignoring, that they were disciples of Jesus, cf. ver. 13. Both the use of ποῖος and the position of ὑμεῖς mark contempt.

8. πλησθείς πν. ἁγίου] Cf. Luke xii. 11, 12. See too xix. 1 n.

9. εἰ] 'if', used with great rhetorical skill here, instead M. of ἐπεί: '*if*...for a *good* deed...we are being *tried*'.

ἀνακρινόμεθα] ἀνάκρισις at Athens was a preliminary enquiry to see whether an action would lie. Here, xii. 19, and Luke xxiii. 14, of examination by a judge.

ἐπ' εὐεργεσίᾳ] Emphatic,—as benefactors, not male-factors.

ἐν τίνι] 'wherein' or 'in whom', i.e. in what or in whom is the healing power which has made him whole, cf. iii. 6 n. and xi. 14 ῥήματα ἐν οἷς σωθήσῃ; Soph. *Ajax* 519 ἐν σοὶ πᾶσ' ἔγωγε σώζομαι. Practically ἐν = 'by'.

σέσωσται] The word can bear a double meaning, cf. ver. 12 ἡ σωτηρία and σωθῆναι. The bodily healing is the work of Him, who also heals the soul. Cf. the Collect for St Luke's Day, 'that by the wholesome medicine of the doctrine delivered by him, all the diseases of our souls may be healed'; Matt. i. 21 'Thou shalt call his name Jesus, for he shall save (αὐτὸς σώσει) his people from their sins'.

10. ὅν...ὅν...] The repeated word emphasizes the antithesis.

ἐν τούτῳ] After ὅν...ὅν and before οὗτος at the be-ginning of the next sentence, clearly masculine = 'in Him'.

11. ὁ λίθος] Ps. cxviii. 22 λίθον ὃν ἀπεδοκίμασαν οἱ οἰκο-δομοῦντες, οὗτος ἐγενήθη εἰς κεφ. γωνίας. Jesus had used this quotation of Himself Matt. xxi. 42; cf. 1 Pet. ii. 7. The 'head of the corner' was the highest corner-stone, of great importance in supporting the roof.

12. ἡ σωτηρία] Absolutely, 'the salvation', i.e. the pro-mised salvation which Messiah is to bring, cf. Mal. iv. 2.

ἐν ἄλλῳ...ἕτερον] ἄλλος, 'one more', ἕτερος, 'one of two'. Salvation is not to be found '*in any besides,* for indeed there does not even exist *a second* name...'.

13. παρρησίαν] 'frank', 'free', 'fearless speech', cf. vv. 29, 31. παρρησιάζεσθαι is also frequently used of the preaching of the Apostles, cf. ix. 27, 28, xiii. 46, xiv. 3.

ἰδιῶται] A. and R.V. 'ignorant', which conveys a wrong idea. The word in classical Gk = (1) a private person, (2) one who is without special or professional knowledge of a subject, 'a layman', e.g. Thuc. II. 48. That it does not F. M. mean 'ignorant' cf. Plat. *Legg.* 830 A ἀνδρῶν σοφῶν, ἰδιωτῶν La. τε καὶ ποιητῶν. Here, like ἀγράμματος, it describes men who had never studied in the rabbinic schools, and had no special knowledge of rabbinic teaching.

ἐπεγίνωσκον] 'began to take notice of them', 'began to recognize who they were'.

16. ὅτι μὲν] answered by ἀλλὰ ver. 17.

γνωστὸν] A. and R.V. 'notable'. γνωστὸν is opposed to δοξαστὸν (e.g. Plat. *Rep.* 479 D), as that which is the *object of knowledge* to that which is the *object of opinion.* The healing was a fact about which definite knowledge was attainable; it was not a matter of mere conjecture.

17. ἀπειλησώμεθα...μηκέτι λαλεῖν] 'Let us threaten them', i.e. 'order them with threats, no longer...'. T. R. has ἀπειλῇ ἀπειλησώμεθα 'straitly threaten'.

Text
אABD.

τούτῳ] *non dignantur appellare nomen Iesu,* cf. v. 28. B. It is "an instance of that avoidance of the name of Christ, which makes the Talmud refer to Him most frequently as Pelonî—'so and so'."

F.

19. ἐνώπιον τοῦ θεοῦ] *coram Deo.* ἐνώπιον, ἐναντίον, ἔμπροσθεν, ἔναντι followed by θεοῦ or κυρίου are very frequent in O.T. The phrase expresses a belief in the immediate presence of Jehovah as viewing, judging, or attesting something; cf. vii. 46, viii. 21, x. 33; hence it is used in asseverations, e.g. Gal. i. 20 ἰδοὺ ἐνώπιον τοῦ θεοῦ ὅτι οὐ ψεύδομαι, and adjurations, e.g. 2 Tim. ii. 14 διαμαρτύρομαι ἐν. τοῦ κυρίου. Here that which is 'just in the sight of God' is appealed to as something higher than human justice.

H.

With Peter's answer cf. Socrates' words (Plato *Apol.* 17), ἐγὼ ὑμᾶς, ὦ ἄνδρες Ἀθηναῖοι, ἀσπάζομαι μὲν καὶ φιλῶ, πείσομαι δὲ τῷ θεῷ μᾶλλον ἢ ὑμῖν.

21. μηδὲν εὑρίσκοντες τὸ πῶς...] The words τὸ πῶς... are explanatory of the positive part of μηδὲν: 'not finding anything, i.e. any means of punishing them...', cf. xxii. 30 n.

They asked themselves πῶς κολασώμεθα αὐτούς; to that question they could find no answer 'owing to the people', i.e. because they feared an outbreak of indignation.

24. ὁμοθυμαδὸν] A strong word, 'with one impulse', with united eagerness': cf. v. 12, vii. 57, xv. 25. It is frequent in the Acts, but only used once elsewhere in N.T.

M.
Baum.
La. B. A.

εἶπαν] 'they said'. The words which follow are clearly not a general and fixed form of prayer, but refer definitely to the special circumstances. We may therefore suppose them to be uttered by some one Apostle, the rest of those present assenting to them, and possibly audibly joining in the well-known words of the Psalm.

Δέσποτα] The word seems to imply the ascription of supreme power and authority. It describes the relation of a master to servants or slaves, cf. δούλοις ver. 29, Luke ii. 29 νῦν ἀπολύεις τὸν δοῦλόν σου, δέσποτα; 2 Pet. ii. 1 τὸν ἀγοράσαντα αὐτοὺς δεσπότην ἀρνούμενοι. It is only used elsewhere of God in Jude 4 and Rev. vi. 10.

ὁ ποιήσας] cf. Gen. i. 1 ἐν ἀρχῇ ἐποίησεν ὁ θεὸς τὸν οὐρανὸν καὶ τὴν γῆν, and for the full phrase Ex. xx. 11.

25. ὁ τοῦ πατρὸς...] T.R. omits τοῦ πατρὸς ἡμῶν and πν. ἁγίου. The text given 'doubtless contains a primitive error'. 'A confusion of lines ending successively with ΔΙΑ ΔΑΔ ΔΙΑ may have produced πν. ἁγίου too high up, and caused the loss of one διά', a view supported by R.V. which gives 'by the Holy Ghost *by* the mouth of...'. *Westcott and Hort. Westcott.*

Δαυείδ] Throughout the Acts the Psalms are spoken of as written by David, in accordance with the common usage of speaking of them as 'the Psalms of David', he having been the great psalmist and the author of very many of them.

The reference is to Ps. ii. 1.

ἐφρύαξαν] (1) 'to neigh eagerly' or 'violently' of horses, (2) 'to be proud', 'haughty'.

ἔθνη...] The explanation is given in ver. 27. ἔθνη = the Romans; λαοί = the Jews (commonly called in LXX. ὁ λαός, the plural in ver. 27 perhaps referring to the 12 tribes); βασιλεῖς = Herod; ἄρχοντες = Pilate.

The distinction between ἔθνη = 'the nations', *gentes*, all non-Jewish peoples, 'Gentiles', and λαός = 'the people', 'the chosen people', must be most carefully noticed in the Acts. Cf. the use of *populus* = 'the Roman people' opposed to *gentes* Lucan *Phars.* I. 82, 83.

27. συνήχθησαν...Ἡρώδης τε καὶ Π. Π.] Luke alone (Luke xxiii. 12) mentions that in this matter Herod and Pilate 'were made friends together, for before they were at enmity'.

Herod Antipas was son of Herod the Great and tetrarch of Galilee and Peraea (xiii. 1). See Mark vi. 14—28; Luke iii. 19, 20, ix. 7, xiii. 31, 32. He was subsequently persuaded by his wife Herodias to go to Rome to obtain the title of king, but was opposed by his nephew Herod Agrippa, who had great influence with Caligula, and banished to Lugdunum A.D. 39. He died in exile.

Pontius Pilatus was appointed A.D. 25 sixth *procurator* of Judaea, which on the deposition of Archelaus, A.D. 6, had been attached to the province of Syria. A.D. 36 he was sent to Rome by Vitellius, governor of Syria, to answer a

charge brought against him by the Samaritans. His name
Pontius suggests a connection with the great Samnite
family of the Pontii, and Pilatus is perhaps=*pileatus*
('wearing the *pileus*' or cap worn by manumitted slaves)
and so may indicate that he was a *libertinus*.

ὃν ἔχρισας] i.e. at His baptism, cf. ii. 22 n. § 2.

28. ποιῆσαι] Inf. of purpose. The sentence is somewhat concisely put: they came together to bring about the
death of Jesus, and so (unwittingly) 'to do all that thy
hand...', cf. ii. 23 n.

29. ἔπιδε] occurs only twice in N.T., but is specially
used in classical Greek of the gods: it signifies to 'regard
with attention', either with a view to bless (cf. Luke i. 25
ἐπεῖδεν) or to punish. Cf. Hom. *Od.* XVII. 487 θεοὶ...ἀνθρώ-
πων ὕβριν τε καὶ εὐνομίην ἐφορῶντες.

30. ἐν τῷ ἐκτείνειν] *dum extendis* B., and so R.V. 'while
thou stretchest forth'. Better 'in stretching out' (or, as
A.V. 'by'); God gives His protection in stretching out His
arm.

The phrase 'with a stretched-out arm', ἐν βραχίονι
ὑψηλῷ, is common in O.T., e.g. Ex. vi. 6; Ps. cxxxvi. 12
ἐν χειρὶ κραταιᾷ καὶ ἐν β. ὑψ., where the use of ἐν is clear.

καὶ σημεῖα...γίνεσθαι] Subordinate to ἐν τῷ, and so
closely connected with τὴν χ. ἐκτείνειν: the miracles are the
visible proof of the outstretched arm. A. and R.V. put a
stop after ἴασιν and make γίνεσθαι depend on δός.

31. ἐσαλεύθη] Used of the effect of an earthquake xvi.
26: for 'earthquake' as a sign of the Divine Presence cf.
Ps. cxiv. 7 ἀπὸ προσώπου κυρίου ἐσαλεύθη ἡ γῆ: Is. ii. 19, 21.
See too Virg. *Aen.* III. 90.

ἐλάλουν...παρρησίας] Luke, with simple skill, describes
the fulfilment of their prayer in the very words of the
prayer ver. 29. Note the emphatic position of μετὰ παρρησίας, and cf. xxviii. 31.

32. καρδία καὶ ψυχὴ μία] *in credendis et agendis.
Egregius character.* B. So too others distinguish between
καρδία, the seat of thought and intelligence, and ψυχή, the
seat of the active affections and impulses. Such distinctions
are however hard to maintain, cf. 1 Chron. xii. 38 'the rest
of Israel were of one heart (ψυχὴ μία) to make David king';
2 Chron. xxx. 12 'the hand of God was to give them one
heart (καρδίαν μίαν) to do the commandments'.

The expression, with emphatic fulness, describes complete unanimity of thought and feeling, resulting naturally,
and not as a matter of enforced rule, in their considering

all believers as brothers, who could have no separate interests in heaven or on earth.

οὐδὲ εἷς] Much stronger than οὐδείς. For the fact cf. ii. 44 n.

ἔλεγεν] 'said', i.e. 'reckoned' or 'considered'.

33. ἀπεδίδουν] 'gave', A. and R.V. inadequately. The word indicates 'giving back', 'duly delivering' something entrusted to you. It is used for 'paying' a debt, Matt. xviii. 25; Luke vii. 42, for 'duly rendering' an account, Matt. xii. 36. The 'witness of the resurrection' was the special charge entrusted to the Apostles: they were bound 'duly to deliver' it.

τοῦ κυρ. Ἰησ. τῆς ἀναστάσεως] T. R. has τῆς ἀναστ. τοῦ κυρ. Ἰησ. In the text the second gen. explains and defines the first: their testimony was 'of the Lord Jesus' that is, of 'his resurrection'.

χάρις] Clearly=*gratia Dei*, as vi. 8 and St Paul *passim*. The proof of its presence is given in the next words 'For none was in want'. In the similar summary ii. 47 χάρις is definitely described as 'favour *with the people*', but that cannot affect it here, where it is used absolutely.

35. παρὰ τοὺς πόδας] To be taken literally, for teachers among the Jews (cf. xxii. 3 n.) and magistrates among the Romans sat on a raised seat, cf. Cic. *pro Flacco* c. 28 *ante pedes praetoris in foro expensum est auri pondo centum.* At the same time the words convey the ideas of submission and deference. [Quoted by A.]

36. Ἰωσήφ] T. R. Ἰωσῆς. The case of Joseph Barnabas is specially mentioned because of the important position Barnabas subsequently takes in the Acts, but the fact of its being mentioned at all shews that there can have been no absolute rule as to the sale of property.

For **ἐπικληθείς** cf. i. 23 n.

Υἱὸς Παρακλήσεως] A.V. 'son of consolation'; R.V. more accurately 'son of exhortation'. The sense of 'encourage', 'exhort' is certainly the first and most usual sense of παρακαλεῖν and παράκλησις. The phrase here clearly describes one who was remarkable in speaking for his power of 'encouraging', 'cheering', or 'exhorting'; cf. xi. 23 where παρεκάλει 'exhorted' is used of Barnabas, and 1 Cor. xiv. 3, where it is said that a preacher speaketh either 'instruction' (οἰκοδομήν) or 'exhortation' (παράκλησιν) or 'consolation' (παραμυθίαν).

παράκλησις is also used ix. 31, xiii. 15, xv. 31, and both
A. and R. V. give three different renderings, viz. 'com-
fort', 'exhortation' and 'consolation', though in all three
cases the word 'encouragement' would be suitable. In
2 Cor. i. 3—7 the sense of 'encouragement' is clearly
marked, e.g. παρακαλεῖν τοὺς ἐν θλίψει. In Luke ii. 25
προσδεχόμενος παράκλησιν τοῦ 'Ισραήλ = 'waiting for the encouragement of Israel', i.e. by the coming of Messiah.

The verb παρακαλεῖν is very frequent in the Acts and
means either to 'invite', 'beseech', e.g. xvi. 9 or 'to encourage', e.g. xx. 12.

παράκλησις ubi desides excitat est hortatio, ubi tris-
titiae medetur est solatium. B.

A. H.   Λευείτης] Levites were not allowed to hold land (Numb.
xviii. 20), but the Mosaic laws about the division of the
land seem to have been neglected after the Captivity.

Κύπριος τῷ γένει] Cf. xviii. 2 Ποντικὸν τῷ γένει;
xviii. 24 'Αλεξανδρεὺς τ. γ., in all three cases of *Jews*, the
phrase indicating their place of birth.

CHAPTER V.

1. 'Ανανίας] The Hebrew name of Shadrach (Dan.
i. 6, iii. 13), found in the *Benedicite*, = 'God is gracious'.
Σαπφείρη probably = 'beautiful'.

2. ἐνοσφίσατο] 'set apart', not to be handed over with
the rest. The same word is used of Achan taking for himself some of the dedicated spoil of Jericho, cf. Josh. vii. 1,
where 'committed a trespass in the accursed thing' is in
LXX. ἐνοσφίσαντο ἀπὸ τοῦ ἀναθέματος.

3. ὁ Σατανᾶς] A Hebrew word = 'adversary'. For
the sense cf. Luke xxii. 3 εἰσῆλθεν δὲ Σατανᾶς εἰς 'Ιούδαν,
and John viii. 44 'he is a liar and the father of it'.

The question addressed to Ananias implies that he might
have resisted.

ψεύσασθαί σε] 'so that thou shouldest cheat'; cf. ver. 21
ἀπέστειλαν...ἀχθῆναι αὐτούς.

So Valck.   ψεύσασθαι τὸ πνεῦμα : ἐψεύσω θεῷ] ψ. τινά is directly
in M.   'to cheat' or 'deceive a person'; ψ. τινί is 'to lie' or 'cheat
in the presence of a person', suggesting the idea of an insult or outrage against him.

οὐδεὶς ψευδόμενος θεὸν ψεύδεται, ψεύδεται θεῷ ὅστις ψεύδεται.

τὸ πνεῦμα τὸ ἅγ.] i.e. as present in the Apostles. The
Holy Spirit had been given them to guide them 'into all

truth' (John xvi. 13); an attempt to deceive them is an
attempt to deceive Him, or, as in ver. 9, 'to make trial' of
Him.

4. ἐξουσίᾳ] i. 7 n.

τί ὅτι] *quid est quod?* Cf. Luke ii. 49 τί ὅτι ἐζητεῖτέ με;
The form of question expresses some astonishment or indignation.

5. ἐξέψυξεν] Only here and xii. 23 in N. T., apparently
connoting a violent, not peaceful death. Classical Gk has
ἀποψύχω *animam agere.*

καὶ ἐγένετο φόβος...] Emphatically repeated ver. 11.

τοὺς ἀκούοντας] Probably as at ver. 11 'those who
heard of it': had the phrase referred only to those present
we should expect 'those who saw it'.

6. οἱ νεώτεροι]=οἱ νεανίσκοι ver. 10, the younger members of the congregation.

συνέστειλαν] A. V. 'wound him up', R.V. 'wrapped
him round'. The word means 'draw together', 'pack up',
and here describes the 'putting together' of the extended
limbs and 'wrapping up' of the body for carrying it out.
The regular word for 'arranging' a corpse for burial is
περιστέλλω, *compono.*

ἐξενέγκαντες] 'having carried him out', a regular word
in connection with burial, which with the Jews, as with the
Greeks and Romans, took place *outside* the city walls—a
rule founded partly on a reasonable regard for health,
partly on fear of ceremonial defilement (Numb. xix. 11).

7. ἐγένετο δὲ...] The construction is ' But it happened M.
—an interval of about three hours—and his wife came in '.
We should say 'it happened that'.
    That διάστημα is not the nom. to ἐγένετο but parentheti-
cal is shewn by comparing Luke ix. 28 ἐγένετο δὲ μετὰ τοὺς
λόγους τούτους ὡσεὶ ἡμέραι ὀκτὼ καὶ...ἀνέβη.

8. ἀπεκρίθη] iii. 12 n. Peter answers her expectant
looks with a question.

τοσούτου] Pointing to it. **ἀπέδοσθε:** plural, 'ye' not
'thou'.

9. οἱ πόδες] A dramatic form of expression, cf. Is. lii. 7
'How beautiful upon the mountains are the feet of him...'.
Alford remarks that the young men were probably bare-
footed and would not be *heard* coming.

11. τὴν ἐκκλησίαν] Here first used in the Acts of the
'assembly of believers'. The word is only found twice in

the Gospels: Matt. xvi. 18 'I will build my church', and
xviii. 17. It was however a well-known term for the ' congregation' of Israel, cf. vii. 38 n. In the Acts it is used of
any 'assembly', as xix. 32, but usually of the body of believers in any one place or town.

12—16. A brief description of the state of the Church
(viz. rapid growth and increasing influence due to the miracles wrought by the Apostles), introduced to explain the
strong and decisive action of the high-priest and rulers
described ver. 17.

That this is the connection is clear from the use of the
imperfect tense vv. 12—16, contrasted with the dramatic
ἀναστάς of ver. 17 and subsequent aorists. The imperfects
describe a state of things during a period of some duration:
the aorists express the single action which resulted from
that state of things.

The paragraph describes,

(1) The miracles wrought by the Apostles.
(2) The gathering of all believers in Solomon's porch.
(3) [1] The fact that, though none of the rest (i.e. the
priests and rulers) dared to join them, yet the people mag-
nified them.
(4) The great increase of believers, naturally resulting
(ὥστε) in a great public manifestation, viz. the placing
sick folk in the streets by the inhabitants of Jerusalem
and even the bringing them in great numbers from neighbouring cities.

It was this public manifestation which at last roused the
'envy' of the rulers.

H. M.   **12.** πάντες] i.e. all the believers, cf. ii. 1.

τῇ Στοᾷ Σολ.] iii. 11 n.

13. τῶν δὲ λοιπῶν] δέ is not adversative, but merely a
particle of transition here. So too μᾶλλον δέ, and συνήρχετο
δέ ver. 16.

W.   λοιπῶν is not opposed to the believers mentioned before,
but to λαός which follows. The opposition of the rulers
and the λαός has already been referred to iv. 21. Others,
who contrast λοιπῶν with πάντες and make it='non-
believers', are driven to render κολλᾶσθαι 'obtrude on
them', 'interfere with them', whereas it always denotes
close *friendly* intercourse, cf. ix. 26, x. 28, xvii. 34.

15. πλατείας] sc. ὁδούς.

---

[1] I do not understand the punctuation in the text, and adopt the
usual punctuation, removing the colon after αὐτοῖς and placing it
after λαός.

κραβάττων] *grabatus*, said to be a Macedonian word=
' a camp-bed'.

ἵνα...κἄν ἡ σκιὰ ἐπισκιάσει] T. R. *ἐπισκιάσῃ.* The construction in the text is that which is common with ὅπως in
classical Greek.

κἄν = καὶ ἐάν; the sentence fully expressed would be,
' that the shadow—*even if* only the shadow—of Peter...', =
' that *at any rate* the shadow...'.

16. ὀχλουμένους] The same word as ' vexed'; the root Curtius.
expresses ' restless movement'.

17. ἀναστάς] A pictorial word representing the commencement of vigorous action.   It is frequent in Luke and
the Acts and is sometimes to be taken literally, e. g. ver. 34,
ix. 11 *ἀνάστα πορεύθητι*, sometimes, as here, metaphorically,
e. g. ix. 18 *ἀναστὰς ἐβαπτίσθη*; xi. 7 *ἀναστὰς θῦσον*; xxii. 16
ἀναστὰς βάπτισαι; in both cases it vividly depicts *action*.
The similar use of *ἀνέστην* is also very common.

πάντες] i. e. those mentioned iv. 6 and other Sadducees.

αἵρεσις]=(1) ' a choosing', (2) ' a set of philosophic or
religious principles chosen', (3) as here, ' those who have
so chosen certain principles', ' a school', ' a sect'.   It is
applied to the Pharisees, xv. 5, xxvi. 5.   The Christians
were regarded as ' a sect' by the Jews, xxiv. 14, xxviii. 22.
The word does not in itself imply condemnation as ' heresy'
does, but a bad sense naturally soon attaches itself to the
word as implying division and disunion, cf. its use by Tertullus xxiv. 5 and Paul's objection to the word xxiv. 14.

ζήλου] A.V. ' indignation', R. V. ' jealousy'.   The word
(from ζέω) indicates ' eager action', and according to the
context bears a bad sense=' jealousy', or a good sense=
' emulation'.

18. ἐν τηρ. δημοσίᾳ] ' in the public prison': not as
A.V. ' the common prison', giving a somewhat wrong idea.
Cf. Thuc. v. 18 *τὸ δημόσιον.*

20. σταθέντες] cf. ii. 14 n.   The word is not only pictorial but suggests the idea of firmness.   Cf. too the emphatic
clearness of *ἐν τῷ ἱερῷ* and *πάντα*.

τῆς ζωῆς ταύτης] Cf. xiii. 26 ὁ λόγος τῆς σωτηρίας ταύτης.
' This life', ' this salvation'=the life, the salvation, which
Jesus came to give and which it is the duty of the Apostles
to preach.   Here the word ' life' suggests an antithesis to
the denial by the Sadducees of a life after death.

21. ὑπὸ τὸν ὄρθρον] *sub lucem.*

πᾶσαν τὴν γερουσίαν] The γερουσία of Sparta and
Senatus of Rome are well known. The word γερουσία is
used in 2 Macc. of the Sanhedrin, which is also called πρεσβυτέριον, cf. iv. 5 n. But here, as the Sanhedrin has been
specially mentioned, probably the word does not describe
any official body but is used generally to indicate men of
age and experience who, though not members of the Sanhedrin, may have been summoned to its meetings on occasions
of importance.

24. οἱ ἀρχιερεῖς] The heads of the twenty-four courses
of priests, and possibly the relatives of the high-priest, cf.
iv. 6. The word is used loosely, cf. xix. 14.

τί ἂν γένοιτο τοῦτο] The question τί γενήσεται τοῦτο
(' what will be the end' or 'result of this') put obliquely.

26. οὐ μετὰ βίας] Emphatic by position. R. V. therefore rightly, ' *but* not with violence'.

28. παραγγελίᾳ παρ.] cf. vii. 34 n.

ἐπαγαγεῖν...] i.e. to make them responsible for His
death, cf. Matt. xxvii. 25; and for the expression 2 Sam.
i. 16; Matt. xxiii. 35.

τοῦ ἀνθρώπου τούτου] cf. iv. 17 n.

29—31. θεῷ...ὁ θεὸς...ὃν ὑμεῖς...τοῦτον ὁ θεός] Note the
emphasis of these words.

30. ἤγειρεν] Without ἐκ νεκρῶν (like ἀνίστημι iii. 22,
26) = 'raised up', 'brought forward', cf. Luke i. 69 ἤγειρε
κέρας σωτηρίας ἡμῖν; Acts xiii. 22 ἤγειρεν αὐτοῖς τὸν Δαυείδ.
So   The reference is to His birth and coming forward as Mes-
Lange.   siah. The order of events is this : God raised Him up;
you crucified Him; God exalted Him.

διεχειρίσασθε] cf. xxvi. 21. The word connotes violence
and injustice: 'made away with violently'. The words
κρεμ. ἐπὶ ξύλου pointedly call attention to His treatment as a
malefactor and accursed man, cf. Deut. xxi. 23 κεκατηραμέ-
νος ὑπὸ θεοῦ πᾶς κρεμάμενος ἐπὶ ξύλου: Gal. iii. 13.

31. ἀρχηγὸν] iii. 15 n. Here clearly 'Prince'.

(τοῦ) δοῦναι] 'to give', i.e. that He may give, in His
character of Prince and Saviour. The passage must be
compared with Luke xxiv. 47, 48, where Jesus gives His
parting injunctions to the Apostles and orders that there
be proclaimed as by heralds (κηρυχθῆναι) 'repentance'—the
condition He imposes as a Prince, and 'remission of sins'
—the reward He offers as a Saviour. He then adds ὑμεῖς
μάρτυρες τούτων, to which here ἡμεῖς ἐσμὲν μάρτυρες τῶν
ῥημάτων τούτων accurately corresponds. Finally He says,
'and behold I send the promise of my Father (i.e. the

Holy Spirit) upon you', and so here Peter speaks of the
Holy Spirit as actually sent and present in them, joining
them as a ' witness' to the events they relate.

32. ῥημάτων] Not ' sayings' but ' things expressed in
words', 'history', 'story'; cf. Luke ii. 15 τὸ ῥῆμα τὸ γεγο-
νός, and the important instance Acts x. 37.

34. **Φαρισαῖος**]=' separated', the name of an important Jewish sect; they believed (1) that an oral law had been
given to Moses in addition to the written law, and had been
handed down by tradition; (2) that the actual law needed to
be supplemented by the explanations of the great doctors,
which established ' a hedge round the law' and enjoined an
immense number of minute ritual observances; (3) in opposition to the Sadducees, that there is a future life.

Γαμαλιήλ] Grandson of the great teacher Hillel;
afterwards president of the Sanhedrin; known as 'the
glory of the law'; one of the seven Rabbis to whom the
higher title of Rabban was given: teacher of St Paul, xxii. 3.

νομοδιδάσκαλος] So νομικός Matt. xxii. 35.   A teacher
or expounder of the Mosaic law.

παντὶ τῷ λαῷ] Ethic dat. = ' in the opinion of', cf.
Eur. *Hec.* 309 ἡμῖν δ' Ἀχιλλεὺς ἄξιος τιμῆς, and vii. 20 n.

τοὺς ἀνθρώπους] T. R. τοὺς ἀποστόλους.   Gamaliel
would certainly not call them 'Apostles': the reading of
the text is much more vigorous and real.

36. **Θευδᾶς**] Gamaliel clearly speaks of the revolt of Jos. *Ant.*
Theudas as preceding that of Judas.   On the other hand xx. 5. 1,
Josephus describes a revolt very similar to this one and full in
headed by a Theudas in A.D. 44, and therefore subsequent to A.
this speech.   Commentators therefore either (1) assume a
historical error here, (2) or, not unreasonably, consider that
among the many risings which took place in Judaea about
the time of the birth of Jesus, there may have been another W
insurgent leader of that name.

λέγων εἶναί τινα ἑαυτόν] cf. viii. 9; Gal. vi. 3 εἰ γὰρ δοκεῖ
τις εἶναί τι μηδὲν ὤν; Soph. *El.* 939 ηὔχεις τις εἶναι, the
nom. after the verb being more classical.   The use of
' somebody'=' some great person', as opposed to ' a no-
body', is common in many languages.   From the use however of almost the same phrase of Simon Magus (viii. 9)
it would seem that Theudas is described as having claimed
to be more than human, possibly to be the promised Messiah.   Jos. *Ant.*
                                                   xviii. 1.
37. **Ἰούδας ὁ Γαλ.**]   In Josephus called Ἰούδ. ὁ Γαυ- 1, given
λανίτης, having been born in the city of Gamala in Gaulani- in A.

tis. His insurrection was in connection with ' the taxing', and he maintained that God alone was the king of Israel. His followers known as Gaulonites seem to have passed into the well-known Zealots.

ἐν ταῖς...] i. e. the celebrated 'registration' or 'enrolment' with a view to taxation referred to Luke ii. 2, which took place A.D. 6 under the prefecture of P. Sulpicius Quirinus.

38, 39. ἐὰν ᾖ ἐξ ἀνθ....εἰ δὲ ἐκ θεοῦ ἐστίν] ' in case it be... if it is'. εἰ with ind. represents a thing as less conditional and more possible than ἐὰν with subj. It must not be inferred however that Gamaliel indicates the second alternative as more likely to be true ; the change of construction only indicates that he puts forward one of two alternatives, as the one the *possibility* of which he wishes to be considered, as being the foundation of his argument.

La. A. dubiously.

39. θεόμαχοι] *Il.* VI. 129 οὐκ ἂν ἔγωγε θεοῖσιν ἐπουρανίοισι μαχοίμην.

41. κατηξιώθησαν ἀτιμασθῆναι] Oxymoron.

τοῦ ὀνόματος] iii. 6 n.

42. κατ᾽ οἶκον] ii. 46 n.

εὐαγγ. τὸν χριστὸν Ἰησ.] ' preaching the Messiah, even Jesus'.

CHAPTER VI.

1. γογγυσμὸς] Imitative reduplicated word = ' murmuring'.

Ἑλληνιστῶν] from Ἑλληνίζω ' to imitate or use the manners, customs, or language of the Greeks' [cf. Λακωνίζω, Μηδίζω, Ἰουδαΐζω (Gal. ii. 14), Φιλιππίζω] = those Jews who, having settled out of Palestine, habitually spoke Greek, and probably adopted many foreign customs, whereas Ἑβραῖοι = those Jews who, continuing to live in Palestine, spoke Syro-Chaldaic, and were more strict in their observance of the laws of Moses.

2. οὐκ ἀρεστόν ἐστιν] *non placet*, a somewhat authoritative phrase, cf. ver. 5, ἤρεσεν, *placuit*, of the adoption of the proposition by the assembly.

διακονεῖν τραπέζαις] Note the emphatic position of τραπέζαις. The Apostles do not object to ' serve', but to ' serve tables': they desire to confine themselves to the ' service of the word' (τῇ διακονίᾳ τοῦ λόγου).

The seven men here appointed are usually called ' the seven Deacons', but there is no authority for this in N. T., where they are only alluded to as ' the seven' (cf. xxi. 8). Their ' ministry' is distinctly opposed to the ' ministry of

the word', and it therefore seems clear that they are not
to be identified with that class of Christian ministers called
διάκονοι (1 Tim. iii. 8; Phil. i. 1) after whom 'Deacons' are
named.

The words διάκονος, διακονεῖν, διακονία are used (1) in the
Gospels, usually of ministering to bodily or temporal wants,
e.g. Matt. iv. 11; Luke x. 40, (2) in the Acts and Epistles,
usually of ministering to spiritual wants, e.g. Paul calls
himself διάκονος Χριστοῦ, δ. εὐαγγελίου. Lastly διάκονος is
used in a special sense of a definitely appointed minister =
'a Deacon' e.g. Phil. i. 1, σὺν ἐπισκόποις καὶ διακόνοις.

τραπέζαις] Used with some indignation = 'food', 'eating
and drinking'. τράπεζα is also used of the table of a money-
changer (e.g. Matt. xxi. 12), and τραπεζίτης = 'a banker',
but here the connection with διακονεῖν precludes the explanation 'tables at which the alms were distributed in small
coins'.

*H.
Lumby,
&c.*

3. μαρτυρουμένους] i.e. of acknowledged good life and
character, cf. x. 22, xvi. 2, xxii. 12.

οὓς καταστήσομεν] 'whom we *may* appoint', A. and
R. V. rightly. The future describes the second action as
subsequent to and dependent on the first; cf. the use of
ὅπως and ἵνα with the fut. ind. To render ' whom we *will*
appoint' would convey a wrong idea, cf. vii. 40 οἳ προπορεύσονται.

5. Στέφανον...] Notice with reference to the cause of
their appointment that all bear Greek names. Seven is a
sacred number. Of none except Stephen and Philip (cf.
viii. 5, xxi. 8) is there anything further mentioned in
N.T. Nicolaus has been identified with the founder of the
sect of 'the Nicolaitans' mentioned Rev. ii. 6, 15, but this
seems conjectural.

6. ἐπέθηκαν...] The laying-on of hands was used in
blessing, cf. Gen. xlviii. 14—20; Matt. xix. 13; at the
appointment of Joshua, Numb. xxvii. 18, and in *healing* by
Jesus, Mark vi. 5. The act seems symbolical of the trans-
mission of some divine power, cf. Acts viii. 17, ix. 17, xiii. 3,
xix. 6, xxviii. 8. It is employed in the Church of England at
Confirmation and Ordination.

7. ὄχλος...ὑπήκουον] iii. 11 n.

8. χάριτος] as iv. 33. *Gratia Dei δύναμιν efficit: δύναμιν demonstrant τέρατα καὶ σημεῖα.*

9. συναγωγῆς] 'place of meeting'. The institution of
'synagogues' dates from the Captivity. They were so

*Eders-
heim, I.
431—450.*

arranged that the congregation turned towards Jerusalem, and at the end opposite them was an ark or chest containing the Book of the Law. Towards the middle was a pulpit in which the reader stood and the preacher sat. Each synagogue had a 'minister' or attendant (ὑπηρέτης Luke iv. 20), and was under the management of a college of elders (πρεσβύτεροι Luke vii. 3 ; ἀρχισυνάγωγοι Acts xiii. 15), with a president ὁ ἀρχισυνάγωγος. There was a fixed liturgy, a reading of a first lesson from 'the Law' and a second from 'the Prophets' (cf. xiii. 15), and afterwards the Derash or exposition. It is said that there were 480 synagogues in Jerusalem, but the number is untrustworthy.

So M.

Λιβερτίνων] *libertinorum.* Probably descendants of the Jews taken to Rome as captives by Pompeius, who had there gained their freedom, and perhaps also proselytes of the freedman class, cf. ii. 10 n.

Three synagogues seem to be described : (1) of the Libertini, (2) of the men of Alexandria and Cyrene, both African cities, (3) of the men of Cilicia and Asia, who are joined together, as τῶν ἀπὸ clearly shews.

συνζητοῦντες] Used of the 'questionings' of the Pharisees and Scribes (Mark viii. 11, ix. 14): cf. too ix. 29.

τῶν ἀπὸ Κιλ.] Therefore probably including Paul. Tarsus is the capital of Cilicia.

10. ἀντιστῆναι τῇ σοφίᾳ] Cf. the promise of Jesus Luke xxi. 15 ἐγὼ δώσω ὑμῖν στόμα καὶ σοφίαν ᾗ οὐ δυνήσονται ...ἀντιστῆναι.

11. ὑπέβαλον] *subornarunt.* The word indicates putting forward in an underhand way for purposes of fraud.

ἀκηκόαμεν...] As in the case of the false witnesses against Jesus (Matt. xxvi. 60, 61), the falsehood of these witnesses would consist in misrepresenting what Stephen had actually said. He had doubtless spoken of the transitory nature of the Mosaic law and the Temple worship, and this they distort. Hence they are distinctly spoken of as 'false' or 'lying' (ψευδεῖς), because 'a lie that is half the truth is ever the blackest of lies'.

13. τοῦ τόπου τοῦ ἁγ.] i.e. the Temple, cf. xxi. 28. The emphatic position of the adjective marks the *special* holiness of the place, cf. i. 25 n.

14. ὁ Ναζ. οὗτος] οὗτος is contemptuous, cf. vii. 40, xix. 26.

καταλύσει] The word used Matt. xxvi. 61 δύναμαι καταλῦσαι τὸν ναόν. Stephen (vii. 48) points out that God ' dwelleth not in (buildings) made with hands'.

παρέδωκεν] *tradidit*, cf. Juv. xiv. 102 *Tradidit arcano quodcunque volumine Moses.*

15. εἶδαν...] Cf. Ex. xxxiv. 30; 2 Cor. iii. 7. Tennyson, *The Two Voices*, 'God's glory smote him on the face'.

CHAPTER VII.

The speech of Stephen must be considered in reference to the twofold charge (vers. 13, 14) to which it is an answer. The argument is throughout from Scripture, and is twofold, but the two threads are not kept distinct, but interwoven.

(1) He meets the charge of 'speaking against this Holy Place'—a charge no doubt founded on the fact of his having taught that worship in the Temple was not essential to the worship of God—by shewing that the worship of God is not confined to Jerusalem or the Jewish temple, this being proved by reference,

a. to His dealings with the patriarchs and people when in foreign lands, in Mesopotamia (ver. 2) and in Egypt (vers. 9—28);

b. to His appearing to Moses 'in the desert of Sinai' (ver. 30);

c. to the fact that all places are holy where God is (ver. 33);

d. to the 'church in the wilderness' (ver. 38);

e. to the fact that it was not until Solomon's time that the Temple was built, and that even that was not the real dwelling of the Most High (ver. 47), as is shewn by a quotation from Isaiah (vers. 48, 49).

(2) As regards the charge of changing 'the customs which Moses delivered', he points out that God had had many dealings with their fathers *before* the giving of the law (e.g. in the covenant of circumcision ver. 8), and that, far from contradicting Moses, Jesus is the very successor whose coming Moses had foretold (ver. 37). He describes Moses at length in words which clearly point him out as the type of Jesus: he was the divinely appointed redeemer of Israel (ver. 35), their saviour (ver. 25); the manner in which the Israelites again and again rejected him (vers. 25, 27, 35, 39) is typical of their rejection of Jesus. As he dwells on this theme the speaker, who began with calm and sober narrative, becomes gradually (as he remembers that his accusers are the children and representatives of those who consistently rejected Moses and the prophets) more argumentative and passionate, until at ver. 51 he breaks out into indignant invective and arraigns his accusers on the very charge which they were bringing against

himself—'Not I, but you, you are the men who received the law and *did not keep it*'.

The speech however is not wholly apologetic, but also constructive. Stephen prepares the way for Paul: he grasps the idea of a religion not exclusive but universal: he anticipates the final declaration of Paul in the Acts, viz. that the Jews will reject and the Gentiles accept the truth offered to them.

2. ὁ θεὸς τῆς δόξης] i.e. the God who reveals Himself in Glory. 'Glory'=the Shechinah, a visible radiance, which indicated the presence of God, and was believed to rest especially on the mercy-seat between the cherubim; cf. ver. 55; Luke ii. 9; Ex. xxiv. 16.   By commencing with these words Stephen at once refutes the charge of vi. 11.

Μεσοποταμία]=γῇ Χαλδαίων ver. 4, used loosely for the district beyond the Euphrates.   In Gen. xi. 31 it is 'Ur of the Chaldees'—a district of Mesopotamia N.E. of Haran.

Χαρράν] 'Haran' Gen. xi. 31; *Carrae*, an ancient town in Mesopotamia not far from Edessa.   Here Crassus met his death B.C. 53 after his defeat by the Parthians, cf. Luc. I. 104 *miserando funere Crassus | Assyrias Latio maculavit sanguine Carras.*

ὤφθη...πρὶν...καὶ εἶπεν...] The quotation is verbatim from LXX. Gen. xii. 1, where however the revelation is said to have been made *in* Haran.   In several instances however Stephen refers to traditions not identical with the statements in our present Pentateuch.   In Gen. xv. 7; Neh. ix. 7 the removal of Abraham from Ur is clearly referred to divine direction.

3. ἣν ἄν σοι δείξω] 'whichever I shall shew thee': *non norat Abram quae terra foret*, Heb. xi. 8.   B.

4. μετὰ τὸ ἀποθανεῖν...] In Gen. xi. 26—xii. 4 it is stated that Abraham was born when Terah was 70 years old, and that he left Haran when 75, Terah dying in Haran at the age of 205, and therefore 60 years *after* Abraham's departure. 'Stephen therefore follows an independent tradition'.

H.

μετῴκισεν] sc. ὁ θεός.

A.

5. οὐκ ἔδωκεν...] A perfectly natural expression: the 'burial-ground' which Abraham acquired (cf. ver. 16) could hardly be reckoned ' an inheritance '.

H.

The rendering of οὐκ ἔδωκεν 'had not yet given ' is downright mistranslation.   To lay stress on ἔδωκεν and explain *non ex donatione divina accepit Abram, quia emit* implies a singularly narrow view of God's gifts.

B. and
so de W.
&c.

For βῆμα ποδός cf. Deut. ii. 5; Cic. *ad Att.* XIII. 2 *pedem ubi ponat in suo non habet.*   II.

ἐπηγγείλατο...] Gen. xvii. 8, xlviii. 4.

6. ἐλάλησεν...] A free quotation of LXX. Gen. xv. 13, 14 which ends with the words μετὰ δὲ ταῦτα ἐξελεύσονται ὧδε μετὰ ἀποσκευῆς πολλῆς. The words καὶ λατρ. μοι ἐν τῷ τόπῳ τούτῳ (i.e. in Canaan) seem to be a reminiscence of Ex. iii. 12 καὶ λατρεύσετε τῷ θεῷ ἐν τῷ ὄρει τούτῳ (Horeb). The addition is natural, for in Gen. xv. 14 it is clear that ' they shall come out' refers to a coming out into Canaan, although the ὧδε of LXX. is not represented in the Hebrew.

πάροικον] 'sojourning'. The word indicates residence in a country which is not of a permanent character nor attended with full rights of citizenship. Cf. vii. 29, xiii. 17; Deut. xxvi. 5 κατέβη εἰς Αἴγυπτον καὶ παρῴκησεν ἐκεῖ; Eph. ii. 19 where ξένοι καὶ πάροικοι are opposed to συμπολῖται καὶ οἰκεῖοι; this life is 'a sojourning' 1 Pet. i. 17; we are all 'sojourners' 1 Pet. ii. 11.

ἔτη τετρακόσια] So too in round numbers Gen. xv. 13. The exact period of 430 years is given Ex. xii. 40; Gal. iii. 17. This includes the whole period from the giving of the promise to the Exodus (the period from the going down of Jacob into Egypt being 215 years), the 'sojourn' of the patriarchs in Canaan as well as of their descendants in Egypt. ἔτη τετρακόσια does not go merely with κακώσουσιν.

δουλώσουσιν] sc. οἱ ἀλλότριοι inferred from ἐν γῇ ἀλλοτρίᾳ.

7. κρινῶ ἐγώ] Emphatic. *Ego—Deus.*

8. διαθήκην περιτομῆς] A covenant of which circumcision was to be the outward sign. Gen. xvii. 9—14.

In classical Greek διαθήκη is almost always 'a testamentary disposition', 'a will', συνθήκη being 'a covenant' or 'agreement'. On the other hand in LXX. and N. T. διαθήκη is regularly='a covenant', and from its being rendered into Latin as '*testamentum*' we have our curious phrases 'The Old' and 'The New Testament' meaning the Old and New Dispensation or Covenant. 'The LXX. translators and New Testament writers probably preferred διαθήκη as better expressing the *free grace* of God than συνθήκη'.   Light. *ad Gal.* iii. 16.

οὕτως] 'thus', i.e. after this covenant had been made, and as an earnest of its fulfilment.

For the facts cf. Gen. xxi. 3, xxv. 26, xxix. 31—xxx. 21, xxxvii. 28.

9. ζηλώσαντες] cf. Gen. xxxvii. 11 ἐζήλωσαν. ἀπέδοντο

Gen. xxxvii. 28. ἦν ὁ θ. μετ' αὐτοῦ, cf. Gen. xxxix. 21 ἦν Κύριος μετὰ Ἰωσήφ.

10. Cf. Gen. xli. 37 et seq.

Φαραὼ βασ. Αἰγ.] Pharaoh is not a name but a title borne by the kings of Egypt. It corresponds with the P-RA or PH-RA of the hieroglyphics, which means 'the sun'.

Grotius.   ἡγούμενον] '*vice regis cuncta regentem.* Gen. xli. 43'.

11. χορτάσματα] 'Fodder for their cattle' (cf. χορτάζω), the word used in LXX. Gen. xxiv. 25, 32, xlii. 27 and trans-
M.   lated 'provender'. It was the first necessity of existence for great owners of flocks and herds like the patriarchs.

12. ἀκούσας...] Gen. xlii. 2 ἰδοὺ ἀκήκοα ὅτι ἐστὶ σῖτος ἐν Αἰγύπτῳ.

14. ἐν ψυχαῖς......] 'in', i.e. consisting in. The Heb. text Gen. xlvi. 26 gives the number who 'came with Jacob' as 66, and then ver. 27, reckoning in Jacob and Joseph with his two sons, gives the whole number as 70. The LXX. in ver. 27, reckoning in some grandchildren of Joseph, gives the number as 75.

16. μετετέθησαν] sc. αὐτὸς καὶ οἱ πάτερες ἡμῶν. Accord-ing to Gen. xlix. 30, l. 13, Jacob was buried 'in the cave of the field of Machpelah which is before Mamre' ('the same is Hebron in the land of Canaan' Gen. xxiii. 19): Joseph was embalmed (Gen. l. 26), taken away at the Exodus (Ex. xiii. 19), and ultimately buried at Shechem (Josh. xxiv. 32). Of the other patriarchs Scripture records nothing as to their burial.

ᾧ ὦν. Ἀβρ.] Gen. xxiii. 3—20. Abraham bought a burying-place at Hebron from Ephron. Jacob (Gen. xxxiii. 19) bought a field, not a burying-place, 'at Shalem, a city of Shechem' 'at the hand of the children of Hamor, Shechem's
A; so   father'. 'The two accounts are certainly here confused'.
La. H.
τιμῆς ἀργυρίου] Gen. xxiii. 16 'four hundred shekels of silver, current money with the merchant': Gen. xxxiii. 19 (of Jacob's purchase) 'an hundred pieces of money'.

17. καθὼς] 'as', not 'when': *as* the time drew near *so* the people....

τῆς ἐπαγγελίας] Cf. vers. 6, 7; and ii. 33 n.

ηὔξησεν, ἐπληθύνθη, ἀνέστη......Ἰωσήφ] LXX. Ex. i. 7.

M. refer-   **18.** ὃς οὐκ ᾔδει τὸν Ἰ.] i.e. who knew nothing of the
ring to   history and services of Joseph. 'The previous dynasty
Knobel   had been that of the Hyksos: the new king was Ahmes who
s. Ex. i.   drove out the Hyksos'.
8.

19. κατασοφ. τὸ γένος] σοφίζεσθαι 'to use subtle, unfair means' is intrans. but like many verbs (cf. καταπονεῖν ver. 24, καταδυναστεύω x. 38) becomes trans. when compounded with κατά = 'to injure by using subtlety'. In Ex. i. 10 it is rendered 'let us deal wisely with them'.

ἐκάκωσεν...τοῦ ποιεῖν...] 'so that he caused' or 'by causing their children to be exposed'. The genitive describes that in which the κάκωσις consisted (cf. iii. 12 n.), its purpose being expressed in the words εἰς τὸ μὴ ζ. **ζωογονεῖσθαι** = 'kept alive', cf. Ex. i. 17 ἐζωογόνουν τὰ ἄρσενα.

20. ἀστεῖος τῷ θεῷ] 'fair (in appearance) to God', i.e. 'before' or 'in the sight of God', θεῷ being an Eth. Dat. Cf. Aesch. *Ag.* 352 θεοῖς ἀναμπλάκητος 'guiltless in the sight of heaven'. A. and R.V. render 'exceeding fair', treating the phrase as a Hebrew method of expressing *extreme* fairness, cf. Jon. iii. 3 πόλις μεγάλη τῷ θεῷ; Gen. x. 9; 1 Sam. xvi. 12 ἀγαθὸς ὁράσει Κυρίῳ, 'of a beautiful countenance and *goodly to look to*'.

ἀστεῖος lit. 'belonging to the city', *urbanus;* 'witty'; then 'elegant', 'pretty', *lepidus:* it is applied to Moses LXX. Ex. ii. 2, and Heb. xi. 23 'a proper child' ἀστεῖον παιδίον.

μῆνας τρεῖς] Ex. ii. 2; **ἀνείλατο** Ex. ii. 5; **ἑαυτῇ εἰς ὑ.** Ex. ii. 10. The succeeding quotations up to ver. 35 are from the same chapter and the beginning of c. iii.

21. ἀνείλατο] *sustulit*, the opposite of ἐκτιθέναι, ἔκθετον ποιεῖν, *exponere*.

τοῦ πατρός] Amram; Ex. vi. 29.

22. πάσῃ σοφ. Αἰγ.] which was proverbial, cf. 1 Kings iv. 30; Her. II. 160 τοὺς σοφωτάτους ἀνθρώπων Αἰγυπτίους. The priestly caste were especially renowned for their M. knowledge of Natural Science (and Magic), Astronomy, Medicine and Mathematics.

δυνατὸς ἐν λόγ. καὶ ἔργοις] The phrase used of Jesus Luke xxiv. 19. δυν. ἐν λόγ. must not be taken as referring to 'rhetorical skill' or 'eloquence' (cf. Ex. iv. 10 'I am slow of speech and of a slow tongue'), but to the weight and wisdom of the matter of his words, spoken or written.

23. τεσσερακονταετὴς χρόνος] The life of Moses is given as divided into three periods, each of 40 years. His first appearance before Pharaoh (Ex. vii. 7) is 40 years after this, and his death 40 years later, when he was 'an hundred and twenty years old' (Deut. xxxiv. 7).

ἐπὶ καρδίαν ἀνέβη] Same words 1 Cor. ii. 9: a LXX. M. phrase: e.g. Jer. iii. 16 οὐκ ἀναβήσεται ἐπὶ καρδίαν.

τοὺς ἀδελφοὺς] *motivum amoris.* B. ἐπισκέψασθαι, 'visit', but also connoting care, consideration, or regard for those 'visited', cf. xv. 36; Luke i. 68; Matt. xxv. 36.

24. ἐποίησεν ἐκδίκησιν] 'wrought an avenging', 'avenged'. ἐκδίκησιν ποιεῖν, ἐκδικεῖν are common in N.T. in this sense, e.g. Rom. xii. 19; so ἔκδικος 'one who exacts vengeance' Rom. xiii. 4.

τῷ καταπονουμένῳ] Present: 'the man who was on the point of being overcome'.

τὸν Αἰγυπτ.] As in the use of αὐτοῖς ver. 26, a familiarity with the facts of the story is assumed in his hearers.

25. ἐνόμιζεν δὲ] Not in Exodus, but a comment of Stephen's, who is drawing a parallel to the similar rejection of Jesus. Note the rhetorical power of οἱ δὲ οὐ συνῆκαν, and cf. ver. 53 καὶ οὐκ ἐφυλάξατε.

αὐτοῖς] Ex. ii. 13 'two among the Hebrews'.

26. συνήλλασσεν] Imperfect: A. and R.V. 'would have set them at one again'.

29. Μαδιάμ] Probably the peninsula on which is Mount Sinai.

υἱοὺς δύο] His father-in-law was Jethro Ex. iii. 1; his wife Zipporah Ex. ii. 21; his sons Gershom and Eliezer Ex. ii. 22, xviii. 4.

30. Σινᾶ] Ex. iii. 1 'Horeb'. Both were probably peaks of one mountain range. The names are used almost indifferently. "Horeb is probably 'the Mountain of the Dried-up Ground'; Sinai 'the Mountain of the Thorn'."

Stanley, Sinai and Palestine.

βάτου] "the wild Acacia (*Mimosa nilotica*), under the name of 'sŭnt', everywhere represents the 'seneh' or 'senna' of the Burning Bush".

Stanley. speaking of the Desert of Sinai.

ἄγγελος] but ver. 31 the voice is of 'Jehovah', and ver. 32 the presence of 'God' is asserted. So too in Ex. iii. 2—4.

33. λῦσον...] So too Josh. v. 15. The priests who ministered in the temple were bare-footed. Moslems still enter their mosques bare-footed. Cf. too Juv. VI. 158 *observant ubi festa mero pede sabbata reges.*

Note carefully the importance of these words for Stephen's argument as to 'the holy place'.

34. ἰδὼν εἶδον] rendered in Ex. iii. 7 'I have surely seen'. The Gk represents the Hebrew idiom, cf. Heb. vi. 14; and Ps. xl. 1 ὑπομένων ὑπέμεινα, *expectans expectavi,* 'I waited patiently'. Repetition or reduplication is one of the earliest and most universal methods of expressing emphasis: the particular emphasis must be judged from the

context. Cf. Plat. *Symp.* 195 B φεύγων φυγῇ; *Soph.* 231 B
ἡ γένει γενναία σοφιστική; Soph. *O. T.* 1469 ὦ γονῇ γενναῖε;
Acts ii. 30 ὅρκῳ ὤμοσεν; ii. 35 ὑποπόδιον τῶν ποδῶν; v. 28
παραγγελίᾳ παρηγγείλαμεν 'we straitly charged you'; xxiii.
14 ἀναθέματι ἀνεθεματίσαμεν; xxviii. 26; Luke xxii. 15 ἐπι-
θυμίᾳ ἐπεθύμησα.

35. τοῦτον...τοῦτον...] Note the emphatic and rhetorical
repetition; and οὗτος...οὗτος...οὗτος vers. 36, 37, 38. The
object is to place the personality of Moses as the divinely
appointed saviour of Israel in marked contrast with the
treatment he received. The parallel thus drawn between
Moses and Jesus is clear; cf. too ἠρνήσαντο with ἠρνήσασθε
iii. 13, and λυτρωτὴν with λύτρωσις 'redemption' Luke i. 68,
ii. 38; Heb. ix. 12.
Note also the contrast in the clauses,
τίς σε κατέστησεν ἄρχοντα καὶ δικαστήν;
ὁ θεὸς ἀπέσταλκε καὶ ἄρχοντα καὶ λυτρωτήν.

ἠρνήσαντο] with ref. to ver. 27. Note the plural and
cf. ver. 41 ἐμοσχοποίησαν. *Unius hominis dicta et facta ad-* B.
scribuntur etiam illis qui eodem sunt animo.

38. τῇ ἐκκλ.] v. 11 n. The reference is to the assembly held for the giving of the commandments, Ex. xix.

ὁ γενόμενος μετὰ τοῦ ἀγγ...καὶ τῶν πατέρων] i.e. he acted
as an intermediary between them; he received (ἐδέξατο) the
law from the angel to give (δοῦναι) to their fathers. So
Moses is called ὁ μεσίτης 'the mediator' Gal. iii. 19; and
Jesus is κρείττονος διαθήκης μεσίτης Heb. viii. 6.

τοῦ ἀγγέλου] in Exodus, 'Jehovah'. The substitution De
belongs 'to later theology'.   Wette.

ζῶντα] 'living', i.e. possessing vitality and force, not
dead, cf. Heb. iv. 12 ζῶν γὰρ ὁ λόγος τοῦ θ.; 1 Pet. i. 23.
This answers the charge of speaking 'against the law'. See
too Soph. *O. T.* 481 τὰ δ' ἀεὶ ζῶντα περιποτᾶται of oracles
which remain in force and effectual; *Ant.* 457 ζῇ ταῦτα of
laws.

40. εἰπόντες] Ex. xxxii. 1, 4. For the pillar of fire
that had hitherto gone before them, cf. Ex. xiii. 21.

οἳ προπορεύσονται] A.V. rightly 'to go before us'. Cf.
vi. 3 n. R.V. alters to 'which shall go before us', without
reason.

ὁ γὰρ Μ. οὗτος...οὐκ οἴδαμεν...] οὗτος, contemptuous, cf.
vi. 14 n. Note the vigorous change of construction; cf.
Aesch. *S. c. Theb.* 678
ἀνδροῖν δ' ὁμαίμοιν θάνατος ὧδ' αὐτόκτονος—
οὐκ ἔστι γῆρας τοῦδε τοῦ μιάσματος.

41. ἐμοσχοποίησαν] The Egyptians worshipped the bull Apis at Memphis, regarding him as the symbol of Osiris, the Sun. Cf. too the golden calves set up by Jeroboam 1 Kings xii. 28: and the winged bulls discovered at Nineveh.

Aaron made the calf, but it was at the people's request: hence the plural, cf. Ex. xxxii. 35 'the Lord plagued the people, because they made the calf, which Aaron made'.

42. ἔστρεψεν] intrans. like ἀναστρέφω v. 22, xv. 16. ἐστράφησαν Israelitae (ver. 39), ἔστρεψεν Deus.

A.   **λατρεύειν...**] 'This fact is not mentioned in the Pentateuch. In after times we have frequent traces of star-worship, e.g. 2 Kings xvii. 16, xxi. 3, 5. See also Deut. iv. 19'.

ἐν Βίβλῳ τῶν προφ.] The Jews divided their Scriptures into 'the Law, the Prophets, and the Psalms' (or Hagiographa), Luke xxiv. 44, or less accurately into 'the Law and Smith's the Prophets', cf. xxiv. 14, xxviii. 23. 'The Law'=the *Dict. of* five books of Moses. 'The prophets' are thus enumerated: *the Bible.*

| Elder | Joshua, Judges, 1 and 2 Samuel, 1 and 2 Kings. | Later | Greater | Isaiah, Jeremiah, Ezekiel. |
| | | | Lesser | The twelve minor prophets. |

The Hagiographa includes the rest of the Hebrew Canon. The quotation here is from Amos v. 25, and apparently the Rabbis regarded the twelve minor Prophets as a single book, La. W. so that probably the words 'the prophets' should be taken II. here in this narrower sense ; cf. xiii. 40 where a quotation from Habakkuk is referred to as ' in the prophets'.

μή...] μή interrogative expects the answer, No. 'Did ye offer me...? No. Ye actually (καί) took up....'

43. ἀνελάβετε] 'took up', i.e. after each halt, to carry it with you instead of the tabernacle of Jehovah.

σκηνήν] 'tent', used as a moveable temple: the word is frequently applied to 'the tabernacle', cf. ver. 44.

Μολόχ] The Hebrew here gives 'your king'. Molech (as the name is elsewhere rightly spelt) means 'king'. He was an Ammonite deity to whom children were offered. The image is said to have been ox-headed, with arms outstretched (in which the children were placed) and hollow so as to be heated underneath: hence perhaps the phrase 'pass through the fire to Molech', Lev. xviii. 21, xx. 2; 2 Kings xxiii. 10.

τὸ ἄστρον...] The Heb. has *Chiun* for 'Ρομφά or 'Ρεφάν.
'Chiun' has been considered to mean 'Saturn'.   Among
Egyptian divinities however two are found of foreign origin,
Renpu and Ken: they occur together and form a pair,
being male and female. The names so curiously correspond
to 'Rompha' and 'Chiun' that it would seem that in some
reference to them is to be found the explanation of the
remarkable variation of the Hebrew and LXX.

'Ρομφά
B
'Ρομφάμ
א¹
'Ρεφάν
CE.
Smith's
Dict.,
s.v.
Rem-
phan.

τὸ ἄστρον probably refers to some symbol or type (cf.
τύπους) under which the god was worshipped.

Βαβυλῶνος] Δαμασκοῦ, LXX. with Heb. The date of
the 'removal to Babylon' is 588 B.C. in the reign of Nebu-
chadnezzar.

44. ἡ σκηνὴ τοῦ μαρτ.] Verbally the mention of 'the
tabernacle of Moloch' seems to suggest the mention of the
real 'tabernacle', but the connection of thought is loose :
a fresh division of the speech begins here : Stephen passes
on from the conduct of the Israelites to his other argument
that God is not necessarily worshipped in a particular spot.

The tabernacle is called 'the tabernacle of the testimony' because it contained 'the ark of the testimony' (Ex.
xxv. 22), which contained the two 'tables of testimony'
(Ex. xxxi. 37), or 'witness' to God's government of Israel.

κατὰ τὸν τύπον] Ex. xxv. 40 ὅρα ποιήσεις κατὰ τὸν
τύπον τὸν δεδειγμένον σοι· ἐν τῷ ὄρει.

45. 'Ιησοῦ] ii. 22 n.

εἰσήγαγον διαδεξ....ἕως τῶν ἡμ. Δ.] 'brought in (i.e. to
Canaan) having received it in their turn...up to the days
of David', a slightly careless but perfectly clear phrase=
'received it and brought it into Canaan, where it remained
up to the days of David'.

ἐν τῇ κατασχέσει] 'in' or 'at the time of their taking
possession of the nations'. For the 'nations' cf. Ex. iii. 8 ;
Josh. iii. 10.

46. ᾐτήσατο] 'asked', but did not obtain permission,
2 Sam. vii. 2 *et seq*.

εὑρεῖν σκήνωμα...] LXX. Psalm cxxxii. 5. Σολομῶν...
1 Kings vi. 14.

48. ἀλλ' οὐχ ὁ ὕψ....] The same thought in Solomon's
prayer at the dedication of the temple, 1 Kings viii. 27:
cf. too Acts xvii. 24. Note the emphatic position of οὐ, and
the use of ὁ ὕψιστος for God in contrast with χειροποίητα—
'*conveniens appellatio. Hunc nulla moles capit*'.   B.

ὁ προφ.] Is. lxvi. 1, almost *verbatim*.

49. ποῖον] Not 'what', but 'what manner', 'what sort of house?' The word expresses scorn, and is so used frequently in classical Greek. Cf. iv. 7 and ποία χάρις Luke vi. 32, 33, 34.

51. σκληροτράχηλοι...] There is no need to suppose 'an interruption from the audience' to account for this outburst: the growing warmth of the speech naturally leads up to it.

Both the epithets used are frequently applied to the Israelites in O.T., e.g. Ex. xxxii. 9; Lev. xxvi. 41. 'Circumcision' as a sign of purification and dedication to God can naturally be used metaphorically of the heart.

ὑμεῖς] Emphatic. 'You, not I'; cf. immediately afterwards ὑμῶν, ὑμεῖς, ὑμῶν, ὑμεῖς.

τῷ πνεύματι...] Apparently a recollection of Is. lxiii. 10 ἠπείθησαν καὶ παρώξυναν τὸ πν. τὸ ἅγιον αὐτοῦ. ἀντιπίπτετε (=in adversum ruitis. B.) is a very strong word, not found elsewhere in N.T., but used of Israel Numb. xxvii. 14.

52. τίνα τῶν προφητῶν...] Cf. Luke xi. 47.

προδόται] as the accomplices of Judas. φονεῖς as urging on Pilate.

53. οἵτινες] 'yes, you who'. 'The use of οἵτινες instead of οἱ so very frequent in the Acts and Epistles, occurs when the clause introduced by it contains a *further explanation* of the position or classification of the person or persons alluded to, and not when the relative serves for simple identification'. Cf. viii. 15, ix. 35, x. 41, 47.

ἐλάβετε...εἰς διαταγὰς ἀγγ.] 'received the law as an ordinance of angels'; εἰς='for', 'so as to be', 'as'. Cf. Heb. xi. 8 λαμβάνειν εἰς κληρονομίαν. The expression is distinctly intended to glorify the law and so enhance their guilt in not keeping it. It was no human ordinance but received by them to be treated as an 'ordinance of angels'. In the O.T. the law is spoken as given directly by God, cf. the first verse of chapters xi.—xxvii. in Leviticus; 'And the Lord spake unto Moses, saying': The mention of angels in connection with it is first found in the poetical passage Deut. xxxiii. 2, but occupied a very prominent place in later rabbinical speculation. In Gal. iii. 19 Paul refers to the law as διαταγεὶς δι' ἀγγέλων 'ordered through the medium of angels'. This substitution of 'angels', where the O.T. speaks directly of God, seems due to an artificial idea of reverence similar to that which forbade the use of the actual name of Jehovah.

The only other possible rendering of this passage is 'received the law into the administration of angels', which might be considered a condensed phrase = 'received from

angels the law which was given them to administer'. The
words διαταγή, διατάσσειν do not however describe 'administration' by an intervening agent, but distinctly 'ordering'
by a superior, cf. Rom. xiii. 2 τῇ τοῦ θεοῦ διαταγῇ ἀνθέστη-
κεν; Luke viii. 55 διέταξεν αὐτῇ δοθῆναι; Acts xviii. 2,
xxiii. 31, xxiv. 23.

55. Ἰησοῦν ἑστῶτα...] cf. Matt. xxvi. 64 'sitting';
Mark xvi. 19 ' sat on the right hand of God'. Gregory the
Great is happy in his comment: ' *Stephanus stantem vidit
quem adjutorem habuit*'; cf. Coll. for St Stephen's Day:
' O blessed Jesus, who standest at the right hand of God to
succour all those that suffer for Thee'.

56. θεωρῶ] a strong word, implying clear vivid vision ;
cf. viii. 13 n.

τὸν υἱὸν τοῦ ἀνθρώπου] This name for the Messiah (cf. A. II.
Dan. vii. 13) is often applied by Jesus to Himself, but never La.
in N.T. applied to Him by any one else, except here, where
there seems to be a reference to His own promise Matt.
xxvi. 64.

53. ἔξω τῆς πολ.] Lev. xxiv. 14, and for the law as to
stoning for blasphemy, ver. 16.
We know too little about the Sanhedrin to decide
whether they were acting within their legal rights or not,
but cf. John xviii. 31. Probably the exact limits of their
authority as opposed to that of the Roman Procurator were
ill-defined and variable.

οἱ μάρτυρες...] In order to cast the first stones, cf. Deut.
xvii. 7.

Σαύλου] "Like Theaetetus means 'asked' (of God)". P.
Note the effect of the repetition of ἐλιθοβόλουν.

59. ἐπικαλούμενον] Regular word for calling upon a *god*
for aid. Translate, ' calling upon (the Lord Jesus) and
saying ' Lord Jesus...'. The only acc. that can be grammatically supplied after ἐπικαλ. is τὸν κύρ. Ἰησοῦν. Bentley's
conjecture that ΘΝ is lost after the final ΟΝ is unnecessary.
For the 'invocation' of Jesus cf. ix. 14, xxii. 16.

60. μὴ στήσῃς αὐτοῖς...] 'do not establish (make fixed,
irremoveable) for them (Eth. Dat.) their sin'. ἱστάναι τινὶ
ἁμαρτίαν is the opposite of ἀφιέναι τινὶ ἁμαρτίαν. For the
prayer cf. the dying words of Jesus (Luke xxiii. 34) πάτερ,
ἄφες αὐτοῖς.

ἐκοιμήθη] cf. xiii. 36. The metaphor is common to all
languages, but the word is used here in striking contrast
with the scene just described. Note too the cadence of the W. on
word expressing rest and repose, and cf. the last word of the xxviii.
Acts, ἀκωλύτως. 31.

130   *ACTS OF THE APOSTLES.* [VIII. 1

CHAPTER VIII.

1. Σαῦλος δὲ...] Rightly appended to the preceding narrative in R.V., and not cut off from it as in A.V. The historian leaves our eyes fixed on him who is from this point to be the central figure of the narrative. That this is done purposely is marked by the reference to Saul vii. 58, and the repeated reference to his activity which immediately follows here, Σαῦλος δὲ ἐλυμαίνετο....

ἐν ἐκείνῃ τῇ ἡμ.] 'on that day' R.V.; not 'at that time', as A.V. The persecution took place (ἐγένετο) then and there. *Non differebant adversarii.* B.

Σαμαρίας] The district between Galilee on the N., and Judaea on the S. Its capital was Samaria, 'the watch-mountain', built by Omri B.C. 925 (1 Kings xvi. 24). It was afterwards named Sebaste by Herod the Great in honour of Augustus (Σεβαστός). Most of the inhabitants had been carried away by Shalmaneser B.C. 721 (2 Kings xvii. 6) and afterwards by Esarhaddon, who replaced them by settlers from Babylon, Hamath, &c. (2 Kings xvii. 24). The mixed race (ἀλλογενεῖς Luke xvii. 18) which subsequently grew up were regarded by the Jews with peculiar hatred, John iv. 9 et seq.

2. συνεκόμισαν] Cf. Soph. *Aj.* 1048 οὗτος, σὲ φωνῶ τόνδε τὸν νεκρὸν χεροῖν | μὴ συγκομίζειν.

εὐλαβεῖς] 'devout', 'god-fearing'. The word only occurs in N.T. three times elsewhere; Luke ii. 25 (of Simeon); Acts ii. 5, and xxii. 12, and in each case is applied to Jews. It is certain that the word here indicates that Jews as well as Christians took part in the burial. Had Christians alone been meant, μαθηταί would have been used. It is not however necessary to confine the word here to Jews because of πάντες in ver. 1; πάντες διεσπάρ. merely describes a *general* dispersion; many Christians were left, cf. ver. 3.

κοπετός] Lamentation, consisting chiefly in beating the breast, cf. *planctus* (πλήγνυμι).

3. ἐλυμαίνετο] A very strong word, implying not only injury but insult. Frequent in Demosthenes. Only here in N.T. but found Ps. lxxx. 13 of a wild boar destroying a vineyard—ἐλυμήνατο αὐτὸν σῦς ἐκ δρυμοῦ. Cf. ix. 21 πορθήσας.

σύρων] 'haling', A. and R.V. (=hauling). Cf. Plaut. *Poen.* III. 5. 45 *collo obtorto ad praetorem trahor.*

5. εἰς τὴν πόλιν τῆς Σαμ.] 'the city of Samaria'. T.R.
omits τὴν; if so, we should render 'a city of (the district of) Samaria', and the words could not refer to the capital.

Text
ΝΑΒ.

4, 5. εὐαγγελιζόμενοι, ἐκήρυσσεν] It is dangerous to distinguish words too minutely. Of the various words however used for 'preaching',

λαλεῖν τὸν λόγον merely expresses without emphasis the utterance of the word ;

εὐαγγελίζεσθαι τὸν λόγον draws attention to the character of the word (1) as a message conveying *news*, (2) as conveying *good* news. It is distinctly a *missionary* word and, as such, very frequent in the Acts.

κηρύσσειν calls attention to the character of the speaker as ' a herald', and suggests the idea of some great person he is charged to proclaim. Hence the special use of the word in Matt., Mark, and Luke, of John the Baptist, and its use in the Acts here followed by τὸν χρ.; by τὸν Ἰησ. ix. 20, xix. 3; by Μωυσῆν xv. 21 ; by τὴν βασιλείαν τοῦ θεοῦ xx. 25.

διδάσκειν is the word specially used of Jesus in all the Evangelists, and suggests His special name ὁ διδάσκαλος. It certainly implies *authority* in the speaker. Cf. Matt. vii. 29.

Φίλιππος] the deacon; called 'the Evangelist' xxi. 8, clearly from his special power of 'preaching'.

6. προσεῖχον] sc. τὸν νοῦν, as often in classical Greek = ' attended to'.

7. πολλοὶ γάρ...] T.R. πολλῶν, an obvious correction. Text ℵABCE. The construction is loose, 'For many of those having unclean spirits, shouting...they (the spirits) went out'. The nom. is perhaps due to an unconscious tendency in the writer to make this clause strictly parallel with the next, which begins πολλοὶ δέ.

παραλελυμένοι] 'palsied', i.e. paralysed; lit. 'loosened at the side', i.e. having no power to contract and so exert the muscles which regulate the limbs.

9. Σίμων] Usually called ' Simon Magus'. There are See A. many legends about him but nothing is really known; e.g. Justin Martyr relates that he subsequently went to Rome, performed miracles and had a statue erected to him with the inscription *Simoni Deo Sancto;* but in this he was undoubtedly mistaken, as a stone found in the Tiber A. D. 1574 bears the inscription SEMONI SANCO DEO FIDIO SACRUM, *Sancus* being a Sabine name for Hercules, and *Semo* = Semihomo (ἡμίθεος) ' a hero'.

μαγεύων] The Magi were the priestly class under the Median and Persian empires. The founding of their order is ascribed to Zoroaster. Their influence and learning were very great. Hence the word is used in a good sense,

Matt. ii. 1, 'There came wise men (μάγοι) from the East'.
But, as their scientific knowledge was most frequently used
to impose on the vulgar, the word has generally a bad sense
in Greek, as here and xiii. 6 and in our 'magic'.

ἐξιστάνων...ἐξεστακέναι ver. 11...ἐξίστατο ver. 13] This
marked repetition clearly indicates that the 'amazement'
produced by Simon on the Samaritans was exactly the
same effect which was produced on him by Philip. The
'belief' spoken of ver. 13 is the result of this amazement
not of any real conversion.

10.   ἀπὸ μικροῦ...] cf. xxvi. 22 ; Heb. viii. 11.

N. La.
Milman,
Hist. Ch.
Bk II.c.5.

ἡ Δύναμις τοῦ θεοῦ ἡ καλουμένη Μεγάλη] There seems
at this time to have been a belief current in Oriental speculation that certain 'powers' (δυνάμεις) or emanations of The
Godhead were revealed or became incarnate in the person
of men. The 'power' described in the text is marked with
emphatic clearness as 'the one which is called Great'—the
one which beyond all others was considered to mark divinity.
This being so, it seems that Simon is described as supposed to
be little less than himself divine. With this later traditions
about him agree, for Jerome (in Matt. c. 24) states that Simon
said 'Ego sum sermo Dei,...ego omnipotens, ego omnia Dei'.

The theory of divine emanations rises to considerable
importance in later Gnostic speculations. δύναμις is used
of 'a being endowed with power' parallel to ἄγγελος, Rom.
viii. 38.

13.   προσκαρτερῶν τῷ Φ.] i.e. persistently clinging to,
or keeping with Philip ; cf. x. 7.

θεωρῶν] This word, which is frequent in the Acts,
always seems to describe clear vision (cf. vii. 56 n.), whether
physical (as here, iii. 16, xvii. 16), or mental (xxvii. 10), or
a combination of both (iv. 13, xvii. 22).

14.   Πέτρον καὶ Ἰωάνην] See iii. 1 n. So Jesus sent
out the Apostles 'two and two' (Mark vi. 7), and also the
Seventy (Luke x. 1). Cf. xiii. 2 'Barnabas and Saul';
xv. 22 'Judas and Silas'; so too xv. 39 Paul takes with him
Silas, and Barnabas Mark.

15.   καταβάντες] 'having come down'; partly of the
actual descent from the high ground of Jerusalem (Mt Zion
is 2535 feet above the level of the Mediterranean), partly
with the idea of going down from the centre or capital of a
country to a provincial town; cf. ver. 5 κατελθών; καταβαίνουσαν ver. 26; ἀνέβη εἰς Ἱερουσαλήμ xi. 2; κατῆλθον xi. 27.

ὅπως λάβωσιν πν. ἁγ.] For the words πνεῦμα ἅγιον
cf. xix. 1 n. Clearly here, and elsewhere in the Acts, this

' receiving the Holy Spirit' is described as accompanied by certain signs obvious to eye and ear—*singularia dona, qui-* Calvin *bus Dominus initio Evangelii quosdam esse praeditos voluit* in A. *ad ornandum Christi regnum.* Cf. ἰδών ver. 18; and the effects mentioned, as for example λαλεῖν γλώσσαις x. 44—48; προφητεύειν xix. 6.

16. For βεβαπτισμένοι... cf. ii. 38 n.

18. προσήνεγκεν χρήματα] Hence our word ' Simony ' applied to trafficking in things sacred.

20. τὸ ἀργύριόν σου...] Not necessarily a curse on Simon, who may repent (ver. 22) and possibly be pardoned. Grammatically the words may fairly be regarded as a brief and vehement expression, which put more carefully would be, ' Thy money perish, even as thou art now perishing', ' art now treading the path that leads to perdition'. The words are not ' Perish thou', or ' Perish thou with thy money', but ' Perish thy money with thee'.

εἴη εἰς] A pregnant construction: ' go to destruction and stay there', cf. ver. 23 εἰς χολὴν...ὄντα ' hast fallen into and art now in'; vii. 4 εἰς ἣν κατοικεῖτε ; Luke xi. 7 εἰς τὴν κοίτην εἰσίν.

τὴν δωρεάν] Emphatic.

κτᾶσθαι] ' to acquire', ' gain possession of' : κέκτημαι= ' I possess', ' own'.

21. ἐν τῷ λόγῳ τούτῳ] A. and R.V. ' in this matter'— Ast in M. *ipsa causa de qua disceptatur.*

ἡ γὰρ καρδία...] Ps. lxxviii. 37 ἡ δὲ καρδία αὐτῶν οὐκ εὐθεῖα μετ' αὐτοῦ. εὐθύς passes from the meaning of mathematically straight, cf. ix. 11, to that of moral uprightness or ' rectitude'. Cf. xiii. 10, where it is to be seen in a transition state.

22. εἰ ἄρα] 'if haply' ; ' to see if possibly'; *si forte.* The expression indicates that the possibility is small. Cf. Mark xi. 13 ἦλθεν εἰ ἄρα εὑρήσει τι. A still stronger form is εἰ ἄρα γε xvii. 27.

23. χολὴν πικρίας καὶ σύνδεσμον ἀδικίας] The gen. in each case defines and makes clear the metaphorical word. The ' gall' or ' poison', with which he is filled, is defined as πικρία 'a bitter, malignant disposition' (cf. Rom. iii. 14 ; Heb. xii. 15) into which he has fallen, and the ' fetters' which bind him are his own ' unrighteousness' or ' iniquity'.

χολὴν πικ. cf. ῥίζα ἄνω φύουσα ἐν χολῇ καὶ πικρίᾳ Deut. xxix. 18. συνδ. ἀδ. Is. lviii. 6.

24. ὑμεῖς] Emphatic.

25. κώμας εὐηγγ.] The verb is allowed to take an acc. from the general sense of 'instructing' contained in it. Cf. xiv. 21, xvi. 10.

26. κατὰ μεσημ.] 'toward the south' A. and R.V.; he was to proceed ' with his face to the south', cf. xxvii. 12 n.

Γάζαν] 'The Strong' city, at the extreme S.W. of Palestine towards Egypt, two miles from the sea; in the portion of Judah, but soon taken by the Philistines, and made one of their five cities; taken by Alexander the Great after a siege of five months; destroyed by the Jewish king Alexander Jannaeus B.C. 96, and re-built by Gabinius B.C. 56; is now known as Ghuzzeh and has 15,000 inhabitants.

αὕτη] 'This (i. e. the particular road you are to take) is desert', i. e. leads through the desert. αὕτη refers to the principal noun of the sentence, ὁδός, not to Γάζαν, and the words are part of the angelic direction to Philip, pointing out to him which of the roads to Gaza he was to take, viz. ' the desert road'.

If αὕτη refers to Γάζα, the words must be treated as a parenthetical remark of the writer, perfectly unnecessary, and also, as regards the condition of Gaza, untrue.

(margin: V. Lange; and so M. Baum. A.)

27. ἀνάστηθι καὶ πορεύου ver. 26: **ἀναστὰς ἐπορεύθη** ver. 27] *Specimen obedientiae.*

Αἰθίοψ] Ps. lxviii. 31. **εὐνοῦχος**: frequently employed by Eastern sovereigns in high posts.

Κανδάκης] Like 'Pharaoh', 'Caesar', this was not a name, but the title borne by the queens of Aethiopia. Their capital was Meroe on the upper Nile.

γάζης] A Persian word used of ' the royal treasure': common in Latin, *gaza.*

ὃς ἐλ. προσκυνήσων εἰς 'I.] cf. John xii. 20. He was clearly already a convert to Judaism.

28. ἀνεγίνωσκεν] In its proper sense 'reading aloud', cf. ἤκουσεν below. It would probably be from the LXX. version, naturally well known in Egypt.

30. ἆρά γε] 'Dost thou really?'implying that he does not.

γιν. ἃ ἀναγινώσκεις;] *quae legis, ea intellegis?*—a play on words. Cf. the famous saying of Julian with reference to the Christian writings ἀνέγνων, ἔγνων, κατέγνων, and the retort ἀνέγνως ἀλλ' οὐκ ἔγνως· εἰ γὰρ ἔγνως οὐκ ἂν κατέγνως.

(margin: F. W. M. &c.)

31. πῶς γὰρ ἄν...] γάρ, *elegans particula, hoc sensu: quid quaeris?* B. 'You need not ask, for how should I be able?' The sentence in its first half expresses hopelessness: a gleam of hope and possibility comes in with the words ἐὰν μή....

32.   ἡ δὲ περιοχὴ τῆς γραφῆς ἥν] 'the contents of the passage (of Scripture) which...'.   For γραφή 'a passage (of Scripture)' cf. i. 16 n.   'Where the reference is to the sacred writings as a whole the plural γραφαί is universally found'.   Therefore the Vulgate, *locus scripturae quem legebat*, and A.V. 'the place of the scripture', cannot be right.

(margin: A. M. W. La. du Light. Gal. iii. 22.)

ὡς πρόβατον...]   Is. liii. 7, 8.   The quotation is from LXX. which differs considerably from the Hebrew.

A.V. gives :

'He was taken from prison and from judgment :
And who shall declare his generation ?
For he was cut off out of the land of the living :
For the transgression of my people was he stricken'.

This should be thus rendered and explained: He (i. e. Jehovah's Servant) was taken away (=cut off, i.e. by a violent death) through oppression and judgment (i. e. through an oppressive judgment), and as for his generation (i.e. contemporaries), who considered that he was cut off ...that for the transgression of my people he was stricken? (i.e. no one of his contemporaries meditated on the truth that the Divine Envoy's life was cut short for the sins of the people.)

(margin: Cheyne, ad loc. and so R.V.)

This explanation of the Hebrew gives enough light to make clear the *general* meaning of the Greek, viz.: 'he was humiliated, but who can describe (the wickedness of) his contemporaries, in that he was put to death ?'

(margin: A. La. de W.)

The words ἡ κρίσις αὐτοῦ ἤρθη cannot possibly however be brought into conformity with the Hebrew. The meaning seems to be, 'by his humiliation, his sentence (i. e. to death) was done away with', i. e. because he humbled himself to death he is now exalted and the sentence of death has been annulled.   Cf. Phil. ii. 8 ἐταπείνωσεν ἑαυτόν, γενόμενος ὑπήκοος μέχρι θανάτου...διὸ καὶ ὁ θεὸς αὐτὸν ὑπερύψωσεν.

(margin: So La. M. W. B.)

35.   ἀνοίξας τὸ στόμα] used only to introduce some weighty utterance, cf. Matt. v. 2, before the Sermon on the Mount, and below x. 34.

εὐηγγ. τὸν Ἰησοῦν] i. e. described the life of Jesus, and pointed out its correspondence with the account of Messiah given in Isaiah.

37.   T.R. reads εἶπε δὲ ὁ Φίλιππος, Εἰ πιστεύεις ἐξ ὅλης τῆς καρδίας, ἔξεστιν.   ἀποκριθεὶς δὲ εἶπε, Πιστεύω τὸν υἱὸν τοῦ θεοῦ εἶναι τὸν Ἰησοῦν Χριστόν.

(margin: Not in ℵABCG H.)

'The insertion seems to have been made to suit the formularies of the baptismal liturgies'.   The phrase τὸν Ἰησοῦν Χριστόν could not have been written by Luke, see ii. 22 n.

(margin: A.)

38. κατέβ. ἐς τὸ ὕδωρ] Literally, actual immersion
being practised, see the account of the baptism of Jesus
(Matt. iii. 16) and the rubric in the Baptismal Service, 'if...
the child may well endure it, he (the Priest) shall *dip* it in
the water discreetly and warily'. The *Teaching of the
Twelve Apostles* c. 7 prescribes that it shall be if possible
'in running water' (ἐν ὕδατι ζῶντι), failing that in other
water, cold if possible, but if not in warm : only as a last
alternative may water be 'poured thrice on the head'.

39. πνεῦμα Κυρίου...] 'the Spirit of the Lord...'.
Clearly a miraculous removal of Philip is described, cf.
1 Kings xviii. 12 πνεῦμα Κυρίου ἀρεῖ σε, 2 Kings ii. 16 μήποτε
ἦρεν αὐτὸν πνεῦμα Κυρίου: for ἥρπασεν = *abripuit*, cf. 2 Cor.
xii. 2; 1 Thess. iv. 17.

χαίρων] Note its position.
40. εὑρέθη εἰς ˮΑζ.] Pregnant construction. 'Was
carried to and found at A.'

Azotus, Ashdod, is 60 miles W. of Jerusalem, 35 N. of
Gaza, and was one of the five cities of the Philistines and
noted for the worship of Dagon, 1 Sam. v.

Καισαρίαν] 'the city of Caesar', called *C. Palaestinae*
to distinguish it from other cities of the same name (e.g.
C. Philippi), originally Turris Stratonis, but largely improved
by Herod the Great and called Caesarea in honour of Augustus. It is 55 miles N.W. of Jerusalem, on the coast S. of
Mt Carmel. It possessed a fine harbour made at great cost
by Herod. It was the chief city of Palestine (*Judaeae caput*
Tac. *Hist.* II. 79), and the residence of the Roman Procurator (cf. xxiii. 23, xxiv. 27).

CHAPTER IX.

1. ἐνπνέων ἀπ. καὶ φόνου] The genitives indicate that
in which the 'breath' consisted: it was 'a breath of threa-
tening and murder'. So in the Anthology πόθου, ἐρώτων,
χαρίτων πνεῖν. The cognate acc. is more common in classical Greek, e.g. πῦρ, φόνον, κότον πνεῖν.

2. ἐπιστολὰς] 'By decrees of Julius Caesar and Augustus the high priest and Sanhedrin at Jerusalem had jurisdiction over Jews resident in foreign cities'.

II. refer-
ring to
Biscoe,
c. 6,
pt. 2

Δαμασκὸν] About 150 miles N.E. of Jerusalem ; one
of the oldest cities in the world, situated in a singularly
fertile plain watered by the Barada (Abana, 2 Kings v. 12)
on the direct line of traffic between Tyre and the East.
First mentioned Gen. xiv. 15 : taken by David but lost by
Solomon, and the capital of a great Syrian power until taken

by Tiglath-Pileser king of Assyria (2 Kings xvi. 9) B.C. 740.
It was soon rebuilt, but its greatness was eclipsed by that
of Antioch. At this time it was in the possession of Arctas v. W.
(2 Cor. xi. 32) an Arabian prince tributary to the Romans, *ad loc.*
who may have been favourable to Jewish authority. It was and on ix. 24.
taken in A.D. 634 by the Mahometan Arabs and became the
metropolis of the Mahometan world. It has still 150,000
inhabitants. Josephus mentions that 10,000 Jews were B. J.
butchered in it by Nero. II. 25.

τῆς ὁδοῦ] 'the way', κατ' ἐξοχήν: the way pointed out
by God, which leads through faith in Christ to salvation.
So xix. 9, xxii. 4, and xvi. 17 ὁδ. σωτηρίας; xviii. 25 ὁδ.
κυρίου. It is opposed to αἵρεσις xxiv. 14 q. v.

3. ἐν δὲ τῷ...] Paul's conversion is described by himself xxii. 6—12, and xxvi. 12—19. The variations in the
three accounts are considerable and relate (1) to the words
spoken by Jesus, (2) to the effect produced on Paul's companions.

(1) In c. xxvi. very much more is said to have been
spoken by Jesus, but it is not improbable that Paul there in
his speech unites to the words actually heard by him the
fuller explanation of them subsequently divinely communicated by Ananias and in other visions.

(2) As regards his companions,

(*a*) ἱστήκεισαν ἐνεοί here has been contrasted with
xxvi. 14 πάντων καταπεσόντων ἡμῶν εἰς τὴν γῆν, but the
points of time referred to are different. Here the position
of Paul's companions *after* the vision is described in the
words 'they were standing speechless': in xxvi. 14 their act
on the *first* appearance of the vision is described—'they and
Paul (ἡμῶν) fell to the ground', i.e. the act is parallel to the
πεσών of ver. 4 in this account.

(*b*) Here they are described as ἀκούοντες μὲν τῆς φ.
μηδένα δὲ θεωροῦντες, but xxii. 9 τὸ μὲν φῶς ἐθεάσαντο τὴν δὲ
φ. οὐκ ἤκουσαν τοῦ λαλοῦντός μοι. It will be observed however that there is no real inconsistency. What Paul hears
and sees is definite: what they hear and see is indefinite.
They heard the φωνή, 'the utterance', but did not hear
'the utterance *of him who spake to me*', i.e. the actual
words which Paul heard. They 'saw the light' but saw
'no person' (μηδένα), whereas Paul saw Jesus.

In any case the variations are a proof of the honesty of
the writer. Variation in a repeated account is natural, but
the artificial introduction of this natural variation with a
view to deceive is very hard to imagine.

Paul himself refers to this event as establishing his claim
to be an Apostle, i.e. one who had seen the Lord and

received his commission directly from Him. 1 Cor. ix. 1, xv. 8, 9; Gal. i. 12, 16.

περιήστραψεν φῶς] It was 'about mid-day' (xxii. 6) and the light was 'above the brightness of the sun' (xxvi. 13). περιήστ. indicates that the light flashed around him suddenly and unexpectedly like lightning.

4. ἤκουσεν φωνήν] but ver. 7 ἀκούοντες φωνῆς. It is ex-
As La. tremely hazardous to draw the distinction that ἀκ. φωνήν =
W. &c. 'to hear and understand', ἀκ. φωνῆς = 'to hear' merely. For xxii. 7 Paul says ἤκουσα φωνῆς λεγούσης and then xxvi. 14 ἤκουσα φωνὴν λέγ., shewing that the constructions are simple equivalents.

Σαούλ Σαούλ] The Hebrew form of the word (cf. xxvi. 14) used in all three accounts and by Ananias (ver. 17, xxii. 13) but not elsewhere. The repetition of the word expresses solemn emphasis; cf. Matt. xxiii. 37 'O Jerusalem, Jerusalem'; Luke x. 41 'Martha, Martha'.

με] Jesus identifies Himself with His followers, cf. Luke
Augus- x. 16.   *Caput pro membris clamabat.*
tine in M.

5. ἐγώ...σύ] Very emphatic antithesis, lost in English.

διώκεις] Here T.R. adds 'without the authority of any
de Greek codex' σκληρόν σοι πρὸς κέντρα λακτίζειν (from xxvi. 14).
Wette. τρέμων τε καὶ θαμβῶν εἶπε, Κύριε, τί με θέλεις ποιῆσαι; καὶ ὁ Κύριος πρὸς αὐτόν.

7. ἱστήκεισαν] 'were standing'; it is used as the im-
perfect of ἔστηκα 'I stand' (cf. i. 11, xxvi. 6). The word certainly indicates an upright position, and could not refer to men prostrate on the ground: to explain 'had halted',
As W. 'had ceased to move forward', and so to reconcile it with xxvi. 14, is impossible and needless.

11. ὁ κύριος] Jesus, cf. ver. 17.

C. & H. ῥύμην τήν...] "We are allowed to bear in mind that the
and so thoroughfares of Eastern cities do not change, and to be-
Stanley, lieve that the 'straight street', which still extends through
Sin. and Damascus in long perspective from the Eastern gate, is the
Pal. street where Ananias spoke to Paul".

ῥύμη, here merely 'street' as xii. 10; Matt. vi. 2, though Luke xiv. 21 πλατείας καὶ ῥ. = (broad) 'streets and lanes'.

Σαῦλον ὀνόματι T.] 'one S. by name, a man of Tarsus'. Tarsus on the Cydnus, 12 miles from its mouth, was the capital of the Roman province of Cilicia. It ranked with Athens and Alexandria as a celebrated school of philosophy and literature. It was an *urbs libera*, i.e. a city enjoying

the right of local self-government.   Paul himself speaks of
it as οὐκ ἄσημος πόλις xxi. 39.

12. ἀναβλέψῃ] 'see again', 'recover his sight'. A.
and R.V. 'receive his sight'.

13. ἁγίοις] The same word as '*sanctus*' 'saint': here
first used = 'Christians'.   Very common in St Paul's
Epistles.

15. σκεῦος ἐκλογῆς] Gen. of quality: 'vessel' or 'instrument of choosing', i.e. 'chosen vessel'.   The object for
which the vessel is to be used is expressed in τοῦ βαστάσαι
'to carry my name...'.

ἐθνῶν] Cf. iv. 25 n. *Gentes primo ponuntur: nam* B.
Paulus gentium apostolus.

βασιλέων] Agrippa (xxvi. 2): Nero.

16. ἐγὼ γὰρ......] With the main verb πορεύου: 'Go v. Lange.
(without fear)...for I will shew him what he must *himself*
suffer' (so that you need not fear that he will do injury to
you).   This brings out the clear contrast between ὅσα κακὰ
τοῖς ἁγ. ἐποίησε (ver. 13) and ὅσα δεῖ αὐτὸν παθεῖν, it being
remembered that ποιεῖν and πάσχειν are strongly antithetical words.   *Patitur Paulus quae fecerat Saulus.*   For 'the
things he suffered' cf. 2 Cor. xi. 23—28.

ὑποδείξω] = to point out beforehand, especially by way of
warning.   Cf. Matt. iii. 7; Luke iii. 7 τίς ὑπέδειξεν ὑμῖν
φυγεῖν; Luke xii. 5.

18. ἀπέπεσαν...ὡς λεπίδες] 'there fell from his eyes as
it were scales'.   The Gk does not indicate that 'scales' or
'something like scales' actually fell from the eyes, but that
what Paul experienced was the 'falling away' of 'a sort of
scale' or 'film', which had previously obscured his vision.
For λεπίδες, cf. Tobit xi. 13 ἐλεπίσθη...ἀπὸ τῶν ὀφθαλμῶν
τὰ λευκώματα, 'the white film peeled from his eyes', and
Pope, *Messiah*, 39
   'He from thick films shall purge the visual ray
   And on the sightless eyeball pour the day'.

19. ἡμέρας τινάς] A short period, cf. x. 48, xvi. 12,
xxiv. 24.   Luke apparently knows nothing of the journey
into 'Arabia' which Paul tells us (Gal. i. 16) followed
'immediately' after his conversion, he returning from it to
Damascus, and only going up to Jerusalem 'after three
years'.   It would seem also that Luke was not aware of
the length of this interval, as the phrase ἡμ. ἱκαναί (ver. 23)
is a very vague one (cf. ver. 43 n.), though not absolutely
inconsistent with the existence of a considerable interval.

Cf. 1 Kings ii. 38 where the words 'many days' are in the
next verse referred to as 'three years' (though LXX. gives
τρία ἔτη in both places).

Paul's own account of this period Gal. i. 13—24 is to be
carefully compared, and it should be borne in mind, (1)
v. Light-
foot, Ex.
ad loc. that, whereas Luke 'derives his information at second
hand', the Epistle to the Galatians is written by an 'eye-
witness and actor in the scenes which he describes', and (2)
that the *object* of the two writers is different: Luke desires
to give a historical narrative of the *outward* facts of Paul's
career, Paul to explain the facts of his *inward* spiritual
history. 'The two accounts are not contradictory, but the
impression left by St Luke's narrative needs correcting by
the precise and authentic statement of St Paul'.

21. ὁ πορθήσας] The word similarly used of himself
by Paul, Gal. i. 13 ἐπόρθουν αὐτὴν (τὴν ἐκκλησίαν). It is a
military word.

22. συνβιβάζων] Just as συνίημι 'to put together'
means 'to comprehend', 'understand', so συμβιβάζω 'to
bring together' is used of bringing several facts together
and deducing the logical inference, 'proving'. Thus:

It was foretold that Messiah should do certain things;

Jesus has done these things;

Therefore Jesus is Messiah.

The word exactly describes the method of argument continually employed by the Apostles, cf. xvii. 3.

24. παρετηροῦντο] i.e. the Jews. Cf. 2 Cor. xi. 32,
where Paul says it was ὁ ἐθνάρχης Ἀρέτα τοῦ βασιλέως, 'the
governor of Aretas the king (of Arabia)': the Jews probably
applied for and obtained the assistance of the governor.

25. διὰ τοῦ τείχους] 2 Cor. xi. 33 διὰ θυρίδος...διὰ τοῦ
τείχους. Paul was let down through the window of a house
standing upon the town wall: cf. Josh. ii. 15, where Rahab
aids the spies to escape from Jericho, 'she let them down
by a cord through the window: for her house was upon the
town wall, and she dwelt upon the wall'.

σφυρίδι] T.R. σπυρίδι; the word used Matt. xv. 37;
Mark viii. 8: the Latin *sporta*, whence *sportula:* a plaited
basket for holding provisions.

27. ἐπιλαβόμενος] Pictorial, cf. xvii. 19: 'having taken
him by the hand'.

πρὸς τοὺς ἀποστόλους] Paul (Gal. i. 18) tells us that
he went up 'to visit' or 'become acquainted with (ἱστορῆσαι)
Cephas' with whom he abode fifteen days, and adds 'other
of the Apostles saw I none save James the Lord's brother'.
Luke clearly possesses only inexact knowledge of this period.

28. ἦν......εἰς Ἰερουσαλήμ] T. R. *ἐν.* The phrase εἰς clearly means 'he was with them *in* Jerusalem going in and ABCEL P. out with them', i.e. in close personal intercourse with them, cf. the use of εἰσῆλθεν καὶ ἐξῆλθεν i. 21. The words ἦν εἰς go together, and the use of εἰς, in preference to ἐν, is probably due to the intervention of the verbs expressing motion.

Paul (Gal. i. 22) says that he was 'unknown by face to the churches in Judaea', and it is to be observed that Luke describes the present visit as abruptly terminated, and strictly confined to Jerusalem itself.

30. κατήγαγον] 'brought down', i.e. to the sea-coast. Caesarea, used absolutely, clearly refers to the best-known Caesarea on the coast. The whole phrase indicates a voyage *by sea* to Tarsus, though ἐξαπέστειλαν does not by itself imply 'a sending off by sea'; it is a favourite word of Luke As A. (e.g. xi. 22, xvii. 14) = 'send away' whether by sea or land. and Light-

In Gal. i. 21 Paul says ἔπειτα ἦλθον εἰς τὰ κλίματα τῆς foot Συρίας καὶ τῆς Κιλικίας, but it is not therefore necessary to state. assume that he travelled *by land* through Syria to Cilicia and Tarsus. He merely states that the next period of his life was spent in the district which he describes as that of 'Syria and Cilicia', the name of Syria being probably v. Light- placed first on account of its greater importance as a foot, ad loc. province.

Paul next visited Jerusalem 'after fourteen years'. Gal. ii. 1.

31. εἶχεν εἰρήνην] The Jews had at this time (A.D. 39, 40) troubles enough of their own in connection with the decision of Caligula to place his statue in the Holy of Holies. Cf. Tac. *Hist.* v. 9 *Jussi a Caio Caesare effigiem ejus in templo locare, arma potius sumpserunt: quem motum Caesaris mors diremit.*

οἰκοδομουμένη] This interesting word is used in the N. T. (1) in its literal sense 'to build', (2) metaphorically, (*a*) as here, of the 'building' of a non-material fabric, such as the Church, (*b*) in the more secondary sense of spiritual 'instruction', 'advancement', 'strengthening', which attaches to the words 'edify' and 'edification', which we have derived from it through its Latin rendering *aedifico.*

It occurs eleven times in Luke and *always* in its literal sense: the only passage in the Gospels where it is not so used is Matt. xvi. 18, where it is used by Jesus, as here, of the Church, ἐπὶ ταύτῃ τῇ πέτρᾳ οἰκοδομήσω τὴν ἐκκλησίαν μου. It is used in its third sense Acts xx. 32. It and οἰκοδομή are frequent in St Paul's Epistles (cf. 1 Cor. xiv.), *always* in a metaphorical and often in a secondary sense.

The use of this and similar words with a gradually
developing meaning deserves attention, as serving possibly
to throw valuable light on the comparative order in point
of time of the books of the N.T. Certainly the use of οἰκο-
δομῶ points to an early origin of the Synoptic Gospels or
their common source.

τῷ φόβῳ] The dat. expresses the rule or standard by
which they regulated their course, cf. xxi. 21 περιπατεῖν
τοῖς ἔθεσι.

τῇ παρακλήσει...] cf. iv. 36 n. The 'encouragement' of
the Holy Spirit is described as aiding or guiding them in
their progress.

The term παράκλητος is applied to the Holy Spirit only
by St John (xiv. 16, 26, xv. 26, xvi. 7) and is there rendered
'Comforter', the margin in R.V. however giving 'Helper'
or 'Advocate'.

32. Λύδδαν] In O.T. Lod (1 Chron. viii. 12) near
Joppa; afterwards Diospolis.

34. ἰᾶταί σε 'Ιησοῦς] *Grata Lucae medico paronomasia.*
Cf. iv. 30 ἴασιν and 'Ιησοῦ last words of two parallel clauses;
x. 38 'Ιησοῦς ὃς διῆλθεν ἰώμενος.

στρῶσον σεαυτῷ] Note the aorist. Now, forthwith, do
thyself what others have hitherto done for thee.

35. τὸν Σαρῶνα] Not a place, but, as the article shews,
the district called Sharon (ὁ Σάρων, Is. xxxiii. 9), the famous
plain extending along the coast from Caesarea to Joppa, cf.
Sol. Song ii. 1.

οἵτινες] 'and they', or 'who also', cf. vii. 53 n.

36. 'Ιόππῃ] Now Jaffa, the port (cf. 2 Chron. ii. 16) of
Jerusalem on the Mediterranean.

M.   **Ταβειθά**] An Aramaic word = 'a gazelle', a term often
used of women in Oriental poetry. Δορκάς is strictly a fem.
adj. = 'the creature with the beautiful look' or 'eyes' from
δέρκομαι.

37. λούσαντες] Cf. *Il.* xviii. 350 καὶ τότε δὴ λοῦσάν τε
καὶ ἤλειψαν λίπ' ἐλαίῳ ; Virg. *Aen.* vi. 219 *corpusque lavant
frigentis et unguunt.*

39. ἐπιδεικνύμεναι] Not merely 'shewing', as A. and
R.V., but 'displaying', 'exhibiting'. The word conveys
the idea of 'shewing with pride', 'satisfaction', v. Lex.

χιτῶνας καὶ ἱμάτια] The two great divisions of clothes;
the χιτών, an *under* garment fitting close, the ἱμάτιον, an
outer garment loose and flowing. In Latin *tunica* and *toga.*

ὅσα] Not merely ἅ 'which', but 'all which': they were numerous.

40. ἐκβαλὼν ἔξω πάντας] The reference to the account of the raising of Jairus' daughter by Jesus Luke viii. 54 is misleading, as the insertion there of the words ἐκβαλὼν ἔξω πάντας καὶ is without authority.

43. ἱκανάς] This adj. is very frequent in the Acts. It is employed to describe (1) time, (2) number, (3) size. Derived from ἱκνέομαι it indicates that which 'does not fall short', 'is adequate', 'sufficient', and it has a purely relative value. For example, when applied to time it might describe ten days, ten months, or ten years : it merely describes the time as not out of relation to what you would expect, though it certainly suggests rather a long than a short time. Here for instance ἱκ. ἡμ. might refer to a month and so xviii. 18; but viii. 11 ἱκ. χρόνῳ could hardly be so short a period, and Luke viii. 27 χρόνῳ ἱκ. might mean 'many years'. So too when applied to numbers e.g. xi. 24, 26, xiv. 21, the adj. must be considered in relation to the number of inhabitants in the cities mentioned. As applied to size the vagueness of φῶς ἱκ. xxii. 6 is obvious.

βυρσεῖ] Classical Greek βυρσοδέψης. The trade was v. Γ. held unclean by the Jews. The word seems added inten- c. 15. tionally and emphatically at the end, in connection with the event which follows.

CHAPTER X.

1. Κορνήλιος] Probably the descendant of some freedman of the great Cornelian family.

ἑκατοντάρχης] The *centuria* is one of the oldest divisions of the Roman army, and its officer was *centurio* 'leader of a hundred' : the 'full legion' (*justa legio*) at this time consisted of 60 centuries or 10 cohorts.

'The Roman centurions in the N. T. always appear in a II. favourable light. See Matt. viii. 5; Luke vii. 2, xxiii. 47 ; Acts xxvii. 3'.

σπείρης] Like *globus* = 'a band of men', probably here 'a cohort', as xxi. 31.

τῆς καλ. Ἰταλικῆς] Probably as consisting of native Italians, not troops levied in the Provinces. Such a cohort would naturally be stationed at Caesarea, the seat of the Roman governor.

2. καὶ φοβ. τὸν θ.] The addition of these words to the *general* epithet 'pious' seems to shew that they are intended M.

to *particularize* Cornelius as not merely a god-fearing man,
but as 'fearing God', i. e. the God of the Jews (cf. xiii. 16,
26), and so a Proselyte of the Gate, i.e. uncircumcised. Cf.
too the use of σεβόμενος clearly in the same sense xvii. 4, 17.

τῷ λαῷ] i.e. the Jews (cf. iv. 25 n.), and so confirming
the view that τὸν θ. before and τοῦ θ. after it must refer to
Jehovah. Moreover τοῦ θ. ver. 3 is certainly Jehovah.

4. ἀνέβησαν] 'rose' or 'went up', i.e. like the smoke
or savour of an offering or incense. For the metaphor,
applied to prayer cf. Ps. cxli. 2, and to alms Phil. iv. 18.

La.   εἰς μνημόσυνον] 'so as to be a memorial', so as to remind
God of thee. μνημόσυνον is used in LXX. Lev. ii. 2, 9, 16
of the portion of the meat-offering which was actually
burnt.

6. παρὰ θάλασσαν] Outside the town and near the sea,
on account of his trade.

7. προσκ. αὐτῷ] Classical, cf. Dem. 1386, 6 θεραπαίνας
τὰς Νεαίρᾳ τότε προσκαρτερούσας.

9. τῇ ἐπαύριον] 1st day they set out; 2nd about noon
reach Joppa; 3rd return with Peter; 4th reach Caesarea
again. Joppa was 28 miles from Caesarea.

Smith's   ἀνέβη ἐπὶ τὸ δῶμα] 'went up on to the house', i.e. on
Dict.,   to the roof of the house. The flat roofs of Oriental houses
s.v.   were used for many purposes, e.g. drying corn, hanging up
House.   linen, as places of recreation in the evening and as sleeping
places at night (1 Sam. ix. 25, 26; 2 Sam. xi. 2, xvi. 22;
Prov. xxi. 9) ; as places of devotion and even idolatrous
worship (2 Kings xxiii. 12; Jer. xxxii. 29).

ὥραν ἕκτην] iii. 1 n.

10. αὐτῶν] i.e. the people of the house, those whose
business it was.

ἔκστασις] The word represents a state in which a man,
to a greater or less extent, ceases to be under the control of
conscious reason and intelligence: he 'passes out of himself'
(ἐξίσταται) and needs 'to come to himself' again (cf. xii. 11
ἐν ἑαυτῷ γενόμενος). It may describe the effect of awe and
amazement (cf. iii. 10 θάμβος καὶ ἔκ., viii. 9, 11, 13), or fear
(Mark xvi. 8 τρόμος καὶ ἔκ.), or as here and xxii. 17 a complete loss of outward consciousness, 'a trance'.

11. θεωρεῖ] Graphic present.

τέσσαρσιν ἀρχαῖς καθιέμενον] R.V. rightly 'let down
(being lowered) by four corners' lit. 'beginnings'. In
English we say 'ends' not 'beginnings'.

Alford says that this would certainly require the article —'the four corners'. He is wrong : a sheet so let down has not necessarily *four* ends or corners : it might be lowered by 3, 5, 6 or any number of ends, and therefore you can say ' by four ends' or 'corners' without adding the article. His rendering 'a rope-end' is impossible: ἀρχή cannot mean the 'end of a rope', except where a rope has been already mentioned, e. g. Eur. *Hipp.* 772 πεισμάτων ἀρχάς.

13. ἀναστάς] v. 17 n.

14. μηδαμῶς] not οὐδαμῶς: a protest, not a refusal. Cf. the similar conduct of Peter, Matt. xvi. 22 ἴλεώς σοι, κύριε· οὐ μὴ ἔσται σοι τοῦτο; John xiii. 8 οὐ μὴ νίψῃς τοὺς πόδας μου.

οὐδέποτε...πᾶν] A Hebraism common in N.T., e.g. Matt. xxiv. 22 οὐκ ἂν ἐσώθη πᾶσα σάρξ. Cf. *Teaching of the Twelve Apostles*, c. ii. οὐ μισήσεις πάντα ἄνθρωπον.

κοινόν] Identical with ἀκάθαρτον, cf. Mark vii. 2 κοιναῖς χερσί, τοῦτ᾽ ἔστιν ἀνίπτοις. That which is 'common', 'shared by all', is opposed to that which is 'peculiar', 'possessed by few'; hence the word acquires the contemptuous sense of 'ordinary', 'vulgar', or, as here, is applied to food not specially pronounced 'clean'. For 'unclean' animals cf. Lev. xi.

For the sense of this passage and the use of κοινόω and καθαρίζω cf. carefully Mark vii. 18, 19, where Jesus distinctly asserts that 'nothing that goeth into a man can defile (κοινῶσαι) him', and Mark (who is said to have derived much information from Peter) adds the remarkable comment 'This he said, making all meats clean (καθαρίζων)'*.

* A.V. here follows T. R. καθαρίζον and sacrifices all sense. Cf. F.

15. ἃ ὁ θεὸς...] 'what God made' or 'declared clean', i.e. by thus offering them to thee.

16. ἐπὶ τρίς] Thus emphasizing the command. Cf. Gen. xli. 32.

17. διηπόρει—διενθυμουμένου] ver. 19. Luke is singularly fond of verbs compounded with διά, cf. διηπορούντο ii. 12; διαχλευάζοντες ii. 13; διαπονούμενοι iv. 2; διατηρεῖν xv. 29; Luke ii. 51; διακατηλέγχετο xviii. 28; διαγογγύζω Luke xv. 2, xix. 7; διαγρηγορεῖν Luke ix. 32, and many others. The preposition strengthens and emphasizes the verb: it adds the idea of *thoroughness*.

τί ἂν εἴη] 'what it could be', i.e. imply. The phrase expresses more doubt and uncertainty than τί εἴη, 'what it was'.

146   *ACTS OF THE APOSTLES.*   [x. 20

20. διακρινόμενος] This verb in the middle is consistently used in N.T. (*e.g.* Matt. xxi. 21; Rom. iv. 20, xiv. 23 ; James i. 6) of 'being divided in mind', 'being in doubt', 'wavering', cf. Tennyson 'hither and thither dividing the swift mind', Virg. *Aen.* IV. 285 *animum nunc huc nunc dividit illuc.*

In xi. 12 where these words are repeated the active is used, μηδὲν διακρίναντα, and R.V. substitutes for 'nothing doubting' the rendering 'making no distinction', in accordance with the regular usage of the active, e.g. xv. 9 ὁ θεὸς...οὐδὲν διέκρινεν. The difference is curious, and though in xi. 12 the reading is uncertain, some MSS. giving μ. διακρινόμενον, others omitting the words, still the preponderance of authority for μ. διακρίναντα is very considerable, and it is not easy to get rid of the words as an interpolation due to an incorrect recollection of the present passage.

Perhaps we may say that here the idea dwelt on is Peter's own *internal* doubt, whereas in xi. 12 the result of such doubt in his *active conduct to others* is contemplated. Here the command is ' Go, without letting the distinction between Jew and Gentile perplex your mind'; in xi. 12 it is 'Go, without letting that distinction cause you to hesitate in action'.

22. μαρτυρούμενος] cf. vi. 3.

τοῦ ἔθνους τῶν 'I.] Not λαοῦ, for the speaker is not a Jew.

ἐχρηματίσθη] Also of a divine communication Luke ii. 26 ἦν αὐτῷ κεχρηματισμένον ὑπὸ τοῦ πνεύματος; Heb. xi. 7 πίστει χρηματισθεὶς Νῶε.

24. τοὺς ἀναγκ. φίλους] So in Latin *necessarius*, and *necessitudo* of close, intimate friendship.

25. ὡς δὲ ἐγένετο τοῦ εἰσελθεῖν] The editors seem to regard the gen. as inexplicable. It appears however that the genitive gives the contents of the action contained in the verb: it is parallel to, though more difficult than, the constructions commented on iii. 12, vii. 19. The thing which took place is defined as consisting in Peter's entry.

εἰσελθεῖν here of entering the house; ver. 27 εἰσῆλθεν of entering a particular room.

προσεκύνησεν] *Adoravit: non addidit Lucas, 'eum'. Euphemia.* B.

The word does not necessarily imply worship, but is often used of Oriental prostration, e.g. Herod. VII. 136 προσκυνέειν βασιλέα προσπίτνοντας. Such prostration would how-

ever be unnatural in a Roman centurion, and Peter clearly
regards the act as implying worship.
Jesus *accepts* such worship, e.g. Matt. viii. 2.

27. συνομιλῶν] A. and R.V. 'as he talked with them'.
ὁμιλέω is only found in N.T. four times (Luke xxiv. 14, 15;
Acts xx. 11, xxiv. 26), and always in the sense of 'converse'.
Cf. our word 'Homily'.

28. ὡς ἀθέμιτον...] There is no such prohibition in
the Mosaic law; it seems due to the teaching of the Rabbis
exaggerating the danger of defilement. 'Any contact with Eders-
a heathen might involve such defilement, that on coming ᶜᵉⁱᵐ,
from the market an orthodox Jew would have to immerse'. Vol. II.,
Though no doubt frequently modified in practice, especi- p. 15.
ally outside Palestine, yet there is abundant evidence of
Jewish exclusiveness, cf. Juv. xiv. 103 *non monstrare vias
eadem nisi sacra colenti;* Tac. *Hist.* v. 5 *adversus omnes
alios hostile odium, separati epulis, discreti cubilibus.*

κολλᾶσθαι ἤ προσ.] κολλᾶσθαι (cf. v. 13 n.) indicates
close intimacy and is much stronger than προσέρχεσθαι.
What was forbidden was not merely 'intimacy', but any
'coming near' a Gentile.

κἀμοὶ ὁ θ....] A.V. straightforwardly gives 'but'; R.V.
has 'and yet', which is the same thing in a roundabout
way. The only possible rendering of καί here is 'and'.
Possibly we should explain: '*Ye* know that..., and to *me* it M, and
was God who shewed...', i.e. I know the Jewish law as well as ⁿᵉᵃʳˡʸ
you do, and a divine revelation alone explains my conduct.

29. τίνι λόγῳ] Plat. *Gorg.* 512 c τίνι δικαίῳ λόγῳ τοῦ M.
μηχανοποιοῦ καταφρονεῖς;

30. ἀπὸ τετάρτης ἡμέρας...] Lit. 'From the fourth
day up to this hour I was during the ninth hour praying',
or as R.V. 'I was keeping the ninth hour of prayer'; i.e.
four days ago (*quarto abhinc die*) reckoning up to this
hour (at which I am speaking to you) I was keeping...'.
A person speaking at 3 p.m. on Friday would refer to
3 p.m. on Tuesday as ἀπὸ τετάρτης ἡμ. μ. τ. τ. ὥρας, according to the Jewish method of reckoning in both days. Cf.
ver. 9 n.

T.R. has ἤμην νηστεύων καὶ τὴν ἐν. ὥρ. προσευχόμενος.

λαμπρᾷ] cf. i. 11; Mark ix. 3. The epithet indicates a
heavenly radiance.

33. καλῶς ἐποίησας] A formula of expressing thanks.
Cf. Phil. iv. 14 καλῶς ἐποιήσατε συνκοινωνήσαντές μου τῇ
θλίψει. Andoc. *de Myst.* 40 εἰπεῖν οὖν τὸν Εὔφημον ὅτι
καλῶς ποιήσειεν εἰπών, 'that E. said he was much obliged for
the information'.

34. ἀνοίξας...] viii. 35 n.

ἐπ' ἀληθείας...] The purport of this speech is this: 'I now see that *all* men, without distinction of nation, are acceptable to God (i.e. He is willing to accept or welcome them). His message on this subject (τὸν λόγον) He sent to the children of Israel proclaiming peace (to be obtained) through Jesus the Messiah, yes, Jesus who is Lord (not of one nation only but) of *all* men. You (ὑμεῖς) know the story of the events which took place (τὸ γενόμενον ῥῆμα), how Jesus of Nazareth was 'anointed' by God and so declared to be Messiah, His commission being demonstrated by the works which He performed (vers. 37, 38), and we (καὶ ἡμεῖς) are the witnesses to that life, and to the facts of His death and resurrection (vers. 39—41); we are commanded to proclaim Him as the universal judge, even as Him to whom all the prophets bear witness, that He is the Saviour of *all* who believe on Him'.

Observe the emphasis of ἐν παντὶ ἔθνει; πάντων κύριος; πάντα τὸν πιστεύοντα. Jesus is Messiah, and Messiah is the Saviour of all men—this is the essence of the whole speech. *Jesus est Christus, Christus est omnium Salvator.*

H. M.
W. La.
and so
A.V.
and
R.V.'
Most editors read τὸν λόγον ὅν and make λόγον, ῥῆμα, Ἰησοῦν all governed by οἴδατε and in apposition, the words οὗτός...κύριος, which contain the gist of the speech, being placed in a parenthesis. This is extremely harsh as regards grammar, ignores the marked difference between λόγος and ῥῆμα, and yields no satisfactory sense.

ὅν is omitted in AB and may easily be a repetition of the final ον in λόγον. Even if it is retained, the stop after αὐτῷ ἐστίν should be removed, and λόγον be governed by κατα-
So A.
de W.
λαμβάνομαι—'I apprehend that all...are acceptable, the message which...'

καταλαμβάνομαι] Exactly 'I apprehend', i.e. 'seize hold' or 'grasp with my mind'. Certain words had only been words before to him: now he *really grasps* their meaning..

προσωπολήμπτης] Only here; but cf. Luke xx. 21 οὐ λαμβάνεις πρόσωπον; Gal. ii. 6 πρόσωπον θεὸς ἀνθρώπου οὐ λαμβάνει. In Deut. x. 17 God οὐ θαυμάζει πρόσωπον οὐδὲ οὐ μὴ λάβῃ δῶρον, and so 2 Chron. xix. 7; Ps. lxxxii. 2 of evil
Light.
ad Gal.
ii. 6.
Lange.
judges πρόσωπα ἁμαρτωλῶν λαμβάνετε. The phrase indicates paying regard to the external circumstances or accidental qualities of a man as opposed to his intrinsic character. To shew special favour to a Jew, merely because he was a Jew, would be πρόσωπον λαμβάνειν.

35. δεκτὸς] A.V. 'accepted with'; R.V. 'acceptable to'. The word can=not merely *acceptabilis* but *acceptus*, cf. Luke iv. 19, 24; Phil. iv. 18 θυσίαν δεκτὴν εὐάρεστον τῷ θ.

36. τὸν λόγον...] A recollection of Ps. cvii. 20 ἀπέστειλε τὸν λ. αὐτοῦ καὶ ἰάσατο αὐτούς. λόγος is the regular word for the divine message which was delivered by Jesus, e.g. ὁ λ. τοῦ θ. iv. 31, viii. 14; ὁ λ. τοῦ κυρίου viii. 25; ὁ λ. τῆς σωτηρίας xiii. 26; ὁ λ. τῆς χάριτος xiv. 3 or simply ὁ λόγος xvi. 32.

εὐαγγ. εἰρήνην] A recollection of Is. lii. 7 πόδες εὐαγγελιζομένου ἀκοὴν εἰρήνης. The peace is peace with God.

διὰ 'Ι.] 'through Jesus', i.e. as the messenger.

οὗτος] 'He, yes he'—very emphatic. If any one will place a comma after Χριστοῦ and substitute ὅς for οὗτος, he will at once see the emphatic force of οὗτος. The four words οὗτός ἐστι πάντων κύριος contain the very gist and essence of Peter's argument. Their strong simplicity is admirable merely as an instance of rhetorical power. Printed as an unmeaning parenthesis in our English Version their whole power is lost.

37. τὸ γενόμενον ῥῆμα] cf. v. 32 n. Perhaps 'the story that was enacted' would fairly express the meaning.

ἀρξάμενος] So ℵABCDE; T.R. ἀρξάμενον. The word is so frequently used adverbially that possibly it is used here as a pure adverb or else Luke may have commenced to write 'beginning with Galilee...how Jesus (nominative) was anointed and then went about'.

ἀπὸ τῆς Γαλ.] Luke iv. 14.

38. 'Ιησοῦν...αὐτόν] The acc. thrown prominently forward and then the pronoun inserted pleonastically after the verb. Great emphasis is thus thrown on 'Ι. τὸν Ναζ., it being Peter's object to emphasize the fact that Jesus, the man 'Jesus of Nazareth', was declared to be the Messiah.

ἔχρισεν] ii. 22 n.

καταδυναστευομένους] vii. 19 n.

τοῦ διαβόλου]='the False Accuser', 'Slanderer'. Cf. διαβάλλω; διαβολή.

39. καὶ ἡμεῖς] answering to ὑμεῖς ver. 37. The historical part of Peter's speech is an appeal (1) to what his hearers know; (2) to what the Apostles are witnesses of. For μάρτυρες cf. i. 22 n.

ἀνεῖλαν...] ii. 23 n.: v. 30 n.

41. ἡμῖν, οἵτινες...] 'even to us, for we (vii. 53 n.)...'. For the 'eating and drinking' cf. Luke xxiv. 41, 43.

42. παρήγγειλεν] i.e. ὁ θεός, clearly. Throughout it is the action of God which is dwelt on: God sends Jesus the Messiah, and commands the Apostles to proclaim and bear

αὐτός
ℵAHP.
οὗτος
BCDEG.

witness to the fact. Moreover οὗτος (i.e. Jesus) could not refer to the nom. of παρήγγειλεν. T. R. reads αὐτός, thus probably making 'Jesus' nom. to παρ.: in which case the reference would be to the command of Jesus Matt. xxviii. 19.

43. πιστεύοντα εἰς αὐτόν] Of the person towards whom the belief is directed, in whose existence and personality it rests. So the Nicene Creed πιστεύομεν εἰς ἕνα θεόν: *Credo in Deum.* So too πιστεύω ἐπὶ τὸν κύριον ix. 42, xi. 17. A distinction is usually drawn between these phrases and πιστεύω σοι which is said to = *credo tibi* 'I believe' or 'trust you', but the distinction cannot be maintained, cf. v. 14, xvi. 34, xviii. 8, πιστεύειν τῷ θεῷ, τῷ κυρίῳ.

45. οἱ ἐκ περιτομῆς πιστοί] 'those who from circumcision had believed', i.e. those who, having been Jews, had become Christians. Cf. xi. 2; Gal. ii. 12 τοὺς ἐκ περιτομῆς of the Judaizing party. They believed that as a preliminary to being accepted as Christians, i.e. believers in the Messiah, it was necessary to be circumcised and accept the Mosaic Law.

τὰ ἔθνη] 'the Gentiles': *ab exemplo ad omnes concluditur.* B.

46. ἀπεκρίθη] cf. iii. 12 n. The 'answer' was not necessarily to their openly expressed questions, but to their visible doubt and amazement.

47. μήτι τὸ ὕδωρ...] 'Surely no one can withhold the water...?' For μήτι cf. Luke vi. 39 μήτι δύναται τυφλὸς τυφλὸν ὁδηγεῖν; Mark xiv. 19 μήτι ἐγώ;

Note the article, '*the* water'. Hitherto the 'gift of the Holy Spirit' had followed the *human* act of baptism as a visible sign of *God's* presence in those baptized (cf. ii. 38, viii. 16, 17). Now the conditions were reversed: *God's* presence had been made clear; it therefore rested with them to do their part. Of the two requisites of baptism, water and the Spirit (cf. xi. 16), the Spirit had been given, *the* water could not be withheld.

κωλῦσαι] Cf. Luke vi. 29 τὸν χιτῶνα μὴ κωλύσῃς.

48. ἐν τῷ ὀνόματι...] ii. 38 n.

CHAPTER XI.

1. ἔθνη ἐδέξαντο] Sense construction, cf. iii. 11 n.

2. διεκρίνοντο] The idea of the word is 'division' and so 'contention': cf. Herod. ix. 58 μάχῃ διακριθῆναι πρός τινα.

3. ἄνδρας ἀκρ. ἔχοντας] Not ἔθνη: the phrase is contemptuous, cf. the use of the adj. 'uncircumcised' in O. T., e.g. 1 Sam. xvii. 26; 2 Sam. i. 20.

συνέφαγεν] So involving the danger of eating some
'unclean' animal, or meat improperly killed. ' To this day F.
orthodox Jews submit to any inconvenience rather than
touch meat killed by a Gentile butcher'.

4. ἀρξάμενος...] The careful particularity of ἀρξάμενος,
of ἐξετίθετο, and of καθεξῆς (Luke i. 3), and the full repetition of the whole narrative, part of it being indeed given Baum.
three times (x. 3—6, 30—32, xi. 13, 14), make it clear that
Luke attaches much importance to it. The case of Cornelius was a test case of primary importance. The question,
whether to become a Christian it was necessary first to
accept the Mosaic law, was the first great difficulty of the
early Church, cf. xv. 1 and Gal. *passim.*

6. κατενόουν καὶ εἶδον] ' I was considering it (i.e. try-
ing to understand what it was) and then I saw (aorist)'.

12. διακρίναντα] Cf. x. 20 n.

13. τὸν ἄγγελον] Peter would probably say ' *an* angel',
but Luke who knows that his readers are already acquainted
with the story, not unnaturally writes ' *the* angel'.

15. ἐν ἀρχῇ] Originally, i.e. at the first outpouring of
the Spirit at Pentecost.

16. Ἰωάνης μὲν...] Cf. i. 5 n. The point of the quotation is this : Jesus promised to us as a special gift baptism
with the Holy Spirit ; that gift He has visibly bestowed on
the Gentiles exactly as it was bestowed on us ; surely we
are bound to admit to the external rite those who have
received the reality of baptism.

17. αὐτοῖς...πιστεύσασιν] ' to them as to us having
believed', or ' because of belief'. Both in grammar and
sense πιστ. seems properly taken both with αὐτοῖς and ἡμῖν:
' belief' in both cases was the condition of receiving the
gift. A. and R.V. give ' when *we* believed'.

ἐγὼ τίς...] Really a double question (1) ' Who was I
that I should...', cf. Ex. iii. 11 τίς εἰμι ἐγὼ ὅτι πορεύσομαι;
(2) ' was I able to...'. Observe the emphatic position of
ἐγώ heightening the contrast and emphasizing the argument : it is not ' who was I?' but ' I, who was I?'

18. ἡσύχασαν] Negative: their opposition ceased.
ἐδόξασαν, positive: their praise began.

ἄρα] *ergo*, ' then', ' so then': the word draws an inference, cf. Luke xi. 20 ἄρα ἔφθασεν ἐφ' ὑμᾶς, xi. 48 ἄρα μαρτυ-
ρεῖτε, and ἄρα οὖν commonly in St Paul at the beginning of
a sentence or clause (e.g. Rom. v. 18), a position which ἄρα
cannot occupy in classical Greek.

τὴν μετάνοιαν εἰς ζ.] 'the repentance (which leads) to
life', the repentance which it was the special mission of
Jesus to offer, cf. v. 31 n.

19. οἱ μὲν οὖν διασπαρέντες] Luke markedly connects
this with viii. 4 οἱ μὲν οὖν διασπαρέντες διῆλθον. From that
point we have the description of one set of incidents, which
arose out of the dispersion and persecution consequent on
the death of Stephen : here our attention is definitely recalled to the same point, that we may trace the same cause
acting in another direction, viz. in the spread of the Gospel to Antioch, the first great scene of St Paul's labours and
the centre from which he commences those missionary
journeys, the record of which composes the chief part of the
remainder of the Acts.

θλίψεως] From θλίβω (akin to τρίβω); cf. *tribulum*
whence 'tribulation'.

ἐπὶ Στεφάνῳ] 'about S.', as the original cause of it, cf.
iii. 10 n. Andoc. *de Myst.* 25 τῶν φυγόντων ἐπὶ τοῖς μυστη-
ρίοις.

Φοινίκης] A plain 120 m. long by 15 broad, on the sea-
coast to the W. of Lebanon, its chief cities being Tyre and
Sidon.

A. F.   **Ἀντιοχείας]** On the Orontes, 15 m. from its port
Seleucia, one of the most important cities of antiquity.
It was built B.C. 301 by Seleucus Nicator, and became the
capital of Syria and residence of the imperial legate. After-
wards one of the five patriarchates with Jerusalem, Rome,
Constantinople and Alexandria.

20. Κυρηναῖοι] ii. 10 n.

καὶ πρὸς τοὺς Ἑλληνιστάς] 'also to the Grecians', i.e.
as well as to the Jews mentioned ver. 19. But this is not
sense, for the term Ἰουδαῖος includes Ἑλληνιστής.

v. A. M.   The readings demand attention.
La. W.   καὶ is found in אAB but omitted in DEHLP.

"Ἕλληνας is found in A (which however reads "Ἕλληνας
wrongly ix. 29), D¹ (where it has been altered to Ἑλληνιστάς)
and א³ as a correction of εὐαγγελιστάς.

Ἕλληνας   Ἑλληνιστάς is found in BD²EHLP.
given in
R.V.,   The objections to Ἑλληνιστάς, notwithstanding its great
Eus.,   mss. authority, are almost insuperable, for (1) the Hellenists
Chrys.,   (vi. 1 n.) had always been accepted as members of the church,
Grotius,   see the list in ch. ii., and preaching to them would certainly
Lach-
mann,   not be mentioned specially or have given occasion to the
Tischen-   sending of Barnabas; (2) they were Ἰουδαῖοι and cannot be
dorf,   opposed to them as they are here : the opposite of Ἑλλη-
M. A. N.
La. F.   νιστής is Ἑβραῖος.
&c.

The reading'Ελληνιστάς seems due to a belief that the
conversion of Cornelius was the *first* case of the conversion
of a Gentile, whereas, if "Ελληνας be read here, we seem to
have a prior instance of such conversion, for the words which
describe the commission and conduct of Barnabas are Λ.
thought to indicate that what had happened at Antioch
startled and surprised the Church at Jerusalem. But
(1) although the case of Cornelius was first in *importance*
(as Luke clearly indicates by the position and length of his
narrative) it is not necessary to assume that it was first in
point of *time;* (2) even assuming that the case of Cornelius
was already known, it would surely be natural to send a
commissioner to examine and report on the working of the
newly-accepted principle in practice.

It is also urged against "Ελληνας that xiv. 27 when Paul
and Barnabas return to Antioch they bring back news that
' God had opened a door of faith to the Gentiles', and that
there would be no need to proclaim this if the same thing
had happened at Antioch itself. It will be observed however that the words in xiv. 27 are not the announcement of
a new *principle*, but of a new *fact*, viz. successful missionary
work among the Gentiles of Asia Minor, which would naturally be good news to the Gentile converts in Antioch.

As a proof that 'Ελληνιστάς is a correction, observe that
all the MSS. which read it omit καί *except* B, which retains
καί. This is remarkable. Any one altering "Ελληνας to 'Ελληνιστάς would naturally omit καί, for ' also to the Grecians'
is obviously not sense (see above). How then is it possible
to account for the reading of B, except on the supposition
that καὶ πρὸς τοὺς 'Ελληνιστάς is an *incomplete* correction
from καὶ πρὸς τοὺς"Ελληνας?

21. χεὶρ Κυρίου] 'the hand of Jehovah', i.e. His visibly
exerted strength; cf. iv. 30, xiii. 11; Luke i. 66 καὶ χεὶρ K.
ἦν μετ' αὐτοῦ. The phrase is graphic, and common in O.T.,
e.g. Ex. ix. 3; Is. lix. 1.

22. περὶ αὐτῶν] i.e. the new converts.

ἐξαπέστειλαν] Clearly as a commissioner to examine and
report. The narrative does not seem to indicate surprise
or opposition, as when the case of Cornelius was reported, v. N.
but rather describes the conduct of those, who regarded with
natural interest the practical working on a large scale of a
principle already accepted.

23. χάριν...ἐχάρη] *Suavis paronomasia;* grace brings
gladness. Cf. Luke i. 28 Χαῖρε, κεχαριτωμένη.

τὴν τοῦ θεοῦ] Emphatic, cf. i. 25 n.

παρεκάλει] iv. 36 n.

προθέσει] 'purpose', cf. xxvii. 13.

26. συναχθῆναι ἐν τῇ ἐκκλ.] 'assembled (with the other believers) in the church'.

W. χρηματίσαι] '(1) *negotiari*, (2) *ita ut* nomen *inde adipiscaris*, (3) *denominari*: cf. Rom. vii. 3 μοιχαλὶς χρηματίσει'.

V. H. W.   Χριστιανούς] About this word two points are clear:
La.   (1) It was not employed by the Christians of themselves, being only found in N. T. here, Acts xxvi. 28 (contemptuously), and 1 Pet. iv. 16. The 'believers' are οἱ μαθηταί, οἱ ἅγιοι, οἱ πιστοί, οἱ ἀδελφοί.
        (2) It was not invented by the Jews, who would not apply the term 'followers of the Messiah' to those who they maintained were the followers of the man Jesus, who was *not* the Messiah. The Jews called them 'Nazarenes' or 'Galilaeans'.
        The word is formed on the analogy of *Pompeiani, Caesariani,* Ἡρωδιανοί (Matt. xxii. 16), and so means 'partizans' or 'followers of Christus'. It is found Tac. *Ann.* xv. 44 *quos vulgus Christianos appellabat. Auctor ejus nominis Christus....* It was also spelt *Chrestiani*, and Suet. *Claud.* 25) has *Chrestus*, apparently connecting it with χρηστός, and cf. Fr. chrétien = chrestien.
        It is a remarkable word, being 'written in Hebrew and Greek and Latin', for it refers to the Hebrew belief in a Messiah, it is a Greek word, and it is formed as a Latin adjective.

27. ἐν ταύταις...] i.e. during the stay of Paul and Barnabas at Antioch.

κατῆλθον] Jerusalem being regarded as the central point; viii. 15 n.

προφῆται] Both in N. T. and O. T. the word 'prophet' is not limited to its modern sense of one who '*foretells* the future', but is used in a wider sense of one who 'declares' or 'forth tells the will of God', and refers either to the present, past, or future. In N. T. it is clearly applied to persons possessing some *special inspiration*. In 1 Cor. xiv. 'prophecy' is distinguished from γλώσσαις λαλεῖν as being intelligent and intelligible, and (ver. 3) its objects are defined as οἰκοδομὴν καὶ παράκλησιν καὶ παραμυθίαν. The term is frequent in the Acts, cf. xiii. 1 π. καὶ διδάσκαλοι; xv. 32 π. ὄντες...παρεκάλεσαν καὶ ἐπεστήριξαν.

28. ἀναστάς] v. 17 n. Ἄγαβος, also xxi. 10.

J. Ant.   λιμὸν...] We have no knowledge of any *universal*
XX. 5. 2. famine in the reign of Claudius, but Josephus speaks of 'the great famine' in Judaea A.D. 44, and describes how pro-

visions were purchased for the Jews from Egypt by Izates king of Adiabene and his mother Helena, who were Jewish proselytes. Famines in various places however characterized the reign of Claudius, and Suet. *Claud.* 10 speaks of *assiduas sterilitates;* cf. too Suet. 18; Tac. *Ann.* XII. 43.

λιμός fem. is Doric, from which dialect many forms W. passed into Hellenistic Greek. Cf. xii. 4 πιάσας for πιέσας.

Κλαυδίου] Roman emperor 41—54 A.D.; born B.C. 10; son of Drusus the brother of the Emperor Tiberius; predecessor of Nero.

29. τῶν δὲ μαθητῶν] Strict grammar would require οἱ μαθ. as nom. to ὥρισαν, but the gen. is due to τις occurring in the intervening clause καθὼς εὐπορεῖτό τις. 'But the disciples according to every one's means determined each of them to send with a view to help...'.

The complexity of the sentence is due to Luke's desire to insert so much, viz. (1) the general determination, ὥρισαν, (2) the rule which determined the amount of the contributions, καθὼς εὐπορεῖτό τις, (3) the individual interest excited, ἕκαστος αὐτῶν.

30. τοὺς πρεσβυτέρους] Here mentioned for the first time. They probably occupy a similar position in the church to the 'elders' in the Jewish synagogue. The 'elders' naturally become marked off in all communities (cf. vi. 11 τὸν λαὸν καὶ τοὺς πρεσβ., and the words *senatus,* γερουσία, alderman, πρεσβυτέριον xxii. 5), and the 'elders' were treated with especial reverence by the Jews and spoken of as a separate body, *v.* O. T. *passim.* The word soon begins to indicate not so much superior age as superior position. The Apostles appointed 'elders' in every city xiv. 23: they ranked next to the Apostles (xv. 2, 4, 6), and are also called ἐπίσκοποι 'overseers' (xx. 17 compared with xx. 28).

From the word our 'priest' is derived, being, like the French *prêtre,* a contracted form of 'presbyter'; some confusion has arisen from the fact that 'priest' is the ordinary rendering of ἱερεύς, which is quite distinct in meaning from πρεσβύτερος.

Σαύλου] St Paul in Gal. does not mention this visit.

CHAPTER XII.

1. κατ' ἐκεῖνον...] i.e. about the time of the mission of Barnabas and Paul.

ἐπέβαλεν τὰς χ.] to be taken literally: 'laid his hands on', κακῶσαι giving the object of his doing so. It is not merely = ἐπεχείρησεν, 'attempted', cf. iv. 3, v. 18.

'Ηρῴδης ὁ β.] Herod Agrippa, son of Aristobulus and Berenice, grandson of Herod the Great, educated at Rome. Caligula at his accession (A.D. 37) gave him the tetrarchy of Trachonitis and the title of king, subsequently adding Galilee and Peraea. He was at Rome at the death of Caligula, and aided Claudius in acquiring the empire; in return for his services Samaria and Judaea were added to his government. He is described by Josephus as a pleasant, vain man, very anxious to secure popularity with the Jews, whose rites he scrupulously observed (τὰ πάτρια καθαρῶς ἐτήρει).

J. Ant.
xix. 7. 3.

2. 'Ιάκωβον] Son of Zebedee, Matt. iv. 21. Specially chosen with John and Peter to be present at the raising of Jairus' daughter (Mark v. 37), at the transfiguration (Matt. xvii. 1), and the agony in the garden (Matt. xxvi. 37). Of him and John Jesus had specially said 'Ye shall indeed drink of my cup' (Matt. xx. 23). He is the only Apostle whose death is mentioned in N.T.

μαχαίρῃ] By beheading; cf. the case of John the Baptist Matt. xiv. 10.

W.

3. προσέθετο συλλαβεῖν] 'A Hebraism. See Luke xx. 12 προσέθετο πέμψαι'; Gen. iv. 2 προσέθηκε τεκεῖν; xxxviii. 26 προσέθετο τοῦ γνῶναι.

τῶν ἀζύμων] 'bread not made with yeast' (ζέω and 'yeast' being from one root). It was to remind the Israelites of the *haste* with which they left Egypt and ate the first passover (Ex. xii. 34, 39). It was eaten for seven days after the eating of the passover lamb on the 14th of Nisan (Ex. xii. 14; Lev. xxiii. 6).

4. τέσσαρσιν τετρ.] Four bodies of four men, each of which would be on duty for six hours out of the twenty-four. The Romans divided the night into four 'watches' (*vigiliae*), and so perhaps each 'quaternion' would take one 'watch' of the night. Two of the soldiers were chained to Peter, and perhaps two kept watch outside the cell, but it is an error to identify these with the πρώτη φυλακή καὶ δευτέρα of ver. 10, as the words φυλακή and διελθόντες do not admit this.

As M. A.
do.

μετὰ τὸ π.] Clearly not merely the 14th of Nisan, the day of the eating the passover lamb, but the whole passover week, for the reference to αἱ ἡμ. τῶν ἀζ. and the imperfect ἐτηρεῖτο ver. 5 imply a duration of several days, and Luke himself defines τὸ πάσχα, cf. Luke xxii. 1 ἡ ἑορτὴ τῶν ἀζύμων ἡ λεγομένη πάσχα.

M. W. A.   *Non judicant die festo* was a Jewish rule.

ἀναγαγεῖν] Herod would take his place on the raised

judgment-seat (βῆμα, *tribunal*) and the prisoner be *led up* to it, and there condemned in the presence of and for the pleasure of the Jews (τῷ λαῷ; Ethic Dat. embracing both these ideas). Cf. John xix. 13—16.

5. ὁ μὲν οὖν Π....] 'So then P. was being guarded... *and* prayer was being made......*but* when Herod was about...'.

The clause προσευχὴ δὲ... is *parallel* to ὁ μὲν οὖν Π...., the *antithesis* to which is ὅτε δὲ.... Both A. and R.V. are in error here; cf. ii. 41 n.

6. δεδεμένος ἁλ. δυσίν] cf. xxviii. 16, 20. The prisoner was chained by the wrist usually to one soldier, here for more security to two. Cf. Sen. *Ep.* 5 *eadem catena et militem et custodiam copulat.*

7. ἐπέστη] cf. verse 10 ἀπέστη. Both words connote La. suddenness. Cf. Luke ii. 9 ἄγγελος Κυρίου ἐπέστη. The 2nd aorist of ἐφίστημι occurs seven times in Luke, eight times in the Acts, and nowhere else in N.T.

οἰκήματι] 'a room in a house', 'chamber', but frequently used euphemistically='a cell', 'a prison', e.g. Dem. 890.

8. ζῶσαι] 'put on thy girdle', worn round the Che- Eders-thoneth (χιτών). 'It was not a hasty escape as in Hor. *Sat.* heim, 1. i. 2. 132 *Discincta tunica fugiendum est ac pede nudo'. H. Cf. too ἄζωστος='hurried' Hes. *Op.* 343.

10. διελθόντες...] 'when they were past the first and second ward', A. and R.V. rightly.

The word διελθόντες suggests 'traversing a place', and so seems to necessitate rendering φυλακή, 'ward': otherwise it might='guard', 'body of men on guard'.

αὐτομάτη] So of things without life, *Il.* v. 749 αὐτόμαται δὲ πύλαι μύκον οὐρανοῦ.

11. ἐν ἑαυτῷ γεν.] Peter had hitherto regarded the impressions he had received as visionary and unreal, as similar to those received x. 10 when he was in an 'ecstasy'; now having 'come to himself', i.e. finding himself in his ordinary everyday waking state, he perceives that they are real.

12. συνιδών] cf. xiv. 6; 'having viewed and comprehended the case', having grasped the situation; so Dem. 17 πάντα δὴ ταῦτα δεῖ συνιδόντας ἅπαντας βοηθεῖν....

Μαρίας] Otherwise unknown. In Col. iv. 10 Μάρκος ὁ ἀνεψιὸς Βαρνάβα is rendered in A.V. 'sister's son to B.', thus making Mary sister of Barnabas, but the rendering of ἀνεψιός is quite arbitrary, and R.V. rightly gives 'cousin'.

'John surnamed Mark' is generally identified with Mark the Evangelist. As with Saul, so with him, his Hebrew name ceases to be used generally, cf. xiii. 5, 13 'John', but xv. 39; 2 Tim. iv. 11; Philem. 24 'Mark'. Notwithstanding his desertion of Paul recorded in the Acts he was with him during his first imprisonment at Rome, cf. Col. iv. 10. Ancient testimony agrees in making him the ἑρμηνευτής of Peter, cf. 1 Pet. v. 13 Μάρκος ὁ υἱός μου.

13. κρούσαντος, ὑπακοῦσαι] Both classical in this sense. Cf. Xen. *Symp.* I. 11 κρούσας τὴν θύραν εἶπε τῷ ὑπακούσαντι.

τὴν θύραν τοῦ πυλῶνος] From this phrase it is clear that πυλών 'gateway', 'gate', is a more inclusive term than θύρα 'door': the words are often however used indifferently, cf. ver. 14.

15. Μαίνῃ] cf. xxvi. 24.

διϊσχυρίζετο] Classical. A very strong word, 'kept confidently affirming'.

ὁ ἄγγελος] It was a popular belief among the Jews that each man had 'a guardian angel'. Cf. the *genius* of the Romans, and Hor. *Ep.* II. 2. 188

> *Genius, natale comes qui temperat astrum,*
> *naturae deus humanae, mortalis in unum*
> *quodque caput, voltu mutabilis, albus et ater.*

And Pind. *Ol.* 13. 148 δαίμων γενέθλιος.
Matt. xviii. 10 is important as regards the validity of this belief.

17. κατασείσας] cf. xiii. 16, xix. 33, xxi. 40, of a speaker, who indicates by a downward movement of the hand a desire for silence.

For James v. F. *ad* xv. 13.
v. Lightfoot, *ad loc.*
Ἰακώβῳ] cf. xv. 13, xxi. 18, president of the Church at Jerusalem; specially mentioned by Paul (Gal. i. 19) as seen by him and 'a brother of the Lord', and an 'Apostle' (but not therefore one of the Twelve, or to be identified with 'James of Alphaeus').

18. οὐκ ὀλίγος] Litotes; cf. xix. 11 οὐ τὰς τυχούσας. The phrase occurs eight times in the Acts; e.g. xv. 2.

τί ἄρα...] 'what could have become of P.'; τί ἄρα expresses much more doubt and astonishment than τί; cf. Luke i. 66 τί ἄρα τὸ παιδίον τοῦτο ἔσται;

19. ἀνακρίνας] iv. 9 n. **ἀπαχθῆναι** here absolutely. ='to be led away, to execution'; cf. Matt. xxvii. 31 ἀπήγαγον αὐτὸν εἰς τὸ σταυρῶσαι; Dem. 736, 2 ἀπαγαγεῖν τοῖς ἕνδεκα. So too *duci*, cf. Plin. *ad Traj.* 96 (of the Christians) *Confitentes iterum ac tertio interrogavi, supplicium minatus: perseverantes duci jussi.*

20. θυμομαχῶν] Late Gk, = 'to fight passionately', but de W.M.
Herod could have no power to go to *war* with Tyre and
Sidon, and so here='have an angry quarrel with'. A.
and R.V. 'was highly displeased with'.

Τυρίοις καὶ Σ.] Both cities are on the coast; Tyre is
20 m. S. of Sidon, of which it was a colony, though it became more important than the mother city; it was almost
the first commercial city of the ancient world. The main
part of the town was on an island half a mile from the shore.
It was taken by Alexander (B.C. 322) after a siege of seven
months, and never regained its former consequence.

τὸν ἐπὶ τοῦ κοιτῶνος] *praefectus cubiculo, cubicularius,*
'chamberlain'—an officer who from his opportunities of
personal access might naturally obtain great influence
with a monarch.

διὰ τὸ τρέφεσθαι…] They were large commercial cities
with an amount of territory not proportioned to their
population, and so looked largely to Palestine for their food-
supply, cf. 1 Kings v. 9; Ezek. xxvii. 17. Herod might
render this importation of food very difficult.

21. τακτῇ…] Josephus gives a full account of Herod's *Ant.*
death. The occasion he describes as a festival held in $\frac{XIX. 8. 2.}{given\ in}$
honour of the emperor: on the second day Herod having A.
put on a robe all of silver tissue (στολὴν ἐνδυσάμενος ἐξ
ἀργύρου πεποιημένην πᾶσαν) came into the theatre at day-
break, and, the rays of the sun striking full on this robe,
it gave forth a marvellous radiance (θαυμασίως ἀπέστιλβεν)
striking awe and terror into the beholders. Thereupon
flatterers hailed him as a god with the words Εὐμενὴς εἴης.
He did not rebuke them, but shortly afterwards observed
an owl (βουβῶνα) perched on a rope above his head and at
once took it for a messenger of evil (ἄγγελον…εὐθὺς ἐνόησε
κακῶν εἶναι); he was presently seized with pain in the pit
of his stomach and died (γαστρὸς ἀλγήμασι διεργασθεὶς) five
days later after continuous suffering.

ἐπὶ τοῦ βήματος] From Jos. we know that this took
place in the theatre, which was often used for public assem-
blies (cf. xix. 29). βῆμα, originally the platform in the
Pnyx at Athens from which the orators spoke, is frequently
used for the raised seat or platform (*suggestus, tribunal*) of
a Roman magistrate or officer; cf. Matt. xxvii. 19; Acts
xviii. 12, xxv. 6.

ἐδημηγόρει] *Contionabatur:* he addressed the ambassa-
dors in a 'public harangue' before the assembly.

23. ἐπάταξεν…ἄγγελος Κυρίου] cf. xii. 7 ἄγγελος Κυρίου
…πατάξας: *observanda antithesis.*

160   *ACTS OF THE APOSTLES.* [XII. 23

For the 'angel of Jehovah', cf. 2 Kings xix. 35, of the destruction of Sennacherib, ἐξῆλθεν ἀγγ. Κ. καὶ ἐπάταξεν; also 1 Chron. xxi. 15.

v. F. ad σκωληκόβρωτος] Apparently this disease, whatever it
loc. was, was regarded as a divine judgment on the pride of tyrants. Cf. 2 Macc. ix. where the death of Antiochus Epiphanes is described, the disease being spoken of as σπλάγχνων ἀλγηδὼν καὶ πικραὶ τῶν ἔνδον βάσανοι,......ὥστε ἐκ τοῦ σώματος σκώληκας ἀναζεῖν, and it is emphatically de-
Ant. scribed as a punishment of his pride and cruelty. Herod
xvii.6.5. the Great according to Josephus died of σῆψις σκώληκας ἐμποιοῦσα. Cf. too Herod. iv. 205 ἡ Φερετίμη ζῶσα εὐλέων ἐξέζεσεν, where it is mentioned as a divine punishment.

At this point begins the history of St Paul's three missionary journeys, and the rest of the Acts is confined to
de W. an account of his life. 'Each journey is commenced from Antioch and ends with a visit to Jerusalem, each is illus-trated with a speech, the first before Jews (xiii. 16—41), the second before Gentiles (xvii. 22—31), the third before Christians (xx. 18—35)'.

CHAPTER XIII.

1. προφῆται καὶ διδ.] xi. 27 n.

Συμεὼν ... Μαναήν] Unknown. Μαναήν = Menahem (2 Kings xv. 14).

σύντροφος] V. *collactaneus;* R.V. 'foster-brother'. A.V. 'brought up with'. There are no grounds for deciding between the two senses.

So M. ὅ τε Βαρνάβας...καὶ Σαῦλος] The marked insertion of the other names between these two names, hitherto men-tioned in close connection (e.g. xii. 25), is curious. It would seem that Luke before describing their special 'sepa-ration' for their missionary work, is desirous to point out that previously they were not 'separated' from, but only two among the other 'prophets and teachers' at Antioch.

'Ηρώδου] iv. 27 n.

2. λειτουργούντων] In classical Greek 'to undertake the performance of one of those public services' (λειτουργίαι) such as the equipment of a trireme, which fell in turn on all wealthy Athenian citizens: in LXX. used of 'minister-ing' in the temple, e.g. 1 Sam. ii. 11; Ex. xxviii. 39 (43), cf. Heb. x. 11: here apparently of 'worship' generally, cf. our word 'liturgy', and 'service' in the phrase 'Morning Service'.

'Fasting' and 'prayer' are continually connected, cf. x. 30; 1 Sam. vii. 5, 6; Dan. ix. 3.

ἀφορίσατε δή] δή gives vigorous emphasis to the command. Cf. xv. 36; Luke ii. 15 διελθωμεν δή, and the frequent use of ἄγε δή, φέρε δή, &c.
Paul speaks of himself (Rom. i. 1) as ἀφωρισμένος εἰς εὐαγγέλιον θεοῦ.

ὅ] εἰς is to be repeated before the pronoun, cf. ver. 39 ἀπὸ πάντων ὧν; Stallb. Plat. *Phaed.* 76 D ἐν τούτῳ ἀπόλλυμεν ὧπερ καὶ λαμβάνομεν—*non iteratur praepositio ἐν more loquendi paene legitimo;* Soph. *O. C.* 749.

4. αὐτοὶ μὲν οὖν] The antithesis is διελθόντες δέ, cf. ii. 41 n.

ὑπὸ τοῦ ἁγ. πν.] Note this repeated reference to the source of their authority, and cf. ver. 9.

Σελευκίαν] Seleucia 'by the sea', as it was called to distinguish it from other cities of the same name, was founded B.C. 300 by Seleucus Nicator at the mouth of the Orontes.

Κύπρον] The birthplace of Barnabas, cf. iv. 36. The number of Jews was so great there, that A.D. 116 they rose upon the native inhabitants and massacred, it is said, 240,000.

5. Σαλαμῖνα] The principal town of the island, on the E. coast in what is now the harbour of Famagousta; said to have been built by Teucer, son of Telamon king of Salamis, whom his father refused to receive home after the death of Ajax, and to have been called after that famous island, cf. Hor. *Od.* I. 7. 29 *ambiguam tellure nova Salamina futuram.*

κατήγγελλον...] It was Paul's regular practice to enter the synagogues and preach, cf. xiv. 1, xvii. 2 κατὰ τὸ εἰωθός, xviii. 4, 19, xix. 8. His rule in preaching the Gospel was, 'to the Jew first and also to the Greek', Rom. i. 16; cf. Acts xiii. 46 ὑμῖν πρῶτον.
Jesus in the same way preached after reading the lesson, cf. Luke iv. 20. For the synagogue worship, vi. 9 n.

ὑπηρέτην] Probably in the same sense as Luke iv. 20, where it is used of the 'minister' (Chazzan) or 'assistant' of the synagogue, cf. vi. 9 n.

6. Πάφου] New Paphos on the W. coast, 8 m. N. of the old Paphos celebrated for the worship of Venus.

μάγον] viii. 9 n.

Βαριησοῦς] 'son of Jesus' or 'Joshua', cf. i. 23 n.

ἀνθυπάτῳ] 'proconsul'. Under the emperors the provinces were divided into two classes, imperial and senatorial.

The former were usually such as needed the presence of a
military force and were governed by a military officer
(*legatus*) immediately subordinate to the emperor : for the
latter the governors were nominally appointed by the senate
and termed proconsuls, that term being applied to them
' though they had only been praetors '.

Cyprus had been an imperial province but had been
restored to the senate by Augustus in exchange for Dal-
matia.   General Cesnola discovered an inscription in
Cyprus with the words

ΕΠΙΠΑΤΛΟΤ...

ΤΠΑΤΟΤ

the letters ΑΝΘ being probably to be supplied.

7. συνετῷ] from συνίημι ('I put together', 'grasp',
' understand') indicates the possession of sound sense and
sagacity.   Amid the decay of belief in their own mythology
many inquiring minds at Rome turned their attention to the
consideration of foreign religions, and especially that of the
Jews.   Hence the influence obtained even with 'sensible'
men by such impostors as Barjesus, cf. Juv. VI. 543 *Arca-
nam Judaea tremens mendicat in aurem | interpres legum
Solymarum.*

8. Ἐλύμας]   Probably an Arabic word = μάγος 'the
wise man' : still found in the Turkish title *Ulemah.*

διαστρέψαι]= 'to pervert', 'turn aside', or into a wrong
direction some one who is taking the direct road to an
object, cf. ver. 10 διαστρέφων ; Luke ix. 41 γενεὰ διεστραμ-
μένη.

9. ὁ καὶ Παῦλος]   Up to this point the Apostle has
always been called by his Hebrew name Σαῦλος, hencefor-
ward he is always called by his Roman name, Παῦλος.   It is
clear that S. Luke notes the change of name as important
and marking an epoch; it would seem that his non-Jewish
name is thus introduced at the commencement of his missionary labours as the Apostle of the Gentiles, in order to
indicate that the narrative is no longer concerned with a
comparatively unknown Jew, but with one who, under the
name of Paul, was to win a wider and universal fame.

Many connect the name with Sergius Paulus (*ob tam
magnae insigne victoriae*, Aug.), but in the text no such connection seems hinted at, and the similarity of the Latin
name to the Hebrew one is probably its real origin (cf. i.
23 n.).   It may have been always borne by the Apostle,
though hitherto, while among Jews, not generally used.

Augustine remarks *nomen elegit ut se ostenderet parvum,*
but as a proper name the word rather suggested the glories

W. F.
from Dio
Cassius,
LIII. 13.

Dio Cas-
sius, LIII.
12.

La. from
'Cesno-
la, *Cy-
prus, its
Ancient
Cities.*
London,
1877'.

v. F.

E. g. Je-
rome,
Augus-
tine, B.
Baum.

Aug. *de
Spir. et
Lit.* c. 7.

of the Aemilian family, and even to us recalls the name of Hor. *Od.*
another Paulus, who was 'lavish of his noble life'. I. 12. 38.

10. παντὸς...πάσης...πάσης] Note the emphasis.

ῥᾳδιουργίας]='acting lightly', 'easily', 'without principle', cf. *ῥᾳδιούργημα* xviii. 14.

τὰς ὁδοὺς...τὰς εὐθ.] The adj. emphatic by position. The opposite expression is 'crooked ways', Ps. cxxv. 5; Prov. ii. 15. Isaiah had specially foretold of Messiah that 'the crooked shall be made straight' (Is. xl. 4, xlii. 16 *τὰ σκολιὰ εἰς εὐθεῖαν*; cf. Luke iii. 5).

11. χεὶρ Κυρίου] xi. 21 n. Cf. Job xix. 21 χεὶρ γὰρ Κ. ἡ ἀψαμένη μού ἐστιν.

12. ἐπὶ τῇ...] For ἐπὶ cf. iii. 10 n. κυρίου is the objective gen.: 'teaching about the Lord'.

13. ἀναχθέντες] 'having put out to sea', classical, and thirteen times in the Acts, cf. too Luke viii. 22 *ἀνήχθησαν*. The Greeks regarded the coast line as lying low: from it you go *up* inland (*ἀναβαίνειν*) or *up* on to the 'high seas' (*ἀνάγεσθαι*), the opposite words being *καταβαίνειν, κατάγεσθαι*.

οἱ περὶ Π.] 'Paul and his companions': so Plat. *Crat.* 440 c οἱ περὶ Ἡράκλειτον. Note that now Paul becomes the main figure, and contrast his *secondary* position ix. 27, xi. 30, xiii. 1, 2.

Πέργην] On the river Cestrus 7½ m. from its mouth. Pamphylia lies along the coast between Cilicia on the E. and Lycia on the W.

Ἰωάνης...] Cf. xv. 38.

14. Ἀντιόχειαν] Like the great Antioch built by Seleucus Nicator and named after his father; made a 'free city.' 189 B.C., and a colony by Augustus, who called it Caesarea.

τῶν σαββάτων] Heb. word='day of rest', cf. Gen. ii. 3.

15. προφητῶν] 'The Prophets were not read in the H. from Brown's *Ant. of the Jews,* I. 610. synagogues till B. c. 163, when they were substituted for the Law, which was prohibited by Antiochus Epiphanes. After the removal of that prohibition by the Maccabees, both Law and Prophets were read'.

'On the Sabbath at least seven persons were called on to Edersheim, I. 443. read successively portions of the Law'.

λόγος παρακλήσεως] iv. 36 n. Any Rabbi or distinguished stranger might be called on to preach: ordination was not requisite. Cf. the case of Jesus, Luke iv. 16 *et seq.*

The outline of Paul's discourse is this: as God has shewn special care for Israel in the past (16—22), so He has now

sent to Israel the promised Saviour—Jesus (23).   The message of this salvation, long promised to our fathers, has
been sent to *us* (26).   The Jews at Jerusalem did not recognize Jesus as the Messiah but crucified Him as had been
foretold.   God has however proved His claims by raising
Him from the dead (27—30), and of this fact we, the Apostles,
are witnesses, and accordingly preach to you that Jesus is
the Saviour whom the Scriptures foretell (31—37), and warn
you to give heed to our message (38—41).

16. καὶ οἱ φοβ. τ. θεόν] Cf. x. 2 n.; not Israelites,
but proselytes, as is clearly shewn by comparing ver. 43.

17. τούτου] deictic.

ἐξελέξατο] Cf. i. 2 n. and Deut. iv. 37 *ἐξελέξατο τὸ
σπέρμα αὐτῶν*; Ps. lxxxix. 3 *διεθέμην διαθήκην τοῖς ἐκλεκτοῖς
μου*.   Israel was 'the chosen' people.

M. **ὕψωσεν]** 'raised', i.e. increased in numbers, strength,
and dignity,—the last especially in connection with their
miraculous delivery.   So the sojourn in Egypt and delivery
from it are referred to with grateful pride, Ps. cv. 23—38.
A. and R.V. 'exalted'.

παροικίᾳ] vii. 6 n.

μετὰ βραχίονος...] Ex. vi. 6 *λυτρώσομαι ὑμᾶς ἐν βραχίονι
ὑψηλῷ*.

18. καὶ ὡς...] This reading makes ὡς = 'when', but
the alternative reading is much simpler, placing a καί before
καθελών and making ὡς = 'about', as in A. and R.V.

ἐτροποφόρησεν] 'suffered he their manners' A. and R.V.
For the meaning of the word cf. Cic. *ad Att.* XIII. 29 *In hoc
τὸν τῦφόν μου πρὸς θεῶν τροποφόρησον*; Schol. Arist. *Ran.*
1432 ἢ μὴ καταδέξασθαι ἢ καταδεξαμένους τροποφορεῖν.
There is a distinct reference to Deut. i. 31 *τροποφορήσει
σε κύριος ὁ θεός σου, ὡς εἴ τις τροποφορήσαι ἄνθρωπος τὸν υἱὸν
αὐτοῦ, κατὰ πᾶσαν τὴν ὁδόν...*

τροπ. The original Hebrew word means simply 'to bear'
in ℵBC² ('carry'; or 'endure' 'be patient with'), and both in the
DHLP. LXX. and here *ἐτροφοφόρησεν* is also read.   Whether it
τροφ. means merely 'nourished' (= *ἔθρεψεν* Hesych.), or 'bare
in AC¹E them as a nursing father' (R.V. in margin), *ἐτροφοφόρησεν*
ἐτροφ. seems clearly required by the sense here (and also in Deut.
is given i. 31), for the Apostle is dwelling not on the *perversity* of
in A. M. Israel but on the *care* and affection of God for them: *ἐτρο-
H.B.W.
F. de W. ποφόρησεν* distinctly is out of place.

Tulit *Deus populum Israeliticum in deserto beneficentissi-
ma, eaque plane singulari ratione, quae proprie illi conveni-
ret aetati tenellae, qua populus non ipse se tulit, ut homo*

adultus, sed Deus eum, ut parvulum necdum sibi suppetentem, gestavit. B.   Cf. Is. lxiii. 9; and especially Num. xi. 12.

19. ἕπτα ἔθνη...] Cf. Deut. vii. 1.

κατεκληρονόμησεν] 'gave (them) as an inheritance': T.R. without any authority *κατεκληροδότησεν* 'divided to them by lot'.

20. ὡς ἔτεσι...] The text seems to mean that the whole of the events from God's 'choosing' Israel, i.e. from His covenant with Abraham up to the entrance into Canaan, took place in 'about 450 years'. For the dat. cf. viii. 11 *ἱκανῷ χρόνῳ.* Text in ℵ ABC and followed by W. B. R. V.

T.R. places these words after *μετὰ ταῦτα,* thus making the period of the Judges 450 years. This was the popular chronology, and the figure is apparently obtained by adding together the dates assigned in the O.T. to the various Judges including Eli; this method of calculation however does not take into account that several Judges may have been contemporaneous, and is inconsistent with 1 K. vi. 1, where Solomon's temple is said to have been begun 480 years after the departure from Egypt. Cf. Jos. Ant. viii. 3. 1.

Many consider that the reading given in the text is a correction, and that the reading of T.R. (following E, G, H) is right, Paul having used the popular, though probably inaccurate, chronology. e.g. F.A. N. de W.

ἔδωκεν κριτὰς] Judges ii. 16.

21. ᾐτήσαντο βασιλέα] 1 Sam. viii. 5. **ἔδωκεν...**1 Sam. ix. 1 *et seq.*

ἔτη τεσσεράκοντα] The time is not given in O.T.; Josephus however tells us that Saul reigned 18 years during the lifetime of Samuel, and 22 after his death. Ant. vi. 14. 9.

22. μεταστήσας] 'having removed him from his office', i.e. by the sentence of deposition recorded 1 Sam. xv. 23. Cf. Luke xvi. 4 ὅταν μετασταθῶ τῆς οἰκονομίας.

εὗρον...] A combination of Ps. lxxxix. 20 *εὗρον Δαυὶδ τὸν δοῦλόν μου, ἐν ἐλέει ἁγίῳ ἔχρισα αὐτόν,* and 1 Sam. xiii. 14 *ζητήσει κύριος ἑαυτῷ ἄνθρωπον κατὰ τὴν καρδίαν αὐτοῦ καὶ ἐντελεῖται κύριος αὐτῷ...*

23. τούτου] Emphatic. ' Of this man from the seed...'

κατ' ἐπαγγελίαν...] The promise is to be found 2 Sam. vii. 12; Ps. cxxxii. 11, both passages being Messianically interpreted.

The verb *ἄγω* is found in Zech. iii. 8 of the sending of Messiah *ἄγω τὸν δοῦλόν μου ἀνατολήν* ('the Branch').   T.R. has *ἤγειρεν.* ἤγαγεν in ℵABE HLP.

24. προκηρύξαντος] As a herald before a king.

πρὸ προσώπου] 'before', 'in front of', with a recollection of Mal. iii. 1 (the passage quoted Mt. xi. 10) ἐξαποστέλλω τὸν ἄγγελόν μου, καὶ ἐπιβλέψεται ὁδὸν πρὸ προσώπου μου.

25. ὡς δὲ ἐπλήρου...] Paul's favourite metaphor from the race-course, cf. xx. 24; 2 Tim. iv. 7 τὸν δρόμον τετέλεκα; Gal. ii. 2. An inscription found at Tarsus refers to the completion of the stadium there. Note the imperfects.

Corpus Insc. Gr. III. 209, No. 4437.

οὐκ εἰμὶ ἐγώ] A. and R.V. rightly 'I am not he', i.e. He whom you expect, the Messiah. Cf. the question put to him; John i. 25 τί οὖν βαπτίζεις, εἰ σὺ οὐκ εἶ ὁ χριστός;

ἀλλ' ἰδοὺ...] John i. 27.

So La.M.

26. ἡμῖν] 'To us': emphatic. The message of this salvation, of the salvation brought by Jesus the Saviour (cf. ver. 23 σωτῆρα 'Ιησοῦν), long promised to our fathers (cf. ver. 32), has been sent *to us*, in our day (cf. n. on ἡμῶν ver. 32). The clause which follows, viz. οἱ γὰρ..., does not give the reason *why* this is so, but tells *how* it is so. γάρ introduces the narrative which explains the message.

ἡμῖν ℵAD and so R.V.

T.R. has ὑμῖν, thus drawing a contrast between the Jews of Antioch and the Jews dwelling at Jerusalem—'we come to *you* with this message because the Jews at Jerusalem rejected it'. But it seems impossible that Paul at this emphatic point in his speech, marked as emphatic by the repeated personal address (ἄνδρες ἀδ...), should explain why he was preaching to the Jews of Antioch and not to those of Jerusalem. Nowhere else is such a distinction drawn between the two classes, nor is it drawn here, for Paul pointedly addresses his hearers as υἱοὶ γένους 'Αβραάμ, i.e. as in common with all other Jews, children of the promise now fulfilled. The introduction of such a distinction between two classes of Jews mars the whole meaning of the speech, which is not a justification of Paul's presence in Antioch but a great argument that Jesus is the Messiah.

27. τοῦτον] i.e. Jesus the Saviour, implicitly referred to in τῆς σωτ. ταύτης and the subject of the whole discourse.

ἀγνοήσαντες] A mild word, purposely chosen, as suggesting unwilling error, cf. iii. 17. It governs both τοῦτον and τὰς φωνὰς (as A. and R.V.) : they failed to recognize Jesus and they failed to recognize the prophetic utterances about a suffering rather than a triumphant Messiah. Others take καὶ almost = 'also' and joining ἀγνοήσαντες with ἐπλήρωσαν.

v. A.

28. μηδεμίαν αἰτίαν...] Cf. Pilate's words Luke xxiii. 22 οὐδὲν αἴτιον θανάτου εὗρον ἐν αὐτῷ.

εὑρόντες] *etsi quaesiere* B. pointedly, but wrongly: it is
not Paul's object to suggest the guilt of the Jews at Jerusalem.

32. ὑμᾶς] acc. after εὐαγγ. as a verb of teaching, cf.
viii. 40; τὴν ἐπαγγελίαν is the second acc. of the thing
taught, 'we teach you the promise, how, that is, God has
fulfilled it...'.

ἡμῶν] T.R. αὐτῶν ἡμῖν, rightly as regards sense, but
without any authority. 'It can hardly be doubted that W. & H.
ἡμῶν is a primitive corruption of ἡμῖν'. Indeed ἡμῖν is
necessary to the sense : 'the promise made to the fathers,
that (promise) God has fulfilled to the children, having for
us raised up...', or 'to the children, even us, by raising
up...'.

ἀναστήσας Ἰησοῦν] as iii. 22, vii. 37 ; certainly not As A. M.
'having raised him from the dead', for the Psalm imme- Luther,
diately quoted, which refers to the *sending* of Messiah, mus,&c.
would have no relevance. Paul refers to the 'raising up of
Jesus' i.e. the sending of Him as Messiah as fulfilling one
prophecy, and the 'raising Him from the dead' as fulfilling
another. The two are separate acts, though forming part La. de
of one divine purpose, and the one is the natural and ne- W.
cessary complement of the other, as the use of the same verb
seems to indicate (cf. below the repeated words δώσω, δώσεις;
τὰ ὅσια, τὸν ὅσιον).

33. υἱός...] Verbatim from Ps. ii. 7. For δευτέρῳ D has So F. M.
πρώτῳ, which is not improbably right, the first Psalm being de W.
regarded by the Jews as introductory, and the second one dorf.
counted as 'the first'.

34. μηκέτι μέλλοντα...] Cf. carefully Rom. vi. 9 'Christ
being raised from the dead dieth no more'.

δώσω...] Is. lv. 3 διαθήσομαι ὑμῖν διαθήκην αἰώνιον, τὰ
ὅσια Δαυὶδ τὰ πιστά. Translate 'I will give to you (the
Israelites) the holy promises of David that are sure'. τὰ
ὅσια is the noun, τὰ πιστά the predicate, marked by its position as emphatic. What 'the holy promises of David' are
is immediately made clear by the second quotation, which
refers to 'the Holy One', i.e. Messiah, the great Son of
David.

35. διότι...] 'Because...': Paul immediately justifies
his application of τὰ ὅσια Δ. to the Messiah by referring to
Ps. xvi. 10 which, he says, shews that the 'holy promises
of David' cannot merely mean that David was God's holy
one, for the Holy One spoken of is described as 'not seeing

corruption', and so cannot be David who died, but must be the Son of David who had been raised from the dead.

36. γενεᾷ ἰδίᾳ...] Of the various ways in which these words may grammatically be taken, the clearest sense is obtained by rendering, 'Having served his own generation, by the will of God fell asleep...and saw corruption'. Thus the words are taken in their natural order and we have a double distinction marked between David and Jesus, for (1) Jesus 'is of service' to *all* generations, and (2) 'by the will of God He fell asleep' but did *not* 'see corruption'.

A.

προσετέθη...] 'An expression arising from the practice of burying families together'. Cf. Gen. xv. 15; Judges ii. 10.

39. ἀπὸ πάντων ὧν] i.e. ἀφ' ὧν, cf. ver. 2 n.   δικαιόω= 'to make' or 'declare righteous': δικαιοῦται ἀπὸ...='is justified (by being set free) from...' The believer receives 'remission of sins', and so is freed from them and 'made righteous'.

Opposed to Jesus in whom (ἐν τούτῳ) is to be found justification from all sin, is the law of Moses in which (ἐν νόμῳ) no justification is possible, according to Paul's constant argument (e.g. Gal. iii. 11) that no man can keep the Law or be 'declared righteous' under it, but that for thus being made 'righteous' forgiveness of sin through Jesus is needed.

40. ἐν τοῖς προφήταις] vii. 42 n. The quotation is almost verbatim from LXX. Hab. i. 5.   The immediate reference of the prophecy is to the Babylonian captivity.   For 'ye despisers' the Heb. has 'among the nations'.

See F.

42. αὐτῶν] i.e. clearly Paul and Barnabas, the nom. to παρεκάλουν being 'those in the synagogue'.

T.R. without any authority ἐξιόντων δὲ ἐκ τῆς συναγωγῆς τῶν Ἰουδαίων, παρεκάλουν τὰ ἔθνη.   The correction is due to some one who considered that the Jews were opposed to the Apostles from the first, whereas the reverse is described as being the case.

A. F.

εἰς τὸ μεταξὺ σ.] 'the following sabbath', a late use of μεταξύ, e.g. Plutarch *Inst. Lac.* 42 Φίλιππον...καὶ μεταξὺ δ' Ἀλέξανδρον τὸν υἱόν.

43. λυθείσης...] Apparently subsequently to the departure of Paul and Barnabas.

46. ἦν ἀναγκαῖον...] Cf. the command of Jesus i. 8.   See too iii. 26 n., xiii. 5 n.

κρίνετε ἑαυτοὺς] Emphatic, 'ye judge yourselves': it is your own choice.

47. οὕτω γὰρ...] The quotation almost verbatim from LXX. Is. xlix, 6.

Paul states that this Messianic passage (1) declares that Messiah is sent not only to the Jews but to the Gentiles, (2) is therefore a direct injunction from God as to their conduct in preaching. For εἰς φῶς ἐθνῶν cf. Luke ii. 32 φῶς εἰς ἀποκάλυψιν ἐθνῶν.

48. ὅσοι ἦσαν τεταγμένοι...] 'as many as were ordained' A. and R.V. The word τεταγμένοι is distinctly passive, = 'placed in a certain position' or 'order'. To the Jews, who of their own choice rejected God's word, are opposed the Gentiles who believed; but, as the term τὰ ἔθνη La. was too wide, the historian adds a correcting and limiting phrase, 'such of them, that is, as had been appointed', 'marshalled' 'placed in the ranks of those who were on the road toward (εἰς) eternal life'.

Luke is simply recording *a fact;* he describes certain Gentiles as τεταγμένοι εἰς ζ. αἰ.; he uses a participle passive to describe their position, but there is no shadow of an indication that the question of 'predestination' was before his mind. He could not have used simpler language. Certain men were in a certain position: he states that they were in that position, but by whom placed there, or why, or how, he does not say. Cf. the use of the passive forms προσεκληρώθησαν xvii. 4, ἀντιτασσομένων xviii. 6.

For the use of τάσσω cf. xviii. 6 ἀντιτασσομένων; Luke vii. 8 ὑπὸ ἐξουσίαν τασσόμενος; 1 Cor. xvi. 15 εἰς διακονίαν τοῖς ἁγίοις ἔταξαν ἑαυτούς; Rom. xiii. 1 αἱ οὖσαι ἐξουσίαι ὑπὸ θεοῦ τεταγμέναι εἰσίν.

V. has *praeordinati*, unfairly: Aug. *destinati*, a much too strong word: A. 'disposed', an ambiguous term: H. 'who had set themselves to attain that great end', cf. xx. 13.

50. τὰς σεβομένας γ....] Proselytes of distinction, as xvii. 12. For σεβομένας cf. x. 1 n.

51. ἐκτιναξάμενοι] Cf. xviii. 6 and the command of Jesus, Mt. x. 14 ἐκτινάξατε τὸν κονιορτὸν τῶν ποδῶν ὑμῶν. It is a sign of the rejection of all intercourse.

Ἰκόνιον] Four or five days' journey S.E. of Antioch, on the table-land of Lycaonia, at the meeting-point of several Roman roads. It was reckoned at various times as in Pisidia, Lycaonia, or Phrygia. Still a large town *Konieh* with 30,000 inhabitants.

52. οἵ τε μαθηταί...] 'Another joyful peroration; like W. and a calm after a storm. See viii. 4, ix. 31, xii. 24'.   so H.

CHAPTER XIV.

Text אA
BC.

2. ἀπειθήσαντες] T.R. has ἀπειθοῦντες: the aorist is much better,='those who disbelieved' i.e. when Paul preached. R.V. gives 'that were disobedient'. No doubt strictly ἀπειθέω='disobey', ἀπιστέω='disbelieve'; but these distinctions cannot be accurately maintained; cf. xix. 9 ἠπείθουν with xxviii. 24 ἠπίστουν. Moreover in John iii. 36 the opposite of ὁ πιστεύων εἰς τὸν υἱόν is ὁ ἀπειθῶν τῷ υἱῷ, 'he that disbelieveth'. In the Greek language 'belief' and 'obedience' were regarded as almost the same thing and represented by a single word—πείθομαι.

3. ἱκανὸν μὲν οὖν...] The antithesis is *not* ἐσχίσθη δὲ (as A. and R.V.) but ὡς δὲ ἐγένετο, cf. ii. 41 n. The sense is clear. 'For a considerable time they stayed, God giving them clear witness *and* the multitude being divided so that they were not actually molested, *but* when they found that they were going to be attacked...they took refuge'.

ἐπὶ] iii. 10 n.

Text
ABDEP.

διδόντι] T.R. καὶ διδόντι marring the sense. The Lord 'bears witness to the word of His grace *by* granting': διδόντι is subordinate to μαρτυροῦντι.

v. Lightfoot, *Gal.*
Excursus.

4. τοῖς ἀποστόλοις] i.e. Paul and Barnabas (cf. ver. 14), here so called for the first time. The term 'apostle' was not confined to 'the twelve', whom our usage designates 'The Apostles'. The word was in use among the Jews to indicate any one sent on a mission by some central authority, and was especially applied to those who were sent from Jerusalem to collect the temple tribute. To be an 'apostle of Jesus', a direct commission from Him would be needed; this Paul had received, and probably Barnabas. Moreover to have seen the risen Jesus was essential to their first duty; cf. i. 8 n.

A. M.

5. ὡς ἐγένετο ὁρμή] 'when there was an assault made' A.V.; 'onset' R.V. It is clear however from συνιδόντες κατέφυγον that no 'assault' or 'onset' took place; ὁρμή therefore is better taken with the infinitives='eagerness' or 'impulse to outrage'; cf. Thuc. IV. 4 σχολάζουσιν ὁρμὴ ἐπέπεσεν ἐκτειχίσαι τὸ χωρίον; Dem. 309. 4 εἰς ὁρμὴν τοῦ τὰ δέοντα ποιεῖν.

τοῖς ἄρχουσιν αὐτῶν] Not τοῖς ἄρχουσιν absolutely (cf. xvi. 19) 'the magistrates', for they would not take part in such a proceeding, but, as the addition of αὐτῶν shews, 'the rulers of the Jews'. Cf. xiii. 27 οἱ ἄρχοντες αὐτῶν; as it had been with Jesus, so it was with His followers.

λιθοβολῆσαι] Cf. vii. 58 n.

6. συνιδόντες] xii. 12. καθέφυγον: *confugerunt*, cf. the command of Jesus Mt. x. 23.

Λυκαονίας] A high table-land, ill watered, bleak, but suited for sheep pasture. Both Lystra and Derbe are S.-E. from Iconium but their exact site is unknown. Lystra was probably the birthplace of Timothy, cf. xvi. 1.

8. ἐκάθητο] 'used to sit', probably in some public place regularly: cf. ἤκουε 'used to listen', i. e. to Paul when speaking to the people.

9. ἀτενίσας] i. 10 n. Of Paul, xiii. 9, xxiii. 1.

πίστιν τοῦ σωθῆναι] The gen. describes not only the aim but the result of the faith. Faith to be healed is the cause of healing, cf. iii. 16; Luke vii. 50 ἡ πίστις σου σέσωκέ σε.

σωθῆναι (cf. iv. 10 n.) primarily of bodily healing, but also conveying the idea of spiritual healing.

10. ἥλατο] 'he leapt up' suddenly, and 'was walking'.

11. Λυκαονιστί] lit. 'in Lycaonian fashion', i.e. in the Lycaonian speech. So Ἑλληνιστί συνιέναι 'to understand Gk', and Δωριστί, Φρυγιστί, Λυδιστί applied to styles of music.

What the Lycaonian speech or dialect was we do not know. Living in a mountainous and secluded district they probably only used Gk in their intercourse with strangers, as Welshmen might use English. It is clear that the Apostles did not understand the cry that was raised, or they would have protested at once.

οἱ θεοί...] One of the oldest of beliefs, cf. Hom. *Od.* XVII. 484

καί τε θεοὶ ξείνοισιν ἐοικότες ἀλλοδαποῖσιν
παντοῖοι τελέθοντες ἐπιστρωφῶσι πόληας.

It was in the neighbouring country of Phrygia that Philemon and Baucis were fabled to have entertained the two divinities here mentioned, Jupiter and Mercury, cf. Ov. *Met.* VIII. 626.

12. τὸν Β. Δία] Perhaps from his more imposing N. appearance. Paul (2 Cor. x. 10) says of himself ἡ παρουσία τοῦ σώματος ἀσθενής; and cf. 2 Cor. xii. 7 ἐδόθη μοι σκόλοψ τῇ σαρκί; Gal. iv. 14. Tradition, probably exaggerating these references, describes him as μικρὸς τῷ μεγέθει, ψιλὸς *Acta* τὴν κεφαλήν, ἀγκύλος ταῖς κνήμαις, but it is clear from the *Pauli et* comparison of him to Hermes that the writer had no idea *Theclae.* of his presence being mean or contemptible, for Hermes, the herald of the gods, is a beautiful figure.

ὁ ἡγ. τοῦ λόγου] Hermes was the inventor of speech, cf. ἑρμηνεύω; Hor. *Od.* I. 10. 1 *Mercuri...... | qui feros cultus hominum recentum | voce formasti catus.*

13. τοῦ ὄντος...] ⁻ The god is identified with his temple, which was 'before the city'.

στέμματα] Regularly used in sacrifices: worn by the priests, carried by the attendants, placed on the victim.

A. W.   τοὺς πυλῶνας] Some say 'the gates of the house where the Apostles were', but if so the plural is strange, cf. xii. 13. It can only be conjecture, but it seems better to refer to the gates of the temple of Zeus, the altar being in front of the v.Renan. temple: this gives great force to τούτων in ver. 15, which thus becomes deictic and vigorous.

14. διαρρήξαντες τὰ ἱμάτια] A sign of grief and horror, cf. 2 Kings xviii. 37, xix. 1; Matt. xxvi. 65.

15. ὁμοιοπαθεῖς] 'of like passions' A. and R.V., the word 'passions' being used in a technical sense as in Art. I., where God is described as 'without body, parts or passions'. The rendering here is however hardly happy, as the ancients always represented the gods as influenced like men by love, anger, hate and those feelings which are usually termed 'passions'. The word ὁμοιοπαθής is of far wider meaning, and describes one who is in the possession of a like nature, and therefore has like feelings or sensations, is affected in the same way by the same things, as heat and cold, pleasure and pain, disease and death.

The word may be well illustrated from Shakespeare, *Merch. of Ven.* III. 1, 'Hath not a Jew eyes? Hath not a Jew hands, organs, dimensions, senses, affections, passions? fed with the same food', &c.

ἀπὸ τούτων...] Cf. 1 Thess. i. 9 ἐπιστρέψατε πρὸς τὸν θεὸν ἀπὸ τῶν εἰδώλων, δουλεύειν θεῷ ζῶντι καὶ ἀληθινῷ.

τούτων is deictic. Paul points to the heathen temple and its altar and images, and calls them 'these vain things', i.e. things which do not represent reality, cf. 1 Cor. viii. 4 οἴδαμεν ὅτι εἴδωλον οὐδέν.

Text AB   θεὸν ζῶντα] 'a living God', opposed to the 'vain', non-
CDE.   existent gods of the heathen. T.R. has τὸν θ. τὸν ζῶντα, probably as seeming more precise and emphatic. Paul however very frequently has θεὸς ζῶν, e.g. 2 Cor. vi. 16; Rom. ix. 26, where he is quoting from Hos. i. 10 κληθήσονται υἱοὶ θεοῦ ζῶντος; and so regularly in LXX. with no article. Cf. too in illustration of the phrase the well-known Hebrew method of confirming an oath, 'Jehovah liveth', e.g. Hos. iv. 15 μὴ ὀμνύετε ζῶντα Κύριον; Jer. iv. 2 ὀμόσῃ ζῇ Κύριος.

ὃς ἐποίησεν...] Gen. i. 1 ἐν ἀρχῇ ἐποίησεν ὁ θεὸς τὸν οὐρανὸν καὶ τὴν γῆν. Ps. cxlvi. 6 τὸν ποιήσαντα τὸν οὐ. καὶ τὴν γῆν, τὴν θάλασσαν καὶ πάντα τὰ ἐν αὐτοῖς.

It will be observed that to the men of Lycaonia, though

Paul quotes O.T., he does not rest his argument upon it,
as when addressing Jews, but on the witness that nature
bears to God. For this cf. the fine passage Cic. *Tusc.* I. 28,
and Rom. i. 20; Ps. xix. 1.

17. ἀγαθουργῶν...διδούς...ἐμπιπλῶν] Notice the three M.
participles, the second subordinate to and explaining · the
first, and the third the second, 'He gave witness of Himself
by doing good, that is, by giving rains, &c., in that way
filling....'

οὐρανόθεν] Not otiose: *caelum sedes Dei.* B.

ὑετούς] It has been pointed out that the district was A.
one which was liable to suffer from drought, and · that the
wells were of unusual depth.

εὐφροσύνης] Specially used in Gk of the cheerfulness
which attends a banquet—'good cheer'.

18. τοῦ μὴ θύειν] gen. dependent on κατέπαυσαν, 'made
to cease from sacrificing', μὴ being redundant as commonly
after verbs containing a negative idea like *forbidding* or
stopping.

19. ἐπῆλθαν δὲ...] Probably after some interval; the
narrative is here very brief.

λιθάσαντες] Cf. 2 Cor. xi. 25, ἅπαξ ἐλιθάσθην. The attack is evidently an irregular proceeding, for a formal or
quasi-formal stoning for blasphemy would have been outside
the city, cf. vii. 58.

20. ἀναστάς...] Luke clearly describes a sudden, miraculous recovery.

Δέρβην] The exact site is unknown, but it was probably to the E. of Lycaonia, near the pass called 'the Cilician gates'. Their return over the same road by which
they had come must have been intentional, for their natural
road to Antioch would have been by the Cilician gates, or a
similar pass over Mt Taurus, the very road taken by Paul
in passing from Antioch to Derbe at the commencement of
his second missionary journey, cf. xv. 41—xvi. 1.

22. καὶ ὅτι...] 'and saying that...'; Luke draws special
attention to this point in their exhortation, which he gives
verbatim, the quotation being marked by ὅτι, cf. xv. 1.

ἡμᾶς] 'we': the speakers are subject to the same conditions as their hearers: 'we' is more sympathetic than 'you'.
It is quite unreasonable to infer the presence of Luke from As A.
the use of 'we' here. does.

23. χειροτονήσαντες] lit. 'having voted for', strictly by
election by show of hands in a public assembly, but here
used generally: 'appointed': cf. x. 41 προκεχειροτονημένοις.

αὐτοῖς: Ethic Dat. For 'presbyters' xi. 30 n.

κατ' ἐκκλησίαν] κατά is distributive.

παρέθεντο] Cf. xx. 32; Luke xxiii. 46 Πάτερ εἰς χεῖράς σου παρατίθεμαι τὸ πνεῦμά μου. The word is not so classical as παρακατατίθεσθαι = 'to place a deposit (παρακαταθήκη) with any one', 'give to be taken care of', e.g. of money with a banker; hence generally 'to entrust'.

24. 'Ατταλίαν] W. from Perga at the mouth of the river Catarrhactes, near the borders of Lycia; at this time the capital of Pamphylia; built by Attalus II. king of Pergamus.

27. ὅσα] 'all the things that', implying that they were many.

μετ' αὐτῶν] Cf. the promise of Jesus καὶ ἰδού, ἐγὼ μεθ' ὑμῶν εἰμί. The phrase expresses the presence and implies the assistance of God.

ἤνοιξεν...] Cf. 1 Cor. xvi. 9 θύρα γάρ μοι ἀνέῳγε μεγάλη; 2 Cor. ii. 12 θύρα ἀνεῳγμένη; Col. iv. 3 ἵνα ὁ θεὸς ἀνοίξῃ ἡμῖν θύραν τοῦ λόγου. The phrase expresses in a vivid and pictorial form the result of their first missionary journey.

θύραν πίστεως] i.e. a full opportunity of belief and so of entrance or admittance into all the blessings attending on that belief.

28. οὐκ ὀλίγον] cf. xii. 18, implies a considerable time, e.g. a year or more.

CHAPTER XV.

1. καὶ τινες...] This visit of Paul to Jerusalem is usually identified with the one he describes Gal. ii. 1—10, fourteen years after his conversion.

The question, whether for admission to the Christian Church it was necessary first to accept the Jewish Law, and especially, as a sign of that acceptance, to submit to circumcision, might appear to have been settled by the case of Cornelius and the discussion which ensued upon it; but it would seem that many still regarded that case as exceptional and by no means clearly establishing a general principle. The question revived again in full vigour, even after the present decision, and is the cause of the Epistle to the Galatians, in which Paul establishes the freedom of the Gentiles. It must be remembered, with regard to the great importance which this question assumed, that the Jews considered themselves a peculiarly privileged people, and even those who acknowledged Jesus as the Messiah

may not unnaturally have held that those Gentiles who
accepted the Jewish Messiah were also bound to accept
the Jewish Law.

τινές] Paul describes these men as παρεισάκτους ψευδ-
αδέλφους, οἵτινες παρεισῆλθον κατασκοπῆσαι τὴν ἐλευθερίαν
ἡμῶν. Gal. ii. 4.

ἐδίδασκον] Note the imperfect, and also that the word
implies a definite purpose.

ὅτι] Introducing their very words, cf. xiv. 22.

τῷ ἔθει] Cf. τὰ ἔθη vi. 14; same as τὸν νόμον ver. 5. Dat.
of the rule by which.

2. στάσεως] A strong word, used = 'uproar', 'riot'
xix. 40: 'sedition' Luke xxiii. 25. Here 'a division between
two opposing parties', cf. xxiii. 7. It is the well-known
classical word for an outbreak between the democratic and
oligarchical parties in a state.

ἔταξαν] sc. οἱ ἀδελφοὶ from ver. 1. Paul says (Gal. ii. 2)
ἀνέβην δὲ κατ᾽ ἀποκάλυψιν: Luke gives the *external*, Paul the
internal history.

καί τινας ἄλλους] e.g. Titus; Gal. ii. 13.

3. προπεμφθέντες] The verb signifies 'to accompany
some one setting out on a journey a part of the way' as a
mark of affection and honour. Cf. xx. 38, xxi. 5.

4. παρεδέχθησαν...] The narrative is by no means
clear, but seems to mark three main points:

(1) A public reception by the whole Church of Paul
and Barnabas.

(2) The raising in a definite form by 'certain converts
from among the Pharisees' of the question of circumcision,
but whether at the first reception or later is not clear.

(3) A subsequent meeting of the whole (vers. 12, 22)
Church to decide the question.

Paul's own account is (Gal. ii. 2) καὶ ἀνεθέμην αὐτοῖς τὸ
εὐαγγέλιον ὃ κηρύσσω ἐν τοῖς ἔθνεσιν, κατ᾽ ἰδίαν δὲ τοῖς δοκοῦσιν,
μή πως εἰς κενὸν τρέχω ἢ ἔδραμον.

Alford fairly observes, 'Paul did not lay before the So N.
whole assembly *the Gospel which he preached among the* Light-
Gentiles, viz. the indifference of the Mosaic Law to their foot.
salvation (Gal. i. 7—9), for fear of its being hastily repudiated and so his own work hindered (μή πως...). But he
did so in private interviews with the chief Apostles'. Cf.
his conduct xxi. 18.

τῆς ἐκκ. καὶ...] The words καὶ τῶν ἀποστ. καὶ τῶν
πρεσβ. are added because the 'Apostles and elders' would
naturally take a prominent part in the reception, and their

presence is therefore specially noted. So ver. 6 they are
mentioned *without* the Church, because the decision of the
question would naturally be left with them, though as we
see from vers. 12, 22, 'the Church' was present and agreed
in the decision.

5. αὐτούς] The converted Gentiles.

6. τοῦ λόγου τούτου] The subject under consideration,
cf. viii. 21 n.

7. Πέτρος] Here last mentioned in the Acts.

ἀφ' ἡμερῶν ἀρχαίων] About 15 years before. The phrase
seems to refer to the 'early days' of the Church, cf. xi. 15,
ἐν ἀρχῇ referring to Pentecost; xxi. 16 ἀρχαίῳ μαθητῇ. It
seems designedly chosen to indicate that the acceptance
of Gentiles was no *new, novel* principle.

8. καρδιογνώστης] *qui cor non carnem spectat.* B.

9. καθαρίσας] Markedly recalling the word used x. 15.
God had taken away the 'uncleanness' of their hearts.

10. ἐπιθεῖναι] The inf. completes the notion of the
verb by explaining wherein the 'tempting' consists: the
πειρασμός is defined as ἐπιθεῖναι...; it is an extension of the
epexegetic inf. and may fairly be rendered 'tempt by
placing...': cf. ver. 14 ἐπεσκέψατο λαβεῖν, where the 'regard'
is defined as 'a taking...'; Luke i. 25 ἐπεῖδεν ἀφελεῖν.

For πειράζετε τὸν θ. cf. Ex. xvii. 7 (where 'Massah' is in
LXX. Πειρασμός); Deut. vi. 16; Matt. iv. 7; 1 Cor. x. 9.
The phrase expresses acting without trust in God, refusing
to follow His guidance till He has been *tried* or *tested* by
some overt proof, such as the sending water from the
rock in Horeb, or the vision sent to Peter at Joppa.

ζυγόν] i.e. the burden of fulfilling the Law; ζυγὸν δουλείας
Gal. v. 1. Opposed to it is the 'easy yoke' (ζυγὸς χρηστός
Matt. xi. 30) of Jesus.

11. διὰ τῆς χάρ. τ. κ. Ἰησ.] With σωθῆναι not with
πιστεύομεν. The words are thrown forward for emphasis:
'not through the Law, but by grace...'.

12. Βαρνάβα καὶ Π.] Notice the reversion to this order,
possibly because the events take place in Jerusalem, where
as yet Barnabas was better known than Paul. So too ver. 25.

ἐξηγουμένων ὅσα...] Paul and Barnabas simply report
the facts. The Council discuss and decide. The triple
repetition of ὅσα ἐποίησεν ὁ θεός (xiv. 27, xv. 4) is noteworthy. Throughout Paul does not argue, but appeals to
the facts as a visible proof of God's presence.

13. ἀπεκρίθη] 'answered', i.e. spoke in reply to the

general expectation of a closing opinion from the president
after the debate.

14. Συμεών] Found also 2 Pet. i. 1 ; a by-form of
Simon. James uses Peter's Hebrew name.

ἐπεσκέψατο λαβεῖν] A. and R.V. 'did visit the Gentiles
to take...'; but the sense of 'regard', 'consideration' is
stronger here in ἐπεσκέψατο (cf. vii. 23 n.) than that of
'visit'. It is='shewed regard' or 'consideration in taking'.

ἐξ ἐθνῶν λαὸν] *Egregium paradoxon.* B. Cf. x. 2 n.
Israel is no longer to be alone 'the people': from 'the
nations' God may take Himself a people—the Israel of God,
not after the flesh but after the spirit.

τῷ ὀν. αὐτοῦ] i.e. to be called 'God's people', 'the Israel
of God' (Gal. vi. 16). Cf. ver. 17.

15. οἱ λόγοι] Plural: 'the utterances', of which he
proceeds to select one.

16. μετὰ ταῦτα...] From LXX. Amos ix. 11, 12 ἐν τῇ
ἡμέρᾳ ἐκείνῃ ἀναστήσω τὴν σκηνὴν Δαυὶδ τὴν πεπτωκυῖαν, καὶ
ἀνοικοδομήσω τὰ πεπτωκότα αὐτῆς, καὶ τὰ κατεσκαμμένα αὐτῆς
ἀναστήσω...ending with λέγει Κύριος ὁ ποιῶν ταῦτα πάντα.

The passage of Amos refers in the first instance to the
restoration of the Davidic empire (instead of the 'house of
David' it speaks poetically of 'the fallen tent'): secondly, it
refers to the Messiah's kingdom ('the throne of David his
father' Luke i. 32).

17. ὅπως ἂν ἐκζητήσωσιν οἱ κατάλοιποι...] In Amos
A.V., following the Hebrew, has 'that they may possess the
remnant of Edom', referring probably to the slaughter M.
already inflicted on Edom by Amaziah (2 Kings xiv. 7).

Certainly, though the general Messianic reference of the F. and so
passage be undisputed, the Hebrew text 'that they (the even
Jews) may possess' is 'much less apposite to the purpose Baum.
of the speaker' than the LXX. version.

ἐφ᾽ οὓς...] A Hebrew expression, for those who acknow- M.
ledge Jehovah as Lord, 'God's people', cf. Deut. xxviii. 10;
Is. lxiii. 19.

17, 18. λέγει Κύριος ποιῶν ταῦτα γνωστὰ ἀπ᾽ αἰ.] So אBC.
'saith Jehovah, making these things known from of old'.
By omitting the article before ποιῶν and adding the words Omit ὁ
γνωστὰ ἀπ᾽ αἰῶνος James incorporates with the quotation אB.
certain explanatory words of his own, intended to shew
that the extension of Messiah's kingdom to the heathen 'is
not a chance occurrence or trivial, but much rather God's Baum. i.
determined act'. 440.

T. R. reads ὁ ποιῶν ταῦτα πάντα. γνωστὰ ἀπ᾽ αἰῶνός ἐστι
τῷ θεῷ πάντα τὰ ἔργα αὐτοῦ. The addition seems due to a A.

P. 12

desire to make the words γνωστὰ ἀπ' αἰ. intelligible: not
being found in Amos they would be regarded as a separate
sentence needing some addition to give sense.

For ἀπ' αἰῶνος cf. iii. 21 τῶν ἀγίων ἀπ' αἰῶνος προφητῶν,
and Luke i. 70, and for the whole phrase Is. xlv. 21.

19. ἐγὼ κρίνω] *Ego censeo.* Not ' my sentence is', as
A.V., but 'I judge' ('my judgement is' R.V.): James
expresses his own ' judgment', not the ' sentence' or ' decision' of the assembly, which is given ver. 22.

20. ἐπιστεῖλαι...τοῦ ἀπέχεσθαι] The gen. gives the
' aim' or the ' contents' of the ' letter'. For ἐπιστεῖλαι cf.
ἐπιστολήν ver. 30, and ἐπέστειλα ὑμῖν Heb. xiii. 22. It is
safer to render ἐπιστεῖλαι 'write' and ἐπιστολή 'letter' (as
A. and R.V.), but the sense of 'enjoin', 'injunction'
strongly attaches to both words, cf. our use of ' message'
and 'mandate'.

τῶν ἀλ. τῶν εἰδώλων] By a comparison with ver. 29, xxi.
25 clearly = εἰδωλόθυτα 'meat sacrificed to idols'. Lit. 'the
pollutions of idols' from the late Greek ἀλισγεῖν, 'to pollute'.
With the ancients sacrifice was always accompanied by
feasting: the parts not burnt on the altar or taken by the
priests afforded the materials for a feast or were sold.
Paul in 1 Cor. viii. clearly lays down his view with regard
to eating or not eating such meat: in no case will he 'make
a brother to offend', though such meat is really but as other
meat.

The four things specially prohibited are those referred
to as ' *defiling*' in Lev. xvii. and xviii. and forbidden not
only to Jews but to 'strangers that sojourn in the land',
M. de W. and it is probable that the same prohibitions were enforced
Baum. on all 'proselytes of the gate'.

(1) τῶν ἀλ. τῶν εἰδώλων, cf. Lev. xvii. 1—9. Of all
beasts killed the blood was to be offered to the Lord, and
the offering to devils was prohibited.

(2) and (3) τοῦ πνικτοῦ καὶ τοῦ αἵμ. cf. Lev. xvii. 10—
16. No blood was to be eaten, and consequently no flesh
of anything of which the blood was not ' poured out'.

(4) τῆς πορνείας, cf. Lev. xviii. 1—18. All forms of uncleanness forbidden.

With regard to the classing of a *moral* offence apparently
on an equal footing with other merely *ritual* offences, it
should be remembered (1) that πορνεία was hardly looked
upon as wrong by the ancient Gentile world, (2) that to the
Jews the distinction between *moral* and *ceremonial* offences
was hardly as clear as it is to us; they regarded all the
offences mentioned as direct violations of divine laws.

21. Μωυσῆς γὰρ] i.e. they are to abstain because their

conduct would give offence. The prohibitions enforced by
Moses on 'strangers', and consequently by the Jews on all
proselytes, were so well known to all their Jewish brethren
that to neglect them would cause offence. They are a
minimum with less than which the Jewish Christians could
not be satisfied—τὰ ἐπάναγκες ver. 28. Some explain the
words as an apology to the Jews 'present for requiring so
little : *nec est metuendum ne Moses antiquetur, habet enim
ille....* Erasmus, and so N. Baum.

22. ἔδοξε] A regular word at the commencement of
decrees.

ἔδοξε τοῖς ἀποστόλοις...ἐκλεξαμένους...πέμψαι...γράψαν-
τες] An instance of loose sense construction. The first
participle is attracted from the dat. into the acc. by the
proximity of the inf., and the second is in the nomin. by a
reversion to the logical nom. of the sentence (ἔδοξε τοῖς
ἀποστόλοις = 'the Apostles determined').

'Ἰούδαν]. Not otherwise known. Silas is an abbrevia- v. W.
tion for Silvanus (cf. Lucas=Lucanus, Epaphras=Epaphro-
ditus &c.) as he is called 1 Thess. i. 1; 2 Cor. i. 19: he accompanied Paul in his second missionary journey, cf. xv. 40.

23. καὶ οἱ πρεσ. ἀδελφοί] T.R. has καὶ οἱ ἀδελφοί with poor Text ℵΑ
authority. The embassy had been sent to 'the Apostles and BCD.
elders' (ver. 2) ; it is answered by 'the Apostles and elders',
and in the reply the word ἀδελφοί is added to emphasize the
unity of feeling which the letter was intended to produce ;
it is from 'brethren to brethren', from Jewish Christians
at Jerusalem to Gentile Christians at Antioch. Translate
'The Apostles and elders, brethren to the brethren...'
R.V. gives 'The Apostles and elder brethren'—a meaning-
less phrase.

ἀδελφοί...τοῖς ἀδελφοῖς...χαίρειν] *Fratres Fratribus
Salutem.* *Auspicata salutatio, fratrum enim* τὸ αὐτὸ φρονεῖν,
cf. 2 Cor. ii. 13 ἀδελφοί, τὸ αὐτὸ φρονεῖτε.

For χαίρειν=*salutem* at the beginning of a letter, cf.
xxiii. 26; James i. 1.

24. ἀνασκευάζοντες] Only here in LXX. and N.T. It
is the opposite of κατασκευάζειν 'to equip', 'furnish', and
='unfurnish', 'destroy', 'subvert' (as A. and R.V.); it
is especially used as a *rhetorical* term of 'destructive arguments', cf. Ar. *Rhet.* II. 24. 4 τὸ δεινώσει κατασκευάζειν ἢ
ἀνασκευάζειν; Quint. II. 4. 18 *opus destruendi confirmandi-
que quod ἀνασκευή et κατασκευή vocatur.*

The rendering 'turning up the foundations' is totally Given by
wrong, cf. Thuc. I. 18, IV. 116, and Poppo *ad loc.* A. F. M.

οἷς οὐ διεστειλάμεθα] Observe the forcible brevity:

12—2

weakened in A.V. 'to whom we gave no *such* command-
ment'. R.V. omits 'such'.

26. παραδεδωκόσι] 'hazarded' A. and R.V. The word
= 'to give' or 'place out of your own power into that of
another'. By their actions they had 'placed their lives out
of their own power'. Cf. Thuc. v.16 τύχῃ αὐτὸν παραδίδωσιν.
Optime rem commissam curant, qui suam vitam non curant.

ὑπὲρ τοῦ ὁν.] iii. 6 n.

27. αὐτοὺς διὰ λόγου] Personally, and by word of
mouth.

28. ἔδοξεν...] The words express a distinct belief that
the Holy Spirit was present and inspired their resolution
(cf. John xvi. 13), and there seems also a reference to the
fact that the right of the Gentiles had been proved by the
'gift of the Holy Spirit', cf. ver. 8, x. 47, xi. 15.

29. εὖ πράξετε] A.V. 'ye shall do well', an ambiguous
rendering, as 'do well' may = 'act rightly' or, 'fare well',
whereas εὖ πράττειν can only mean the latter, and so R.V.
rightly 'it shall be well with you'. Cf. Plato *Protag.* 333ᴅ
εἰ εὖ πράττουσιν ἀδικοῦντες; Dem. 469. 14 εὖ ἐποίησεν ὑμᾶς εὖ
πράττων.

ἔρρωσθε] *Valete.*

31. τῇ παρακλήσει] Contained, that is, in the letter;
this 'encouragement' the bearers of the letter repeat and
increase by their spoken words (διὰ λόγου π. παρεκάλεσαν).

33. ποιήσαντες δὲ χρόνον] cf. Dem. 392 οὐκ ἀνέμειναν
τὸν κήρυκα οὐδ' ἐποίησαν χρόνον οὐδένα.

Text fol-
lows ℵ A
ᴮᴱᴵᴸᴸ
P.
After ver. 33 T.R. with *very poor* authority inserts ἔδοξε
δὲ τῷ Σίλᾳ ἐπιμεῖναι αὐτοῦ, an addition apparently to explain
ver. 40. But the μετά τινας ἡμέρας of ver. 36 allows for a
considerable interval during which he may have returned
from Jerusalem.

36. μετὰ δέ...] Commencement of Paul's second missionary journey.

ἐπιστρέψαντες δὴ ἐπισκεψώμεθα] For δή (*particula exci-
tandi*) cf. xiii. 2 n. Note the vigour of the repeated ἐπι-.

37. ἐβούλετο] *volebat* 'wished'; ἠξίου, *aequum censebat*
'thought right'; but probably there is no real difference of
meaning between the two verbs, ἠξίου...μὴ being simply =
'refused', 'objected'. To note 'characteristic mildness' in
the one and 'characteristic vehemence' in the other is
imaginative.

As F.

37, 38. συμπαραλαβεῖν, μὴ συνπαραλαμβάνειν] *simul
assumere, non simul assumere. Contradictio sententiarum
viride expressa.* B.

Note too the emphasis with which τοῦτον is added pleonastically at the end. Its force is best felt by reading over the Greek without it. Even in the indirect form in which the historian gives it, the refusal is instinct with energy— 'One who deserted us before, and went not on with us! No, I will not take *him*'.

Mark was subsequently reconciled with Paul; Col. iv. 10; 2 Tim. iv. 11; Philemon 24.

39. παροξυσμὸς] 'irritation'; the word is a strong one, but has not necessarily a bad sense, cf. xvii. 16 παρωξύνετο; Heb. x. 24 εἰς παροξυσμὸν ἀγάπης καὶ καλῶν ἔργων; but on the other hand 1 Cor. xiii. 5 ἀγάπη...οὐ παροξύνεται.

40. παραδοθεὶς] Cf. xiv. 26.

41. διήρχετο...] His way would be by the Gulf of Ia. F. Issus through 'the Syrian gates', a narrow road between steep rocks and the sea, and then inland, probably past Tarsus and over Mt Taurus by the ' Cilician gates'.

CHAPTER XVI.

1. Τιμόθεος] Probably a native of Lystra (to which ἐκεῖ must refer), not of Derbe, as has been wrongly inferred from xx. 4. His mother's name was Eunice 2 Tim. i. 5. He had probably been converted on his former visit by Paul, who calls him τέκνον μου ἀγαπητὸν καὶ πιστὸν ἐν κυρίῳ. 1 Cor. iv. 17.

2. ἐμαρτυρεῖτο] vi. 3 n.

3. λαβὼν περιέτεμεν] To be taken literally: any Israelite might perform the rite.

διὰ τοὺς Ἰουδαίους...] Clearly not Christian Jews (for them the Jerusalem ' decrees' referred to ver. 4 would have sufficed), but Jews generally. Paul saw that in preaching So M.La. to the Jews, if Timothy was to be of any use to him, he Baum.F. must be circumcised: they would not have associated with one who was uncircumcised or allowed him to preach in the synagogues. He circumcised him ' because of the Jews, for they all knew that his father was a Greek', and therefore that he was not circumcised.

The refusal of Paul to circumcise Titus (Gal. ii. 3) is quite different. Titus, who was a Greek, had gone up with Paul on the mission referred to in the last chapter. A demand had been made that he should be circumcised. To have complied would have been fatal to the cause of Gentile freedom, which Paul was sent to represent. *Idem non est semper idem.*

4. παρεδίδοσαν] 'they kept handing over': the decrees had been entrusted to them; it was their duty to 'pass them on', 'deliver them'.

6. διῆλθον δὲ...] 'They went through the Phrygian and Galatian district having been hindered (i.e. because they had been hindered) from preaching in Asia'.

Had they kept on in the direction in which they were going, following the great line of traffic to the West, they would have reached Ephesus, the chief city of proconsular Asia (ii. 9, vi. 9), but their progress was 'barred' by a divine prohibition and they turned off either to the N. or N.W. T.R. has διελθόντες δὲ τὴν Φ. καὶ τὴν Γ. χώραν obscuring and probably altering the sense; cf. A.V.

διῆλθον ℵABCD E.

καὶ Γαλ. **τὴν Φρυγίαν καὶ Γαλ. χ.**] Not two districts (as reading of T.R. makes it) but one: it was 'the country which could be termed indifferently Phrygia or Galatia. It was in fact the land originally inhabited by Phrygians but subsequently occupied by Gauls'. See however xviii. 23.

ℵABCD. Lightfoot.

Galatia is the land of the Γαλάται, Κέλται or *Galli*, the same race who B.C. 390 sacked Rome, and in B.C. 279 poured over Greece: a portion of this latter body, instead of proceeding S., turned E. and crossed the Hellespont into Asia, where they finally occupied the territory called Galatia. It was made a Roman province B.C. 25.

So Lightfoot. F. A. W. N.

The Churches of Galatia to which Paul addressed his Epistle were probably founded during this journey, though Luke gives no hint of it. It may be noted however that the narrative here is extremely brief, the writer being clearly anxious to pass on to the preaching of Paul in Europe.

e.g. Lange, M.

Others consider that Paul uses the word 'Galatians' in an official sense = 'inhabitants of the Roman province of Galatia' and that the Epistle is addressed to the Churches of Lycaonia, which formed part of that province.

7. κατὰ τὴν M.] R.V. rightly 'over against': with it opposite them.

τὸ πνεῦμα Ἰησοῦ] T.R. with poor authority omits Ἰησοῦ. R.V. gives the 'Spirit of Jesus'. The exact expression occurs nowhere else, but cf. Phil. i. 19 τοῦ πν. Ἰησοῦ Χριστοῦ; Romans viii. 9 πνεῦμα Χριστοῦ. In all these cases R.V. gives 'Spirit' not 'spirit'.

8. παρελθόντες] A. and R.V. 'passing by', which may either mean 'neglecting' or 'passing along the edge of'.

M. La. A. F. give 'neglecting'.

It is certainly natural to take the word literally and not metaphorically, as merely describing their route (cf. διῆλθον, ἐλθόντες, κατέβησαν) 'having passed along the side of Mysia', 'skirted it', keeping it, that is, on their right. In

this case Mysia must = Mysia Minor which belonged to Bithynia, whereas Mysia Major was part of the province of Asia.

Τρωάδα] Alexandria Troas, S.W. of Troy on the sea-
coast, a Roman colony.

9. ὅραμα] Hitherto they had been simply 'hindered',
'forbidden' to approach certain places; now there is a
positive direction.

10. ἐζητήσαμεν] '*We* sought'. The introduction of
the first person plural, in a writer with such considerable
literary skill as Luke, cannot be set down to the inartistic
incorporation of some narrative written by an actual companion of Paul, but clearly indicates the presence of Luke
himself. The use of it ceases xvii. 1 when Paul leaves
Philippi, and is resumed six or seven years later (xx. 5) on
his sailing from Philippi, and continued to the end of the
Acts.

συνβιβάζοντες] ix. 22 n.   ἀναχθέντες xiii. 13 n.

11. εὐθυδρομήσαμεν] expresses a straight run with
the wind well astern: the journey *from* Neapolis (xx. 6)
took *five* days.

Σαμοθράκην] A small island opposite the mouth of the
Hebrus, distant about 38 m.; celebrated for the worship of
the Cabiri.

Νέαν Πόλιν] Just opposite Thasos; at this time be-   M. La.
longing to Thrace, but from Vespasian's time to Macedonia.

12. Φιλίππους] Founded by Philip, father of Alexander the Great, on the site of the old Krenides, 'Wells';
near the sources of the river Gangites or Gangas, which
flows into the Strymon, about 30 m. distant. On the
intervening plain took place the battle of Philippi B.C.
42. The city lies on the great *Via Egnatia* (see xvii. 1 n.).
Augustus, as Philip had done, recognized the strategical importance of its position and founded a Roman colony there,
Colonia Augusta Julia Philippensis.

ἥτις...] 'for it is, first in the district, a city of Macedonia,
a colony'.

Whatever the exact meaning of these words, it is clear   So Light-
that the clause, introduced by the explanatory ἥτις, is in-   foot (q.
tended to call attention to the fact that Paul had reached   v.), La.
the place to which he had been specially directed in ver. 9.

It seems plainer to take τῆς μερίδος M. = 'that portion'
or 'district of Macedonia' than to make μερίδος = 'province'
and render 'the province Macedonia'. 'Macedonia' is the
Roman province of that name (including Macedonia proper,

Illyricum, Epirus, and Thessaly) which had been divided
after its conquest 168 B.C. by Aemilius Paulus into four
districts, of which one, *Macedonia Prima*, between the Strymon and the Nestus, had Amphipolis for its capital, but
whether this district still existed and is referred to by the
words τῆς μερίδος is doubtful.

The word πρώτη cannot = 'chief city', as it otherwise
naturally should, for Amphipolis was the chief city of that
district and Thessalonica of the whole of Macedonia. It
remains therefore to explain it with Erasmus: *prima occur-
rit a Neapoli petentibus Macedoniam*. Passing from Neapolis
the traveller has to cross the lofty ridge of Symbolum before
entering Macedonia, and the first city he comes to is Philippi.

So Light-
foot.

It must be admitted however that the use of πρῶτος in
this sense without any words to make it clear is unexampled.

κολωνία] *colonia*. A colony consisted of a body of Roman citizens publicly sent out to occupy some town, usually
important on military grounds, who in their new home
still continued to enjoy the full rights of Roman citizens.
Cicero calls colonies *propugnacula imperii*, and Aulus Gel-
lius (xvi. 13) describes them as 'offshoots' or 'miniature
copies of the Roman people'—*quasi propagatae...pop. Romani
quasi effigies parvae simulacraque*. The name is still found
in 'Lincoln', 'Cologne' (=*Köln*).

13.   παρὰ ποταμὸν] The Gangites. The term προσευχή is applied to any 'place of prayer', whether a building,
or open space as here (cf. ἐνομίζομεν). It was a well-known
term, cf. the sneer in Juv. III. 296 *in qua te quaero proseucha?*
The choice of a spot by a river had probably reference to
ceremonial washings. A decree of Halicarnassus allowed
the Jews τὰς προσευχὰς ποιεῖσθαι πρὸς τῇ θαλάσσῃ κατὰ τὸ
πάτριον ἔθος. Cf. Ps. cxxxvii. 1, 'By the waters of Babylon...'.

v. reff. in
A.

Jos. *Ant.*
xIV. 10.
23.

καθίσαντες ἐλαλοῦμεν] *Non statim se contulere ad docen-
dum* B., and so others speak of it as 'informal conversation';
but to *sit* was customary for a preacher (vi. 9 n.), and λαλεῖν
is a regular word for preaching, e. g. xviii. 25, and by no
means denotes 'conversation', 'talk', in N.T. The words
clearly describe preaching.

La. F.

14.   Λυδία] Probably so called from her birthplace being
in Lydia, though 'Lydia' was a common female name.

πορφυρόπωλις] 'The guild of dyers at Thyatira have
left inscriptions still existing'. The celebrity of the purple
dyeing of the neighbourhood is as old as Homer, cf. *Il.* iv.
141,   ὡς δ' ὅτε τίς τ' ἐλέφαντα γυνὴ φοίνικι μιήνῃ
Μῃονὶς ἠὲ Κάειρα, παρήϊον ἔμμεναι ἵππῳ.

A.

Claudian *de Rapt. Pros.* I. 270

> *non sic decus ardet eburnum*
> *Lydia Sidonio quod femina tinxerit ostro.*

Θυατείρων] In N. of Lydia on the river Lycus: one of
the seven Churches mentioned Rev. ii. 18.

διήνοιξεν] A strong word, such as might be used of
opening folding-doors and throwing them wide back. Cf.
Luke xxiv. 45 διήνοιξεν αὐτῶν τὸν νοῦν. It occurs four
times in Luke, three times in the Acts, once elsewhere in
N.T.

15. πιστὶ'ν τῷ κυρ.] 'believing on the Lord', one who La.
really believes on Jesus as Lord. A. and R.V. 'faithful to'—
an ambiguous rendering.

παρεβιάσατο] Cf. Luke xxiv. 29 καὶ παρεβιάσαντο αὐτόν ;
1 Sam. xxviii. 23 οὐκ ἐβουλήθη φαγεῖν καὶ παρεβιάζοντο αὐτόν ;
in all three cases of gentle, hospitable constraint.

16. ἐγένετο δὲ...] i. e. on a subsequent day.

εἰς τὴν προσευχὴν] i. e. the προσευχή already mentioned.
T.R. omits τήν: 'as we went to prayer' A.V.   Text
                                                      ℵABCE.
πνεῦμα πύθωνα] In apposition: T.R.´Πύθωνος. Πύθων   Text
was the name of the serpent slain by Apollo, whence his   ℵABCD.
name of Πύθιος, and the prophetess of Apollo at Delphi
(anciently Πυθώ) was called Πυθία.

Plutarch however tells us that in his day (50—100 A.D. ?)   *de defec-*
the term Πύθωνες was applied to τοὺς ἐγγαστριμύθους Εὐρυ-   *tu Orac.*
κλέας or 'ventriloquist prophets', and so too Hesychius   p. 414.
explains the word. It is also used in LXX., cf. Lev. xix. 31
οὐκ ἐπακολουθήσετε ἐγγαστριμύθοις, and xx. 6, 27, where
A. and R.V. give 'that have a familiar spirit'; and of the
witch of Endor 1 Sam. xxviii. 7 γυναῖκα ἐγγ.

The derivation of the word is unknown. Bengel (as the
ancients probably thought) says *ex quo* πύθεσθαι *datur.*
Lange gives the root *budh*, 'depth', whence βύθος, *puteus;*
Curtius doubtfully the same root as *pus, putidus.*

17. ἔκραζεν...] So too the unclean spirits recognize
Jesus, e.g. Mark i. 24, iii. 11.

18, 19. καὶ ἐξῆλθεν...ὅτι ἐξῆλθεν] Note the simple skill
of this repetition, not reproduced in A. or R.V. Render,
'departed'.

19. εἵλκυσαν] denotes violence. Cf. Plaut. *Poen.* III. 5.
45 *obtorto collo ad praetorem trahor.*

εἰς τὴν ἀγοράν] i.e. into the forum, near which would
be the courts of law.

τοὺς ἄρχοντας] 'the magistrates', a general term; the actual magistrates before whom they were brought are immediately specified as τοῖς στρατηγοῖς, which is the Gk rendering of *praetor*. Colonies were actually governed by *duumviri*, who occupied a position similar to that of the consuls at Rome, but we learn from Cicero that at Capua *cum in ceteris coloniis Duumviri appellentur, hi se Praetores appellari volebant*, and it is probable that the same vanity was not uncommon, cf. the contemptuous *Lusco praetore* Hor. *Sat.* I. 5. 34.

de Leg. Agr. 34.

20. οὗτοι οἱ ἄνθρωποι] Contemptuous.

ἐκταράσσουσιν...] *Suberat utilitas privata, publica ostenditur.* B.

Ἰουδαῖοι ὑπάρχ.] Used to excite prejudice in strong opposition to Ῥωμαίοις οὖσιν. For the unpopularity of the Jews cf. xviii. 17, xix. 34; Tac. *Hist.* v. 5 *Caetera instituta sinistra, foeda, pravitate valuere....Apud ipsos fides obstinata...adversus omnes alios hostile odium*, and cf. Juv. xiv. 96—106 and Mayor *ad loc.*

It will be observed that their accusers speak of them as Jews, and it is most probable that the Christians were for some time confused with the Jews in the general estimation.

21. ἔθη...] The exact nature of this the first charge made against Christians before a Roman magistrate should be noted. It is that they preach 'unlawful customs', i.e. the practice of things unlawful. No Roman magistrate would deal with abstract theological questions (cf. xviii. 15): religion only became a subject for the magistrate, when it (1) might tend to create a breach of the peace (cf. ἐκταράσσουσιν), (2) or tend to the encouragement of illegal acts, especially to the formation of secret sects, organizations, &c.

22. περιρήξαντες] *Summove, lictor, despolia, verbera*, might be the order. Cf. Liv. II. 55 *Consules spoliari hominem et virgas expediri jubent. Provoco, inquit, ad populum, Volero... Quo ferocius clamitabat, eo infestius circumscindere* (cf. περιρήξ.) *et spoliare lictor.* So Dion. Halic. has περικαταρρῆξαι in this sense. ῥαβδίζειν=*virgis caedere*.

Brissonius, de Formulis.

lib. IX. p. 440.

24. ἠσφαλίσατο] Cf. ἀσφαλῶς τηρεῖν above.

τὸ ξύλον] 'used at Sparta (Herod. IX. 37), Athens (Ar. *Eq.* 366), Rome (Plaut. *Capt.* III. 70
    nam noctu nervo vinctus custodibitur)'.

H.

25. ὕμνουν] Clearly connotes thanksgiving, cf. Is. xii. 4 καὶ ἐρεῖς ἐν τῇ ἡμέρᾳ ἐκείνῃ, Ὑμνεῖτε κύριον...; Dan. iii. 23 (Shadrach, Meshech and Abednego) περιεπάτουν ἐν μέσῳ τῆς φλογὸς ὑμνοῦντες τὸν θεόν.
    Crus in nervo cor in caelo. W.

Altered from Tertullian.

ἐπηκροῶντο] ἀκροάομαι = 'hear' 'listen to with pleasure', especially of listening to a recitation, music or the like: ἐπακρ. also suggests the idea of attention. Cf. ἀκούω = 'hear', ἐπακούω = 'hear attentively'.

27. ἑαυτὸν ἀναιρεῖν] It was near Philippi that Brutus committed suicide. For the fact that it was so frequent as to become almost a 'national usage' under the empire cf. Merivale c. 64.

For the punishment of those who had allowed a prisoner to escape cf. xii. 19.

30, 31. Κύριοι...τὸν κύριον] *Non agnoscunt se dominos.* B.

σωθῶ] In the same sense as ὁδὸν σωτηρίας ver. 17, and σώζω throughout the Acts. The keeper was acquainted with the purport of their preaching.

31. σὺ καὶ ὁ οἶκός σου] These words are added to supplement and make more correct (*per Epanorthosin*) the statement πίστ. καὶ σωθήσῃ. Cf. xi. 14.

R.V. rightly, 'Believe...and thou shalt be saved, thou and thy house'.

A.V. wrongly, Believe...and thou shalt be saved, and thy house'.

33. ἔλουσεν...καὶ ἐβαπτίσθη] Chrys. *Hom.* xxxvi. 2 ἔλουσεν αὐτοὺς καὶ ἐλούθη· ἐκείνους μὲν ἀπὸ τῶν πληγῶν ἔλουσεν, αὐτὸς δὲ ἀπὸ τῶν ἁμαρτιῶν ἐλούθη.

Both acts would perhaps take place at a well in the courtyard, cf. προαγαγὼν ἔξω.

34. ἀναγαγών] Perhaps his house was *over* the prison.

παρέθηκεν τράπεζαν] Cf. *Od.* v. 92 ὡς ἄρα φωνήσασα θεὰ παρέθηκε τράπεζαν. The tables being small and easily moveable, were actually placed before the guest.

πανοικεί] Not classical, but cf. πανοικησίᾳ (Thuc. II. 16, III. 57), πανδημεί, πανστρατιᾷ.

πεπιστ. τῷ θεῷ] Hitherto he had been a heathen. The words could not have been used of a converted Jew.

35. τοὺς ῥαβδούχους] = 'fasces-bearers', regular Gk for *lictor.* Cicero appears to suggest that the lictors of the *de Leg.* duumviri should have carried *baculi* not the *fasces— Agr.* 34. 'anteibant lictores, non cum baculis, sed, ut hic praetoribus anteeunt, cum fascibus duobus'.

37. δείραντες...] Note the rhetorical power of this verse. First the statement of the wrong done (δείραντες): then the threefold aggravation of it by the circumstances under which it was done, (1) δημοσίᾳ, (2) ἀκατακρίτους, (3) ἀνθ. Ῥωμαίους ὑπ.: then the wrongful imprisonment; and lastly the enhancement of the injury by the inadequate reparation offered, which was (1) λάθρᾳ, not δημοσίᾳ, (2) not offered personally, cf. αὐτοὶ ἐξαγαγέτωσαν, (3) without courtesy, cf. ἐκβάλλουσιν.

δείραντες] Cic. *in Verr.* v. 66 *Facinus est vincire civem Romanum, scelus verberare;* v. 57 *illa vox et imploratio, Civis Romanus sum, quae saepe ultimis in terris opem inter barbaros et salutem tulit.*
This immunity was secured by the Lex Valeria B.C. 500 and the Lex Porcia B.C. 248.
The praetors do not question Paul's claim, nor does Claudius Lysias xxii. 27. A false claim might be punished with death, cf. Suet. *Claud.* 25 *civitatem Romanam usurpantes...securi percussit.*

Ῥωμαίους ὑπ.] Cf. xxii. 28. How Paul was 'free-born' we do not know; certainly not merely as citizen of Tarsus, which was only an *urbs libera.* Of Silas we know nothing.

ἐκβάλλουσιν] '*cast* us out', a strong word; cf. ἐξαγαγέτωσαν, '*conduct* us out'.

οὐ γάρ] γάρ is the γάρ so frequent in answers: the question it answers here is implied in the indignant protest which precedes. 'They propose to do this! Shall they do it? No, indeed'. So too οὐ γὰρ οὖν.

αὐτοί] In person, not by sending their attendants.

39. παρεκάλεσαν] Cf. v. 15; Luke xv. 28: 'invited', 'besought', its earlier sense. In ver. 40 as usual 'encouraged', 'exhorted'.

40. ἐξῆλθαν] '*they* went out': not Luke.

CHAPTER XVII.

1. διοδεύσαντες] The ὁδός was the *via Egnatia,* so called from Egnatia, on the coast of Apulia, where the Appian road reaches the sea. It passes from that point to Brundisium, and then leads from Dyrrhachium to Byzantium. It was the great road from the W. to the E.

Ἀμφίπολιν] On the left bank of the Strymon, just below L. Cercinitis, 3 m. from the sea: the river flows almost round it, whence its name. On account of its situation it was an important town in Gk history, several times colonized by the Athenians and recaptured by the Thracians. Acquired by Philip B.C. 358. An *urbs libera* and capital of Macedonia Prima.

'Απολλωνίαν] About 30 m. S.-W. of Amphipolis, half-way to Thessalonica.

Θεσσαλονίκην] Originally Therma, at the head of the Thermaic Gulf; Cassander largely increased it and called it Thessalonica after his wife, the sister of Alexander the Great. It is still the second city of European Turkey, with 70,000 inhabitants, and called Saloniki.

ἦν συναγωγὴ] T.R. ἦν ἡ συν. In either case the town Text is distinguished from the other towns mentioned, in which ℵABD. there was no synagogue. This implies the existence of but few Jews in Macedonia.

2. διελέξατο] Used 9 times in the Acts, 3 times in the v. de W. rest of N.T. The word originally indicates an *interchange* of words, conversation; it is then used of reasoning or arguing by means of question and answer—the 'dialectic method' as illustrated in the Dialogues of Plato. In Luke however the word has lost this meaning, and does not imply discussion, though sometimes conveying the idea not merely of 'reasoning' but 'arguing', 'disputing', as perhaps here; ver. 17, xviii. 19, xxiv. 12. In other places it is simply = 'discourse', as xx. 7, 9.

ἀπὸ τῶν γραφῶν......] A most important description of the Apostolic method of teaching, cf. ix. 22 n.
Paul first 'expounds' (διανοίγει xvi. 14 n.) and 'brings forward' (παρατίθεται) passages of 'the Scriptures', i.e. of the O.T., to shew that the Messiah (ὁ χριστός) must do certain things. He then shews that Jesus did these things, and so draws his conclusion 'that this man is the Messiah (ὅτι οὗτος ὁ χ.), even Jesus whom I preach to you'.
For παρατιθέμενος = 'bring forward', 'quote as evidence', cf. Plat. *Polit.* 275 B τὸν μῦθον παρεθέμεθα, ἵν' ἐνδείξαιτο......

3. τὸν χρ. ἔδει παθεῖν] Luke xxiv. 26 οὐχὶ ταῦτα ἔδει παθεῖν τὸν χριστόν; and cf. iii. 18 n.

4. προσεκληρώθησαν] Strictly passive, 'were allotted to', but A. and R.V. probably rightly 'consorted', cf. n. on τεταγμένοι xiii. 48.

5. τῶν ἀγοραίων] The ἀγορά was the natural resort of those who had nothing to do, cf. Matt. xx. 4. Hence ἀγοραῖοι = 'idlers', 'good-for-nothing fellows', cf. Plat. *Prot.* 347 c τῶν φαύλων καὶ ἀγοραίων ἀνθρώπων; Xen. *Hell.* vi. 2. 23 τὸν ἀγοραῖον ὄχλον; Dem. 269 περίτριμμα ἀγορᾶς, where it is put side by side with σπερμολόγος (cf. xvii. 18 n.). So *sub-rostrani, subbasilicani.*

'Ἰάσονος] A common name in Thessaly; or possibly he was a Jew and it is here a Gk form of Joshua or Jesus, as in 2 Macc. i. 7.

εἰς τὸν δῆμον] Thessalonica was an *urbs libera*, retaining its own government (cf. τὸν δῆμον) and its own magistrates (cf. τοὺς πολιτάρχας).

6. τοὺς πολιτάρχας] It is noteworthy that this word, which never occurs in Gk literature (πολίταρχος occurs once in Aeneas Tacticus), is found in the verbal form in an inscription of about the date 69—79 A.D. found on an arch at Thessalonica, which begins πολειταρχούντων Σωσιπάτρου... and names seven such politarchs.

'Now in the British Museum'. Cooke.

The word literally = 'burgomasters', and is formed on the analogy of Βοιωτάρχαι, 'Ασιάρχαι.

οἱ τὴν οἰκ...] Note, in this the second instance of accusation before non-Jewish magistrates, (1) the exaggeration, (2) that the charge is not made on religious grounds but for disturbance and treason. Cf. xxiv. 5.

7. οὓς ὑποδέδεκται 'I.] Added because he is the prisoner, and they are justifying their apprehension of him. ὑποδέχεσθαι is especially used of 'receiving with hospitality', cf. Luke x. 38 ὑπεδέξατο αὐτὸν εἰς τὸν οἶκον αὐτῆς.

καὶ οὗτοι...] A charge against all Christians as guilty of treason. Under the emperors to accuse any one of treason (*majestatis deferre; laesae majestatis accusare*) was the surest method of procuring a conviction. To acknowledge allegiance to another king would be treason and render the offender liable to the *Lex Julia de Majestate* (cf. τῶν δογμάτων Καίσαρος). The Jews here bring the same charge against His disciples which they had brought against Jesus, cf. Luke xxiii. 2 κωλύοντα Καίσαρι φόρους διδόναι λέγοντα ἑαυτὸν χριστὸν βασιλέα εἶναι.

Although the emperors never ventured to assume the title *rex* at Rome, in the Eastern provinces they were regularly termed βασιλεύς.

ἕτερον] 'different' i. e. from Caesar.

9. λαβόντες τὸ ἱκανὸν] The Roman law would be in force even in an *urbs libera*, and this is clearly the Gk for the legal Roman phrase *satis accipere* or *exigere* 'to take security', the opposite of *satis dare*, 'to go bail', 'give security'. Probably security for the departure of Paul was required.

10. Βέροιαν] About 60 m. S.W. from Thessalonica, near Pella.

A. 11. εὐγενέστεροι] that is, in disposition: 'stirred up not to envy but to inquiry'.

προθυμίας] 'readiness of mind' A. and R.V., but the word is stronger = 'heartiness', 'eagerness'.

τὸ καθ' ἡμέραν] So in the Lord's Prayer, Luke xi. 3 *τὸν ἄρτον ἡμῶν τὸν ἐπιούσιον δίδου ἡμῖν τὸ καθ' ἡμέραν* 'day by day'.

ἀνακρίνοντες] implies careful and often judicial examination into facts, e.g. Thuc. i. 95 Παυσανίαν ἀνακρινοῦντες ὧν πέρι ἐπυνθάνοντο. Cf. iv. 9 n.

For the sense cf. John v. 39 *ἐρευνᾶτε τὰς γραφὰς...*

ταῦτα]   Paul's statements: **οὕτως**, as he stated them.

13. οἱ ἀπὸ Θεσσ. 'I.]   *Const. praegnans.* They are regarded not merely as 'the Jews in Thessalonica' but as 'the Jews who *went from* Thessalonica to Beroea'.

κἀκεῖ] with *σαλεύοντες*, 'stirring up the people there too' i. e. as they had done at Thessalonica.

14. ἕως ἐπὶ...] 'as far as to...'.   T.R. *ὡς ἐπὶ...*, which does not imply that it was a *feint*, Paul actually going by land (as A.V. seems to think, 'to go as it were to the sea'), but *ὡς* merely expresses their *intention* or *thought*. *ὡς* seems a correction, *ὡς* being misunderstood.   ἕως omit D.

He would probably reach the sea at Dium.

[margin: ἕως NBE, ὡς HLP.]

15. καθιστάνοντες] so classical of 'conducting to' a place, e. g. Thuc. iv. 78 οἱ δὲ Περαιβοὶ αὐτὸν...κατέστησαν ἐς Δῖον.

ἵνα...ἔλθωσιν]   Cf. xviii. 5; they joined him at Corinth.

16. ἐν δὲ ταῖς 'Αθ.]   Athens had been captured by Sulla B.C. 86 and suffered greatly.   Her renown was however great as a place of education: she was 'the classic university of the ancient world'.

[margin: Merivale. c. 56.]

παρωξύνετο] xv. 39 n.

κατείδωλον] 'wholly given to idolatry' A.V., but R.V. rightly, 'full of idols', i.e. statues, &c. For the formation of the word cf. *καταβόστρυχος νεανίας* Eur. *Phoen.* 146; *κατάδενδρος; κατάμπελος; κατάχρυσος.*

For the fact cf. Xen. *de Rep. Ath.* where he describes Athens as ὅλη βωμός, ὅλη θῦμα θεοῖς καὶ ἀνάθημα, and Livy xlv. 27 alludes to *simulacra deorum hominumque omni genere et materiae et artium insignia.*   *[margin: La.]*

17. διελέγετο μὲν οὖν...]   The sense of this passage is lost in A.V., and is not clear in R.V. or in the text as punctuated.

Before coming to the *special* event which he wishes to narrate at length, Luke by means of several parallel clauses, loosely connected, describes the *general* condition of things preceding it.   These clauses have their verbs in the imperfect (διελέγετο, συνέβαλλον, ἔλεγον, εὐηγγελίζετο), the special event being markedly introduced by two aorists (ἐπιλαβόμενοι ἤγαγον).

While he was thus waiting in Athens Paul's spirit was gradually provoked by the number of idols he saw. In consequence of this (1) he used to discourse not only in the synagogue but in the market-place with those who came up. (2) Among those (τινὲς δὲ καὶ) who thus entered into conversation with him Luke notes that there were some philosophers. (3) The general opinion of him was contemptuous. But at last 'they (i.e. the people generally) took him and conducted him...'.

It is to be noted that the antithesis to διελέγετο μὲν is ἐπιλαβόμενοι δὲ (for which T.R. has ἐπιλαβ. τε), cf. ii. 41 n., and that the clause τινὲς δὲ τῶν 'Επ....συνέβαλλον αὐτῷ is almost parenthetical* (cf. xii. 5, xiii. 5 for similar clauses with δὲ, intervening between μὲν and the antithetical δέ), and in no case are 'the philosophers' to be regarded as the people described ver. 19 as 'taking hold of Paul', for Paul's speech was certainly not addressed to 'the philosophers', who could not possibly be called δεισιδαιμονεστέρους or have had the remarks in vv. 24, 29 addressed to them, but was made to the 'men of Athens' generally.

ἐν τῇ ἀγορᾷ] S.W. of the Acropolis, between it and the Areopagus and the Pnyx. Especially in the forenoon (the time known as πλήθουσα ἀγορά) it was a place of general resort, both for business and pleasure. It was here that Socrates 'argued' (διελέγετο) or 'reasoned' with all who came up to him. Cf. Plat. *Gorg.* 469 D πληθούσης ἀγορᾶς ἐκεῖ φανερὸς ἦν.

18. 'Επικουρίων...] The Epicurean and Stoic schools were at this time the two great rival systems—sharply contrasted both in reality and in popular opinion.

The Epicureans, so called from Epicurus (342—270 B.C.), taught at Athens in the famous gardens of Epicurus.

They considered (1) that the world was created by the fortuitous combinations of indestructible atoms; (2) that the aim of life was pleasure, defined as mental calm or freedom from passion (ἀταραξία), and that the soul perishes with the body; (3) that the gods lived an existence of eternal calm not troubling themselves about men. Lucretius has embodied their philosophy in the greatest of Latin poems, and in a popular form it permeates Horace.

The Stoics were founded by Zeno (360—260 B.C.), who lectured in the στοὰ ποικίλη; but Chrysippus (280—207 B.C.) was held to have really established the system by his great ability. He was, it may be noted, of Soli in Cilicia, and his successor was Zeno of Tarsus.

Their principal doctrines were (1) a theory that the world was due to the transition of a 'constructive fire' (πῦρ τεχνικόν) or 'breath' through air into water and so into

*'Ein sehr flüchtiger Pinselstrich im ganzen Bilde', F. Overbeck.

v. Ritter and Preller.

Diog. L. VII. 156.

solids; (2) that ἀρετή was the one thing desirable, and that
this consisted in living 'conformably to nature' (ὁμολογου-
μένως ζῆν), all other things, e.g. pleasure, pain, health,
wealth, being 'indifferent' (ἀδιάφορα); (3) that God was a
certain living force immanent in nature (τὸ ποιοῦν...τὸν ἐν
τῇ ὕλῃ λόγον), a sort of *natura naturans*, and was known
to men by many names, e.g. εἱμαρμένη, νοῦς, Ζεύς. **Diog. I.. VII. 134.**

καί τινες ἔλεγον...] Probably not the philosophers but
generally some of those who heard Paul.

τί ἄν θέλοι] Cf. x. 17 n. The phrase suggests that
possibly, but only possibly, there was a meaning in his
words.

σπερμολόγος] (1) 'a rook' or 'crow', cf. Ar. *Av.* 578 τότε
χρὴ στρούθων νέφος ἀρθὲν | ἢ σπερμολόγων ἐκ τῶν ἀγρῶν | τὸ
σπέρμ' αὐτῶν ἀνακάψαι.
(2) Eustath. on *Od.* v. 940 says that the Athenians
applied the term to τοὺς περὶ ἐμπόρια καὶ ἀγορὰς διατρίβοντας,
διὰ τὸ ἀναλέγεσθαι τὰ ἐκ τῶν φορτίων ἀναρρέοντα καὶ διαζῆν,
and so it is used of τοὺς οὐδένος λόγου ἀξίους, 'hangers-on',
'good-for-nothing fellows'.

Dem. 269 calls Aeschines σπερμολόγος, περίτριμμα ἀγορᾶς,
ὄλεθρος γραμματεύς, where the meaning is clearly not 'bab-
bler' but 'parasite', 'hanger-on', also with a hit at his
voice (as throughout the speech) and method of speaking.
Cf. Suidas, σπερμολόγον; εὐρυλόγον, ἀκριτόμυθον: Hesychius
too explains the word by φλυαρός.

So here it means (1) a man who hangs about to pick up
odds and ends in the market-place; (2) one who was all
sound without meaning.

ξένων δαιμονίων] The first count against Socrates was
ἀδικεῖ Σωκράτης...καινὰ δαιμόνια εἰσφέρων. **Xen. Mem. 1.**
The plural is generic: Paul preached 'Jesus and His
rising from the dead'; the Athenians considered this to be
an account of some new Eastern divinity (ξένον δαιμ.), and
immediately classed Paul among the 'preachers of new
divinities'.

Many commentators explain the plural by saying that
the Athenians imagined that Ἀνάστασις was the name of a
goddess, but Luke cannot have meant this, as those for
whom he is writing could not possibly so understand the
word, for he has already used it several times of 'the rising
again' of Jesus. **e.g. Chrys. La. Baum.**

καταγγελεύς] Cf. ver. 23, καταγγέλλω.

19. ἐπιλαβόμενοι] Not by any means implying violence,
cf. ix. 27, xxiii. 19; Mark viii. 23 ἐπιλαβόμενος τῆς χειρὸς τοῦ
τυφλοῦ.

P.   13

Dem.
721. 14.

τὸν "Ἄρειον Πάγον] A.V. 'unto Areopagus', adding in the margin 'It was the highest court in Athens'. No doubt the court of Areopagus (ἡ βουλὴ ἡ ἐξ Ἀρ. πάγου) did especially deal with religious offences, but there is not the slightest indication of any judicial hearing here, indeed the polite interrogation δυνάμεθα γνῶναι at the outset precludes it.

The hill is W. of the Acropolis, N. of the Agora, accessible from it by a flighṭ of steps cut out of the rock. Perhaps Paul was taken there for a *quiet* hearing.

20. ξενίζοντα] Cf. Ἑλληνίζω &c., 'act as a stranger', 'to be strange', 'unusual'. τίνα θέλει... cf. ii. 12.

21. Ἀθηναῖοι δὲ...καινότερον] Explanatory remark of the writer.

οἱ ἐπιδημοῦντες ξένοι] For ἐπιδημεῖν cf. ii. 10 n. Athens was much frequented, not only as a town of historical interest, but also as a university by young Romans. Cf. Cic. *de Off.* I. 1 *Quamquam te, Marce fili, annum jam audientem Cratippum idque Athenis abundare oportet praeceptis...*

M.

ηὐκαίρουν] Late Gk, =*vacare alicui rei.*

καινότερον] The Greeks frequently use the comparative, where there is no direct comparison, merely to indicate that the quality described by the adj. is present in an *unusual* degree: cf. next verse δεισιδαιμονεστέρους; xxiv. 4 ἐπὶ πλεῖον; xxiv. 22 ἀκριβέστερον εἰδώς; xxv. 10 κάλλιον ἐπιγινώσκεις; xxv. 14. With καινός however and νέος their fondness for using the comparative is quite singular, and seems to illus-

See also
Stallb.
Euthy-
phro,
sub in.

trate the restless desire for novelty so characteristic of the Athenians and often referred to, e.g. Thuc. III. 38; Dem. 156 πυνθανόμενοι κατὰ τὴν ἀγοράν, εἴ τι λέγεται νεώτερον. *Nova statim sordebant, noviora quaerebantur.* B.

22. σταθεὶς δὲ...] Cf. ii. 14 n. Observe the dramatic power with which Luke calls attention to the great actor (σταθεὶς δὲ Π.) and the great stage (ἐν μέσῳ...) on which he appears. *Amplum Theatrum.* B.

W.

'The temple of the Eumenides was immediately below him :...eastward was the temple of Theseus...he beheld the Propylaea facing him and the Parthenon fronting him from above. The temple of Victory was on his right...Above him towering over the city...was the bronze Colossus of Minerva, armed with spear, shield, and helmet, the champion of Athens'.

δεισιδαιμονεστέρους] δεισιδαίμων is in itself a neutral word, and can be used (1) in a good sense = 'god-fearing', 'reverent', or (2) in a bad sense = 'fearful of the gods', 'superstitious'.

XVII. 23] *NOTES.* 195

A.V. gives 'too superstitious', R.V. 'somewhat superstitious', and V. *superstitiosiores.* These renderings are
however misleading. Paul certainly does not commence with
words of *rebuke:* he makes the unusual regard which the
Athenians paid to religious matters the *point d'appui* of his
address. It seems clearly right therefore to take the word
in a good sense = 'very god-fearing' or 'reverent'. For
this reverent spirit of the Athenians, cf. Pausanias I. 17. 1
οἱ Ἀθηναῖοι θεοὺς εὐσεβοῦσιν ἄλλων πλέον; Soph. *O. C.* 260
τάς γ' Ἀθήνας φασὶ θεοσεβεστάτας.

Chrys.Λ.
Baum.
M. N. H.
F. de W.

At the same time the choice of the peculiar word here
(cf. too its use xxv. 19) seems not unintentional. To the
writer of the Acts the 'reverence' of the Athenians was
'superstition', and, assuming that we have only the *substance* of Paul's speech, it is possible that Luke, writing for
Christians, chooses a word to describe the religious feeling
of the Athenians which at any rate suggests the idea of
superstition.

23. ἀναθεωρῶν] 'passing in review'. **σεβάσματα**, 'objects
of reverence', e.g. temples, altars, &c.

καὶ βωμὸν...] 'among others an altar...' ᾧ ἐπεγέγραπτο
= *inscriptum erat.*

ΑΓΝΩΣΤΩ ΘΕΩ] 'to (i.e. dedicated to) an unknown
god'. The Greek gods had each their own rights and privileges
(e.g. one guarded the sea, another the air; one was a god of
healing, another of war): when therefore some occasion of
prayer or thanksgiving necessitated the dedication of an
altar, it was important to dedicate it to the proper deity,
for otherwise there was grave danger of incurring the anger
of the deity who was thus defrauded of his rights.

So Epimenides in a pestilence, which could not be
attributed to the anger of any special deity, advised the
sacrifice of a sheep τῷ προσήκοντι θεῷ, and to this fact is
assigned the existence at Athens of βωμοὶ ἀνώνυμοι.

Diog.
Laert.
Epim. 3.

So too the chorus in great perplexity Aesch. *Ag.* 155
appeal to Ζεὺς, ὅστις ποτ' ἐστίν, not implying any doubt of
his existence, but not knowing by what title properly to
address him under the circumstances, and so asking him to
accept an *ambiguous* address.

Pausanias I. 1. 4 says that in Athens there are βωμοὶ
Θεῶν ὀνομαζομένων ἀγνώστων, i.e. altars dedicated to a god
not with any definite name but nameless or 'unknown'.

δ...τοῦτο] T.R. ὃν...τοῦτον, probably corrected from an
idea of reverence. 'What' = 'the divinity which', cf. τὸ
θεῖον below.

Text
א¹A¹BD,
ὃν
א³A²
EHLP.

13—2

ἀγνοοῦντες] The keynote of the speech: God unknown hitherto, now revealed. Instead of your needing to appeal to a god one among many and unknown, I proclaim to you God who is (1) *the* God, and (2) is revealed, (*a*) by His works, (*b*) by the special revelation of Jesus.

24. κύριος] *dominus*, here clearly 'owner', 'absolute possessor'.

οὐκ ἐν χειροποιήτοις] Cf. vii. 48 n. The thought is not uncommon in heathen writers, cf. Eur.

Fragm.
ap.
Clem.
Alex.

ποῖος δ' ἂν οἶκος τεκτόνων πλασθεὶς ὕπο
δέμας τὸ θεῖον περιβάλοι τοίχων πτυχαῖς;

Leg. ii.
10.

So too Cicero says that Xerxes is reported to have burnt the temples of the Greeks, *quod parietibus includerent deos....quorum hic mundus omnis templum esset et domus.*

25. ὑπὸ χειρῶν...] Cf. Ps. l. 9 *seq.* 'I will take no bullock...'.

Ulpian
in La.

προσδεόμενος] προσδεῖσθαι = ἔχειν μὲν μέρος, ἔτι δὲ δεῖσθαι πρὸς τὸ τέλειον. This exactly describes the *popular* conception of the gods as needing for their full happiness the offerings of men. On the other hand the Epicureans asserted that the divine nature was self-complete; cf. Lucr. ii. 650 *Divom natura...ipsa suis pollens opibus nihil indiga nostri.*

πᾶσι] 'to all', carefully not 'to all men'. In vv. 24, 25 God is described as the Creator of 'the universe, the heaven and the earth, and all that is in it'; in ver. 26 as the Creator of men and their governor.

So
A.&R.V.
So A. M.
La. de
W.

26. ἐποίησεν] Clearly in its emphatic position 'He made' i.e. created, parallel to ὁ ποιήσας ver. 24. Others give ἐποίησεν κατοικεῖν 'He caused to dwell'; cf. Mark vii. 37 τοὺς κωφοὺς ποιεῖ ἀκούειν.

κατοικεῖν] Inf. of purpose or result, 'so that they should dwell'; cf. below ζητεῖν, which is not joined with καί because it is not parallel to κατοικεῖν, but somewhat subordinate in sequence of thought: not 'so as to dwell...and seek', but 'so as to dwell...so as to seek'.

ἐπὶ παντὸς προσ.] Gen. xi. 8 ἐπὶ πρόσωπον πάσης τῆς γῆς.

27. εἰ ἄρα γε] viii. 22 n.

ψηλαφήσειαν...καὶ εὕροιεν] The two verbs form one compound idea, 'if haply they might by groping find Him': it is not the searching that is problematical but the finding. For ψηλαφάω, cf. *Phaedo* 99 B, where it is used of vague guesses at truth.

καί γε...] 'and that though He is...'.

28.   ἐν αὐτῷ γάρ...] Proving that He is not far from us, and therefore to be taken literally, 'for *in* Him...', but also including the meaning '*by* Him'.   As air is everywhere, and in it and by it we live, so in a fuller sense we live in God and by Him.

ζῶμεν, κινούμεθα, ἐσμέν] Lange remarks that these words So too M. by themselves are in a descending scale; life is more than movement, movement than existence: but taken in their connection here they form an ascending scale and produce a climax; not only our life but movement, not only movement but existence is in God.

τινές...]   Aratus of Soli in Cilicia (flor. B.C. 270) in his astronomical poem τὰ Φαινόμενα, which begins ἐκ Διὸς ἀρχώ-μεσθα, has these exact words.   Cleanthes, the Stoic philosopher (300—220 B.C.), in his Hymn to Ζεύς l. 5 has ἐκ σοῦ γὰρ γένος ἐσμέν.   In both cases Ζεύς is used in a Pantheistic sense, see note on the Stoics ver. 18.

Paul quotes a Gr. poet again in 1 Cor. xv. 33 φθείρουσιν ἤθη χρήσθ' ὁμιλίαι κακαί ; Tit. i. 12 Κρῆτες ἀεὶ ψεῦσται, κακὰ θηρία, γαστέρες ἀργαί.

γένος...] Thrown forward to connect the argument: being His offspring we ought to know that He cannot be like an image, to which we are ourselves unlike and superior.

29.   οὐκ ὀφείλομεν] *Clemens locutio praesertim in prima persona plurali.* B.

χρυσῷ...ὅμοιον] The same protest against anthropomorphism is not uncommon in antiquity, e.g. Xenophanes has

> εἷς θεός ἐντι θεοῖσι καὶ ἀνθρώποισι μέγιστος
> οὔτε δέμας θνητοῖσιν ὁμοίϊος οὔτε νόημα.

Ap. Clem. Alex. Strom. v. p. 601 c.

χαράγματι] 'a thing graven', from χαράσσω.

τέχνης καὶ ἐνθυμ.] *artis* externae, *cogitationes* internae. B.

τὸ θεῖον] Not 'God', because Paul is referring to their ideas of 'the Divine'.

30.   τοὺς χρ. τῆς ἀγνοίας] The time previous to the sending of the 'message' by Jesus which Paul 'proclaims', and also with reference to ἀγνώστῳ, ἀγνοοῦντες ver. 23.

ὑπεριδών] A.V. 'winked at'; R.V. 'overlooked'. Both words suggest an idea of 'pardon', not contained in ὑπερ-ιδεῖν. The word is the opposite of ἐφορᾶν 'to regard', and only occurs here in N.T., but is found in LXX. in the clear sense of 'neglect', e.g. Ps. lv. 1 μὴ ὑπερίδῃς τὴν δέησίν μου; Ps. lxxviii. 62 τὴν κληρονομίαν αὐτοῦ ὑπερεῖδεν; Gen. xlii. 21; Deut. xxii. 1. The word here however must not be pressed,

198   ACTS OF THE APOSTLES. [xvii. 30

as though it contained any *positive* statement as to God's treatment of men in the past: it has merely a *negative* force, serving to bring out more clearly the contrast between the past and God's present definite revelation. One part of an antithetical statement should never be taken alone.

μετανοεῖν, καθότι...] 'to repent, according as...': the warning to repent is in accordance with the declaration of judgment.

μέλλει κρίνειν...] Ps. ix. 8 αὐτὸς κρινεῖ τὴν οἰκουμένην ἐν δικαιοσύνῃ.

31. ἐν ἀνδρὶ ᾧ...] 'by means of the man whom...'; cf. Matt. ix. 34 ἐν ἄρχοντι τῶν δαιμονίων ἐκβάλλει τὰ δαιμόνια.

πίστιν παρασχών] 'having afforded' or 'brought forward proof' (i.e. of this appointment) by having raised...'.
παρέχεσθαι, regularly in Dem. of 'bring forward evidence'.

32. ἀνάστασιν νεκρῶν] 'a resurrection of dead men'; not 'the resurrection of the dead', as R.V. Paul had said nothing about the resurrection of the dead generally, but only spoken of the resurrection of Jesus: his hearers immediately refuse to listen any more to a man who talks about 'a rising again of dead men'. The plural 'men' represents their scornful generalization.

33. οὕτως...] 'Then (cf. vii. 8, xxvii. 44, xxviii. 14) Paul went forth from their midst'. The graphic vigour of these words deserves notice.

Euseb. *Hist.* III. 4.
34. Διο. ὁ 'Αρεοπ.] According to tradition ordained Bishop of Athens by Paul.

CHAPTER XVIII.

1. Κόρινθον] Taken and destroyed by L. Mummius B.C. 146: rebuilt and made a 'colony' by Caesar: capital of the province of Achaia and residence of the proconsul: the chief commercial city of Greece.

2. 'Ιουδαῖον] 'a Jew', not 'a disciple', and therefore probably not at this time a Christian: the reason assigned for Paul's residence with him is not that he was a Christian but that he was 'of the same trade'.

'Ακύλαν] *Aquilam.* For Jews of Pontus cf. ii. 9 n. Aquila and Priscilla went with Paul to Ephesus and stayed there (vv. 18, 26; 1 Cor. xvi. 19), but are referred to as again at Rome, Rom. xvi. 3.

Πρίσκιλλαν] dimin. of *Prisca*, cf. *Livilla, Drusilla.* She is called Πρίσκαν Rom. xvi. 3 (where T.R. wrongly Πρίσκιλλαν).

διὰ τὸ διατετᾱχέναι...] Claudius was Emperor 41—54 A.D. Suetonius says *Judaeos impulsore Chresto assidue* Claud. *tumultuantes Roma expulit.* These ambiguous words may [25.] refer (1) to riots at Rome headed by some one actually called 'Chrestus' (χρηστός), or (2), much more probably, to disturbances due to disputes among the Jews about 'the Christ' (Suet. having mistaken the name and its meaning), and possibly in connection with the new teaching that Jesus was 'the Christ'.

The edict (like the other edict of Claudius against astrologers (Tac. *Ann.* XII. 52) cannot have been strictly enforced, for Jews were numerous in Rome very shortly after this, cf. e.g. xxviii. 15.

3. ὁμότεχνον] The Rabbis enjoined that every father should teach his son a trade, that he might always be able to earn his own bread. The Rabbi Judah says 'He that teacheth not his son a trade, doth the same as if he taught him to be a thief'.

For Paul earning his own living, cf. xx. 34; 1 Thess. ii. 9; 2 Thess. iii. 8. The *Teaching of the Twelve Apostles* ch. 12 distinctly asserts that those who claim to be prophets or preachers shall earn their own living.

σκηνοποιοί] 'tent-makers'. It is suggested that the word may refer to 'making the material for tents'; the manufacture of a substance called *cilicium*, much used for tents, was much practised in Cilicia, the goats in that region possessing specially thick hair. There is however no authority for rendering σκηνοποιός 'maker of material for tents'.

'The fertile plain on which Tarsus stands is, in harvest Cooke time, still studded with these hair-cloth tents'. with ref. to Beau-

5. συνείχετο τῷ λόγῳ] T.R. with poor authority τῷ fort πνεύματι. *Kara-*
mania,
R.V. renders 'was constrained', as though the arrival 273. of Silas and Timothy had caused this increased vigour, whereas the imperfect clearly expresses that when they arrived 'they found Paul wholly occupied with the word'.

For συνέχομαι, cf. xxviii. 8; Luke viii. 37 φόβῳ μεγάλῳ συνείχοντο; Thuc. II. 49 τῇ δίψῃ ἀπαύστῳ ξυνεχόμενοι. The word expresses a *firm* hold.

6. ἐκτιναξάμενος] Cf. xiii. 51 n.   Neh. v. 13.

τὸ αἷμα...] Cf. Ezek. xxxiii. 4 τὸ αἷμα αὐτοῦ ἐπὶ τῆς κεφαλῆς αὐτοῦ ἔσται. The words here are not a curse but

(1) a warning, (2) a solemn disclaimer of responsibility, cf.
xx. 26; Ezek. xxxiii. 8, 9; 2 Sam. i. 16.

εἰς τὰ ἔθνη] i.e. here at Corinth, cf. ver. 19.

II.   **7.** ἐκεῖθεν] from the synagogue. The house of Justus
he enters probably for the purpose of preaching. There is
no indication of his leaving either his residence or his work
with Aquila.

Τιτίου Ἰούστου] MSS. vary much; some give Τίτου,
others omit the word. Perhaps the word is due to the final
v. Δ. M. τι in ὀνόματι being written twice and τι taken as a contrac-
tion for Titus, Justus being elsewhere only a second name,
cf. i. 23; Col. iv. 11.

8. Κρίσπος] 1 Cor. i. 14.

9. μὴ φοβοῦ] Is. xliii. 5.

λάλει καὶ μὴ σιωπήσῃς] The double form expresses
emphasis.   Cf. John i. 3, 20; Acts xiii. 11 τυφλὸς μὴ βλέπων
τὸν ἥλιον.

10. διότι ἐγώ...] Cf. x. 38; Judg. vi. 16; Jer. i. 8.

λαός] Cf. iv. 25 n., not Jews but 'a chosen people', i.e.
chosen from among the heathen.

11. ἐκάθισεν] Cf. Luke xxiv. 49 καθίσατε ἐν τῇ πόλει;
'remain', 'tarry'. The two Epistles to the Thessalonians
are generally assigned to this period.

12. Γαλλίωνος] brother of Seneca and uncle of Lucan;
his original name was M. Annaeus Novatus until he was
Quest. adopted by the rhetorician Gallio. Seneca describes him
Nat. 4, as possessing *comitatem et incompositam suavitatem*, and
Praef. adds, *Nemo enim mortalium uni tam dulcis est quam hic
omnibus.* So too Statius *Silv.* II. 7. 32 *dulcem Gallionem.*

ἀνθυπάτου] xiii. 6 n. Achaia had been a senatorial
province: Tiberius made it an imperial one (Tac. *Ann.* I. 76),
but Claudius gave it back to the senate (Suet. *Claud.* 25).

Ἀχαίας] By Homer the Greeks generally are termed
Ἀχαιοί, but in classical times the name is confined to the
inhabitants of a narrow strip of land to the N. of Pelopon-
nesus; the Achaeans however become again important with
the formation of the Achaean league B.C. 281, and on the
final reduction of Greece B.C. 146 the term was applied to
the Roman province, which embraced the whole of Greece
proper. Beyond it was 'Macedonia', cf. xvi. 12 n.

βῆμα] xii. 21 n.

13. παρὰ τὸν νόμον] The Jews designedly use an
ambiguous phrase 'contrary to the law' desiring to induce
Gallio to put Paul on his trial: he however rightly distin-

guishes between Roman law, which he was bound to administer, and Jewish law (νόμου τοῦ καθ' ὑμᾶς), with which
he had nothing to do. Observe the emphatic position of
the words.

14. εἰ μὲν ἦν...εἰ δὲ ζητήματά ἐστιν] 'If it had been
(which it is not)...but if they are (as they are)'.

ἀδίκημα] *injuria*, a general word for anything which La. B.
would form the ground of civil or criminal proceedings.
ῥᾳδιούργημα πονηρόν: a criminal offence.

κατὰ λόγον] Opposite of παρὰ λόγον.

ἀνεσχόμην] *Judaeos sibi molestos innuit.* B. Cf. the
contemptuous plural ζητήματα, and Ἰουδαῖοι without ἄνδρες.

15. λόγου καὶ ὀνομάτων] words not facts; cf. the old
Roman principle—*facta arguebantur, dicta impune erant*
(Tac. *Ann.* I. 72).

The sentence χριστὸς ὁ Ἰησοῦς would give rise to 'questions about a statement (λόγου) and names (ὀνομάτων)'.

ὄψεσθε αὐτοί] Really imperative; 'look to it yourselves';
cp. Matt. xxvii. 4 σὺ ὄψει. So αὐτὸς γνώσει Plat. *Gorg.*
505 c.

17. πάντες] i.e. the bystanders. T.R. adds οἱ"Ελληνες— οἱ"Ελλ.
a correct gloss.   DEHL
                                                                P, text
Σωσθένην τὸν ἀρχ.] Perhaps the successor of Crispus אAB.
ver. 8. Anyhow he seems to have been prominent in bringing forward the charge against Paul.

18. ἀποταξάμενος] Mark vi. 46; Luke ix. 61='bid
farewell'.

κειράμενος...] Without doubt referring to Παῦλος the
main subject, the words καὶ σὺν αὐτῷ...'Ακύλας being parenthetical. Nor is it an objection to this that Aquila is named
after his wife, as, for some unknown reason, the same
order is found ver. 26; Rom. xvi. 3.

The incident seems referred to in order to call attention
to Paul's personal obedience to the Jewish Law.

What the cause or nature of the vow was is not known.
Abstinence from wine and allowing the hair to grow were
common accompaniments of a vow, cf. xxi. 24, 26, and
the description of the vow of the Nazarites, Numb. vi.
Shaving the head would mark the completion of the vow,
and strictly could only be performed in the Temple, the hair
being burnt with the offering. Wordsworth however draws a v. W.
distinction between κειράμενος 'having polled', 'cut shorter', *ad loc.*
and ξυρήσωνται xxi. 24 'shaved', comparing 1 Cor. xi. 6
αἰσχρὸν γυναικὶ τὸ κείρασθαι ἢ ξυρᾶσθαι; and it seems that

one who had taken a Nazarite vow in foreign lands might so *poll* his hair, provided that he kept the hair for burning when the head was finally shaved.

Roman sailors made similar vows, cf. Juv. xii. 81 *gaudent ubi vertice raso | garrula securi narrare pericula nautae.*

Κεγχρεαῖς] The Eastern of the two ports of Corinth (*bimaris Corinthi* Hor. *Od.* i. 7. 2), 70 stades from the city: Lechaeum was the W. port.

19. κἀκείνους κατέλιπεν αὐτοῦ] i.e. Aquila and Priscilla. The words somewhat anticipate Paul's actual departure, but Luke is desirous to pass on to the action of the central figure (cf. αὐτός).

Omit
אABE. **21. ἀποταξάμενος**] T.R. has ἀπετάξατο αὐτοῖς εἰπών, Δεῖ με πάντως τὴν ἑορτὴν τὴν ἐρχομένην ποιῆσαι εἰς Ἱεροσόλυμα, πάλιν δὲ...

22. ἀναβάς] Clearly to Jerusalem, cf. viii. 15 n.

23. ἐξῆλθεν] Commencement of the third missionary journey, ending at Jerusalem (xxi. 16). For ἡ Γαλ. χώρα, which is here distinguished from Phrygia, see xvi. 6 n.

24. Ἀλεξανδρεύς] Alexander founded Alexandria b. c. 332, and himself planted a colony of Jews there; at this time they formed a third of the population. It was the great meeting-point of Judaism and Hellenism, and it was here that the LXX. version of the Old Testament was produced. For Apollos, cf. 1 Cor. i. 12, iii. 5, iv. 6.

See
quot.
in W. **λόγιος**] A.V. 'eloquent'; R.V. 'learned' with 'eloquent' in margin. The word can bear either meaning, but, as the words δύν. ὢν ἐν ταῖς γ. describe *learning*, it seems preferable to render 'eloquent'. Moreover when it means 'learned' it specially means 'learned in history' (ὁ τῆς ἱστορίας ἔμπειρος, Hesych.), a sense not required here.

25. κατηχημένος] lit. 'orally instructed', cf. Luke i. 4. But, as oral instruction was almost the only method used, it = merely 'instructed'.

ζέων τῷ πνεύματι] 'fervent', expresses the effect of 'yeast' or 'ferment'. Cf. Rom. xii. 11 τῷ πνεύματι ζέοντες, and the comparison of the kingdom of God to 'leaven' (ζύμη) Luke xiii. 21.

ἀκριβῶς] A.V. 'diligently' and in next verse 'more perfectly'; R.V. 'carefully' and 'more carefully': but as in ver. 26 the word is clearly objective, referring not to the greater *care* they took but to the greater *accuracy* of their information, we should perhaps render 'accurately' in both cases. The accuracy of Apollos' teaching was only comparative and needed supplementing. Like his master John, he knew much but not all (cf. the account of John's uncertainty about Jesus being the Messiah, Matt. xi. 2; Luke vii. 18).

τὸ βάπτισμα Ἰωάνου] = βάπτισμα μετανοίας (xiii. 24 ; xix. 4), baptism of which repentance was the condition as a preparation for the coming of the Messiah; opposed to it is the baptism by the Messiah Himself ἐν πνεύματι ἁγίῳ καὶ πυρί (Matt. iii. 11; Mark i. 8; Luke iii. 16).

27. προτρεψάμενοι...ἔγραψαν] Clearly 'encouraged him and wrote' as R.V., not 'wrote exhorting the disciples' as A.V. He was eager and they urged him on: *currenti addiderunt calcar.* ^{Calvin} ^{in M.}

τοῖς πεπιστευκόσιν] *Rigavit Apollo non plantavit.* B. Cf. 1 Cor. iii. 6.

διὰ τῆς χάριτος] With συνεβάλετο but placed last for emphasis: his success was due to 'grace': so Paul ascribes his success to the same cause 1 Cor. xv. 10.

28. εὐτόνως] Classical, and Luke xxiii. 10 = *intentis nervis.*

διακατηλέγχετο] A very strong word. ἐλέγχειν merely expresses 'proof', but κατελέγχ. = 'overpower by proof', 'confute', and διακατελ. = 'thoroughly confute'.

CHAPTER XIX.

1. τὰ ἀνωτερικὰ μέρη] the inland part of Asia Minor, see xviii. 23.

2. πιστεύσαντες] A.V. 'since ye believed': R.V. rightly 'when ye believed'. The question asked is whether when they became believers they 'received the Holy Spirit', i.e. clearly the special visible gift of the Holy Spirit as described ch. ii., x. 44—46, and ver. 6 here.

ἀλλ' οὐδ' εἰ πνεῦμα ἅγιον ἔστιν ἠκούσαμεν] 'Nay, we did not even hear whether there is a Holy Spirit'; i.e. at our baptism (cf. aorist ἠκούσαμεν) so far from receiving a Holy Spirit we did not even hear of the existence of a Holy Spirit. ^{A. and so F. 'ignorant of the very name'.}

This, the only possible rendering of the Greek, gives a clear sense. John preached βάπτισμα μετανοίας εἰς ἄφεσιν ἁμαρτιῶν; this baptism these men had received: he also proclaimed a coming Messiah, who should baptize ἐν πνεύματι ἁγίῳ; of this baptism these men had not heard. It is on this point that Paul specially supplements their knowledge, 'John's baptism of repentance', he says, 'was *preparatory* to a belief on one who should come after him, viz., Jesus'.

R.V. gives, 'Nay, we did not so much as hear whether the Holy Ghost was *given*', a rendering which in several ways misrepresents the Gk.

(1) The words πνεῦμα ἅγιον may be used as = (*a*) The Holy Ghost, (β) 'the holy spirit' or 'inspiration' which He produces by His presence, (γ) 'a spirit of holiness', without any special reference to the Holy Ghost. The rendering 'Holy Ghost' is on the other hand far more definite.

(2) The Gk has no article, and though in Paul's question to render 'Did ye receive the Holy Ghost' gives the true sense, because he is definitely referring to the Holy Ghost; yet in the reply to render πν. ἁγ. 'the Holy Ghost' is to *assume* that the words were understood in the sense in which Paul used them.

(3) The rendering 'was given' cannot be supported by John vii. 39 τοῦτο δὲ εἶπε περὶ τοῦ πνεύματος οὗ ἔμελλον λαμβάνειν οἱ πιστεύσαντες εἰς αὐτόν· οὔπω γὰρ ἦν πνεῦμα, where A.V. renders οὔπω ἦν 'was not yet given'. Jesus there had been telling of a great gift which He had to bestow, and the writer adds, 'This He said with reference to the spirit which they were about to receive: for as yet the spirit was not'. The words οὔπω γὰρ ἦν are explanatory of οὗ ἔμελλον λαμβάνειν. John writing long after the spirit had been given, thinks it needful to explain the phrase 'which they were about to receive' by recalling to his hearers the fact that 'as yet the spirit was not', i.e. was not received. 'They were about to receive it' he says 'for as yet it was not (received)'. The addition of the word 'given' in A.V. is legitimate though unnecessary, and the addition of the word 'received' would have been much better.

Here however ἔστι is totally unconnected with ἐλάβετε, so that it is impossible to supply εἰλημμένον. The two verbs that are connected are ἐλάβετε and ἠκούσαμεν, and they are in marked antithesis (ἀλλ' οὐδέ). The addition of the word 'given' destroys the sense. This is at once made clear by altering the form, but not the sense, of the question. 'When you became believers', Paul asks, 'was the Holy Ghost given you?'; to this the revisers make the men reply 'Nay, we did not even hear that the Holy Ghost was given'. The strong antithesis vanishes.

(4) As has been already pointed out, to assume that these men were acquainted with John's Messianic preaching is to assume that they knew exactly what Luke describes Paul as proceeding to teach them: the revisers quit the necessary rendering to destroy the necessary sense.

As D. &c.   Lastly, lest it should be assumed that, as Jews, they must have heard of πνεῦμα ἅγιον, it should be remembered that the phrase only occurs three times in the O.T. and is never used absolutely as here. Cf. Is. lxiii. 10, 11 (and Cheyne *ad loc.*), Ps. li. 13.

It is perhaps necessary to add that in any case the 'was given' of R.V. is a grammatical error; it should have been 'is' or 'has been given', or, if accuracy be desired, 'has been received'.

3. εἰς τί] 'into what?' Their answer was 'into John's baptism', i.e. into repentance. They are now baptized 'into the name of the Lord Jesus', i.e. into an acceptance of Jesus as the Messiah.

εἶπεν] Clearly the words given are but a summary of Paul's argument shewing the merely *preparatory* nature of John's teaching, which only had a meaning in as far as it pointed onward to his *successor*. Notice εἰς τὸν ἐρχόμενον μετ' αὐτόν placed with great emphasis before ἵνα πιστ.

5. εἰς τὸ ὄνομα...] ii. 38 n.

9. ἀποστὰς...] As he had done at Corinth, xviii. 7.

σχολῇ] 'school', *ludus.* (1) Originally='time not occupied by business', (2) then, as such leisure was frequently employed by educated Greeks in philosophic or literary discussion, the word is applied to such discussions, (3) the place in which they are held, 'a lecture-room', 'a school'.

10. ἔτη δύο] xx. 31 Paul speaks of his stay at Ephesus as τριετίαν; here the three months of ver. 8 are to be added, and perhaps the period referred to in vv. 21, 23. Anyhow τριετίαν need not mean more than 'a part of three years', cf. the famous 'after three days' Matt. xxvii. 63.

ὥστε πάντας] To this visit may be referred the foundation of 'the seven churches' in Asia, Rev. i. 11.

11. οὐ τὰς τυχούσας] Litotes, cf. xxviii. 2. In classical Gk. ὁ τυχών='one who meets one by chance', 'any chance' or 'ordinary person'.

12. σουδάρια ἢ σιμικίνθια] *Sudarium*, 'a napkin' or 'handkerchief'; the word used Luke xix. 20; John xi. 44, xx. 7. *Semicinctium*, perhaps a linen apron worn by servants or workmen, and Paul did manual work at Ephesus, cf. xx. 34. ^{Baum. notes this.}

These words, transliterated from Latin, are interesting historically; the Roman conquest could not have been superficial when such words as these had passed into the ordinary language of Greek-speaking countries.

13. τῶν περιερχ. Ἰ. ἐξορκιστῶν] For the practice of exorcism by the Jews on those 'possessed' cf. Matt. xii. 27. ^{v. Edersheim, App. 16.}

Ant.
VIII. 2. 5.
Josephus relates traditions as to the skill of Solomon in expelling demons who caused various diseases, and says that his formulae and words of exorcism were known in his day.

ὁρκίζω ὑμᾶς τὸν 'I.] Cf. Mark v. 7 ὁρκίζω σε τὸν θεόν; 1 Thess. v. 27 ἐνορκίζω ὑμᾶς τὸν κύριον. ὑμᾶς is the direct acc. after the verb, τὸν 'Ιησοῦν the cognate accusative giving the words of the adjuration (ὅρκος) with which the person adjures (ὁρκίζω).

14. ἀρχιερέως] ' a chief-priest', cf. v. 24 n.

As W.
and
others.
15. γινώσκω...ἐπίσταμαι] ' know...know' A. and R.V. rightly. It is easy, but unsafe, to say that γινώσκω = ' acknowledge', i.e. as recognizing His power, whereas ἐπίσταμαι = ' know' merely expresses acquaintance with a fact. The change of the word seems due to a natural tendency to variation, cf. xx. 15, where τῇ ἐπιούσῃ, τῇ ἑτέρᾳ, τῇ ἐχομένῃ = ' on the next day'.

ὑμεῖς] Thrown forward contemptuously.

Text
אABD.
16. ἀμφοτέρων] T. R. αὐτῶν, an obvious correction to suit ἑπτὰ above. Two sons only would seem to have been present on this occasion.

So A. La.
Baumg.

As M.
18. τῶν πεπιστευκότων] 'believers', absolutely, cf. xviii. 27, xxi. 20, 25. They had embraced Christianity but had not hitherto given up their evil practices. Not 'those who believed owing to the event', which would rather require the aorist.

πράξεις] 'deeds' A. and R.V., but rather ' dealings', viz. with the magicians.

19. ἱκανοὶ δὲ...] Apparently contrasted with the ' many believers' who confessed their dealings with magicians are the ' considerable number of those who dealt in magical arts', i.e. actual magicians, who burnt their books as a sign of relinquishing their art.

τὰ περίεργα] i.e. things better left alone, not meddled with; cf. Plat. *Apol.* 19 B Σωκράτης ἀδικεῖ καὶ περιεργάζεται ζητῶν τά τε ὑπὸ γῆς καὶ τὰ ἐπουράνια. So too Ecclesiasticus iii. 23.

v. A. F.
βίβλους] i.e. magical books. Pieces of parchment containing words copied from a mysterious inscription on the figure of Artemis were well known under the name of 'Εφέσια γράμματα, and supposed to act as charms.

ἀργυρίου] i.e. 50,000 drachmae, the drachma being the standard silver coin (so now a 'shilling', 'franc', 'mark') representing the Latin *denarius* = eightpence or ninepence.

20.   κατὰ κράτος] Only here in N.T. A frequent military term in classical Greek, e.g. Thuc. VIII. 100 πόλιν ἐλεῖν κατὰ κράτος.

21.   δεῖ με καὶ 'Ρώμην ἰδεῖν] The emphasis of this almost rhythmical phrase is distinct. The Apostle sees before him the final goal of his labours. Cf. xxiii. 11 n. For his desire to visit Rome cf. Rom. i. 13: the Epistle to the Romans was probably written from Corinth shortly after this. v. Baum. ii. 27.

22.   "Ἔραστος. The same name 2 Tim. iv. 20; Rom. xvi. 23.

εἰς τὴν 'Ασίαν] 'in Asia', A. and R.V. But from the fact that the words are not 'in Ephesus' it would seem that the phrase implies movement from Ephesus into other parts of Asia, or at any rate that his stay had *reference to* parts of Asia outside Ephesus. Cf. xxii. 5 n.

24.   ναούς] Apparently small models of the temple, portable, and placed in houses or even worn as amulets. Wordsworth refers to similar Παλλάδια περιαντόφορα. *Athens and Attica,* c. 16 n.
Ephesus, near the mouth of the Cayster, was the capital of the province of Asia, and at this time the most important city of Asia Minor. The temple of Artemis, built in the 6th century B.C., was burnt down by Herostratus on the night of Alexander's birth (Oct. 13—14 B.C. 356), but was restored and reckoned one of the wonders of the world.
The Ephesian Artemis (quite distinct from "Αρτεμις = *Diana*) was an Asiatic deity: the image (see below ver. 35) was swathed like a mummy, and πολύμαστος, probably symbolizing the fructifying powers of nature.

26.   ὁ Παῦλος οὗτος] Contemptuous, cf. vi. 14.

οὐκ εἰσὶν θεοί...] One of the most striking differences between the Jews and most heathen nations as regards religion was that the latter used 'images' or 'idols', which the common people certainly identified with the gods themselves, whereas to the Jews the making of an idol was most strictly forbidden, cf. Ex. xx. 4; Ps. cxxxv. 15—18 and the description of the 'making of a god' (cf. οἱ διὰ χειρῶν γιγν.) Isaiah xliv. 9—17. Tac. *Hist.* v. 6 *Judaei...nulla simulacra urbibus suis nedum templis sinunt.*

27.   μέρος] 'part', 'part assigned one', and so 'trade', 'business'. ἡμῖν *dat. incommodi,* 'there is risk of our finding our trade....'

ἀλλὰ καὶ] *sed etiam. Efficax sermo, quem utilitas et superstitio acuit.* B.

ἀπελεγμὸν] lit. 'rejection after being examined'; R.V. 'disrepute'.

τῆς μεγάλης θ. 'Αρτ.] The goddess was generally known as ἡ μεγάλη; cf. Xen. *Ephes.* I. p. 15 ὀμνύω τὴν πάτριον ἡμῖν θεόν, τὴν μεγάλην 'Εφεσίων "Αρτεμιν. On an inscription found at Ephesus in 1877 she is styled ἡ μεγίστη θεός.

La. referring to Wood.

Text ℵABE.
τῆς μεγαλειότητος] T.R. has acc. The gen. seems partitive, 'there is likely to be overthrown of her magnificence', cf. Xen. *Hell.* IV. 4; 13 καθελεῖν τῶν τειχῶν; and Diod. Sic. IV. 8 καθαιρεῖν τι τῆς τοῦ θεοῦ δόξης. But R.V. 'that she should even be deposed from her magnificence'.

W.
ἦν ὅλη...] Cf. Apuleius 2, *Diana Ephesia, cujus nomen unicum, multiformi specie, ritu vario, nomine multijugo, totus veneratur orbis.*

29. εἰς τὸ θέατρον] The theatre at Ephesus was colossal and capable of containing 56,000 spectators. 'On inscriptions of Ephesus discovered in 1877 the theatre appears as the well-known place for public meetings...In it were many statues and inscriptions referring to the worship of Artemis'. For a similar use of a theatre, cf. Tac. *Hist.* II. 8 *Antiochensium theatrum ingressus, ubi illis consultare mos est.*

La. and M. referring to Wood.

Γαῖον] *Gaium;* the same name XX. 4. For Aristarchus cf. XX. 4, XXVII. 2; Col. IV. 10; Philem. 24.

31. τῶν 'Ασιαρχῶν] Ten officers elected by the various cities in the province of Asia, whose duty it was to celebrate at their own cost the public games and festivals. The games in honour of Artemis were held in May, which was called after her (ἐπώνυμον τοῦ θείου ὀνόματος). The mention of the Asiarchs here makes it probable that this disturbance took place, as it very naturally might, in that month.

v. Kuin. in W.

Ephesian Insc. in A.

δοῦναι] A. and R.V. 'adventure': the word suggests hazard.

33. συνεβίβασαν] T.R. προεβίβασαν, an obvious correction. The nom. is certainly the same as that of ἔκραζον —' so then they (i.e. the various members of the ὄχλος) kept crying (imperfect)...but at last they pushed forward (aorist) Alexander....'

Text ℵABE. προεβ. HLP.

What the narrative seems to describe is this. The excitement of the multitude had inspired fear among the Jews at Ephesus (unpopular there as at Philippi and Corinth, cf. too ver. 34), for the multitude would not distinguish between Paul and other Jews, and the special teaching with regard

to idols, which had caused the riot, was wholly Jewish.
They therefore tried to put forward (προβαλόντων) one of
their number, Alexander, in the hope that he might get a
hearing and make a defence (ἀπολογεῖσθαι), shewing that
they had nothing to do with Paul. The result was that the
people 'joined in pushing him out of the throng', i.e.
forced him out of the mob on to some raised place, from
which he could address them.

συνεβίβασαν, from βιβάζω the causal of βαίνω='make to
go', seems a graphic word accurately describing the way in
which a mob, when their attention had been directed to a
man, would join in pushing him forward, 'thrust' or
'squeeze' him out. For this use of βιβάζω in compounds
cf. καταβιβάζω, ἐκβιβάζω, προβιβάζω, and συμβιβασθέντες, συμ-
βιβαζόμενον='made to go together' Col. ii. 2, 19.
Meyer renders 'instructed', cf. 1 Cor. ii. 16, and so
R.V. in margin, but this yields no sense.

34. ἐπιγνόντες...φωνὴ ἐγένετο μία] Sense-construction
='having learned...they shouted'. T.R. ἐπιγνόντων with
no authority.

35. ὁ γραμματεύς] 'town-clerk', a very important officer,
keeper of the public records, whose duty it was to draw up
official documents and read them in the public assembly.
Often named on Ephesian inscriptions. The tone of his
speech is 'decidedly legal'.   Baum.

τίς γάρ...] Explaining his conduct: 'I have tried to
quiet you and there is no reason for disturbance, *for*...'.

νεωκόρος (1) 'temple-cleaner', (2) 'guardian of a temple', See A.
(3) frequently applied as a title of honour especially to
Asiatic cities, and so found on coins and inscriptions, the
Ephesian people being described on two inscriptions as
ὁ νεωκόρος δῆμος, and also ν. τῆς Ἀρτέμιδος.

τοῦ διοπετοῦς] 'the image that fell from heaven'; A. and
R.V. 'that fell from Jupiter', giving a distinctly wrong
impression, for διο- merely describes 'the bright sky' (of
which no doubt Ζεύς is king) from the root διϜ found in *dies*
&c., and should no more be translated 'Jupiter' than in
the phrase *sub dio*. διπετής is applied to rivers as being
fed by rain 'fallen from heaven', Hom. *Il.* xvi. 174; *Od.* iv.
477.
The same tradition attached to the statue of Artemis at
Tauris (Eur. *Iph. T.* 977 διοπετὲς ἄγαλμα, οὐρανοῦ πέσημα), ll.
the Palladium of Troy, the Minerva Polias of Athens
(Paus. *Att.* 26 Ἀθήνας ἄγαλμα ἐν τῇ νῦν ἀκροπόλει...φήμη δὲ
ἐς αὐτὸ ἔχει, πεσεῖν ἐκ τοῦ οὐρανοῦ), the Cybele of Pessinus, &c.

P.   14

37. γάρ] explains προπετές—'headstrong, as your conduct has been, *for...*'

οὔτε βλασφημοῦντας] *Apostoli non collegerunt multa
absurda ex mythologia sed proposuerunt veritatem Dei.* B.
rightly. On the other hand Chrysostom τοῦτο ψεῦδος, ταῦτα
μὲν πρὸς τὸν δῆμον.

38. ἀγοραῖοι] sc. *ἥμεραι*. *ἀγοραῖος=forensis*, and as
the law-courts in Rome and other towns were near the
forum or *ἀγορά*, the adj. becomes='having to do with the
law-courts', e.g. *forense genus dicendi*, 'the oratory of the
bar'.

Translate 'court-days are kept', i.e. at certain regular
periods, not in any degree implying that at that particular time court-days were being kept; for in that case
'and there is the proconsul' ought to follow, and the plural
ἀνθύπατοι could not stand, as at no particular time was

W. B.   there more than one proconsul. So too the statement
'there are proconsuls' is general, = there is always a proconsul,
not always the same, but always one.

·In the provinces the proconsul passed round the principal
towns, administering justice, much as the judges in our
Cic.   assize towns. Such 'holding assizes' was *conventus agere*,
2 *Verr.*   which seems = ἀγοραίους ἄγειν.
v. 11. 28.
W.   'The following inscription of the age of Trajan from
an aqueduct of Ephesus happily illustrates the accuracy of
St Luke's language. ἡ φιλοσέβαστος Ἐφεσίων βουλη, καὶ ὁ
νεωκόρος δῆμος καθιέρωσαν ἐπὶ ἀνθυπάτου Πεδουκαίου Πρεισ-
κείνου, ψηφισαμένου Τιβ. Κλ. Ἰταλικοῦ τοῦ γραμματέως του
δῆμου'.

περαι-   **39. εἰ δέ τι περαιτέρω...**] i.e. charges of illegal conduct
τέρω   should have been brought before the regular magistrates,
B.
περ   but 'if you want anything further' (cf. Plat. *Phaed.* 107. 8
ἕτερον   οὐδὲν ζητήσετε περαιτέρω), e.g. to pass any public resolutions
E.
περί   on the subject which is exciting you, then that can be
ἑτέρων   settled at the regular meeting of the assembly. The use of
ℵADHL   ἐννόμῳ suggests the irregularity of the present assembly.
P.

40. στάσεως...] The text here is very uncertain and
the Greek awkward, but the general sense is clear.

στάσεως ἐγκαλεῖσθαι] These words go together, and περὶ
τῆς σήμερον = 'concerning to-day' (cf. ἡ σήμερον ἡμ. xx. 26;
M.   ἡ σήμ. Matt. xi. 23), for if περὶ be taken as governing
στάσεως (R.V. 'concerning this day's riot') not only is its
position very unusual in N.T. but the town-clerk is represented as calling what had happened by the strong word

στάσις, which he would naturally not do, but rather refer to it as συστροφή 'a gathering', as he does immediately after.

περὶ οὗ] 'and as touching it' R.V. The relative has no grammatical antecedent, but refers to the subject before the speaker's mind, and is immediately defined by the explanatory words περὶ τῆς συστροφῆς ταύτης. T.R. omits οὗ after οὗ. Text NABHL P.

ἀποδοῦναι 'to give an account when called upon', *rationem reddere.*

'There was nothing on which the Romans looked with such jealousy as a tumultuous meeting. *Qui coetum et concentum fecerit, capitale sit,* Senec. *Controv.* 3. 8'. F.

CHAPTER XX.

1. ἀσπασάμενος] The word describes the kiss and embrace which accompanied either arrival or departure (cf. xxi. 6, 7, 19); here the latter.

2. τὰ μέρη ἐκεῖνα] i.e. Macedonia; αὐτοὺς the Christians there. From Rom. xv. 19 (written shortly after this) it is inferred that he almost reached Illyricum. The 2nd Ep. to the Corinthians is assigned to this period. F.

τὴν Ἑλλάδα]=Ἀχαίαν xviii. 12. It is the national not the official name. Only here in N.T.

3. ποιήσας...ἐγένετο γνώμης] T.R. has γνώμη, a sense-construction, like xix. 34. He would naturally reach Corinth, to which he had recently sent his two Epistles, and from which he could most easily 'put to sea for Syria' (ἀνάγεσθαι εἰς τ. Συρ.). Text NABE.

τοῦ ὑποστρέφειν] The genitive gives the contents or substance of the γνώμη.

4. συνείπετο δὲ αὐτῷ] T.R. adds ἄχρι τῆς Ἀσίας; but Trophimus went to Jerusalem, xxi. 29, and Aristarchus to Rome, xxvii. 2; Col. iv. 10. Text NB Vulg. ἄχρι τῆς Ἀσ.

Sopater, Gaius, and Secundus are unknown. Σέκουνδος = *Secundus,* ου representing Latin *u* and our oō (as in 'boot'). ADEHL P.

Ἀσιανοί] *ex Asia stricte dicta.* B. Tychicus (for the meaning of name cf. Εὔτυχος ver. 9 and *Faustus*) was a close companion of Paul, cf. Eph. vi. 21; Col. iv. 7; Tit. iii. 12; 2 Tim. iv. 12. Trophimus, cf. xxi. 29; 2 Tim. iv. 20.

5. ἡμᾶς] xvi. 10 n.

6. τὰς ἡμ. τῶν ἀζ.] cf. xii. 3 n. 'Paul left Philippi about April 4, A.D. 58'. La. and so F.

M.

ἄχρι ἡμ. πέντε] The phrase expresses the time up to which their voyage lasted. Cf. Luke ii. 37 χήρα ἕως ἐτῶν ὀγδοηκοντατεσσάρων. D has πεμπταῖοι, a correct explanatory gloss. For the journey, cf. xvi. 11.

7. τῇ μιᾷ τῶν σαββάτων] 'the first day of the week', cf. Luke xxiv. 1; John xx. 1: πρώτῃ σαββάτου Mark xvi. 9: opposed to σάββατα Matt. xxviii. 1: the day of the resurrection: ἡ κυριακὴ ἡμ. Rev. i. 10: specially selected for alms-giving 1 Cor. xvi. 2. This is the first place in which there is any reference to a special observance of the day, it being here clearly marked as a fit day for an ἀγάπη. The use of the cardinal for the ordinal numeral is a Hebrew idiom.

A.

κλάσαι ἄρτον] ii. 42 n. 'The breaking of bread in the Holy Communion was at this time inseparable from the ἀγάπαι. It took place apparently in the evening (after the day's work was ended) and at the end of the assembly after the preaching of the word'.

La. M.

8. ἦσαν δὲ...] Pictorial description, natural in an eyewitness.

ἐν τῷ ὑπερῴῳ] i. 13 n.

9. ἐπὶ τῆς θυρίδος] 'on the window-seat', the window being without glass or frame-work. They sometimes had latticed-doors, as in French houses, to keep out the sun.

Ahaziah met his death in this way, cf. 2 Kings i. 2 'fell down through a lattice in his upper chamber'.

καταφερόμενος...κατενεχθείς] R.V. gives 'borne down... being borne down', utterly hiding the force of the participles: the one expresses the gradual stealing of drowsiness upon him, the other the moment when sleep wholly overpowered him and he fell.

In A.

Arist. *de som. et vig.* 3 τὰ ὑπνωτικὰ...καρηβαρίαν ποιεῖ... καὶ καταφερόμενοι καὶ νυστάζοντες τοῦτο δοκοῦσιν πάσχειν.

ὕπνῳ βαθεῖ] Not 'deep sleep' i.e. sound sleep, but 'strong drowsiness' which ends in sound sleep.

Cook.

10. καταβάς] 'by the outside staircase usual in the East'.

ἐπέπεσεν αὐτῷ] Like Elijah, 1 Kings xvii. 21, and Elisha, 2 Kings iv. 34.

μὴ θορυβεῖσθε] So on the death of Jairus' daughter, Matt. ix. 23 ἰδὼν τοὺς αὐλητὰς καὶ τὸν ὄχλον θορυβούμενον, and Mark v. 38 θεωρεῖ θόρυβον καὶ κλαίοντας καὶ ἀλαλάζοντας where Jesus asks τί θορυβεῖσθε; These passages shew that θορυβεῖσθαι describes the loud and ostentatious lamentation common in the East. 'Make ye no ado' R.V.

ἡ γὰρ ψυχή...] Not at all implying that they had been *mistaken* in supposing him dead. Luke distinctly describes a miraculous restoration to life; cf. the opposition ἤρθη νεκρός verse 9)(ἤγαγον ζῶντα verse 12.

11. κλάσας τὸν ἄρτον] They had came together 'to break bread'; this would have taken place naturally at the end of Paul's discourse but for the interruption; he now therefore resumes the interrupted order of the meeting by 'breaking the bread'.

γευσάμενος] i.e. having eaten a meal, to satisfy hunger, as x. 10.

ὁμιλήσας] x. 27 n. 'conversed'. The word is much less formal than διελέγετο above.

οὕτως] cf. xxvii. 17 = *tum demum :* the word sums up all the preceding participles, 'having done all these things, then, and then only, he departed'. A very frequent classical usage.

13. Ἄσσον] A seaport in Mysia, S. from Troas, opposite Lesbos.

διατεταγμένος] perf. pass. in sense of middle; cf. for the use of the middle 1 Cor. vii. 17 διατάσσομαι; xi. 34 διατάξομαι.

μέλλων...] The distance is about 20 m., and there was La. then a Roman road between Troas and Assos. πεζεύειν 'go afoot' A.V., but the word only means 'go by land' R.V.

14. Μιτυλήνην] Capital of Lesbos on the E. coast.

15. κατηντήσαμεν] as xvi. 1, xviii. 19, 24 'arrived'.

ἄντικρυς Χ. = 'opposite' or 'off Chios', where they would anchor for the night. Chios is an island about 30 m. by 10, 8 m. from the opposite peninsula of Clazomenae.

παρεβάλομεν εἰς Σάμον] T.R. adds καὶ μείναντες ἐν Τρω- Text γυλλίῳ and omits δὲ after τῇ. Trogylium is on the main- ℵABCE. land about 5 m. from Samos. The omission of the reference to Trogylium may be due to an idea that παρεβάλομεν ε. Σ. means 'put in to Samos' i.e. to pass the night, in which case they could not have 'stayed at Trogylium'. But cf. Thuc. III. 32 παραβαλεῖν εἰς Ἰωνίαν 'to cross over to Ionia', which is the meaning of παρεβάλομεν here.

In crossing from Chios to Samos they would 'sail past' Ephesus.

Μίλητον] At one time the most important city of the Ionian Greeks, but at this period quite eclipsed by Ephesus.

About 28 m. S. of Ephesus. Its site is now several miles from the sea owing to the silting-up of the Maeander.

Light-
foot,
Ex. ad
Phil.
i. 1.

17. τοὺς πρεσβυτέρους] called ἐπίσκοποι ver. 28; 'elders' and 'bishops' being in apostolical times interchangeable words.

18. εἶπεν] A great 'Apology' at the close of his three missionary journeys.

In this speech occur many words and phrases also found in Paul's Epistles: these are noted as they occur, and deserve careful attention.

ἀπὸ...'Ασίαν] The clause is thrown forward for emphasis, and goes not with ἐπίστασθε but with πῶς ἐγενόμην.

ἐπέβην] 'set foot in' R.V.; *pedem intuli* B.

πῶς ἐγενόμην] He describes 'how' vv. 19—21. For the phrase cf. 1 Thess. i. 5 οἴδατε οἶοι ἐγενήθημεν ἐν ὑμῖν; ii. 10 ὑμεῖς μάρτυρες...ὡς ὁσίως...ὑμῖν ἐγενήθημεν.

A   **19. δουλεύων**] "With the sole exception of the assertion of our Lord, 'Ye cannot serve God and Mammon' (Matt. vi. 24; Luke xvi. 13), the verb δουλεύω for 'serving God' is used by Paul *only*, and by him six times, e.g. Rom. xvi. 18 and cf. Phil. i. 1; Gal. i. 10".

ταπεινοφροσύνης] Favourite Pauline word, e.g. Phil. ii. 3. "In heathen writers ταπεινός has almost always a bad meaning, 'grovelling', 'abject'.... It was one great result of the life of Christ to raise 'humility' to its proper level; and, if not fresh coined for this purpose, the word ταπεινοφροσύνη now first becomes current through the influence of Christian ethics".

Light-foot, ad loc.

δακρύων] cf. ver. 31; 2 Cor. ii. 4; Phil. iii. 18. 'Tears' under strong emotion, whether sorrowful or the reverse, were common with the ancients.

20. οὐδὲν ὑπεστειλάμην] 'I did not (cautiously) hold back' or 'conceal': ὑποστέλλεσθαι is the opposite of παρρησιάξεσθαι, cf. Dem. 54 πάνθ' ἁπλῶς, οὐδὲν ὑποστειλάμενος, πεπαρρησίασμαι; so too 415. The word describes 'caution' As F.W. and 'reserve', cf. Gal. ii. 12. To describe the word as a 'nautical' metaphor is erroneous.

τοῦ μή...] Probably the gen. expresses that in which the 'concealment' would have consisted, viz. in 'not proclaiming...', and so we should render 'by not proclaiming...'; cf. iii. 12 n., vii. 19 n.

Others make τοῦ the direct gen. after ὑπεστειλάμην in the sense of 'shrinking', 'withdrawing', and regard μή as a pleonastic repetition of the negative sense of the verb—'I shrank not from declaring' R.V.

22. ἰδού] Purely adverbial, and so singular, cf. Matt. x. 16 *ἰδού, ἐγὼ ἀποστέλλω ὑμᾶς.*

δεδεμένος τῷ πνεύματι] 'bound in the spirit', i.e. in my spirit, feeling an inward constraint: so with reference to this same journey xix. 21 *ὁ* Π. *ἔθετο ἐν τῷ πν.* It is clearly not 'bound by the Holy Spirit' (*alligatus Spiritu* V.), for 'the Holy Spirit' is specifically mentioned immediately. Not that the sense is affected; Paul looks on the Holy Spirit as directly influencing his spirit; cf. Rom. viii. 16 *τὸ πνεῦμα συμμαρτυρεῖ τῷ πν. ἡμῶν.* The rendering of *τὸ πν. τὸ ἅγιον* 'Holy Ghost' is a distinct loss in this passage.

24. οὐδενὸς λόγου...] A combination of two construc-tions viz. *οὐδενὸς λ. π. τὴν ψ.* and *οὐ ποιοῦμαι τὴν ψ. τιμίαν ἐμαυτῷ.*

T.R. has *ἀλλ' οὐδενὸς λόγον ποιοῦμαι, οὐδὲ ἔχω τὴν ψ. μου τιμ. ἐμ.*

ὡς τελειώσω] 'in order that I may accomplish'. For the metaphor, cf. xiii. 25 n.

T.R. has *ὡς τελειῶσαι =* ' as to accomplish', i.e. in com-parison with accomplishing. It also adds *μετὰ χαρᾶς* after *τὸν δρόμον μου.* Omit *μετὰ χ.* ℵABD. Insert CEHLP.

καὶ τὴν διακ.] Explanatory of *τὸν δρόμον,* 'even my ministry'.

25. οἶδα ὅτι...] In two letters written from Rome (Phil. ii. 24; Philem. 22) Paul expresses his hope of quitting Rome and travelling to the east, but we do not know that he ever did so. Luke certainly here seems to regard this parting as final. In any case *οἶδα* does not ex-press more than Paul's personal conviction: cf. its use xxvi. 27. To lay great emphasis on *πάντες* is to pervert the plain sense. As B. and·W.

ὑμεῖς π. ἐν οἷς διῆλθον] The use of *διῆλθον* shews that not merely the Ephesian elders are meant: in addressing them Paul regards them as representatives of all those in that region among whom he had laboured as a missionary.

26. μαρτύρομαι ὑμῖν] *μαρτύρομαι* does not occur else-where in N.T. except in Paul's Epistles, viz. Gal. v. 3; Eph. iv. 17; 1 Thess. ii. 12.

It means 'I protest', i.e. I assert as in the presence of a witness. The word signifies properly 'to call to witness', and is never, except perhaps in very late Gk, equivalent to *μαρτυρῶ* 'I bear witness'. See too ii. 40 n. Light-foot, Gal. v. 2.

ἐν τῇ σήμερον ἡμέρᾳ] Emphatic: on this the last day that I shall see you. καθαρὸς... cf. xviii. 6 n.

27. τὴν βουλὴν τοῦ θ.] i.e. His purpose of redemption through Jesus the Messiah. The sense is not 'all the counsel of God' absolutely, but ' all His counsel as far as it refers to my work'.

28. προσέχετε ἑαυτοῖς] The same phrase v. 35 ; Luke xii. 1, xvii. 3, xxi. 34 and nowhere else in N.T. Paul however has προσέχειν μύθοις, οἴνῳ, τῇ ἀναγνώσει 1 Tim. i. 4, iii. 8, iv. 13.

τῷ ποιμνίῳ] Cf. Luke xii. 32 μὴ φοβοῦ, τὸ μικρὸν ποίμνιον, and John xxi. 16 ποίμαινε τὰ πρόβατά μου.

ἐπισκόπους] It will be observed that the use of the word here does not necessarily prove that the πρεσβύτεροι (as Luke elsewhere always terms them) were regularly called ἐπίσκοποι: they are so called here not officially but with reference to the special charge laid upon them of 'watching over' and tending the flock committed to them. At the same time there would be special point in the use of ἐπίσκοποι here in connection with ποιμνίῳ, if the word were beginning to be applied to 'the elders' as a title, as it certainly is elsewhere, e.g. Phil. i. 1 σὺν ἐπισκόποις καὶ διακόνοις.

v. Light-foot, ad loc.

τὴν ἐκκ. τοῦ θεοῦ ἦν...] It is impossible to determine the reading here ; the mss. are divided between θεοῦ and κυρίου with some preponderance for the latter.

(1) It is urged for θεοῦ that ἐκκ. τ. θεοῦ occurs 11 times in Paul's epistles, whereas ἐκκ. τ. κυρίου does not occur elsewhere, nor does 'the church of Jesus'. Judging therefore from his regular practice it is argued that Paul must have said 'church of God'. (For this cf. Alford.)

The value of this argument depends however on the opinion that may be formed as to how far Luke gives the very words of a speaker.

Moreover it may be maintained in reply that θεοῦ is a correction to make the passage fit with the well-known phrase, and that the reading κυρίου καὶ θεοῦ points to the introduction of θεοῦ as a gloss.

(2) It is said for θεοῦ that, if θ. be read, the passage would contain a reference to τὸ αἷμα τοῦ θεοῦ and that this would perplex many readers and cause copyists to alter the phrase.

But though such a phrase as τὸ αἷμα τοῦ θεοῦ is certainly contrary to apostolic usage, yet it is well known later and is found e.g. in Ignatius and Tertullian, so that there

θεοῦ
אB,
Vulg.
Syr.
κυρίου
ACDE,
Copt.
Arm.
κυρίου
καὶ θεοῦ
HLP.
For θεοῦ
cf. W.
and H.
Appendix.

So W.

is no reason against a copyist introducing it. Moreover
there would be a strong tendency to read θεοῦ at and after
the Arian controversy from a desire to see Jesus called
θεός.

(3) It is also said for θεοῦ that a comparison with
Psalm lxxiv. 2, to which there is a reference, points to the
nom. to περιεποιήσατο being God. But the reference to the
Psalm (μνήσθητι τῆς συναγωγῆς σου ἧς ἐκτήσω ἀπ' ἀρχῆς) is
slight, and hardly justifies the inference.

Reading κυρίου, as is certainly preferable, the sense is
very simple, 'the Church of the Lord' or 'Master which He
purchased with His own blood' and the words τοῦ κυρίου ἦν...
have great force as assigning a special reason why the
elders should be careful guardians of the Church. And for
the Church being called the 'Church of the Lord' cf. Jesus'
own reference to 'My Church', Matt. xvi. 18.

So M.
de W.
La.
Lumby,
F. Lach-
mann,
Tischen-
dorf,
Baumg.,
&c.

Reading θεοῦ, it is certain that θεοῦ = God the Father.
'The supposition that by the precise designation τοῦ θεοῦ,
standing alone as it does here, with the article and without any adjunct, St Paul (or St Luke) meant Christ, is
unsupported by any analogies of language'.

Dr Hort.

This being so we must render 'the church of the Father
which He purchased through the blood that was His own',
i. e. the blood of Jesus; and the conception of the death of
Christ as a price paid by the Father is in strict accordance
with St Paul's own language (Rom. v. 8, viii. 32); and cf.
The Prayer for those that are to be admitted into Holy
Orders 'Almighty God, our heavenly Father, who hast
purchased to Thyself an universal Church by the precious
blood of Thy dear Son'. It must be allowed however that
such a rendering is forced, and not justified even by the
peculiar position of τοῦ ἰδίου. It is suggested that the
passage contains some primitive error, and that the position
of τοῦ ἰδίου may be accounted for by supposing ΤΙΟΥ to
have dropped out after ΤΟΥΙΔΙΟΥ.

W. and
H.

29. ἄφιξιν] 'departure'; cf. Herod. ix. 76 ἀπέπεμψε
ἐς Αἴγιναν, ἐς τὴν αὐτὴ ἤθελε ἀπικέσθαι. μετὰ δὲ τὴν ἄπιξιν
(departure) τῆς γυναικὸς...ἀπίκοντο (arrived) Μαντινέες.

λύκοι] For the metaphor cf. John x. 12. The 'wolves'
are false teachers, for whose presence at Ephesus cf. 1 Tim.
i. 20; Rev. ii. 2.

μὴ φειδόμενοι] Litotes.

30. διεστραμμένα] xiii. 8 n.

31. γρηγορεῖτε] *verbum pastorale.* Β. τριετίαν xix. 10 n.

νουθετῶν] A. V. 'warn': R. V. rightly 'admonishing'.
The word implies authority on the one side and wrong

doing on the other; cf. 1 Cor. iv. 14 ὡς τέκνα μου ἀγαπητὰ νουθετῶν. Only here, and seven times in Paul's Epistles.

32. παρατίθεμαι] xiv. 23 n.

So all editors.

κυρίῳ only in B, and θεῷ is decidedly preferable.

e.g.
Vulg.
Luther,
B

τῷ δυναμένῳ] 'which is able' A. and R.V. Many refer this to τῷ κυρίῳ, considering the words καὶ τῷ λόγῳ τῆς χ. α. explanatory, and that it is God only who can be spoken of as 'able to build up...', but in reality the whole phrase is one; 'the Lord and the word of His grace' are regarded as *one* in their action.

κληρονομίαν...] There is a comparison between the kingdom of Canaan, which was given as an inheritance to Israel, and the kingdom of Jesus the Messiah, which is the inheritance of all the saints.

κληρονομία is frequent in LXX. of Canaan, and of Israel as God's inheritance. The Israelites are termed οἱ ἡγιασμέ-νοι Deut. xxxiii. 3.

The expression is Pauline, cf. Eph. i. 18 τῆς κληρονομίας αὐτοῦ ἐν τοῖς ἁγίοις.

33. ἱματισμοῦ] Oriental wealth largely consisted in costly raiment. Cf. 2 Kings v. 5; Gen. xxiv. 53; Ps. xlv. 13, 14; Matt. vi. 19, where 'treasure' is referred to as corrupted by the 'moth'.

34. αὗται] Deictic; cf. xxvi. 29, xxviii. 20. *Callosae, ut videbant.* B.

35. πάντα] R.V. 'in all things'; for which cf. 1 Cor. x. 33 κἀγὼ πάντα πᾶσιν ἀρέσκω; Eph. iv. 15. It is certainly equally natural to place the full stop *after* πάντα, and commence the next sentence with the forcible ὑπέδειξα—'an example I set you (by doing so) that...'.

So M.
de W.
Lach.

For ὑπέδειξα = 'shewed by pattern' or 'example', cf. ὑπει-πεῖν, ὑπογράφειν.

ἀντιλαμβάνεσθαι...] Cf. Luke i. 54 ἀντελάβετο Ἰσραὴλ παιδὸς αὐτοῦ: 'to take hold of (so as to afford support, both moral and material) to those who are weak (i.e. either in health, wealth, or religious knowledge)'. The phrase is perfectly general.

Cic. de
Nat. D.
I. 5. 10.

αὐτὸς εἶπεν] 'He himself' or 'The Master said'. Cf. the answer of the Pythagoreans when asked for a proof of their opinions, αὐτὸς ἔφη, *Ipse dixit.*

West-
cott,
Int. to
Gospels.
Ap.

μακάριον...] This is the only saying of Jesus recorded in N.T. not in the Gospels. The best known traditional saying of Jesus is γίνεσθε τραπεζῖται δόκιμοι.

For μακάριον cf. Matt. v. 3—11. For the sense Arist. *Eth.* IV. 1 μᾶλλόν ἐστι τοῦ ἐλευθερίου τὸ διδόναι οἷς δεῖ ἤ λαμ-βάνειν ὅθεν δεῖ—but the reason he assigns is the pleasure of feeling superiority. Sen. *de Ben. Qui dat beneficia, deos imitatur, qui recipit, foeneratores.*

37. κατεφίλουν] A strong word 'were covering with kisses': used also Matt. xxvi. 49.

38. προέπεμπον] xv. 3, xxi. 5.

CHAPTER XXI.

1. ἀποσπασθέντας] *avulsos, non sine desiderio magno, cum vi,* B., but cf. Luke xxii. 41 ἀπεσπάσθη merely = 'He was parted from them', and so R.V. here 'He parted from them'.

Κῶ] Now Stanchio, an island opposite Halicarnassus.

'Ρόδον] The famous island off the S. coast of Caria; at this time a great commercial centre with a university; the Colossus was not at this time standing, having been over-thrown by an earthquake.

Πάταρα] A seaport of Lycia near the mouth of the Xanthus, possessing an oracle of Apollo (*Patareus Apollo* Hor. *Od.* III. 4. 64).

2. εὑρόντες] Hitherto the voyage had been apparently in a small hired boat, at the disposition of Paul and his companions, in which they crept along from island to island, after the fashion of the early Gk mariners, not venturing out into the open sea at all. This they now dismiss and become passengers on board a larger merchantman, which, instead of hugging the coast, was going to stand straight across (διαπερῶν) for Tyre.

3. ἀναφάναντες τὴν Κ.] lit. 'having made C. rise up out of the sea', i.e. having sighted Cyprus. The opposite idiom is γῆν ἀποκρύπτειν (Plat. *Prot.* 338 A); cf. Virg. *Aen.* III. 291 *Phaeacum abscondimus arces;* III. 275 *formidatus nautis aperitur Apollo.*

ἐκεῖσε...ἦν ἀποφ.] 'for there the ship was unlading her M. de W. cargo'. ἐκεῖσε because of the idea of movement and carrying into the town contained in 'unlading'; the words do not describe the *destination* of the vessel, which they clearly wait for and proceed in to Ptolemais.

4. ἀνευρόντες] suggests 'looking for': they were pro-bably few in a large city.

διὰ τοῦ πνεύματος] cf. xx. 23. The Spirit gives them and Paul the same warning of danger. Affection therefore urges them to detain him; duty impels him to go.

5. ἐξαρτίσαι]=*justum numerum explere*, 'fulfil', 'make up an exact number'. The days referred to are 'the seven days' probably required for the unloading of the ship and taking in fresh cargo.

6. εἰς τὰ ἴδια] 'to their homes', cf. John xix. 27 ἔλαβεν ὁ μαθητὴς αὐτὴν εἰς τὰ ἴδια.

7. τὸν πλοῦν διανύσαντες] Not with ἀπὸ Τύρου (as A.V. 'when we had finished our course from Tyre'), for the short journey to Ptolemais would not be specially referred to as 'fully completed' (διανύσαντες). It is better rendered 'but we, having (thereby) completed our voyage, came from Tyre to Ptolemais'.

M. La.
de W.

Πτολεμαΐδα] A bay surrounded by mountains; the best harbour on the coast. Called Accho Judges i. 31; afterwards Ptolemais from one of the kings of Egypt; in the time of the Crusades St Jean d'Acre, or Acre.

8. ἐξελθόντες ἤλθαμεν] 'having gone out from Ptolemais came' i. e. clearly by land.

de W. M.
A.

T.R. after ἐξελθόντες inserts οἱ περὶ τὸν Παῦλον—an addition due 'to the commencement of a lesson' in Church services at this point.

Φιλίππου] viii. 5 n. For 'the seven' vi. 5. For εὐαγγελιστοῦ cf. Eph. iv. 11, from which it appears that the word had a special sense and is not merely = 'preacher'. Probably as the word implies (=one who carries good tidings), they were 'travelling missionaries'. The English 'Evangelist' = 'writer of a gospel'.

N. de W.
M.

10. κατῆλθέν τις...προφ. ὀν. Ἄγ.] mentioned as though not already referred to xi. 28.

11. ἄρας τὴν ζώνην] Symbolical acts are frequently employed by prophets in O.T., e.g. 1 Kings xxii. 11, Zedekiah 'made him horns of iron'; Is. xx. 2. For the particular symbol cf. the prophecy of Jesus about Peter, John xxi. 18. For ζώνη cf. xii. 8 n.

τάδε λέγει...] An authoritative formula, frequent in LXX. e.g. τάδε λέγει κύριος ὁ θεός...Ex. v. 1.

παραδώσουσιν...] Cf. the words of Jesus about Himself Matt. xvii. 22 μέλλει ὁ υἱὸς τοῦ ἀνθρώπου παραδίδοσθαι εἰς χεῖρας ἀνθρώπων; Matt. xx. 19 παραδώσουσιν αὐτὸν τοῖς ἔθνεσιν.

13. τί ποιεῖτε κλαίοντες...] The phrase indicates strong remonstrance, cf. Mark xi. 5 τί ποιεῖτε λύοντες τὸν πῶλον;

συνθρύπτοντες] stronger than θρύπτοντες, lit. 'break in pieces', but almost always = 'make weak', and especially 'enervate', 'unman': they were 'unmanning' or 'weakening Paul's heart,' i. e. determination. R. V. 'breaking my heart' hardly gives the sense.

14. τοῦ κυρίου...] Perhaps with reference to τοῦ κυρίου La. M. 'Ἰησοῦ just before; and so κυρίου = Jesus. On the other hand the expression seems a perfectly general one of acquiescence in the Divine will = 'God's will be done', cf. Matt. vi. 10 H. γενηθήτω τὸ θέλημά σου; Matt. xxvi. 42.

15. ἐπισκευασάμενοι] 'having packed up'; A.V. 'we took up our carriages'; Geneva Version 'trussed up our fardels'.

16. ἄγοντες...] A. and R.V. 'bringing with them Mnason with whom we should lodge', which assumes that Mnason was at Caesarea.

Others, perhaps more accurately, take the Gk as = M. La.B. ἄγοντες παρὰ Μνάσωνα, παρ' ᾧ ξεν. 'bringing us to the house de W. of Mnason, with whom we should lodge'.

ἀρχαίῳ μαθ.] R.V. 'an early disciple', cf. xv. 7 n. or H. possibly 'one of the original disciples' converted at Pentecost, cf. xi. 15 ἐν ἀρχῇ.

17. ἀπεδέξαντο] T.R. ἐδέξαντο. The compound verb Text is peculiar to Luke in N.T.   ℵABCE.

18. σὺν ἡμῖν] Note that Luke is personally present.

πρὸς Ἰάκωβον] Probably to his house. It would seem, from the absence of all reference to them, that none of the apostles were in Jerusalem at this time. The presence of 'all the elders' is noted (as at the council xv. 6), and the observations (vv. 20—25) are throughout in the plural.

19. ἐξηγεῖτο καθ' ἓν ἕκαστον ὧν] The treating of the adverbial expression καθ' ἕν as a direct acc. after the verb is classical, e.g. Dem. 1265 τῶν παρόντων καθ' ἕνα...ἄγοντες.

20. θεωρεῖς] The word indicates actual 'seeing', 'beholding'.

πόσαι μυριάδες] A. and R. V. 'thousands', regarding μυριάς as used indefinitely for any large round number, as it is used Luke xii. 1, ἐπισυναχθεισῶν τῶν μυριάδων τοῦ ὄχλου.

Whether Paul reached Jerusalem by Pentecost (cf. xx. 16) or not is doubtful, but the city was still full (cf. ver. 27) of Jews from a distance: and there is no reason for not including these Jews of the dispersion among the 'many myriads of zealots' whom Paul is said to 'behold', for from ver. 27 we see that 'the Jews of Asia' were chief among those who accused Paul as teaching contempt of the Law to the Jews of the dispersion.

ζηλωταὶ τοῦ νόμου] For ζηλ. i. 13 n. The word is here used in a general sense, as it is used by Paul speaking of himself before his conversion Gal. i. 14 ζηλωτὴς ὑπάρχων τῶν πατρικῶν μου παραδόσεων.

21. κατηχήθησαν] cf. xviii. 25 n. The word certainly describes Paul's opponents as acting with deliberate purpose, and suggests that they were in a position of authority and 'teachers'.

ἀποστασίαν] A strong word: classical Greek, ἀπόστασις.

τοὺς κατὰ τὰ...] The Jews of the dispersion, cf. ii. 9 n.

μὴ περιτέμνειν...] Circumcision was the most distinctive rite of the Mosaic law, and the sign of obedience to it. The charge therefore of teaching Jews 'not to circumcise their children' involved the further charge of teaching them 'not to walk by the customs' of the Mosaic law. The term 'uncircumcised' was used by the Jews with the bitterest contempt, e. g. 1 Sam. xvii. 26 'this uncircumcised Philistine'.

τοῖς ἔθεσιν περιπατεῖν] Cf. ix. 31 n. and note on στοιχεῖς ver. 24.

22. πάντως...] T. R. has πάντως δεῖ πλῆθος συνελθεῖν· ἀκούσονται γὰρ ὅτι ἐλήλυθας.

Text BC¹ Syr. Copt. Arm. Aeth. Insert אAC²DE for the Law.
HLP.

In any case the sense is that Paul is requested to mark in a public and noticeable manner his regard as a born Jew for the Law.

The question of *heathen* converts obeying the Mosaic law had been settled, see ch. xv.; the question here is whether Paul teaches *Jewish* converts to despise the Law: his action clearly marks the reverse. Cf. his own statement of his rule of conduct 1 Cor. ix. 19 ἐγενόμην τοῖς Ἰουδαίοις ὡς Ἰουδαῖος ἵνα Ἰουδαίους κερδήσω...τοῖς ἀνόμοις ὡς ἄνομος ἵνα κερδανῶ τοὺς ἀνόμους.

23. εὐχὴν ἔχοντες...] This vow seems clearly to have been the Nazarite vow, for which cf. Numb. vi. 1—21. It was a vow of 'separation (ἁγνισμός) unto the Lord,' marked (1) by abstinence from wine, (2) by not allowing the hair to be cut: Its completion was marked by several costly sacrifices (Numb. vi. 13—15) in the Temple, and the shaving of the head and burning of the hair upon the altar.

It was considered a work of piety to relieve needy Jews from the expenses connected with this vow, as Paul does here. Josephus mentions that Herod Agrippa so paid the expenses of very many (μάλα συχνούς) Nazarites. *Antiq. xix. 16. 1.*

24.   ἁγνίσθητι...] Paul does not merely pay the expenses of the men, but takes the vow and 'becomes a Nazarite with them'. The word ἁγνίσθητι seems to shew this: it is rendered in A. and R.V. 'purify thyself', but it is the word used in LXX. of those who actually take the Nazarite vow, and there rendered 'separate', cf. Numb. vi. 1 ὃς ἂν εὔξηται εὐχὴν ἀφαγνίσασθαι ἁγνείαν Κυρίῳ; ver. 5 πάσας τὰς ἡμ. τοῦ ἁγνισμοῦ. Lange however considers that ἁγνίσθητι is not used here in a special sense='take the Nazarite vow', but quite generally='perform some ceremony of purification', and this would much simplify the whole passage.

ἵνα ξυρήσονται] A construction unknown to class. Gk but not uncommon in N.T. Cf. the classical use of ὅπως with fut. ind.

στοιχεῖς] 'to walk by a line' or 'rule'; cf. Gal. vi. 16 τῷ κανόνι τούτῳ στοιχήσουσιν. Here strictly used: the rule is 'the Law'.

25.   περὶ δὲ...] Anticipating an objection: 'this only with regard to Jews, with regard to Gentile converts...'.

After κρίναντες T.R. inserts μηδὲν τοιοῦτον τηρεῖν αὐτούς, εἰ μή. *Text ℵAB. Insert CDEHL*

26.   διαγγέλλων...] A.V. 'to signify the accomplishment of the days of the purification', which is misleading as suggesting that the vow was *finished*.

The Gk states that Paul, the day after he took the men into his company (παραλαβών), 'joined them in their separation' (i.e. took upon himself the vow of separation which they had already upon them), and went into the Temple 'to report the fulfilling of the days of separation', naming, that is, the day 'on reaching which (ἕως οὖ) the sacrifice was offered'.

It was ordained that he who was under a Nazarite vow should bring the sacrifice (προσοίσει Numb. vi. 13) on the day when he had fully completed the days of his vow (ᾗ ἂν ἡμέρᾳ πληρώσῃ ἡμέρας εὐχῆς Numb. vi. 13). Paul would report to the priests what would be the day when the vow would come to an end, which, adds the historian, ' was the day on which the sacrifice was offered', of which naturally the priests might require notice.

The past προσηνέχθη is best explained by regarding the words ἕως οὖ...ἡ προσφορά as an explanatory addition of the historian. *deW.,M.*

27. αἱ ἑπτὰ ἡμ.] '*the* seven days' can only naturally refer to the seven days for which Paul had taken the vow, and we must assume that when he joined the four men seven days of their vow were still unfulfilled. Luke's reference to '*the* seven days', though he has not previously mentioned the number, is parallel to his use of the word ἀμφοτέρων xix. 16, where we have no hint previously that only two sons of Sceva were present. The Mishna names 30 days as the least period for which a vow can be taken, but our knowledge on this point is very uncertain. Nor can we determine whether this vow has any connection with the one referred to xviii. 18: Luke certainly marks no connection except the dubious reference to his coming up to Jerusalem 'for sacrifices', xxiv. 17. The whole passage remains very perplexed.

As W thinks.

28. βοηθεῖτε] 'Help', 'To the rescue', as though an outrage were being committed.

κατὰ τοῦ λαοῦ] This part of the charge differs from that against Stephen (vi. 13): Paul's teaching is represented as 'an attack on the chosen people', doing away, that is, with their special privileges.

ἔτι τε καὶ] i.e. not contented with *teaching*, he has *moreover actually* brought Greeks....

Ἕλληνας] Malevolent generalization : he was supposed to have brought *one*, cf. ver. 29.

εἰς τὸ ἱερόν] Clearly, that is, beyond the court of the Gentiles into the court of the Israelites. On the wall which divided them inscriptions in Greek and Latin warned all Gentiles that the penalty of entering was death.

Athenaeum, July 8, 1871: cf. M. F. Such an inscription was found by Clermont-Ganneau built into the walls of a mosque in the Via Dolorosa: μηθένα ἀλλογενῆ εἰσπορεύεσθαι ἐντὸς τοῦ περὶ τὸ ἱερὸν τρυφάκτου καὶ περιβόλου· ὃς δ᾽ ἂν ληφθῇ ἑαυτῷ αἴτιος ἔσται διὰ τὸ ἐξακολουθεῖν θάνατον.

κεκοίνωκεν] cf. x. 14. For Trophimus cf. xx. 4.

29. ἐνόμιζον] Putabant: *Zelotae putantes saepe errant.* B.

30. ἐκλείσθησαν...] i.e. by the Levites, to avoid the pollution of the Temple by Paul's murder.

31. ἀνέβη] 'went up', literally, the Roman guard being stationed (and on festivals kept under arms, cf. ἐξαυτῆς) in the *turris Antonia*, a fort built by Herod on a rock at the N.W. corner of the Temple, commanding the Temple and connected with it by stairs (ἀναβαθμούς ver. 35).

τῷ χιλιάρχῳ...] 'to the tribune of the cohort (stationed there)', i.e. Claudius Lysias, cf. xxiii. 26. Each legion had six tribunes, and as the legion with its full complement (*justa legio*) numbered 6000 men, each tribune had 1000 men: hence the Greek word formed on the analogy of ἑκατοντάρχης. For σπεῖρα cf. x. 1 n.

33. δεθῆναι] cf. xii. 6. The tribune considered Paul to be a leader of assassins.

τίς εἴη καὶ τί ἐστιν...] Probably the change of construction is merely for the sake of variety : τί εἴη πεποιηκώς after τίς εἴη would be very ugly. Most editors draw a distinction : 'he was uncertain who he was, but assumes as certain that he is a malefactor'. T.R. has τίς ἂν εἴη. ^{Text}⟨Text ℵABD.⟩

34. ἐπεφώνουν] A word peculiar to Luke in N.T. For its use here cf. Luke xxiii. 21 ἐπεφώνουν λέγοντες, Σταύρου, σταύρου αὐτόν and Acts xii. 22.

τὴν παρεμβολήν] xxii. 24, xxiii. 10, 16, 32: 'barracks', the soldiers' quarters inside the fort.

36. αἶρε αὐτόν] Cf. Luke xxiii. 18 αἶρε τοῦτον. The full phrase Acts xxii. 22.

37. εἰ ἔξεστίν...] A simple question, 'May I...?' cf. i. 6 n. Bengel remarks *modeste alloquitur*, straining the Greek.

Ἑλληνιστὶ γινώσκεις;] So Xen. *An.* VII. 6. 8 Ἑλληνιστὶ ξυνιέναι; *Cyrop.* VII. 5. 31 Συριστὶ ἐπίστασθαι. Cic. *pro Flacco* 4 *qui Graece nesciunt.*

38. οὐκ ἄρα σὺ εἶ...] 'Thou art not then (as I supposed) the Egyptian....' The sentence asks a question in fact though not in form. οὐκ is emphatic: the centurion hearing Paul speak Greek says, 'I was wrong it seems in taking you for the Egyptian'. A. and R.V. 'Art thou not then the Egyptian?' which would certainly require ἆρ' οὐκ εἶ σύ... ;

ὁ Αἰγύπτιος...] One of the many impostors who, like Theudas (v. 36 n.), arose during this unsettled period. Josephus tells us that he collected 30,000 people on the Mount of Olives to see the walls of Jerusalem fall down before him, and that he was attacked by Felix with great loss, but escaped himself. ^{B. J. II.} ^{13. 5.} ^{Ant. xx.} ^{8. 6.}

The discrepancy between 30,000 and 4000 need not trouble us, as Josephus contradicts himself, in one passage describing 'the majority' of the 30,000 as killed or wounded, in the other stating that 400 were killed and 200 wounded. ^{M. de W.}

τοὺς τετ.] '*the* four thousand'; referred to as well known.

σικαρίων] *sicariorum;* R.V. 'assassins'. Josephus refers to the number of the banditti, to be found even in Jerusalem, wearing concealed daggers (*sicae*) and committing murders with impunity.

39. ἐγὼ ἄνθρωπος μὲν...δέομαι δὲ...] Note the position of μέν : 'I (ἐγώ), as regards your question to me, am a man (ἄνθρωπος μέν)..., but, as regards my question to you, I ask (δέομαι δὲ...)'.

οὐκ ἀσήμου] Litotes. Cf. Eur. *Ion* 8 ἔστιν γὰρ οὐκ ἄσημος Ἑλλήνων πόλις (of Athens).

πόλεως πολίτης] Effective assonance, adding to the emphasis on πολίτης.

40. πολλῆς δὲ σιγῆς] A.V. excellently ' a great silence'. For the scene cf. Virgil's famous lines *Aen.* I. 148—152 *ac veluti magno in populo...*, and for **κατέσεισε...**, Pers. IV. 7 *calidae fecisse silentia turbae | majestate manus.*

τῇ Ἑβραΐδι δ.] Aramaic or Aramaean.

CHAPTER XXII.

1. Two points should be noticed in Paul's speech, (1) his argument that the strength of his former zeal for Judaism gives a measure of the strength of the conviction which had induced him to adopt the course he had taken— a conviction based on direct and repeated revelation; (2) the way in which, while developing this argument, he answers the charge of enmity to 'the people', 'the Law', and 'the Temple', by referring to his Jewish birth and strict Jewish training in the law of their fathers, ver. 3, by his description of Ananias as an observer of the Law, ver. 12, by his reference to the ' God of our fathers', ver. 14, to his prayer ' in the Temple', to his earnest desire to remain and preach in Jerusalem, vv. 19, 20.

ἀδελφοὶ καὶ πατ.] So vii. 2. *Amoris et honoris nomina.*

3. παρὰ τ. π. Γαμ.] Some would join these words with πεπαιδ. but the commencement of each clause seems marked by a participle, γεγεννημένος, ἀνατεθραμμένος, πεπαιδευμένος. Moreover 'brought up in this city at the feet of G.' is one complete fact, 'educated in the strictness of our ancestral law' another.

The Rabbis sat on raised seats, their pupils on low benches or on the ground: it was at the age of 13 that a Jewish boy destined to become a Rabbi entered the school of some great teacher.

Paul gives exactly the same account of his early life, Gal. i. 13, 14.

ἀκρίβειαν] The word expresses 'mathematical accuracy': on this rigid accuracy in observance of the Law the Pharisees prided themselves, cf. xxvi. 5 ἀκριβεστάτην αἵρεσιν; Jos. *Ant.* XVII. 2. 4 ἐπ' ἀκριβώσει μέγα φρονοῦν τοῦ πατρῴου νόμου; *B. J.* II. 8. 18 Φαρισαῖοι οἱ δοκοῦντες μετὰ ἀκριβείας ἐξηγεῖσθαι τὰ νόμιμα.

ζηλωτὴς ὑπάρχων τοῦ θεοῦ] Note carefully the difference between this and ζηλωταὶ τοῦ νόμου ὑπάρχουσιν (xxi. 20).

5. ὁ ἀρχ.] Saul had asked for a commission from 'the high priest' (ix. 1), who at that time was Theophilus. That he was still alive is inferred from this passage, although Ananias was the actual high priest (xxiii. 2).

τὸ πρεσβυτέριον] i. e. the Sanhedrin probably, cf. iv. 5 n.

τοὺς ἐκεῖσε ὄντας] *Constructio praegnans:* those who had fled to Damascus on the prosecution after the death of Stephen, and were in Damascus. This traditional explanation is however very unsatisfactory. It seems better to say that the use is deictic, and almost pictorial: the word represents the speaker as *directing* his thoughts and the attention of his hearers *to* Damascus. Cf. the otherwise inexplicable τηρεῖσθαι τὸν Παῦλον εἰς Καισαρίαν xxv. 4 and xix. 22 n.

7. ἤκουσα φωνῆς: φωνὴν οὐκ ἤκουσαν ver. 9; **ἀκοῦσαι φωνήν** ver. 14] Cf. ix. 4 n.

8. Ἰησοῦς ὁ Ναζωραῖος] But ix. 5, xxvi. 15 'Jesus' only. It is clear that Paul adds the explanatory words ὁ Ναζωραῖος here because, mentioning Jesus for the first time (in ch. xxvi. Jesus had been already referred to as 'Jesus of Nazareth') he finds it necessary to do so for the sake of clearness. Such an addition would be perfectly natural. The instance however shews how hard it may often be to separate *ipsissima verba* from explanatory additions, and it is important to bear this in mind when we come to consider the account of the conversion ch. xxvi.

9. ἐθεάσαντο] T. R. adds καὶ ἔμφοβοι ἐγένοντο. Omit ℵABH.

13. ἀνάβλεψον...ἀνέβλεψα εἰς αὐτόν] R.V. 'receive thy sight...I looked upon him'. The same verb is used ix. 17, 18, where it distinctly is = 'receive sight again', and it should be so rendered here, ἀνέβλεψα εἰς αὐτόν being put shortly for 'I received my sight (and looked) upon him', as R. V. gives in margin.

Of course ἀναβλέπω can mean 'look up', as John ix.
11, but here the meaning of ἀνάβλεψον absolutely determines
the meaning of ἀνέβλεψα.

14. τὸν δίκαιον] Jesus, cf. iii. 14.

M.

16. βάπτισαι] Middle: 'cause thyself to be baptized'.
For καὶ ἀπόλουσαι τὰς ἁμαρτίας cf. the Baptismal Service 'O
God...who didst sanctify water to the mystical *washing
away of sin*', and cf. 1 Cor. vi. 11.

17. ἐγένετο δέ μοι...προσευχομένου μου...γενέσθαι με]
For similar carelessness of style in Hellenistic Gk cf. xv.
22 n.

ὑποστρέψαντι] Cf. ix. 19 n.   **ἐν ἐκστάσει,** cf. x. 10 n.

18. σπεῦσον] He only stayed 15 days, cf. Gal. i. 18.

19. αὐτοὶ ἐπίστανται...] 'they themselves know...':
Paul's reply expresses this argument : the Jews must believe
that my conversion was due to a miraculous and divine
revelation, because *they themselves know* how previously I
hated the Christians.

v. H.

20. μάρτυρος] A.V. 'martyr'; R.V. 'witness'; V.
testis, and cf. Rev. ii. 13 ; xvii. 6 ἐκ τοῦ αἵματος τῶν μαρ-
τύρων Ἰησοῦ, where it certainly is = 'martyrs'. The word
is here seen in a transition state, no longer merely meaning
'witness', but not yet specifically describing one who had
borne witness by his death—'a martyr'.

Text
אABCD
EHLP.

21. εἰς ἔθνη] Emphatic. The 'mission to the Gentiles'
is the 'word' or 'utterance' up to which the Jews listen.

22. καθῆκεν] T. R. καθῆκον with no authority. The
imperfect is vigorous, expressing impatience, 'it was not
fitting' i. e. he ought long ago to have been put to death.
Cf. Ar. *Eccl.* 177 τί ποθ' ἄνδρες οὐχ ἥκουσιν · ὥρα δ' ἦν πάλαι.

23. ῥιπτούντων] 'threw off' R.V.; 'cast off' A.V., for
which cf. Plat. *Rep.* 473 E ῥίψαντας τὰ ἱμάτια, γυμνούς, of
men about to make an attack. Here however there is no
sign of an attack, and the participle is in the present and
the verb frequentative (ῥιπτέω *jacto*, ῥίπτω *jacio*?), so that

A.La.M.
de W. H.

it is better to explain 'tossing about their garments' as a
symbol of excitement and abhorrence. So Chrys. ἐκτινασ-
σόντων. Cf. Ov. *Am.* III. 2. 74 *jactatis signa dedere togis.*

κονιορτὸν...] 2 Sam. xvi. 13; Job ii. 12.

Digest L.
XLVIII.
Tit. 18.

24. ἀνετάζεσθαι] This commencing an 'inquiry' (cf.
'Inquisition') by torture was contrary to Roman law. *Non
esse a tormentis incipiendum, Divus Augustus statuit.*

25. ὡς δὲ προέτειναν...] 'when they had bound him (leaning) forward with thongs', i.e. so that his back was exposed to the lash. R.V. in marg. 'for the thongs', but this needlessly makes ἱμᾶσιν exactly = μάστιξιν.

τὸν ἑστῶτα ἑκατ.] The inferior officer appointed to carry out the tribune's orders. So at the crucifixion Matt. xxvii. 54.

εἰ ἄνθρωπον Ῥωμαῖον...:] xvi. 37 notes.

26. τί μέλλεις ποιεῖν: ὁ γάρ...] The words τί μέλλεις ποιεῖν; contain a warning = 'Be careful'; hence γάρ. T.R. ὅρα τί μ. π. gives the right sense but is less vigorous.

27. σὺ Ῥωμαῖος εἶ;] σύ expresses astonishment and presupposes contempt.

28. κεφαλαίου] Classical = 'principal' as opposed to 'interest', *caput;* or 'a large main sum' (e.g. Dem. 834 τὸ κεφ. τῆς ἐμῆς οὐσίας 'the bulk'), 'a capital sum', as here.
The sale of the Roman citizenship was resorted to by the emperors as a means of filling their exchequer, much as James I. made baronets.
πολιτείαν = *jus civitatis.*

30. τὸ ἀσφαλὲς τὸ τί...] The words τὸ τί...are epexegetic of τὸ ἀσφαλές—'the exact facts, viz. what accusation is brought'. τί is nom. cf. Thuc. I. 95 ἀδικία κατηγορεῖτο; M. Soph. O. C. 529.

ἐκέλευσεν συνελθεῖν] T. R. has ἐλθεῖν, which would mean 'to come to him', whereas συνελθεῖν = 'assemble', probably in their ordinary place of meeting. That they did not 'meet' in the Turris Antonia is clear from καταγαγών, and that it was not inside the Temple is shewn by the presence of Lysias. *Text* ℵABE, ἐλθεῖν HLP. Copt. Aeth.

CHAPTER XXIII.

1. ἀτενίσας...τῷ συνεδρίῳ] Same construction iii. 12. The words indicate that he confronted them boldly, cf. xiii. 9.
Note too ἀδελφοί without the usual (cf. iv. 8, vii. 2, xxii. 1) and respectful καὶ πατέρες.

συνειδήσει] 33 times in Paul's Epistles, three times in Peter's, not elsewhere in N.T. Cod.

πεπολίτευμαι τῷ θ.] The ideal Jewish state was a state under the direct government of God—a theocracy. Paul says 'You accuse me of speaking against the Jews, the Law, &c.; I answer that *in the sight of God*, the ruler and lawgiver of the Jewish nation, *I have acted as a good citizen*'.

230   *ACTS OF THE APOSTLES.* [xxiii. 1

For the metaphor cf. Phil. i. 27 ἀξίως τοῦ εὐαγγελίου τοῦ χριστοῦ πολιτεύεσθε: iii. 20 ἡμῶν τὸ πολίτευμα ἐν οὐρανοῖς ὑπάρχει.

H. M.

2. **'Ανανίας**] Son of Nebedaeus, nominated to the office by Herod, king of Chalcis, A.D. 48: sent to Rome A.D. 52 by Quadratus, prefect of Syria (predecessor of Felix), to answer a charge of rapine and cruelty made against him by the Samaritans, but honourably acquitted. He was murdered about ten years after this.

Jos. B. J. ii. 17. 9.

τύπτειν αὐτοῦ] Cf. the treatment of Jesus, John xviii. 22.

3. **τύπτειν σε...**] Note the indignant emphasis of the position of τύπτειν. Cp. carefully the reply of Jesus.

τοῖχε κεκονιαμένε] Cf. Matt. xxiii. 27 τάφοις κεκονιαμένοις, where the following words explain the phrase. It seems to have been a proverbial expression.

Eders- heim ii. 320.

The stone which marked a grave was 'kept whitened, to warn the passer by against defilement'.

καὶ σὺ...] καί at the commencement of a question expresses indignation or astonishment. 'Dost thou indeed sit...?', or 'What! dost thou sit...?' Cf. καὶ πῶς; &c.

5. **οὐκ ᾔδειν...**] 'I did not know...', the only possible rendering of the Greek.

So Chrysostom: σφόδρα πείθομαι μὴ εἰδέναι αὐτὸν ὅτι ἀρχιερεύς ἐστι· διὰ μακροῦ μὲν ἐπανελθόντα χρόνου, μὴ συγγινόμενον δὲ συνεχῶς Ἰουδαίοις, ὁρῶντα δὲ καὶ ἐκεῖνον ἐν μέσῳ μετὰ πολλῶν καὶ ἑτέρων.

This explanation is the only natural one. Others argue (assuming too much) that Paul must have recognized the High Priest from his position, attire, &c. But Lange points out (1) that the High Priest, not being engaged in the service of the Temple, would not necessarily be distinguishable by his dress; (2) that the assembly was an irregular one, summoned by Lysias, and he may not have been presiding.

Calvin took the words ironically—'a man who so acts could never I thought be the High Priest': others render **B. N. W.** *non reputabam*, and make the words apologetic—'I forgot it was the High Priest'. Both explanations do violence to the Greek. Others have conjectured that Paul was nearsighted, giving an unnatural and forced meaning to ἀτενίσας in ver. 1.

γέγραπται γάρ] 'I did not know, otherwise I should not have spoken as I did, *for...*', cf. Ex. xxii. 18 ἄρχοντα τοῦ λαοῦ σου οὐ κακῶς ἐρεῖς.

6. γνοὺς δὲ...] Luke here in a marked manner points out that it was Paul's *purpose* to introduce dissension into the assembly.

Some regard Luke's account as unsatisfactory and unauthentic. M.Rouss in M.

Many approach very near to the dangerous assertion that the end justifies the means, pointing out that Paul saw no other way of securing the liberty necessary for preaching the Gospel: e.g. Alford, 'he uses in the cause of Truth the maxim so often perverted in the cause of falsehood, *divide et impera*'. And so N. Lange, Lumby, Cook; but see W. on this.

Farrar distinctly condemns Paul's conduct, and takes xxiv. 21 as a virtual confession of error. In the absence of adequate data for forming a fair judgment, we may note (1) that this act of Paul's stands by itself, and is without any parallel in his life or writings; (2) that to found on it such a comment as *bellum haereticorum pax ecclesiae* is to violate the whole teaching of the N. T. Corn. à Lapide.

It will be observed that xxiv. 21 where Paul refers to this event he makes no reference (1) to the motive described in the words γνοὺς δὲ..., (2) to the words ἐγὼ Φαρισαῖός εἰμι. It is therefore possible that Luke has here assigned a motive for Paul's words, or even amplified his description of the occurrence, because he desires to explain to his Gentile readers (cf. the explanation ver. 8) how it was that a statement about 'the resurrection' should have caused so great a diversion in Paul's favour. Paul, in xxiv. 21, refers definitely to his 'one utterance', viz. 'about the resurrection of the dead I am on my trial', and it is certainly natural to assume that the words there given accurately represent the fact, for it was distinctly his belief in the resurrection and consequently in the Messiahship of Jesus which distinguished Paul from other Jews, and it is to the resurrection that he constantly appeals as the very centre of his faith; cf. his speech at Athens and 1 Cor. xv. throughout.

ἐγὼ Φαρ....] This sentence (subject to the above remarks) must be taken as a whole. The words 'I am a Pharisee' are immediately limited and defined by what follows—'I am a Pharisee for I believe in a resurrection'.

Paul and Pharisaism seem to us such opposite ideas that we often forget that to Paul Christianity was the natural development of Judaism. Luke throughout describes him as a pious Jew: see too his own emphatic assertion of agreement with Judaism xxiv. 14, xxvi. 5 (ἔζησα Φαρισαῖος. καὶ νῦν...). He differed from the Jews as regards facts perhaps rather than principles. They looked for a Messiah; he said Jesus is the Messiah. The Pharisees

asserted a resurrection of the dead; Paul said Jesus has
risen from the dead.

υἱὸς Φαρισαίων]   'Perhaps refers rather to his teachers
than his ancestors, being a Hebraism like 'the sons of the
prophets'; cf. Amos vii. 14.'

Lightfoot
Phil. iii.
5.

ἐλπίδος καὶ ἀναστ.]   Probably a hendiadys; 'hope of a
resurrection'.

7. *στάσις*] xv. 2 n.   The Sadducees, iv. 1 n.

8. *μήτε ἄγγ. μήτε...*]   T.R. has *μηδὲ ἄγγ. μήτε*, a correction made in order to join *ἄγγελον* and *πνεῦμα* together
and so make *ἀμφότερα* formally accurate, as it is perfectly
accurate in fact, the denial of the existence of 'either angel
or spirit' being a single tenet.

Text
אABCE.

πνεῦμα is 'any spiritual incorporeal being', but here as
distinguished from *ἄγγελος* perhaps refers, to 'the spirit of
man after death' (*homines defuncti* B.).

For
Jewish
Angelo-
logy
v. Eders-
heim
App. 13.

9. *οὐδὲν...*]   Luke xxiii. 4 *οὐδὲν εὑρίσκω αἴτιον ἐν τῷ
ἀνθρώπῳ τούτῳ.*   A sentence of acquittal.

εἰ δὲ...]   After *ἄγγελος* T.R. adds *μὴ θεομαχῶμεν* from
v. 39.   As punctuated the sentence is generally regarded as
an instance of aposiopesis, 'But if an angel spoke to him
(what then?)', putting a hypothetical case which deserves
consideration.

Text
אABCE.

Surely however *εἰ* is interrogative (i. 6 n.) and a question
should be marked, 'But did an angel speak to him?', referring to Paul's own statement xxii. 6 ff.

11. *ὁ κύριος*] Jesus.

οὕτω σε δεῖ καὶ εἰς ʽΡώμην μ.]   Cf. xix. 21.   It is important to notice these two emphatic phrases.   It is clear that
Luke looks on Paul's preaching at Rome as the crowning
point of his narrative.   *Paulus Romae, apex Evangelii* B.

12. *πεῖν*] = *πιεῖν.*

ἕως οὗ ἀποκτείνωσιν] *ἀποκτ.* is 1st aorist subj. 'until
they shall have killed'; cf. ver. 21 *ἕως οὗ ἀνέλωσιν.*

13. *πλείους τεσσεράκοντα*]   Cf. iv. 22 *πλειόνων τεσσερ.*;
xxiv. 11 *πλείους δώδεκα*; so in class. Gk, e.g. Plat. *Apol.*
17 D *ἔτη πλείω ἑβδομήκοντα*, and in Latin *amplius decem
annos.*

14. *ἀναθέματι ἀνεθεματίσαμεν*]   Emphatic repetition of
the word.   Cf. vii. 34 n.

ἀνάθημα is used in classical Gk of 'a thing set up in a
temple', 'dedicated'—an offering; cf. Luke xxi. 5 *ἀναθήμασιν
κεκόσμηται*, the only place where it occurs in N.T.

But a thing may be 'dedicated' in a good or bad sense
(cf. *auri sacra fames* Virg. *Aen.* iii. 57; *devota arbos* Hor.

Od. III. 4. 27), and so the by-form ἀνάθεμα came to be used in Hellenistic Gk in a bad sense = 'a thing accursed', cf. Josh. vii. 1 ἐνοσφίσαντο ἀπὸ τοῦ ἀναθέματος, Gal. i. 8 ἀνάθεμα ἔστω and ἀναθεματίζειν = 'make accursed', 'curse', cf. Mark xiv. 71 ἀναθ. καὶ ὀμνύναι.

Here the sense is that they solemnly declared themselves ἀνάθεμα, i.e. 'an accursed thing', if they did not kill Paul before eating or drinking.

15.   ὑμεῖς] Emphatic: it anticipates ἡμεῖς δέ.

ἐμφανίσατε...] 'make a statement' or 'declaration to the tribune to induce him (ὅπως) to bring Paul down to you, on the plea that you propose (ὡς μέλλοντας)...'. The words ὡς μέλλοντας...give the substance of the declaration to be made to the tribune.

A. and R.V. 'signify to the chief captain that he bring him', a rendering which suggests that *authority* in the matter belonged to the chief priests, whereas ἐμφανίζειν in no way indicates the possession of authority by the person making the declaration, but rather that the person to whom the declaration is made is himself in authority (cf. xxiv. 1, xxv. 2, 15).

τοῦ ἀνελεῖν] Gen. of purpose, or the thing aimed at.

16.   ὁ υἱὸς...] Quite unknown except here.

παραγενόμενος καὶ εἰσελθὼν] Graphic fulness of description. It is possible however to take παραγ. with what precedes, 'having heard...having come upon them'; but this is not so simple.

18.   ὁ δέσμιος Π.] Probably now in *custodia militaris* (cf. xxviii. 16), a prisoner, but with free access to him, as had been the case since xxii. 30; a relief from the 'two chains' (xxi. 33).

20.   ὡς μέλλων] This must refer to the tribune, and is inconsistent with ver. 15. So R.V. 'bring down Paul...as though thou wouldest inquire': but this cannot be right, for it describes the tribune as giving a reason for bringing Paul down, whereas it is clear that the Jews should give a reason for asking him to do so, as in ver. 15. Moreover Luke could not repeat ver. 15 with so absurd an alteration.

Text ABE, μέλλον-τες T.R., μέλλοντα HLP, μέλλον Χ.

The reading μέλλον (in agreement with συνέδριον) seems to account for the other readings best.

23.   τινὰς δύο] Cf. Luke vii. 19 προσκαλεσάμενος δύο τινὰς τῶν μαθητῶν, 'certain two'; Thuc. VIII. 100 τινὲς δύο νῆες. The expression indicates that they were not specially chosen. Two centurions naturally 'got ready two hundred men'.

στρατιώτας...ἱππεῖς...δεξιολάβους] The words describe
the three varieties of troops which formed a Roman army,
and which would be found in every fraction of an army, e.g.
in the cohort of Lysias. The στρατιῶται were the heavy-
armed legionaries; the ἱππεῖς a portion of the *alae equitum*
attached to every legion, and the δεξιολάβοι formed one of
the many varieties of troops which composed the *auxilia*
or supplementary troops, not Romans, but foreigners armed
with their native weapons, c.g. Balearic slingers, Cretan
archers.

What δεξ. exactly means is unknown. A. and R.V.
'spearmen', and V. *lancearii*. A has δεξιοβόλους, perhaps=
'slingers': Syr. has *dextra jaculantes*.

The size of the escort points to the unsettled nature of
the times, and so perhaps does the night start.

24. κτήνη τε παραστῆσαι] Change to indirect speech,
'and (he ordered them) to provide...'.

κτήνη] *jumenta*, beasts of burden or for riding: asses or
horses, not war-horses.

Φήλικα] *Felicem*. Antonius Felix, procurator of Judaea,
who succeeded Cumanus about A.D. 52, was brother of Pallas the notorious freedman and favourite of Claudius. Ta-
*Hist.*v.9. citus says of his government, *per omnem saevitiam et libidi-*
*Ann.*xii. *nem jus regium servili ingenio exercuit,* and *Judaeae impositus,*
54. *et cuncta malefacta sibi impune ratus tanta potentia subnixo.*
Jos. He was recalled by Nero about 60 or 62 A.D. on the com-
Ant. plaint of the Jews, but protected by the influence of Pallas.
xx. 8. 9.

25. ἐπιστολὴν] Such a letter, containing a summary
of the facts, when a charge was referred to a superior magistrate, was technically termed *elogium*.

τύπον] Like *exemplum* in Latin (cf. Cic. *ad Att.* ix. 6. 3
literae sunt allatae hoc exemplo: Pompeius mare transiit...)
of the 'purport', 'contents' of a letter. So 3 Macc. iii. 30
ὁ μὲν τῆς ἐπιστολῆς τύπος οὕτως ἐγέγραπτο.

26. κρατίστῳ] Cf. i. 1 n. ἡγεμόνι; cf. Matt. xxvii. 2,
Πιλάτῳ τῷ ἡγεμόνι.—The word is general='governor', not
defining the particular rank of the governor. χαίρειν: xv.
23 n.

27. ἐξειλάμην, μαθών] 'I rescued him, having learned',
i.e. when I had learned: Lysias clearly leaves the inference
open that he rescued Paul *because* he was a Roman, though
he did not discover this until *after* he had rescued him and
was about to scourge him—a point about which he is also
silent (*de verberibus tacet.* B.).

μαθών cannot possibly = καὶ ἔμαθον as Grotius and others
take it.

29. ζητήματα...] The distinction which Gallio drew, xviii. 14, 15 n.

30. μηνυθείσης...ἐπιβουλῆς...ἔσεσθαι] A natural combination of two constructions, (1) *μηνυθείσης...ἐπιβουλῆς... ἐσομένης*, (2) *μηνυθέντος...ἐπιβουλὴν...ἔσεσθαι*.

ἐπὶ σοῦ] 'in the presence of', 'before', especially of hearing 'before a judge', cf. xxiv. 20 *ἐπὶ τοῦ συνεδρίου*; xxiv. 21 *ἐφ' ὑμῶν*; xxv. 26, xxvi. 2; so in Latin *apud*, e.g. *apud judices*, *apud senatum*. T.R. adds *ἔρρωσο, Vale*.

31. οἱ μὲν οὖν στρ.] The antithesis to *μέν* is probably xxiv. 1 *μετὰ δέ...*; 'so then the soldiers, &c. &c...., but after five days....' See n. on xxiv. 11.

διὰ νυκτὸς] They could not reach Antipatris that night, but their march continued 'through the night'.

Antipatris, formerly Capharsaba, had been rebuilt by Herod the Great and named after his father: it was 42 m. from Jerusalem and 26 from Caesarea.

33. οἵτινες] Not the same people as the nom. to *ὑπέστρεψαν*, but 'the cavalry' to be supplied from *τοὺς ἱππεῖς*. The sense must override strict grammar, as often in late Gk.

ἀναδόντες] Classical Gk *ἀποδόντες*, *quum reddidissent*.

34. ἐπαρχείας] *Provinciae*. The object of the question of Felix is not clear. It is said that Cilicia was included in the province of Syria and that Felix was desirous of learning whether the case was within his jurisdiction, but it is not easy to see how, even though Cilicia was under the governor of Syria. Felix, who was only procurator of Judaea, would have jurisdiction over it. Luke seems merely to indicate that Felix contented himself for the time with some personal inquiries about Paul.

35. διακούσομαι] Of a *full* hearing, as contrasted with the present brief interrogatory. The rule was: '*qui cum elogio mittuntur, ex integro audiendi sunt.* *Digest* xlviii. 3. 6.

ἐν τῷ πραιτ. τοῦ 'Η.] The palace built by Herod the Great and used as a residence by the Roman governor.

πραιτωρίῳ=praetorio, (1) originally the general's tent in a camp, (2) the residence of a governor or prince, cf. Mark xv. 16 *ἔσω τῆς αὐλῆς, ὅ ἐστι πραιτώριον*; Juv. *Sat.* x. 161 *sedet ad praetoria regis*.

CHAPTER XXIV.

1. πρεσβ. τινῶν] T.R. *τῶν πρεσβ.* 'the elders': in any case it can only have been a deputation. Text ℵABE.

ῥήτορος...] R.V. rightly 'an orator, one Tertullus'. In classical Gk *ῥήτωρ*=a public speaker in the assembly;

in Latin *rhetor* is 'a teacher of rhetoric' and is often opposed to *orator*, one who actually speaks in court or elsewhere. Here however ῥήτωρ is clearly = *orator* or *causidicus*, 'a barrister'.

II. 'The provincials being themselves unacquainted with the law of their rulers, employed Roman advocates to plead for them'. This practice in the provinces (*usus provincialis*, Cic. *pro Cael.* 30) was regarded as good training for young men. Tertullus is a dimin. from Tertius, as Catullus from Catius, Lucullus from Lucius.

2. λέγων] Obviously a summary of the speech. The statement of the case vv. 5—8 could not possibly have been made so briefly.

πολλῆς...] The speaker begins with the regular *captatio benevolentiae*. See Quint. *Inst. Or.* IV. 1. So too Paul ver. 10.

εἰρήνης] Tacitus (*Ann.* XII. 54) does not give this description of the government of Felix, but describes him as secretly encouraging banditti and sharing the plunder, and he was shortly after this accused by the Jews at Rome, cf. xxiii. 24 n.

1A. Anyhow to refer to the 'peace' of a district would be acceptable and usual flattery to a governor. Cf. Ulpian *de officio praesidis: Congruit bono et gravi praesidi ut pacata sit provincia.*

Text ℵABE. **διορθωμάτων**] 'corrections', 'reforms'. T.R. κατορθωμάτων = *recta, recte facta*, a philosophic term; A.V. 'worthy deeds'.

So II. B. A. **προνοίας**] 'providence' A. and R.V., evidently regarding it as used in flattery and representing the Latin *providentia*, *Providentia Caesaris* being common on coins, and *providentia* being used of God in post-Augustan Latin. But surely προνοία is only = *prudentia*, 'wise forethought', 'care'. Cf.

So Lumby. e.g. 2 Macc. iv. 6 ἄνευ βασιλικῆς προνοίας ἀδύνατον τυχεῖν εἰρήνης. So τῆς σαρκὸς πρόνοιαν Rom. xiii. 14 'provision for the flesh', and προνοεῖσθαι 'take thought for' or 'provide' Rom. xii. 17; 2 Cor. viii. 21; 1 Tim. v. 8.

3. πάντη τε καὶ πανταχοῦ] The rhetorical balance of the sentence is increased by taking these words with διορθ. γινομένων. The words which record the virtues of Felix begin with πολλῆς and end with πάντη τε καὶ πανταχοῦ: it is for '*great* peace and improvements *everywhere*' that, says the orator, we must begin by expressing our thanks to-day.

R.V. 'we accept it in all ways and in all places': but surely the speaker in using ἀποδεχόμεθα expresses not their 'acceptance in all places', but their acknowledgment *that*

day and in *that* place of benefits they had in *all* ways and
in *all* places received from Felix. Moreover, 'we accept in
all ways, in *all* places, with *all* thankfulness' is an exaggeration of style which verges on the absurd.

4. ἐνκόπτω] The opposite of προκόπτω, used of pioneers
'clearing a way', = (1) impede a way, (2) delay, interrupt.

συντόμως] 'concisely'; strictly of speakers, then naturally of hearers, 'to hear briefly' or 'in a few words'.

ἐπιεικείᾳ] 'consideration', 'courtesy'. ἐπιεικής is 'a
reasonable man', 'one who makes reasonable concessions';
often opposed to δίκαιος, 'one who insists on his strict
rights'. Ar. *Eth.* v. 10, Plat.*Leg.* 757 D.

5. εὑρόντες γάρ...] Here follows a summary of the
charges against Paul. There is no verb, and it bears the
stamp of a *résumé* of the points urged by Tertullus.

Note the charge of inciting to disorder put strongly forward, cf. xvi. 20 n.

ἄνδρα τοῦτον λοιμόν] So Dem. 794 οὗτος οὖν αὐτὸν ἐξαι-
τήσεται ὁ φαρμακός, ὁ λοιμός; 1 Macc. x. 61 ἄνδρες λοιμοί;
Cic. *pro Sest.* 14. 33 *illa juria ac pestis patriae* (of Clodius).

κατὰ τὴν οἰκ.] xvii. 6 n.

τῶν Ναζωραίων] Here only in the plural and used contemptuously, cf. John i. 46. 'Christians are still called
by this term by Jews and Mahometans'. Elsewhere in
N.T. the adj. merely describes the birthplace of Jesus. W.

αἱρέσεως, v. 17 n.

6. ἐπείρασεν] *verbum aptum ad calumniam.* B. It had
been alleged that he had profaned the Temple (xxi. 28) but
this could not be proved.

After ἐκρατήσαμεν T.R. adds καὶ κατὰ τὸν ἡμέτερον νόμον
ἠθελήσαμεν κρίνειν. παρελθὼν δὲ Λυσίας ὁ χιλίαρχος μετὰ
πολλῆς βίας ἐκ τῶν χειρῶν ἡμῶν ἀπήγαγε, κελεύσας τοὺς κατηγόρους αὐτοῦ ἔρχεσθαι ἐπὶ σέ—an insertion due to the speech
of Tertullus seeming incomplete. Omitted by אABH LP.

8. παρ' οὗ] i.e. from Paul. Examine him, they say,
and he will not be able to deny it: Paul (ver. 20) rejoins
'let them say if they can what crime I have committed'.

The suggestion of a *quaestio per tormenta* is quite un-
warranted. In T.R. οὗ refers to Lysias. La. M. de W. W. Corn. à Lapide. Grotius.

9. συνεπέθεντο] 'joined in the attack'; a strong word.

10. πολλῶν] About seven. For ἔθνει = Jews xxviii. 19 n.

11. δυναμένου σου...] i.e. I address myself with confi-
dence to a judge of your experience, because you will find

out that the crime charged against me was committed only
twelve days ago, and therefore as an experienced judge you
can easily discover the exact truth.

The days may be thus reckoned: 1, arrival in Jerusalem;
2, meeting with James, xxi. 18; 3, taking of the vow, xxi.
26; 7, arrest in the temple ὡς ἔμελλον αἱ ἑπτὰ ἡμ. συντελεῖσθαι; 8, taken before the Sanhedrin xxii. 30; 9, conspiracy of
Jews xxiii. 12; 10, arrival at Antipatris; 11, at Caesarea; 13,
the day when Paul is speaking.

It will be noted that this reckoning makes the 'after
five days' of xxiv. 1 refer, not to Paul's arrival in Caesarea,
but to his despatch from Jerusalem by Lysias; the difficulty
of doing so is much relieved by observing that δέ in xxiv. 1
is the antithesis to μέν xxiii. 31 (v. n.).

13. παραστῆσαι] 'present', 'shew', 'prove'; so classical,
cf. Plato *Rep.* 600 D τοῖς ἐφ' ἑαυτῶν παριστάναι ὡς...

14. ὁμολογῶ δὲ...] Paul, having denied the charge of
disturbance, now proceeds to answer the charge of being 'a
ringleader of the sect of the Nazarenes'. This he does by
declaring that Christianity is not a deviation from Judaism
but the fulfilment of it.

τὴν ὁδὸν ἣν λέγουσιν αἵρ.] For ὁδός cf. ix. 2 n. αἵρεσις
v. 17 n. Paul objects to the term αἵρεσις employed by Tertullus (ver. 5), which he himself elsewhere uses in a bad
sense, e. g. Gal. v. 20, where among the 'works of the flesh'
are διχοστασίαι, αἱρέσεις. The distinction he draws here is
between *the path* which is marked out for a man by God
(*via divinitus prescripta* B.) and *a self-chosen course*, which
a man marks out for himself. Cf. the same distinction in
Newman's hymn: 'I loved to choose and see my path, but
now Lead thou me on'.

τῷ πατρῴῳ θ.] The adj. emphasizes the argument: cf.
v. 30 ὁ θ. τῶν πατέρων; xxii. 3 τοῦ πατρῴου νόμου.

15. ἐλπίδα...ἣν προσδέχονται] Those 'look for a hope'
who look for its fulfilment. Cf. Tit. ii. 13 προσδεχόμενοι
τὴν μακαρίαν ἐλπίδα.

In using the words αὐτοὶ οὗτοι Paul points to his accusers, not regarding them as probably for the most part
Sadducees who denied a resurrection, but as representatives
of the Jewish nation and religion.

A.V. gives 'hope...which they allow', apparently avoid-
ing the difficulty about the Sadducees.

16. ἐν τούτῳ] 'herein', referring to his whole declaration of belief vv. 14, 15.

καὶ αὐτός] 'I also', as well as my accusers and the Jews
whom they represent. 'In all the points just mentioned *I
also* endeavour to live without offence to God or man'.

ἀπρόσκοπον] A.V. excellently 'void of offence', for the
word may have two meanings:
(1) 'not stumbling' i. e. not offending, upright—in this
sense Paul seeks to be ἀπρόσκοπος πρὸς τὸν θεόν.
(2) 'not stumbled against', i. e. not causing offence—in
this sense Paul seeks to be ἀπρόσκοπος πρὸς τοὺς ἀνθρώπους.
The word only occurs twice elsewhere in N.T., both
times used by Paul: viz. in its first meaning Phil. i. 10 ἵνα
ἦτε εἰλικρινεῖς καὶ ἀπρόσκοποι εἰς ἡμέραν Χριστοῦ; in its second
meaning 1 Cor. x. 32 ἀπρόσκοποι καὶ Ἰουδαίοις γίνεσθε καὶ
Ἕλλησι.
ἀσκῶ...παντός might be given as the best statement of
Paul's rule of conduct in dealing with his difficulty between
Jews and Gentiles.

17. δι' ἐτῶν πλειόνων] 'after an interval of several
years'. His last visit was on his return from his second
missionary journey, xviii. 22.

ἐλεημοσύνας] For this collection for the poor in Jerusalem cf. 1 Cor. xvi. 1—4; Rom. xv. 26.

προσφοράς] 'offerings', 'sacrifices', i.e. in the Temple.
The same word xxi. 26.

18. ἐν αἷς] 'in which', i.e. in connection with the offer- Text
ing of the sacrifices. T.R. ἐν οἷς 'herein', i.e. in connec- ℵABF,
tion with these matters generally. ἐν οἷς
HLP.

τινὲς δέ] So ℵABCE. T.R. omits δέ, making τινές nom.
to εὗρον—an obvious correction.
The sentence as given in the text is broken off after
the words πρὸς ἐμέ: 'they (my accusers here present) found
me, I grant, in the Temple performing a religious duty, *not*
creating a disturbance, *but* certain Jews from Asia, who
ought to have been present to-day to support any charge
they had against me—or let these men here (turning to his
accusers) state what illegal act they found me guilty of
when I was arraigned before the Sanhedrin'.
δέ after τινές is opposed to the emphatic οὐ μετὰ ὄχλου
οὐδὲ μ. θ.—'I was not creating disturbance, but certain
Jews from Asia (brought an accusation to that effect)'.
Before stating what the accusation was Paul proceeds paren-
thetically to comment on the absence of his accusers as
indicating the falsity of their charge. Strictly he ought to
have gone on to state what the accusation was, instead of
doing so however he breaks off, and, turning to the San-

hedrists, says '*or* let these men say what I was proved guilty of', the force of '*or*' being this—'The absence of my original accusers shews that they had no case, *or*, if this inference is objected to, then let these men *themselves* (though their evidence is only second-hand) say what...'.

The passage as it stands is instinct with life, and seems to exhibit the abruptness so characteristic of the Pauline Epistles. Cf. xxvi. 9 n.

20.　τί...ἤ = τί ἄλλο...ἤ, 'what...except'.

A.　21.　ἐκέκραξα] Reduplicated aorist. Cf. Numb. xi. 2 ἐκέκραξεν and 'almost always in LXX.'

Bris-　22.　ἀνεβάλετο] When a case was put off for fuller
sonius, hearing the judge AMPLIUS *pronuntiabat*, cf. Cic. *Brut.* 22
de For- *cum consules re audita* AMPLIUS *de consilii sententia pro-*
mulis. *nuntiassent.*

ἀκριβέστερον...] These words assign *a reason* why Felix put off the case, just as the next participle εἴπας assigns *the reason he alleged* for so doing, viz. the need of Lysias' evidence.

Lange.　He did so 'because he had more exact knowledge of the Way', the comparative indicating a more than usually exact knowledge, such as was not unnatural in one who had been so long governor and had a Jewish wife. His knowledge enabled him to see that Paul could not be condemned by a Roman tribunal on the religious question, and he accordingly 'put off' the case, alleging the need of further evidence. He might have acquitted Paul, but he may have wished not to offend the Jews (cf. ver. 27) and trusted that time would afford some chance of getting out of the difficulty, or he may have hoped for a bribe from Paul (cf. ver. 26).

M. II.　Some say εἰδώς = 'now that he had learnt', i.e. he put them off because he had learnt from Paul's speech to understand more clearly what Christianity was. But εἰδώς cannot naturally = *certior factus.*

23.　ἄνεσιν] lit. 'relaxation'; R.V. 'indulgence'—the opposite of strict confinement; the next words serve to explain it.

24.　Δρουσίλλῃ τῇ ἰδίᾳ γυναικί] Suetonius (*Claudius* 28) calls Felix *trium reginarum maritum aut adulterum;* one was a daughter of Juba, king of Mauretania, the third is unknown. Drusilla was a daughter of Herod Agrippa (xii.
A. 1), who killed James; Felix had persuaded her to leave her former husband Aziz, king of Emesa. She perished with her son in an eruption of Vesuvius in the reign of Titus.

ἰδίᾳ　The MSS. authority for ἰδίᾳ is not strong, and it is per-
DC³, haps safer to render merely 'his wife', but the reading is

remarkable considering the history of Felix and Drusilla omit
and the description given of Paul's discourse.

οὔσῃ Ἰουδ.] The words seem to suggest that the inter- αὐτοῦ
view was held on her account as taking a natural interest in Eᴷ¹.
Paul and his teaching.

εἰς Χριστὸν Ἰησοῦν] Probably wrong, cf. ii. 22 n. Ἰησοῦν found in אEL; omitted א°AHP.

25. ἐγκρατείας] 'temperance'. Strictly
σώφρων = one who has got the mastery over his passions.
ἐγκρατής = ... is getting ....
ἀκρατής = ... is losing ....
ἀκόλαστος = ... has lost ....

τὸ νῦν ἔχον] Cf. Tobit vii. 11 τὸ νῦν ἔχον ἡδέως γίνου, Lumby.
'for the present'.

26. χρήματα] He knew that Paul had gone up to Jerusalem with money collections (xxiv. 17). *Lex Julia de* Digest
repetundis praecipit, Ne quis...ob hominem in vincula publica XL. 11. 3
conjiciendum, vinciendum...exire vinculis dimittendum... [XLVIII.
aliquid acceperit. Such laws are of course often a dead in H.
letter.

27. Πόρκιον Φῆστον] *Porcium Festum.* He died after
about two years.

χάριτα καταθέσθαι] Lit. 'to deposit a favour with', i.e.
to do a favour which may as it were stand to your credit,
on which you may at any time draw. The verb is strictly
used of 'depositing with a banker': its metaphorical use is
classical, e.g. Thuc. I. 33 *sub in.* μετὰ ἀειμνήστου μαρτυρίου
τὴν χάριν καταθήσεσθε; I. 138 εὐεργεσίαν ἐς βασιλέα κατέθετο.

CHAPTER XXV.

1. τῇ ἐπαρχείᾳ] Cf. xxiii. 34 n. Strictly Judaea was
not a 'province', but a department of the province of Syria,
but the term is used loosely. Syria was under a *legatus* H. La.
Caesaris, Judaea under a *procurator* (ἐπίτροπος).

2. οἱ πρῶτοι] Not identical with but including οἱ πρεσβύτεροι ver. 15. All 'the chief Jews' would attend to pay
their respects to the new governor.

4. ὁ μὲν οὖν Φ.] Answered by διατρίψας δὲ...ver. 6.
Cf. ii. 41 n.

τηρεῖσθαι] A.V. 'should be kept'; R.V. rightly 'was
kept': the words seem to contain a rebuke of their unusual
request. 'Paul is in custody at Caesarea', said Festus, 'and
I am going there soon: you had better go there too'.

εἰς Καισαρίαν] cf. xxii. 5 n. on ἐκεῖσε.

5. δυνατοί] A.V. 'them…which are able'; R.V. rightly 'which are of power'. Festus orders the proper authorities to go.

ἄτοπον] Cf. Luke xxiii. 41 οὗτος δὲ οὐδὲν ἄτοπον ἔπραξε 'nothing amiss'. So in LXX.

7. αἰτιώματα] What they were, is seen from Paul's reply; cf. too xxiv. 5.

8. εἰς Καίσαρα] An offence against Caesar would render liable to the penalties of *majestas*, 'treason'. Nero was 'the Caesar' A.D. 54—68. 'Caesar' is originally a family name. Augustus was so called as the adopted son of Julius Caesar. It soon became a title = Emperor (cf. its derivatives Kaiser, Czar). Nero was the last emperor who had any hereditary claim to be so called.

9. ἐπ' ἐμοῦ] These words literally mean only 'in my presence', but in connection with κριθῆναι certainly imply 'in my presence as judge', cf. xxiii. 30 n. It is clear however that Festus means Paul to be tried really by the Sanhedrin, for otherwise (1) what favour would he do the Jews? (2) what is the point of Paul's reply 'I stand at Caesar's judgment-seat'?

Festus certainly seems to be laying a snare for Paul. So B., *Hoc Festus speciose addit.*

10. ἑστώς…] i.e. I am a Roman citizen before a Roman tribunal. Festus is the representative of Caesar: the tribunal of Festus is the tribunal of Caesar.

Ulpian in M.

Quae acta gestaque sunt a procuratore Caesaris, sic ab eo comprobantur, atque si a Caesare ipso gesta sunt.

As La. M. de W.

κάλλιον] 'very well' A. and R.V.: not at all implying that he understood the point better than he pretended to, but rather perhaps a polite use of the comparative, cf. xvii. 21 n., and 2 Tim. i. 18 βέλτιον σὺ γινώσκεις.

10, 11. Ἰουδ. οὐδὲν ἠδίκηκα…εἰ μὲν οὖν ἀδικῶ] Paul says 'of offences against the Jews I am not guilty, as you know, and therefore refuse to be sacrificed to a Jewish court: if I am guilty of any crime against Roman law, let it go before a Roman court '.

παραιτοῦμαι] *deprecor.*

δύναται] 'is able', that is, legally.

χαρίσασθαι] iii. 14 n.

12. Καίσαρα ἐπικαλοῦμαι] *Caesarem appello.* In capital cases the Roman law had always allowed an appeal to the people (*provocatio ad populum*). This right of appeal from any magistrate was confirmed by the *Lex Valeria et Horatia*

b.c. 449 and by the *Lex Valeria* b.c. 300. The emperor
represented the Roman people, and so the appeal passed to
him.

Cf. Pliny's conduct with regard to the Christians in *Epist.*
Bithynia: *quos, quia cives Romani erant, adnotavi in urbem* ^{x. 97.}
remittendos.

τοῦ συμβουλίου] Probably the chief officers and personal retinue of the procurator. These constantly acted as
a council of assessors to a Roman governor. They were
technically known as *cohors*, cf. Hor. *Sat.* i. 7. 23 *laudat
Brutum laudatque cohortem; Epist.* iii. 6; Cic. *ad Q. Fr.*
i. 1. 4 *quos aut ex domesticis convictionibus aut ex necessa-
riis apparationibus tecum esse voluisti, qui quasi ex cohorte
praetoris appellari solent.*

13. Ἀγρίππας ὁ βασ.] Son of Herod Agrippa I., brother
of Drusilla and Bernice; the last of the Herods; only 17
when his father died, a.d. 44, and too young to receive his
father's kingdom, Cuspius Fadus being sent as procurator
to Judaea. He was made king of Chalcis a.d. 48; received
the tetrarchies of Philip and Lysanias (Luke iii. 1) a.d. 53.
He was governor of the temple and appointed the high
priest. His title was only a courtesy title, as he was really
a vassal of the Roman empire. He endeavoured to dissuade
the Jews from their great rebellion in 66 a.d., and afterwards retired to Rome, where he died a.d. 100.

Βερνίκη] = Φερενίκη, *Veronica* (and cf. *Victoria*); a noted
beauty; she had originally married her uncle Herod of
Chalcis, but after his death lived with Agrippa. She became ^{Suet. Tit.}
afterwards the mistress of Titus. ^{7.}

ἀσπασάμενοι] So אABEHLP. T.R. ἀσπασόμενοι 'to
salute', which certainly gives a preferable sense.

Agrippa visited the new governor to pay his respects
and to indicate his acknowledgment of Roman supremacy,
much as an Indian prince might do to a new Governor-
general.

14. ἀνέθετο] R.V. 'laid Paul's case before': the verb
is used of communicating something with a view to consul-
tation or receiving an opinion. Cf. Gal. ii. 2 ἀνεθέμην
αὐτοῖς τὸ εὐαγγέλιον...of Paul laying before the Apostles at
Jerusalem an account of the gospel he taught among the
Gentiles.

Festus would do this on account of Agrippa's acquaintance with the Jews and the Jewish religion, cf. xxvi. 3, 27.

16. πρὶν ἤ...ἔχοι] Optative because the sentence passes
into oblique narration. Direct speech would be πρὶν ἄν...ἔχῃ.

τόπον = *locum*, 'opportunity'.

16—2

244   ACTS OF THE APOSTLES. [xxv. 18

Text ℵABC EL, ἐπέφερον HP.

18. αἰτίαν ἔφερον] T.R. ἐπέφερον, which is more classical; cf. Thuc. vi. 76 αἰτίαν εὐπρεπῆ ἐπενεγκόντες.

ὧν ἐγὼ ὑπενόουν πονηρῶν] Festus had suspected some serious charge (1) from the strong feeling shewn by the Jews, (2) from the length of Paul's imprisonment.

19. τῆς ἰδίας δεισιδαιμονίας] Cf. xvii. 22 n. The rendering 'superstition' is certainly wrong: Agrippa, whom Festus addresses, was at any rate professedly a Jew. Festus says '*their own* religion' because as such it did not concern a Roman magistrate.

ἔφασκεν] 'alleged', suggesting that the statement was false, cf. xxiv. 9; Rom. i. 22 φάσκοντες εἶναι σοφοὶ ἐμωράνθησαν.

Text ℵABH P.

20. ἀπορούμενος ... τὴν ... ζήτησιν] T.R. has εἰς before τήν. But ἀπορεῖσθαι can take a direct acc. e.g. Plat. *Crat.* 309 D τὸ πῦρ ἀπορῶ; Thuc. v. 40 ταῦτα ἀποροῦντες. The reason Festus assigns differs from that assigned to him ver. 9.

ἔλεγον εἰ βούλοιτο] Apparently εἰ βούλοιτο is the oblique form of the direct question εἰ βούλει; 'dost thou wish?'—'I said to him, did he wish...'.

21. ἐπικαλεσαμένου τηρηθῆναι] 'having made appeal to be kept'. The 'making appeal' involved a request: hence the infinitive.

Merivale c. xxx.

τοῦ Σεβαστοῦ] The Gk rendering of *Augustus*. Octavian assumed this *agnomen* B.C. 27. The adj. had never been used as a name before, but was applied to things venerable and sacred, cf. Ov. *Fast.* I. 609 sancta vocant augusta patres, augusta vocantur templa. By his successors it was assumed as a title.

Text ℵABCE.

ἀναπέμψω] 'send up' to a central authority, or from a province to the metropolis. T.R. πέμψω.

22. ἐβουλόμην] 'I was wishing'. The expression is a polite request which Festus immediately grants; 'I was wishing to hear him myself too. To-morrow you shall hear him'. The imperfect is due to a tendency, common to many languages, to soften the direct 'I wish' or 'I want'. The imperfect is less direct than the present: 'I was wishing' says Agrippa courteously, and the imperfect implies that, if the wish is inconvenient, it may be taken as withdrawn and no longer existing.

It is usual to quote in illustration Gal. iv. 20 ἤθελον δὲ παρεῖναι and Rom. ix. 3 ηὐχόμην γὰρ ἀνάθεμα εἶναι αὐτός, but in those passages the imperfect is put for the imperfect with ἄν, and ἄν is omitted to make the wish more emphatic and unconditional—in fact the exact opposite of the form of wish here.

23. φαντασίας] 'pomp', 'parade'; cf. Herod. VII. 10 τὰ ὑπερέχοντα ζῷα κεραυνοῖ ὁ θεὸς οὐδ᾽ ἐᾷ φαντάζεσθαι.

ἀκροατήριον] *auditorium*, 'hall of audience'. The hearing was semi-judicial, to obtain materials for a statement of the case to the emperor, cf. ver. 26.

26. τῷ κυρίῳ] *Domino*. *Dominus* = 'master' or 'owner' and, as being specially applied to the relationship of a master to his slaves, the appellation was repudiated by Augustus and Tiberius, but it soon began to be regularly applied to the emperors by the servility of a later age. It is still to be found as a title on the degree lists of the University of Cambridge. *(margin: Suet. Aug. 53. Tib. 27.)*

ἀνακρίσεως] In cases of appeal the judge who allowed the appeal had to send what were termed *litterae dimissoriae* or *apostoli*, containing a statement of the case. So Marcianus: *Post appellationem interpositam litterae dandae sunt ab eo, a quo appellatum est, ad eum qui de appellatione cogniturus est, sive principem sive quem alium. Quas litteras dimissorias sive apostolos appellant.* *(margin: Brissonius, p. 439.)*

CHAPTER XXVI.

1. ἐκτείνας τὴν χεῖρα] An oratorical gesture.

2, 3. ἐπὶ σοῦ...μάλιστα γνώστην ὄντα σε] T.R. adds εἰδώς with no authority. R.V. gives the right sense, 'especially because I know thee to be expert...'. The acc. is governed by the sense of 'thinking' or 'considering', which is the main idea of the sentence.

ἐθῶν] *consuetudinum, in practicis,* ζητημάτων *quaestionum, in theoreticis.* B.

4. τὴν μὲν οὖν...] vv. 2 and 3 contain the preliminary *captatio benevolentiae.* Paul now passes on with the transitional particles μὲν οὖν (ii. 41 n.) to the *narratio* or statement of his case: 'with regard then to my mode of life...'. But at ver. 6 the account of his life is interrupted by a parenthesis, the speaker being desirous of pointing out that his new belief is not opposed to his old belief when a Pharisee, but a legitimate development of it. The account of his life is then markedly resumed, ver. 9, with ἐγὼ μὲν οὖν.... *(margin: La. A.)*

For a very similar instance cf. Dem. 945 πρῶτον μὲν οὖν ἀναγνώσεται τὰς συνθήκας ... καί μοι λαβὲ τὰς συνθήκας...

246 ACTS OF THE APOSTLES. [XXVI. 4

ΣΥΝΘΗΚΑΙ. αἱ μὲν οὖν συνθῆκαι.... Here and ver. 9 μέν,
as frequently when introducing a narrative, has nothing to
answer to it. In ver. 9 A. and R.V. render μὲν οὖν by an
ambiguous 'verily'.

5. Φαρισαῖος] Emphatic by position.

6. καὶ νῦν] '*and* now'. As I was in my youth a Pharisee, *so now also* it is because I have shared the Pharisees'
hope of a Messiah and belief in a resurrection that I am
accused.

ἐπ' ἐλπίδι] The hope is the ground or basis of the
charge. The ' promise...' is the Messiah, as xiii. 32.

7. εἰς ἥν] 'into which', i.e. into the fulfilment of
which.

τὸ δωδεκάφυλον] Only here, but cf. James i. 1 ταῖς
δώδεκα φυλαῖς ταῖς ἐν τῇ διασπορᾷ. The term comprises the
whole of the Jews throughout the world, and expresses a
certain national pride, and sense of national unity in spite
of dispersion.

ἐν ἐκτενείᾳ...] Cf. the instances of Simeon and Anna,
Luke ii. 25—38.

ὑπὸ 'Ιουδαίων] Indignantly last.—A Jew for expecting
Messiah accused by Jews!

8. τί ἄπιστον...] Suddenly turning from the king (cf.
βασιλεῦ) to the whole audience (cf. παρ' ὑμῖν) Paul answers
their unexpressed objection by referring to the resurrection
as a proof that Jesus is the Messiah. They would have
urged : Jesus is not the Messiah, for He was crucified, and
is dead ; Paul replies : Jesus is risen, and why not ? Is it
incredible that God raises the dead?

ἄπιστον εἰ] Possibly merely ' incredible *that*', as θαυμασ-
τὸν εἰ continually ; but it is better to render εἰ 'if', for Paul
is putting the case as a *hypothesis* which is not incredible.

9. ἐγὼ μὲν οὖν...] Resuming the narrative. The
parenthesis of vv. 6, 7, 8 seems to possess great vividness
and reality, and to be such a parenthesis as a powerful and
passionate speaker might introduce naturally arising out of
the statement of facts. The argument of the abrupt question in ver. 8 is not expressed with smooth fulness, but
Paul's arguments often seem abrupt; like a powerful
mathematician he omits several steps in rapidly reaching
his conclusion.

So ap-
parently
A. and
R.V.
Others take ἐγὼ μὲν οὖν... as an answer to the question
contained in ver. 8, explaining ' and indeed there was a
time when I thought the same and persecuted Christianity'.

But (1) such a use of μὲν οὖν in reply needs justification,
(2) the words do not answer the question of ver. 8 at all,
they say 'I did everything to injure the name of Jesus',
(3) the question in ver. 8 is rhetorical and needs no answer.

ἐγώ...ἔδοξα ἐμαυτῷ...τῶν ἁγίων ἐγώ] *Ita egoismus saepe
fallitur.*

Ἰησοῦ τοῦ Ναζ.] The distinctively human name of
Jesus. Paul speaks from the point of view he held before
his conversion : to him then Jesus was 'Jesus the Nazarene',
not ' Jesus the Messiah'.

10. τῶν ἁγίων] Used in the same connection ix. 13.

κατήνεγκα ψῆφον] Not found elsewhere : R.V. 'I gave
my vote against them'. The phrase is much more vivid
and pictorial than κατεψηφίσαμην ; ἀναιρουμένων αὐτῶν is of
course the gen. absolute, but it also supplies the genitive
which has mentally to be supplied as the object of κατήνεγκα
ψῆφον.

Others render κατήνεγκα 'I deposited', i.e. in the urn or M. A.
ballot-box, a rendering which takes all force from the Vulg. *detuli*
passage. *sententiam.*
It is clear that Paul must have been a member of the *tiam.*
Sanhedrin.

11. ἠνάγκαζον βλασφημεῖν] A.V. 'compelled them to
blaspheme' ; R. V. rightly 'I strove to make them blaspheme'. The imperfect sense is not due however to the As A. H.
verb being in the imperfect, for the imperfect merely indi- Cook.
cates that Paul's efforts were repeated, but to the fact that
ἀναγκάζω merely means 'to bring compulsory (not voluntary) motives to bear', and does not indicate whether the
compulsion is effective or not; cf. Gal. vi. 12 ἀναγκάζουσι
περιτέμνεσθαι, 'they try to make you be circumcised'.

βλασφημεῖν i.e. εἰς Ἰησοῦν : the word is the opposite of
εὐφημεῖν.
Cf. Pliny, *Ep.* x. 97, where he writes to Trajan that he
compelled certain men accused of being Christians *male-
dicere Christo*, and adds *quorum nihil cogi posse dicuntur
qui sunt revera Christiani. Ergo dimittendos putavi.*

τὰς ἔξω πόλεις] i.e. outside Palestine.

12. ἐν οἷς] i.e. in connection with their leaving Palestine and my following them beyond it.

ἐξουσίας καὶ ἐπιτροπῆς] A. and R.V. 'authority and
commission'. ἐπιτροπή is any office or duty *entrusted* (ἐπι-
τρέπω) to a person, ἐξουσία the authority attaching to one
holding official position and power.

13. οὐρανόθεν...] ix. 3 φῶς ἀπὸ τοῦ οὐρανοῦ, xxii. 6 φῶς ἱκανόν. For the variations in the three accounts, cf. ix. 4 n. It is clear that Paul here interweaves with the words of Jesus others spoken to him subsequently by Ananias, or communicated to 'him in subsequent visions (cf. ver. 16 ὧν τε ὀφθήσομαί σοι), or which seem necessary to explain the exact meaning of the divine call to his hearers.

Doubtless Paul, believing that from his conversion his divine Master had been in frequent direct communication with him, never thought of critically distinguishing the message conveyed at one time from the similar or fuller message conveyed at another, or the fuller understanding of it which came later. Luke certainly saw nothing unreasonable in giving the words of Jesus here differently, or he would not have left such variations in his three accounts. Deliberate forgery would certainly not have left them as they stand. On the other hand the variations are a direct warning to those who found dogmatic statements on isolated words or phrases of Scripture.

14. τῇ Ἑβρ. διαλέκτῳ] Only in this account : a natural addition, as Paul is probably speaking in Greek.

σκληρόν σοι...] Only here, its introduction in the other accounts being without authority. The proverb is common in Greek, e.g. Aesch. *Ag.* 1624 πρὸς κέντρα μὴ λάκτιζε, and cf. Ter. *Phorm.* I. 2. 27 *quae inscitia est! advorsum stimulum calces!* It is taken from an ox that being pricked with a goad kicks and receives a severer wound. The application here is to Paul's resistance referred to in ver. 9.

16. ἀνάστηθι καὶ στῆθι] Emphatic assonance. Cf. Eph. vi. 13 (quoted below, ver. 22 n.). The latter part of the phrase is from Ezek. ii. 1 Υἱὲ ἀνθρώπου, στῆθι ἐπὶ τοὺς πόδας σου.

προχειρίσασθαι] 'appoint', iii. 20. **ὑπηρέτην**] *ministrum.*

ὧν τε εἶδές με ὧν τε ὀφθήσομαί σοι] 'of what thou hast seen (the present vision) and of the visions in which I shall (hereafter) be seen by thee'. For such visions cf. xviii. 9, xxiii. 11; 2 Cor. xii. 2.

ὧν ὀφθ. = ἐκείνων ἃ ὀφθ., where ἃ is acc. plural, such a use being very common with the neuter plural of pronouns even after intransitive verbs, and ἃ ὁρῶμαί σοι = exactly 'the visions in which I am seen by you'. Cf. Soph. *Oed. T.* 788 ὧν μὲν ἱκόμην ἄτιμον ἐξέπεμψεν. The passive form of the phrase is due to a desire to bring out the *agency of God.*

de W. H.   **17. ἐξαιρούμενος**] 'choosing', not 'delivering' as A. and R.V. The use of τοῦ λαοῦ shews this: when the Jews are referred to as *enemies* they are Ἰουδαῖοι (cf. vv. 7, 21); λαός is their name of honour,—Paul is chosen from the chosen people and from all the world. Cf. ix. 15 ; where he is called σκεῦος ἐκλογῆς, in special reference, as here, to his conversion.

Elsewhere in the Acts (vii. 10, 34, xii. 11, xxiii. 27) the word means 'deliver'. It can bear either meaning: the context must in each case determine the right one. Nor is the reference to Jer. i. 8 and 1 Chron. xvi. 35 sufficiently definite to fix the meaning here, where 'delivering' spoils the sense.

18.   ἀνοῖξαι...] For ἀνοῖξαι ὀφθαλμούς, cf. Is. xlii. 7, and for ἀπὸ σκότους, Is. xlii. 16 ποιήσω αὐτοῖς τὸ σκότος εἰς φῶς.

ἀνοῖξαι is the infinitive of purpose, and τοῦ ἐπιστρέψαι is subordinate to it (='that then they may turn'), τοῦ λαβεῖν being again subordinate to this and expressing the final result aimed at.

πίστει τῇ εἰς ἐμέ] Note the emphatic position of these words and the special emphasis of the words τῇ εἰς ἐμέ.

19.   ὅθεν] i.e. as the conclusion of all this which has been described.

οὐκ ἐγενόμην ἀπειθής] *Litotes: plane statim obedii.* B. For ὀπτασίᾳ cf. ὀπτανόμενος i. 3 n.

20.   πᾶσαν] So אAB omitting εἰς; but surely εἰς is needed and the preceding οἷς may account for its omission. In the text the acc. must represent the *space over which* their teaching extended.

ἄξια τῆς μετ.] Cf. Matt. iii. 8 ποιήσατε οὖν καρπὸν ἄξιον τῆς μετανοίας.

22.   ἕστηκα] *sto*, a picturesque word, expressing immoveable firmness.   Cf. Paul's words Eph. vi. 13 ἀντιστῆναι ἐν τῇ ἡμέρᾳ τῇ πονηρᾷ καὶ ἅπαντα κατεργασάμενοι στῆναι. στῆτε οὖν....

μαρτυρόμενος] 'protesting', אABHLP. T.R. μαρτυρούμενος, which means 'of good repute', cf. vi. 3.

οὐδὲν ἐκτὸς...] Again reverting to his main point, that Christianity is the fulfilment of the Jewish religion, Jesus the Jewish Messiah.

οἱ προφῆται...καὶ Μωνσῆς] So Luke xvi. 29 ἔχουσι Μωσέα καὶ τοὺς προφήτας.   Moses was the greatest of 'those who declared God's will'.   Cf. iii. 22 n.

23.   εἰ] 'whether', not that Paul considered it question- So B.
able, but because it was the question at issue with the Jews.

παθητὸς] V. *passibilis*, 'subject to suffering', as R.V.
in margin. The word='one liable to suffer' (παθεῖν), so
Plut. *Pelop.* 16 τὸ θνητὸν καὶ παθητόν, but, from the well-
known use of παθεῖν in connection with 'the Passion' (e.g.
i. 3) it here specially means 'liable to be put to death'.
A.V. 'should suffer', R.V. 'must suffer', and Beza *fuisse
passurum*, giving a good sense but neglecting the Greek.

La. M.
de W.

εἰ πρῶτος...] A.V. mistranslates and mars the sense,
'should be the first that should rise from the dead, and
should shew light...': R.V. better, 'that he first by the
resurrection of the dead should proclaim light...'. A more
accurate rendering would be 'that he first by *a* resurrection
from the dead...'
Others Paul believed to have risen from the dead, as for
instance Lazarus, but Christ 'first by a resurrection from
the dead proclaimed light', because, while they died afterwards, Christ's rising again was the first instance of that of
which it is the earnest, viz. a resurrection to life everlast-
ing; cf. 1 Cor. xv., and Rom. vi. 9 Χριστὸς ἐγερθεὶς ἐκ νεκρῶν
οὐκέτι ἀποθνήσκει.

φῶς: cf. ver. 18, and Luke ii. 32 φῶς εἰς ἀποκάλυψιν
ἐθνῶν.

24.　**ταῦτα...ἀπολογουμένου**] Present part., shewing that
it was the latter portion of Paul's discourse which provoked
the exclamation of Festus.

As A.

μαίνῃ] 'Thou art mad'. The word does not in any
way describe 'insanity'. It merely represents the opinion
which practical common-sense men often form of the speculations of an enthusiast: it is immediately defined by its
opposite, he who 'is mad' does not speak words 'of reality
and soberness'. An Athenian would have used the word of
any abstruse philosopher.
Cf. the description of a philosophic 'madman' Plato
Phaedr. 249 D ἐξιστάμενος τῶν ἀνθρωπίνων σπουδασμάτων
καὶ πρὸς τῷ θείῳ γιγνόμενος νουθετεῖται μὲν ὑπὸ τῶν πολλῶν
ὡς παρακινῶν, ἐνθουσιάζων δὲ λέληθε τοὺς πολλούς.

τὰ πολλά σε γράμματα] Note the remarkable position
of σέ: *multae illae te litterae*: 'that great learning of thine'.
The word γράμματα no doubt refers to knowledge of the
Hebrew Scriptures (αἱ γραφαί), cf. John vii. 15 πῶς οὗτος
γράμματα οἶδεν μὴ μεμαθηκώς; and γραμματεύς='a scribe'.

La.

25.　**ἀληθείας καὶ σωφρ. ῥήμ.**] The first gen. is objective, the second subjective: the words describe the exact
facts, and are uttered by one in full possession of a con-
trolled reason.

A. and R.V. give σωφροσύνης = 'soberness', but note that σώφρων is from σῶς φρήν, *sobrius* from *so* (= *se*) -*ebrius*.

28. ἐν ὀλίγῳ με πείθεις Χριστιανὸν ποιῆσαι] ποιῆσαι אAB; T.R. with EHLP γενέσθαι, which seems a correction for the more difficult ποιῆσαι.

ἐν ὀλίγῳ is clearly = 'with little (trouble, effort)', ἐν being instrumental, its sense being determined by the use of the phrase in Paul's reply ἐν ὀλ. καὶ ἐν μεγάλῳ = 'with little or with great (trouble)'. It cannot = ἐν ὀλίγῳ χρόνῳ 'quickly', for ἐν μεγάλῳ (so אAB but T.R. ἐν πολλῷ with HLP) could not mean 'in much time'.

The words seem spoken chiefly with reference to Paul's *brief* final appeal directly to Agrippa, and to be a light in-different dismissal of the subject 'not in a jeering tone but La. without real earnestness'—'With little art thou persuading me (so as) to have made me a Christian'. It should be noted that πείθεις does not express the actual effecting of persuasion, but only 'the effort to persuade'. So R.V. rightly gives 'wouldest fain make'.

A has the reading πείθῃ, and this certainly improves Alford the sense and gives ποιῆσαι a more intelligible construction. and 'With little art thou persuaded (cf. οὐ πείθομαι ver. 26) to Lach-mann have made me a Christian'. have this

The use of Χριστιανός is certainly not as 'an offensive reading. appellation': the whole discourse of Paul had been about ὁ As A. χριστός; he had shewn why he believed that the Messiah had come, and Agrippa not unnaturally characterizes one who holds such a belief as Χριστιανός, 'a Messiah-follower'. Agrippa was a Jew, and 'Messiah-follower' would not be used by a Jew as 'an offensive appellation'.

On the other hand it is impossible to take Agrippa's M. de words as sober earnest, 'With thy few words thou art per- W. suading me to become...'. The emphasis on ἐν ὀλίγῳ is too marked to allow this; it also involves the acceptance of γενέσθαι, and then neglects the aorist ('to have become', not 'to become').

29. καὶ ἐν μεγάλῳ] '*or with great*', so δὶς καὶ τρίς, *terque* B. *quaterque*.

31. πράσσει] *agit egitque. Non de una actione sed de tota vita Pauli loquuntur.*

32. ἐδύνατο] ἄν is often omitted with simple verbs such as ἔδει (xxiv. 19), ἐχρῆν &c. So in Latin *poterat, debebat*, instead of *posset, deberet.*

CHAPTER XXVII.

1. ἐκρίθη τοῦ ἀποπλεῖν] The gen. gives the purport of
the decision, cf. iii. 12 n., xx. 3 n.

v. La. **σπείρης Σεβαστῆς]** *cohortis Augustae.* The adj. 'Augus-
tan' applied to troops affords as little means for identifying
them as 'Royal' would now-a-days. All conjectures as to
what the cohort was and who Julius was are worthless.

The words certainly do not mean a cohort of men from
Σεβαστή = Samaria, which would require σπεῖρα Σεβαστηνῶν.

As A. To refer to the *Augustani* of Tac. *Ann.* xiv. 15, troops
W. specially selected by Nero to applaud his artistic perform-
ances, is more than arbitrary.

Possibly the adj. was applied by way of distinction to
one of the cohorts at Caesarea specially attached to the
person of the procurator, who was the representative of 'the
Augustus'.

2. Ἀδραμυντηνῷ] Adramyttium, in Mysia, opposite
Lesbos. The vessel was probably a small coasting vessel
on its way back to Adramyttium for the winter, intending
to touch at various ports on the road (cf. πλεῖν εἰς τοὺς
κατὰ τὴν Ἀσίαν τόπους, i.e. places along the coast of Asia).
At one of these ports Julius hoped to find a larger vessel
bound for Rome, to which he might transfer his prisoners,
for it is highly improbable that he intended to take them to
Adramyttium, and then through the Troad, across the Hellespont and along the *via Egnatia* to Dyrrhachium, and so
by Brundisium to Rome.

C. & H. **3. εἰς Σιδῶνα]** 67 miles.

φιλανθρώπως...χρησάμενος] Cf. Xen. *Mem.* iv. 3. 12
φιλικῶς χρῆσθαι; Dem. 1286. 23 ὑβριστικῶς χρ.

4. ὑπεπλεύσαμεν] Cf. ver. 7, and ver. 16 ὑποδραμόντες;
R.V. 'sailed under the lee of Cyprus', i.e. so that Cyprus
was between us and the wind, on the left hand, and we
were 'sailing through the sea off Cilicia and Pamphylia'.
The direct course would have been straight to Patara keeping to the S. of Cyprus (as Paul had come from Patara, xxi.
1—3), but the Etesian winds from the N.W. were still blowing and would have been dead in their teeth.

Smith. On the coast of Cilicia 'they might expect to be favoured
p. 67. by the land wind, which prevails there during the summer
months, as well as by the current, *which constantly runs to
the westward*, along the S. coast of Asia Minor'.

5. Μύρρα] An important town 2½ miles from the sea:
its port Andriace had an excellent harbour.

6. πλοῖον Ἀλεξανδρινὸν] Rome with its vast population was, like London, mainly dependent on imported corn, the supply from Egypt being especially large. It seems probable that this ship was a corn-ship, cf. ver. 38 n., and its presence at Myrra would be accounted for by the unfavourable winds. Such ships were usually employed for conveying passengers (e.g. Titus returned to Rome in one after the capture of Jerusalem), and a cargo of corn would in no way interfere with this. If the number 276 in ver. 37 be correct it is calculated that the ship must have been of 500 tons burden. *Suet. Tit. 5.*

7. κατὰ τὴν Κνίδον] 130 m. from Myra, a Lacedaemonian colony of great importance, on the promontory of Triopium in Caria; it had two harbours, that on the E. being especially large. It was the scene of the naval defeat of Pisander by Conon B.C. 394.

μὴ προσεῶντος] Up to this point in spite of the continuous N.W. winds they had worked along by tacking, though slowly (βραδυπλοοῦντες) and with difficulty (μόλις), but now 'they lost the advantage of a favouring current, a weather shore and smooth water, and were met by all the force of the wind from the westward'. At this point therefore the wind *stopped their further course* (μὴ προσεῶντος); they could not hold on in the direct course, which would have been 'by the north side of Crete, through the Archipelago, W. by S.' They therefore made for Salmone, the E. promontory of Crete, S.W. by S. from Cnidus. *C. & H.* *Smith, p. 73.*

The rendering προσεῶντος 'permitting us to enter the harbour' seems unreasonable, for (1) Why did they wish to stop at Cnidus? (2) What reason was there for not being able to enter its southern harbour? The word is a ἅπαξ λεγόμενον. *As R.V. in marg. F. M.*

8. παραλεγόμενοι] So *legere oram* in Latin commonly.

μόλις] because the same difficulties would occur as in coasting along to Cnidus.

Καλοὺς Λιμένας] At C. Matala the land 'trends suddenly to the N. and the advantages of a weather shore cease, and their only resource was to make for harbour'. Just E. of Cape Matala is such a harbour, still known as Kalus Limeónas, open to the E. and S.E. and a fair harbour, but not fit to winter in, cf. ver. 12. About a mile to the E. (and also 3 or 4 m. to the E.) ruins have been discovered, which may be those of Lasea, one of the 'hundred cities' of Crete. *Smith. p. 75.* *Smith, App.* *Spratt. Travels in Crete. II. 1—20. London. 1865.*

9. ἐπισφαλοῦς τοῦ πλοὸς] With the ancients navigation ceased in winter. Hesiod fixes the time at the setting *Works and*

Days,
619.
F.

of the Pleiades (about Oct. 20), others fix the latest day at Nov. 11. 'The fast' which is referred to is 'the one fast in the Jewish calendar', i.e. the great Day of Atonement (see Lev. xvi. 29 to end), on the 10th day of the month Tisri, about the time of the autumnal equinox, so that their arrival in Rome, before the period when sailing ceased, was extremely doubtful.

10. ὕβρεως] R.V. 'injury'. The word is a strong one, and indicates violent injury: it is the legal word for 'violent personal assault', and describes what the ship would suffer from the battering and buffeting of the waves.

ὅτι......μέλλειν] Change of construction, accounted for by the number of words intervening.

11. ναυκλήρῳ] The word usually = 'captain and owner'.

12. εἴ πως δύναιντο...] Almost giving in oblique narration their very words, ἐάν πως δυνώμεθα; 'we vote for going... on the chance that we may be able...'.

Φοίνικα] Phoenix, 'the town of palms' (φοῖνιξ): several towns of Crete have palm-trees on their coins.

So A.V.
Vulg.
W. B. H.
M.

λιμένα τῆς Κ. βλέποντα κατὰ λίβα καὶ κατὰ χῶρον] 'a harbour of Crete which faces the S.W. and N.W.'
Λίψ is *Africus*, the African or Libyan wind, Χῶρος the Latin *Caurus* in Gk letters.

The ancients having no compass or exact maps, continually mark direction by the quarter from which a wind blows; indeed they had no other method of marking the points of the compass, except for the four quarters N., S., W. and E.

A harbour 'looks' or 'faces' (or 'has its mouth') *seaward* always, and a harbour βλέπει κατὰ λίβα καὶ κ. χ. when it looks towards the points of the compass indicated by λίψ and χῶρος, i.e. when one side runs towards the S.W. and the other to the N.W., the harbour thus 'looking S.W. and N.W.' and being open from those points.

Smith.

R.V. gives 'looking N.E. and S.E.', an impossible rendering, apparently due to a belief that the harbour referred to must be the harbour of Lutro, which answers that description, and is said to be the only good harbour on the coast.

Two explanations of this rendering are given, which however obtain the desired result by directly contradictory methods :—

F. and so
C. & H.

1. Taking κατὰ λίβα καὶ κ. χ. rightly, but βλέποντα wrongly: it is said that the explanation is to be found in the 'subjectivity of sailors', who 'speak of everything from their own point of view', that is to say, a sailor entering the harbour *ABC* would speak of 'the harbour' (not of 'its sides')

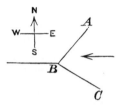

'looking N.W. and S.W.' because the side *AB* runs from *A* to *B* towards the S.W. and *CB* towards the N.W.

But (i) although sailors *naturally* speak of certain phenomena of motion from their own point of view (see xxi. 3 n.) as we talk of 'the sun rising', yet to talk of a harbour as looking landwards because they are sailing into it is *most unnatural:* a harbour can only look seawards. A harbour which you sail into from the W. cannot be said 'to look F. says towards the W.' Has any sailor ever described Torbay as it can. 'looking towards the W.'? Where is the proof of this startling 'subjectivity of sailors' or anyone else? When you enter a cathedral walking northwards does the door you enter by 'look towards the N.'?

(ii) Assuming that it is *conceivable* that any one sailing into a harbour from the W. should describe the harbour as 'looking west', yet it is *inconceivable* that he should describe 'the harbour' (not 'its sides') as 'looking N.W. and S.W.', for the *double* point of view is only possible for any one placed, or mentally placing himself, at the point *B*, and such a person can only describe the sides *BA*, *BC* as looking N.E. and S.E.

2. Taking κατὰ λ. καὶ κ. χ. wrongly but βλέποντα rightly, Smith, as indicating the way the harbour faces from the point *B* Alford. looking *seaward:* it is urged that κατὰ λίβα = 'in a N.E. direction' because the wind from the S.W. blows towards the N.E. and κατὰ indicates the line of motion, which is N.E. So too κ. χῶρον = 'in S.E. direction'.

But (i) no doubt κατὰ ῥόον, κατ' οὖρον, κατ' ἄνεμον are common enough, and mean 'in the direction of a stream, wind, &c.', i.e. down the line of motion of the stream or wind; they cannot however be used except of an object *in motion*, e.g. a ship, and in reference to a stream or wind *actually in movement*. Now a harbour does not *move* and must look κατὰ λίβα whether λίψ is blowing or not: moreover, if λίψ and χῶρος represent, not points of the compass, but winds in motion, then κατὰ λίβα κ α ὶ κατὰ χῶρον involves the assertion that two winds are blowing at the same time.

(ii) βλέπειν κατά τι can only be used of that which is *opposite* you, which you *face;* cf. Luke's own use of κατὰ, κατὰ πρόσωπον (iii. 13); κατὰ τὴν Μυσίαν (xvi. 7) 'with Mysia in front of you'; κατὰ τὴν Κνίδον (xxvii. 7) 'off' or 'opposite Cnidus'; πορεύου κατὰ μεσημβρίαν (viii. 26) 'go with your face towards the south'. If βλέπω κατὰ λίβα can mean 'The S.W. wind is blowing *on my back*', language must cease to be intelligible. Even πορεύομαι κατὰ λίβα would mean 'I go to the S.W.' The only case where κατὰ λίβα could mean 'to the N.E.' would be in such a sentence as ναῦς κατὰ λίβα φέρεται, where λίψ is distinctly referred to as *in movement* and *the cause of movement.*

It will be observed that Luke never reached Phoenix, and that his remark is a mere *obiter dictum* derived from

PHINEKA 〜 LUTRO

Smith,
p. 94.
report, and quite possibly an error. Moreover there is marked on the map a harbour opposite Lutro which does look S.W. and N.W. and has the name Phineka[1].

13. ὑποπνεύσαντος] ὑπό in composition = 'slightly', cf. Hom. *Il.* IV. 423 Ζεφύρου ὑποκινήσαντος; so too ὑποταρβεῖν, ὑποταράσσειν: and *sub* as in *subagrestis, subaccusare.*

τῆς προθέσεως] viz. to reach Phoenix; after passing C. Matala a S. wind would enable them to reach any harbour such as Lutro. κεκρατηκέναι = 'to have got within their
Dr Field. grasp'. Cf. Diod. Sic. XVI. 20 κεκρατηκότες ἤδη τῆς προθέσεως.

ἄραντες] A.V. 'loosing thence'; lit. 'having started' or 'moved'; B. *moventes.* R.V. has 'having weighed anchor', as though the word meant 'to lift', and 'anchor' had to be supplied, but even in classical Gk the word means simply 'to move', and is used transitively or intransitively, and of movement either by sea or land, cf. Thuc. I. 52 ἄραντες τὰς ναῦς; IV. 129 ἄρ. ταῖς ναυσίν; II. 23 ἄραντες περιέπλεον; but II. 12 ἄρας τῷ στρατῷ; II. 23 ἄραντες ἐκ τῶν Ἀχαρνῶν, and II. 98 of land marches.

ἆσσον] 'nearer', 'closer to the shore', an adv. comparative of ἄγχι. Long mistaken for a proper name; cf. V. *cum sustulissent de Asson.*

---

[1] The whole of this note was originally written independently of Wordsworth's note, with which it remarkably agrees.

14. ἔβαλεν] 'dashed' or 'beat', intransitive, or rather reflexive; 'flung (itself)', 'dashed (itself) down', cf. ἐπιδόντες ver. 15, ἐρείσασα ver. 41, ἀπορίψαντας ver. 43.

κατ' αὐτῆς] 'down from it', i.e. from Crete; for the construction cf. the Homeric usage, κατ' Οὐλύμποιο καρήνων, κατ' Ἰδαίων ὀρέων 'down from'.

αὐτῆς naturally refers to Κρήτης, and the wind did actually blow 'down from Crete'; see next note.

κατ' αὐτῆς cannot be 'down on her', i.e. the ship, supplying νεώς, for the ship is πλοῖον throughout, and only ναῦς ver. 41. As A.V.

ἄνεμος...Εὐρακύλων] Whether Euraquilo or Euroclydon represent the right reading, the wind referred to was certainly Euraquilo, 'the N.E. wind', or 'E.N.E. wind', for (1) the wind struck the vessel when off C. Matala and drove her under Cauda, which is about 20 m. S.W. of that point, (2) the sailors feared to be driven on to the Syrtis, and that is exactly where a N.E. wind would have taken them. Εὐρακύ-
λων
אAB.
Εὐρο-
κλύδων
T.R.
with
HLP.

The wind would descend from Mt Ida, which was just above them, '*in heavy squalls and eddies*' and drive the now helpless ship far from the shore'. The words in Italics exactly represent τυφωνικός, which describes the *character* of the gale, just as Εὐρακύλων gives its *direction*. Sir C.
Penrose
in C.& H.
See too
Spratt in
Smith,
p. 97.

Εὐροκλύδων seems to represent a corruption of *Euraquilo*, possibly by Gk sailors, suggesting a false but tempting etymology from κλύζω κλύδων (cf. our 'Charter House' 'cray-*fish*', 'lant*horn*', and other false etymologies).

Euraquilo will be a wind lying between Eurus and Aquilo (cf. Euronotus in Pliny), but, as Aquilo may not be a wind blowing from due N. but is placed by Pliny *inter septentrionem et exortum solstitialem*, it may be rather a wind from E.N.E. than from N.E. N. H.
II. 47.
Smith,
App. 4
and 5.

15. ἀντοφθαλμεῖν] 'face the wind' R.V. The violence of the N.E. gale prevented her getting her head (or 'eyes') enough to the wind to make Phoenix. Great eyes were often painted on the prows of vessels.

ἐπιδόντες ἐφερόμεθα] 'giving (ourselves) up (i.e. to the wind), we were being carried along', i.e. scudded before the gale. Cf. Hom. *Od.* v. 343 σχεδίην ἀνέμοισι φέρεσθαι | κάλλιπε.

16. Καῦδα] or Κλαῦδα, now Govdo. They took advantage of the comparatively smooth water under the lee of Cauda, (1) to get the boat on board, (2) to undergird the vessel. Spratt,
II. 274
in La.

P.   17

μόλις] Doubtless owing to the sea being only comparatively smooth and the boat almost full of water. For
σκάφη 'a small boat', usually towed behind, cf. Cic. *de
Invent.* II. 51 *funiculo qui a puppi religatus scapham annexam
trahebat.*

H.

17. βοηθείαις] What these 'helps' were the participle
ὑποζωννύντες defines : they were ὑποζώματα or cables, passed
round the hull of the ship, and tightly secured on deck, to
prevent the timbers from starting, especially amidships,
where in ancient vessels with one large mast the strain was
very great. Cf. Hor. *Od.* I. 14. 6 *ac sine funibus | vix du-
rare carinae | possint imperiosius | aequor ;* Plat. *Rep.* 616 c.
The technical English word is 'frapping', but the process has only been rarely employed since the early part of
the century, owing to improvements in shipbuilding.

**Smith,
p. 105.**

τὴν Σύρτιν] Clearly the *Syrtis Major*, which derived its
name from the dangerous *sand-banks* (σύρτις from σύρω) in
it. Cf. the description of the fleet of Aeneas in the same
seas, Virg. *Aen.* I. 111 *tres Eurus ab alto | in brevia et syrtes
urget.*

ἐκπέσωσιν] Classical Gk for a ship being driven out of
her course in the deep seas (cf. *ab alto urget* above) on to
shoals, rocks, &c. Cf. Xen. *Anab.* VII. 5. 12 τῶν νεῶν πολλαὶ
ὀκέλλουσι καὶ ἐκπίπτουσιν; Herod. VIII. 13. In Latin *ejicior.*

H.

χαλάσαντες τὸ σκεῦος] 'having lowered (cf. χαλασάντων
ver. 30) the gear'. One point seems clear, viz. that the neut.
sing. σκεῦος denotes a single thing, or a single thing and its
accompaniments, so differing from the collective σκευή (ver.
19)=*supellex.* Cf. the use of the word ix. 15, x. 11, and
Luke viii. 16. Moreover the definite article describes something which was specially '*the* gear' or 'equipment' of
the ship, and this can hardly have been anything but the
mainyard and the mainsail attached to it. It is objected
to this, (1) that to have thus struck sail would have involved
their drifting straight towards the Syrtis; (2) that the vessel
would have rolled and pitched in the most dangerous manner. But (1) by striking the mainsail they would immensely
diminish their speed in the direction of the Syrtis ; (2) they
had still other sails (e.g. the *artemon* ver. 40) with which
to keep the ship steady.

**So W.
who is
very
good.
Smith,
H.**

The following explanation is *a priori* very probable, but
does not immediately arise from the text. To avoid being
driven by Euraquilo right on to the Syrtis the ship would
be laid with her head as near as possible to the wind, i.e.
within about 7 points of the wind[1]. Enough sail would be

**See
C. & H.**

[1] That is to say, a line drawn in the direction of the ship's length

kept 'to keep the ship steady, and by pressing her side down into the water prevent her from rolling violently, and also to turn her bow in the direction of the wind'. Under these conditions, thus close-hauled, a ship drifts in a direction between that of the wind and that in which her bow points, and it is said that 36 miles in 24 hours would be an average distance to drift. Moreover with 'a wind E.N.E. a ship would drift W. by N.' Now, if of 'the 14 days' (ver. 27) one was taken up with reaching Cauda, we have 13 × 36 = 468 miles of drift in a direction W. by N. from Cauda, and as a matter of fact Malta is about 480 miles from Cauda, in exactly that direction.

The explanation is very tempting and the result striking, but it will be observed that it assumes a somewhat even gale steadily blowing in one direction, and hardly agrees with διαφερομένων, ver. 27.

18. ἐκβολήν] *jacturam.* The object was to lighten the ship. So Jonah i. 5 ἐκβολὴν ἐποιήσαντο τῶν σκευῶν...τοῦ κουφισθῆναι ἀπ' αὐτῶν. The ἐκβολή here would be of part of **So R.V.** the cargo, which is the regular use of the word, cf. Aesch. *Ag.* 1008, *S. C. Th.* 755, where the reference is to a merchant flinging overboard part of his cargo to save the rest. Moreover the ἐκβολή on this day is opposed to the 'flinging-out of the furniture' on the next.

ἐποιοῦντο] Notice the imperfect. The process of lightening the ship was *commenced* by this throwing overboard of some of the cargo, and *completed* the next day (cf. ἔριψαν aorist) by flinging out the furniture.

F. asserts that the aorist ἔριψαν must describe a *single* act, and so the flinging overboard a *single* object, e.g. the great mast. But σκευή is a *collective* word = 'furniture', i.e. all the heavy articles of tackling, &c. which were not absolutely necessary.

For ἔριψαν T.R. has ἐρίψαμεν, a correction due to αὐτό- **Text** χειρες, which seems as if it should mean 'with our hands', **אABC.** indicating that on the next day the need was so urgent that Luke and Paul took part in the task. The word is however only one of the graphic words, so common in the Acts, used by the writer to make his readers vividly realize the danger.

20. μήτε δὲ...] And so without a compass they would be ignorant of their course. Cf. Virg. *Aen.* I. 85; III. 195.

λοιπὸν] Neut. adj. used adverbially, 'as regards the future'.

would form an angle of ⅔ of a right angle with the direction of the wind: if the wind were E.N.E. the ship's head would be turned N. by W., the point which lies between N.N.W. and N.

περιηρεῖτο] A very vivid word: 'was being gradually stripped from us', v. Lex.

21. ἀσιτίας] Not 'want of food', for there was corn on board (ver. 38), but 'going without food' (*jejunatio*, V.) owing to want of fires to prepare it with, &c.

σταθείς] Mark the force of this pictorial word amid such a scene; cf. xvii. 22. It is impossible not to recall the *vir justus et propositi tenax*, whom Horace depicts unmoved amid the storms of 'unreposeful Hadria'.

Od. III. 3. 1.

ἔδει μέν] μέν has nothing to answer it; the words 'but you did not listen' are omitted in courtesy.

κερδῆσαι] Does μή pass on to κερδῆσαι, or is the construction ἔδει τε κερδῆσαι?

R.V. carries on μή, rendering 'and have gotten this injury and loss'. But surely κερδῆσαι ζημίαν is a strange phrase if it means merely 'suffer loss', for κέρδος is the direct opposite of ζημία (e.g. Arist. *Eth.* v. 4) and could hardly be thus joined with it without any antithetical force.

So M. A. La. H. de W.

It is better not to carry on μή: 'you ought not to have put to sea, and (you ought by so not putting to sea) to have gained this loss', i. e. not suffered it. A person is said in Gk 'to gain a loss' when, being in danger of incurring it, he by his conduct saves himself from doing so. A merchant, who being in danger of losing 1000*l*. manages to avoid doing so, 'makes a gain of' the 1000*l*.

Cf. Arist. *Mag. Mor.* II. 8 ᾧ κατὰ λόγον ἦν ζημίαν λαβεῖν, τὸν τοιοῦτον κερδάναντα εὐτυχῆ φάμεν. So Cic. *Verr.* II. 1. 12 *lucretur indicia veteris infamiae;* and in Pliny *lucrifacere injuriam.*

23. θεοῦ...ἄγγελος] Note the emphatic position of θεοῦ 'from God...an angel'.

24. κεχάρισται] iii. 14 n., and for the general sense, Gen. xviii. 26.

27. ὡς δὲ τεσσαρ.] 'when the fourteenth night came as we continued to be driven to and fro' (present part.). The fourteenth night is clearly reckoned from the time when they began to be so driven, i.e. from the evening of the day when they left Fair Havens.

A.

διαφερομένων] certainly describes 'drifting to and fro', cf. Philo de *Migr. Abr.* p. 454 ὥσπερ σκάφος ὑπ' ἐναντίων ἀνέμων διαφερόμενον. Smith says 'being driven through the sea of Adria', but the Gk hardly justifies this. F. gives 'tossed hither and thither', but adds 'so it would appear to those on board'—an easy but unsatisfactory explanation.

ἐν τῷ Ἀδρίᾳ] Not merely 'the Adriatic', but the whole
sea between Italy and Greece. Strabo II. p. 123 ὁ Ἰόνιος H.
κόλπος μέρος ἐστὶ τοῦ νῦν Ἀδρίου καλουμένου.

προσάγειν] Intransitive, v. Lex., = 'was approaching'.
'*Lucas optice loquitur nautarum more*'. Cf. Virg. *Aen.* VIII. Kypke.
72 *Provehimus portu, terraeque urbesque recedunt*. So we
talk of 'the sun rising'. The sailors would detect the sound
of breakers, and fear a rocky coast (τραχεῖς τόπους).

29. ἐκ πρύμνης...] The ordinary practice was and is to
anchor by the bows; cf. *Aen.* III. 277 *anchora de prora jacitur*.
With a view to running the ship ashore anchoring from the Smith,
stern would, it is said, be best.   p. 132.

At the Battle of Copenhagen (April, 1801) the fleet so
anchored, and Nelson is reported to have stated 'that he C. & H.
had that morning been reading the 27th chapter of the
Acts'.

30. προφάσει] Dat. used adverbially, cf. Luke xx. 47 καὶ
προφάσει μακρὰ προσεύχονται; Thuc. VI. 76 προφάσει μὲν...
διανοίᾳ δὲ....

ἐκτείνειν] They would carry out the anchors until the
cable was taut. It is contrasted with ῥίψαντες, ver. 29.

31. σωθῆναι οὐ δύνασθε] Cf. ver. 24. *Rejici potest
promissa salus*.

33. ἄχρι δὲ οὗ...] 'up to the time when day was about to
dawn'—during the interval before dawn. Paul urged them
to use this interval for the purpose of taking food, and so
being ready for action at dawn.

34. πρὸς τῆς ὑμ. σωτηρίας] lit. 'from the side of', 'in the
interests of'. Cf. Thuc. III. 59 οὐ πρὸς τῆς ὑμετέρας δόξης;
Dem. 1006 πρὸς ἐμοῦ...τὴν ψῆφον ἔθεσθε. In Latin *ex*, cf. *e
re publica facere*.

οὐδένος γὰρ...] A proverbial expression, cf. Luke xxi. 18;
1 Kings i. 52.

35. λαβὼν ἄρτον εὐχαρίστησεν...καὶ κλάσας] From
the careful way in which Luke refers to each act here it
would seem that he describes something more than the
acts of 'an ordinary pious Jew' when beginning a meal. M. de W.
See ii. 42 n., where it is remarked that since the 'Last
Supper' the 'breaking of bread' had received for believers a
special significance as a remembrance and a hope.

37. ὡς ἑβδομήκοντα ἕξ] T.R. has διακόσιαι for ὡς, and
so R.V. ὡς rests 'on the single evidence of B', and Alford M.
marks it as due to the ω of πλοίῳ and σ (=200) of the
numeral.

38. ἐκβαλλόμενοι τὸν σῖτον] A second ἐκβολή to further lighten the ship, so that she might be run as far on to the land as possible.

As M. A.   That τὸν σῖτον refers to the cargo of corn and not to mere 'provisions' is certain. The casting overboard of 'provisions' could not have been of much service, and the fact that the ship was a trader from Alexandria to Rome removes all doubt.

39. ἐπεγίνωσκον] 'recognize', i.e. as being Melita. Cf. xxviii. 1 ἐπέγνωμεν.

αἰγιαλὸν] 'a beach', R.V. Cf. Matt. xiii. 2 ὁ ὄχλος ἐπὶ τὸν αἰγιαλὸν εἱστήκει; Acts xxi. 5. Not ἀκτή 'a rugged, rocky coast'. Dr Field aptly quotes Xen. *Anab.* vi. 4. 4 λιμὴν δ' ὑπ' αὐτῇ τῇ πέτρᾳ...αἰγιαλὸν ἔχων.

Text BC.   ἐκσῶσαι] 'get the ship safe ashore'. T.R. ἐξῶσαι, 'drive the ship up on to it'.

40. περιελόντες] lit. 'having taken away all round'; strictly used, as there were *four* anchors, which would be in a sort of semicircle round the stern.

εἴων εἰς τὴν θάλασσαν] Not 'they committed themselves unto the sea' as A.V., but 'they left them in the sea'. The notion of 'discarding', 'abandoning', is strong in εἴων and accounts for εἰς with the acc.

C. & H.   ἀνέντες τὰς ζευκτ.] 'The ships of the Greeks and Romans, like those of the early Northmen, were not steered by means of a single rudder, but by *two* paddle-rudders, one on each quarter' ... 'the hinged rudder does not appear on any of the remains of antiquity till a late period in the middle ages'. These paddle-rudders had been 'hoisted up and lashed' while the ship was at anchor, 'to prevent them fouling the anchors'. They were now required to steer the ship straight ashore.

τὸν ἀρτέμωνα] R.V. 'foresail', and so Smith, who gives illustrations of two coins of Commodus with a corn-ship on the obverse with mainsail and foresail set. Cf. Juv. xii. 68 *cucurrit | vestibus extentis et, quod superaverat unum, | velo prora suo*, where the Scholiast explains *artemone solo veli-* v. Smith, *caverunt.* The word does not occur elsewhere in Greek, but App. is found in Italian and French, though the meaning varies.

41. περιπεσόντες δὲ...] The words describe something unexpected which befell them. 'They were making for the beach (cf. κατεῖχον imperfect), but came upon (aorist) a τόπος διθάλασσος and ran the vessel aground'. They never reached the beach but unexpectedly grounded, and to reach the beach was a matter of great difficulty (cf. vv. 42—44). That what happened was unexpected is also clear from the obviously sudden resolution of the soldiers to kill their prisoners: if what happened was what they expected, why did they not propose to kill them before leaving their anchorage?

διθάλασσος is usually applied to a neck or tongue of land lying between two seas or portions of sea, a reef. Dion Chrys. 5, p. 83, mentions among the dangers of the sea τραχέα ('rocks', cf. above τραχεῖς τόπους) καὶ διθάλαττα (? half-sunken reefs), καὶ ταίνιαι (sand-banks), and so Virg. *Aen.* I. 108 refers to *saxa latentia ... dorsum immane mari summo ... brevia et syrtes,* and certainly, if we only regard the text, we should render τόπον διθ. here 'a ridge' or 'reef running out into and dividing the sea', or a 'bank', on to which they ran the ship, because being at the time wholly covered by the water they did not see it (cf. n. on ἐλύετο below).

A fairly strong case is however made out for the ship-wreck having taken place in what is known as 'St Paul's Bay', a little to the N.W. of Valetta. It is pointed out that a ship drifting W. by N. might pass very close to land off Koura Point (where the sailors would hear breakers, ver. 27), and that just beyond the soundings are 20 fathoms, and just beyond 15 fathoms, with a good anchorage. Here they

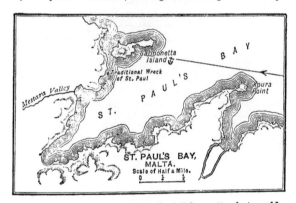

would be just off the little island of Salmonetta, but could not tell that it was an island, it being only separated from the mainland by a channel 100 yards wide. It is considered that this channel is the τόπος διθ. of Luke, and that they

M.

So
Lumby.

ran on some mudbank due to the currents caused by the channel. This is the account of Smith, who however, assuming his view generally to be right, seems clearly wrong in describing the vessel as driven on to the beach, a mistake in which he is followed by A., F., C. and H., &c. For the sense he assigns to τόπος διθ. Smith quotes Strabo II. 5. 12 who calls the Bosporus διθάλαττος τρόπον τινά.

Smith, p. 138.

ἐρείσασα] cf. ver. 14 n. A strong word, 'having planted itself firmly'.

ἐλύετο] Notice the imperfect. For the description cf. Virg. *Aen.* x. 303,

> sed non puppis tua, Tarchon.
> Namque inflicta vadis dorso dum pendet iniquo,
> Anceps sustentata diu fluctusque fatigat,
> Solvitur.

ὑπὸ τῆς βίας] So אAB. T.R. with CHLP adds τῶν κυμάτων, certainly improving the sense.

F.

42. ἵνα τοὺς δεσμώτας...] 'Soldiers were responsible with their own lives for their prisoners'; cf. xii. 19.

44. οὓς μὲν...οὓς δὲ...] So Dem. 248 πόλεις ἃς μὲν ἀναιρῶν εἰς ἃς δὲ τοὺς φυγάδας κατάγων, and this use of the relative is common in later Greek.

CHAPTER XXVIII.

1. Μελιτήνη] This is the reading of B only, and seems due to a clerical error. 'The scribe had written Μελιτη-νησος for Μελιτηηνησος omitting the article: but perceiving his mistake, expunged η̄η̄ and began again thus Μελιτη̄ν̄η̄η-νησος' Dr Field.

T.R. Μελίτη; *Melite*, Malta. That the island was Malta is shewn not only from the name and general probability, but from the fact that a ship of Alexandria (ver. 11) on the way to Puteoli had put in there for the winter, and from the reference to Syracuse (ver. 12) as the first port touched at after leaving it.

Meleda, an island off Illyria, near Ragusa, has been suggested, from a mistaken view of xxvii. 27.

2. οἱ βάρβαροι] Diod. Sic. v. 12 ἔστι δὲ ἡ νῆσος αὕτη Φοινίκων ἄποικος. Their language therefore was probably Punic. The word βάρβαρος is not in the least = 'barbarous' in the modern sense; it is an imitative word and = 'speaking unintelligibly', cf. 1 Cor. xiv. 11. The Greeks applied it to all non-Greek-speaking peoples, cf. Rom. i. 14 "Ελλησί τε καὶ βαρβάροις, and so well known was the use that Plautus,

speaking of a translation of his from Philemon, says *Plautus* Pl. *Trin.* prol. 19.
rortit barbare, i.e. into Latin. Here it probably = 'not
speaking Greek or Latin', the two great languages of the
civilized world at that time.

3. συστρέψαντος τοῦ Π.] *Exemplum αὐτουργίας.* B.

φρυγάνων τι πλῆθος] A. and R.V. 'a bundle of sticks'.
The term φρύγανον can be used of anything useful for kind-
ling a fire. Wood is now very scarce in Malta and there are '1200 to the sq. m.' Cook.
no vipers, but it is now densely populated and carefully
cultivated, and the effect of changed conditions on the existence of plants and animals in a district is well known.

ἀπὸ τῆς θέρμης] Probably 'by reason of the heat': the
viper lay among the sticks or brushwood in a state of
torpor. T.R. with very poor authority reads ἐκ.

καθῆψε] 'laid hold of', i.e. bit. Cf. the promise of Jesus
Mark xvi. 18.

4. φονεύς] They *knew* that he was a prisoner being
taken to Rome on some grave charge, and *inferred* that the
charge was murder.

ἡ δίκη] Like the Latin *Justitia*, an abstraction per- W.
sonified.

οὐκ εἴασεν] Note the past tense. *Jam nullum putant
esse Paulum.* B.

6. πίμπρασθαι] A. and R.V. 'would have swollen'.
The word combines the ideas of 'inflammation and swelling'. πίμπρημι and πρήθω, both having aorist ἔπρησα,
seem connected, though πίμπρημι is usually='burn', and
πρήθω = 'blow up,' 'cause to swell'. Cf. πρεστήρ=(1) a flash
of lightning, (2) a hurricane, (3) a venomous snake, the bite
of which caused both 'inflammation' and 'swelling'; cf.
Lucan ix. 790 *Percussit Prester: illi rubor igneus ora | suc-
cendit tenditque cutem.*

καταπίπτειν...] Cp. Shakespeare *Ant. and Cleop.* v. 2, of H.
Charmian bitten by an asp, 'Tremblingly she stood, and
on the sudden dropped'.

ἄτοπον] 'extraordinary'.

μεταβαλόμενοι...] Cf. the opposite change at Lycaonia
xiv. 11 and xiv. 19.

7. τῷ πρώτῳ τῆς νήσου] 'the governor of the island', Cic. *in Verr.* ii. 4. 18.
which was under the government of a deputy of the praetor
of Sicily. The title is not elsewhere referred to, but is
found on an inscription from the island Gaulus, close to
Malta. Λ(ούκιος), Κλ(αυδίου) υἱὸς, Κ., Προύδηνς, ἱππεὺς Ῥω-

La. from μαίων, πρῶτος Μελιταίων, καὶ πάτρων, ἄρξας καὶ ἀμφιπολεύσας
Böckh,   θεῷ Αὐγούστῳ ἀνέστησεν.
Corpus
Inscr.   Ποπλίῳ] *Publio.* The Gk represents no doubt a com-
Graec.
no. 5754.   mon pronunciation of the name. So *publicus* on inscrip-
tions, often *poblicus* or *poplicus*, being from *populus = popu-
licus.*

ἡμᾶς] Not the whole crew (which would be πάντας ἡμᾶς,
as ver. 2) but, as throughout the narrative, Paul and his
companions, including the writer, cf. ver. 10.

8. πυρετοῖς] 'attacks of fever'; cf. Dem. 1260 πυρετοί
συνεχεῖς. Note the medical terms in connection with Luke.

κατακεῖσθαι] = *cubare* (Hor. *Sat.* i. 9. 18).

So too   10. τιμαῖς] H. objects to the rendering 'honours', and
W.   gives 'presents'; comparing Ecclesiasticus xxxviii. 1 τίμα
ἰατρὸν πρὸς τὰς χρείας τιμαῖς αὐτοῦ; but this is unduly to narrow
the phrase 'honoured us with many honours', though no
doubt among those 'honours' were included actual gifts, such
as 'the needful things' immediately referred to as placed on
board, it being a common practice so to 'honour' a parting
guest; cf. Virg. *Aen.* i. 195 *Vina bonus quae deinde cadis
onerarat Acestes | litore Trinacrio dederatque abeuntibus
heros.*

11. μετὰ τρεῖς μῆνας] i.e. in the early part of February.
Navigation began with spring (Hor. *Od.* i. 4. 2), and spring
commenced on Feb. 9 (Ov. *Fast.* ii. 149).

Smith,   παρασήμῳ] That this is a noun is proved by an
Preface,   inscription found near Lutro, which refers to one Dionysius
p. 7.   of Alexandria, *Gubernator navis parasemo Isopharia.* Διοσκούροις is in apposition to παρασήμῳ, describing what the
παράσημον was; cf. the construction ὀνόματι Ποπλίῳ ver. 7.
Others take the word as an adj.

For Castor and Pollux as guardians of ships cf. Hor.
Od. i. 3. 2 *sic fratres Helenae, lucida sidera (te, navis, regant).*
In thundery weather a pale-blue flame may sometimes be
seen playing round the masts of ships, due to the tendency
of 'points' to produce a discharge of electricity. This was
taken to indicate the presence of the Dioscuri and the safety
of the ship. Italian mariners call it the fire of St Elmo.

12. Συρακούσας] 80 m. from Malta, the chief city of
Sicily, founded B.C. 734.

Text   13. περιελόντες] R.V. in margin 'cast loose', cf. xxvii.
אB as M.   40, but there seems no authority for this absolute use of the
word. T. R. has περιελθόντες, which can hardly mean
'having gone round (Sicily)', but must = 'having made a

circuit' (A.V. 'having fetched a compass'), i.e. having been unable, owing to the winds, to steer direct for Rhegium : the opposite of εὐθυδρομήσαντες.

'Ρήγιον] i. e. 'the place where the land breaks off' (ῥήγ-νυμι), at the extreme S.W. of Italy in Bruttium, opposite Messana.

ἐπιγενομένου] The word might mean 'came after', 'suc- As A. ceeded', i. e. the hitherto adverse wind, but more probably describes a wind that 'blew from right astern' (*ventus secundus*). The distance is 182 m., which would take 26 hours at seven knots or so an hour.

Ποτιόλους] *Puteoli*, Pozzuoli ('Wells'), N. of the bay of Naples, a little E. of Baiae. It was at this time the chief port of Rome, and the regular harbour for the corn-fleet from Alexandria. Portions of the great mole are still visible.

καὶ οὕτως εἰς τὴν 'Ρώμην ἤλθαμεν] The exultant tone of these words is marked. *Paulus Romae captivus : triumphus unicus.* Luke regards Paul's visit to Rome as the crowning point of his career, cf. xix. 21, xxiii. 11. It is this eagerness to reach Rome which makes him slightly anticipate the narrative, which in the next verse reverts to events which happened before their arrival.

It would make the narrative much clearer if the end of a paragraph were marked at ἤλθαμεν. The events related in vv. 15, 16 are regarded not as part of Paul's journey, but as part of the action of the Roman community with which Luke closes his narrative vv. 15—28.

It is hardly safe to draw distinctions between τὴν 'P. here and 'Ρώμην ver. 16, as Bengel does (τὴν 'Ρώμην emphasin habet, ut notetur urbs diu desiderata), for xviii. 2 we have τῆς 'P. where there is no emphasis, but xix. 21, xxiii. 11 no article where there is strong emphasis.

Paul would go from Puteoli to Capua (for the coast road to Sinuessa was made later by Domitian) and there join the great Appian road, constructed by the censor Appius Claudius B.C. 312. From there the distance is about 125 m. He would pass Sinuessa, Minturnae, Formiae, Anxur, and at Templum Feroniae might either proceed by road or by the canal which ran parallel to it through the Pomptine Marshes, to Forum Appii, and from there to Tres Tabernae, Lanuvium and Aricia, entering Rome by the Porta Capena.

See for the route Hor. *Sat.* I. 5, and full information in C. and H., F., &c.

Appii Forum is about 40 m. from Rome, and Tres Tabernae about 30.

In B. **15. θάρσος**] ἔλλογος ὁρμή: θράσος ἄλογος ὁρμή, Ammonius.

16. καθ' ἑαυτὸν] 'by himself', i.e. not with the other prisoners in some public prison. In ver. 23 there is reference to τὴν ξενίαν, 'his lodging', and in ver. 30 to ἴδιον μίσθωμα, 'his own hired room' or 'dwelling'. These two last phrases probably refer to the same thing, it being specially described in ver. 30 as ἴδιον μίσθ. because Luke is there dwelling strongly

C. & H. on the comparative *freedom* enjoyed by Paul. Others argue that ξενία implies 'residence with friends', but this is unduly pressing the Greek.

Omit ℵABI. Insert HLP. After 'Ρώμην T.R. adds, ὁ ἑκατόνταρχος παρέδωκε τοὺς δεσμίους τῷ στρατοπεδάρχῃ, τῷ δὲ Π...

στρατοπεδάρχης = *Praefectus praetorio.* The praetorian cohorts (a select body of household troops, about 10,000

Tac. *Ann.* IV. 2. in number, who served on the body-guard of the emperor) had been collected into one camp by Sejanus, A.D. 23, outside the Porta Viminalis. Afranius Burrus was their commander A.D. 51—62. Before and after him there were two 'prefects', but no argument as to date can be drawn from the use of the singular here, as the singular might merely represent the one *on duty.* They had charge of

Plin. *Ep.* x. 65. prisoners sent to Rome; cf. the rescript of Trajan to Pliny, *vinctus mitti ad praefectos praetorii mei debet.*

17. συνκαλέσασθαι...] Here, as throughout, Paul first appeals to the Jews. As he cannot go to the synagogue, he summons them to him. He desires to make it clear that his appeal to Caesar was forced upon him, and does not arise from any desire to accuse his nation.

παρεδόθην] Practically, though not technically. The violence of the Jews had compelled the Romans to interfere.

La. **19. τοῦ ἔθνους μου**] Not λαοῦ, because he is not considering them as *God's people,* but as *his own nation,* whom he would not wish to accuse before a foreign tribunal.

20. παρεκάλεσα] R.V. 'did I intreat you', but A.V. rightly 'I called for you', i.e. invited you here, as xvi. 15.

τῆς ἐλπίδος τοῦ 'Ι.] Cf. xxvi. 6; the hope of a Messiah.

τὴν ἅλυσιν τ. περίκειμαι] Cf. xxvi. 29. For περίκειμαι cf. Heb. v. 2, περίκειται ἀσθένειαν 'is compassed with infirmity', and so commonly, v. Lex. The acc. is due to the active sense of 'wearing', 'having on', contained in the verb.

As F. states. **21. ἡμεῖς...**] The Jews do not assert that they had never heard of Paul, which would be 'inconceivable'; what they state is, that with reference to the charge against Paul just mentioned by him they had received no letter or report;

the aorists (ἐδεξάμεθα, ἀπήγγειλεν, ἐλάλησεν) shew that their
statement must be so limited, and does not express general
ignorance of Paul and his views; moreover they immediately
acknowledge that they are aware that his views are 'everywhere spoken against'. It was almost impossible that they
should have had knowledge of Paul's appeal to Caesar, for
how could the news have reached Rome before Paul ?

25. τοῦ Παύλου] The personal name instead of the
pronoun for emphasis. Note, too, the strong emphasis of
ῥῆμα ἕν: he had appealed to them 'from morning until
evening': he had appealed to the Jews elsewhere continually
in vain: he has now but 'one word' more to say.

καλῶς] So placed first with strong indignation: cf.
Matt. xv. 7 ὑποκριταί, καλῶς προεφήτευσε περὶ ὑμῶν Ἡσαΐας;
Mark vii. 6.

ὑμῶν] So ℵAB. T.R. ἡμῶν.

26. πορεύθητι...] Accurately from the LXX. Is. vi. 9,
the famous passage which describes the vision and call of
Isaiah. It is the passage quoted by Jesus (at length, Matt.
xiii. 14, and partially Mark iv. 12; Luke viii. 10) when
explaining why He taught the Jews in parables. It is also
quoted John xii. 40, where he refers to the disbelief of the
Jews in Jesus.

ἀκοῇ ἀκούσετε, βλέποντες βλέψετε] Emphatic repetition,
to strengthen the contrast with their 'not understanding'
and 'not seeing (i.e. perceiving)'.

Cf. for the sense Dem. 797, 3 ὁρῶντας μὴ ὁρᾶν καὶ ἀκούοντες μὴ ἀκούειν; Aesch. *Prom.* 448 κλύοντες οὐκ ἤκουον; Soph.
O. R. 371 τυφλὸς τά τ' ὦτα τόν τε νοῦν τά τ' ὄμματ' εἶ.

οὐ μὴ] Strong negation : 'surely ye shall not understand'.

27. ἐπαχύνθη ἡ καρδία] The phrase seems to describe
the negligence and indifference to religion produced by pro-
sperity. Cf. Deut. xxxii. 15 ἔφαγεν Ἰακὼβ καὶ ἐνεπλήσθη, καὶ
ἀπελάκτισεν ὁ ἠγαπημένος, ἐλιπάνθη, ἐπαχύνθη.

ἐκάμμυσαν] The Heb. has 'their eyes besmear' (cf. Is. Cheyne
xxix. 10, xliv. 18), i.e. seal up. *ad loc.*

καὶ ἰάσομαι αὐτούς] T.R. ἰάσωμαι. The future ind. Text
after μή represents the action of the verb as more vividly ℵABH
realized as possible and probable than is the case when the LP, and
subj. follows. The change from the subj. to the ind. here so LXX.
is very forcible and vigorous: it represents the 'healing',
which the Jews refused, as something clearly apprehended
by them to be the purpose of God, and so enhances the
guilt of their refusal.

Cf. Plat. *Rep.* 451 A φοβερὸν καὶ σφαλερὸν...μή...κείσομαι and Stallb. *ad loc.*

28. τὸ σωτήριον τοῦ θ.] Ps. lxvii. 2 τοῦ γνῶναι ἐν τῇ γῇ τὴν ὁδόν σου, ἐν πᾶσιν ἔθνεσιν τὸ σωτήριόν σου.

αὐτοὶ καὶ ἀκούσονται] αὐτοί is vivid and antithetical: ' *They* will also hear (as opposed to your 'hard hearing' and 'not hearing', ver. 27). Cf. Luke vi. 11 αὐτοὶ δὲ ἐπλήσθησαν ἀνοίας.

Omit KADF. T.R. adds here, καὶ ταῦτα αὐτοῦ εἰπόντος, ἀπῆλθον οἱ Ἰουδαῖοι, πολλὴν ἔχοντες ἐν ἑαυτοῖς συζήτησιν, marring the climax.

30. διετίαν] In this period were written the Epistles to the Philippians, Colossians, Ephesians, and to Philemon.

W. **μετὰ πάσης παρρησίας ἀκωλύτως**] παρρ. *fiducia, intrinsecus,* ἀκωλ. *sine impedimento, extrinsecus.* B. The rhythmic cadence of the concluding words is marked (cf. vii. 60 n.). Cf. the end of St Luke's Gospel, καὶ ἦσαν διὰ παντὸς ἐν τῷ ἱερῷ εὐλογοῦντες τὸν θεόν ; also the last words of Dem. *de Cor.* καὶ σωτηρίαν ἀσφαλῆ.

Various arguments have been deduced from the fact that Luke ends his narrative at this point and leaves us without any account of Paul's subsequent history. Some have in consequence regarded the Acts as an unfinished work. It is clear, however, that Luke regards Paul's preaching at Rome as the crown and goal of his career. Rejected by the Jews, the Gospel is for 'a whole two years' preached to the Gentiles in Rome, the capital of the world, *Urbi et Orbi*—this is the climax of the Acts. Moreover the whole style of vv. 25—31 marks a concluded narrative : notice the distinctive τοῦ Παύλου, the emphatic ῥῆμα ἕν, the indignant καλῶς, the full quotation of Isaiah's famous prophecy, the clear διετίαν ὅλην, the description of Jesus as τοῦ κυρίου Ἰησοῦ Χριστοῦ, and, lastly, the closing cadence of μετὰ πάσης παρρησίας ἀκωλύτως.

CAMBRIDGE : PRINTED BY C. J. CLAY, M.A. AND SON, AT THE UNIVERSITY PRESS.

For EU product safety concerns, contact us at Calle de José Abascal, 56–1°, 28003 Madrid, Spain or eugpsr@cambridge.org.

www.ingramcontent.com/pod-product-compliance
Ingram Content Group UK Ltd.
Pitfield, Milton Keynes, MK11 3LW, UK
UKHW010346140625
459647UK00010B/866